Fodor's

SAN DIEGO
19TH EDITION

Where to Stay and Eat
for All Budgets

Must-See Sights
and Local Secrets

Ratings You Can Trust

Fodor's Travel Publications   New York, Toronto, London, Sydney, Auckland
www.fodors.com

FODOR'S SAN DIEGO

Editor: Christina Knight

Editorial Production: David Downing

Editorial Contributors: Rob Aikins, Collin Campbell, Lenore Greiner, Satu Hummasti, Maribeth Mellin, David Nelson, Bobbi Zane

Maps: David Lindroth, *cartographer;* Rebecca Baer and Robert P. Blake, *map editors*

Design: Fabrizio La Rocca, *creative director;* Guido Caroti, *art director;* Melanie Marin, *senior picture editor*

Cover Design: Moon Sun Kim

Production/Manufacturing: Robert B. Shields

Cover Photo (SeaWorld): James Lemass

Nineteenth Edition

ISBN 1–4000–1420–4

ISSN 1053–5950

SPECIAL SALES

This book is available for special discounts for bulk purchases for sales promotions or premiums. Special editions, including personalized covers, excerpts of existing books, and corporate imprints, can be created in large quantities for special needs. For more information, write to Special Markets/Premium Sales, 1745 Broadway, MD 6-2, New York, New York 10019, or e-mail specialmarkets@randomhouse.com.

AN IMPORTANT TIP & AN INVITATION

Although all prices, opening times, and other details in this book are based on information supplied to us at press time, changes occur all the time in the travel world, and Fodor's cannot accept responsibility for facts that become outdated or for inadvertent errors or omissions. So **always confirm information when it matters,** especially if you're making a detour to visit a specific place. Your experiences—positive and negative—matter to us. If we have missed or misstated something, **please write to us.** We follow up on all suggestions. Contact the San Diego editor at editors@fodors.com or c/o Fodor's at 1745 Broadway, New York, NY 10019.

PRINTED IN THE UNITED STATES OF AMERICA

10 9 8 7 6 5 4 3 2 1

DESTINATION SAN DIEGO

More than any other city in California, San Diego embodies the dream of an oceanfront paradise with all the comforts of home. Whose cares can't be cast away while crossing the harbor by ferry or walking barefoot along the Pacific shoreline? The most popular man-made pleasures here are still collaborations with nature, such as the world-famous zoo and marine attractions, and the museums and centers of Balboa Park that lay out the world along the promenade. The scenic cityscape includes a Spanish mission in Old Town and Victorian houses in the downtown Gaslamp Quarter. San Diego basks in warm sunshine, but will never leave you drowsy.

Tim Jarrell, Publisher

CONTENTS

Maps

CloseUps

ABOUT THIS BOOK

The best source for travel advice is a like-minded friend who's just been where you're headed. But with or without that friend, you'll be in great shape to find your way around your destination once you learn to find your way around your Fodor's guide.

RATINGS

Orange stars ★ denote sights and properties that our editors and writers consider the very best in the area covered by the entire book. These, the best of the best, are listed in the Fodor's Choice section in the front of the book. Black stars ★ highlight the sights and properties we deem Highly Recommended, the don't-miss sights within any region. In cities, sights pinpointed with numbered map bullets ❶ in the margins tend to be more important than those without bullets.

SPECIAL SPOTS

Pleasures & Pastimes and text on chapter-title pages focus on experiences that reveal the spirit of the destination. Also watch for Off the Beaten Path sights. Some are out of the way, some are quirky, and all are worthwhile. When the munchies hit, look for Need a Break? suggestions.

TIME IT RIGHT

Check On the Calendar up front and chapters' Timing sections for weather and crowd overviews and best days and times to visit.

SEE IT ALL

Use Fodor's exclusive Great Itineraries as a model for your trip. Either follow those that begin the book, or mix regional itineraries from several chapters. In cities, Good Walks guide you to important sights in each neighborhood; ► indicates the starting points of walks and itineraries in the text and on the map.

BUDGET WELL

Hotel and restaurant price categories from ¢ to $$$$ are defined in the opening pages of each chapter—expect to find a balanced selection for every budget. For attractions, we always give standard adult admission fees; reductions are usually available for children, students, and senior citizens. Look in Discounts & Deals in Smart Travel Tips for information on destination-wide ticket schemes. Want to pay with plastic? AE, D, DC, MC, V following restaurant and hotel listings indicate whether American Express, Discover, Diner's Club, MasterCard, or Visa are accepted.

BASIC INFO

Smart Travel Tips lists travel essentials for the entire area covered by the book; city- and region-specific basics end each chapter. To find the best way to get around, see the transportation section; see individual modes of travel ("Car Travel," "Train Travel") for details.

ON THE MAPS

Maps throughout the book show you what's where and help you find your way around. Black and orange numbered bullets ❶ ❶ in the text correlate to bullets on maps.

BACKGROUND

We give background information within the chapters in the course of explaining sights as well as in CloseUp boxes and in Understanding San Diego at the end of the book. To get in the mood, review the Books & Movies section.

FIND IT FAST

Within the Exploring San Diego chapter, sights are grouped by neighborhood, and neighborhoods are arranged in a roughly clockwise direction. Where to Eat and Where to Stay are also organized by neighborhood—Where to Eat is further divided by cuisine type. The Nightlife & the Arts and Sports & the Outdoors chapters are arranged alphabetically by entertainment type. Shopping is organized by neighborhood. The North County chapter is subdivided by town, and the towns are covered in logical geographical order. The Tijuana, Playas de Rosarito & Ensenada chapter has exploring, dining, lodging, and other options listed under each city. Heads at the top of each page help you find what you need within a chapter.

DON'T FORGET

Restaurants are open for lunch and dinner daily unless we state otherwise; we mention dress only when there's a specific requirement and reservations only when they're essential or not accepted—it's always best to book ahead. Hotels have private baths, phones, TVs, and air-conditioning and operate on the European Plan (a.k.a. EP, meaning without meals). We always list facilities but not whether you'll be charged extra to use them, so when pricing accommodations, find out what's included.

SYMBOLS

Many Listings

★ Fodor's Choice
★ Highly recommended
⊠ Physical address
✛ Directions
⌕ Mailing address
☎ Telephone
🖷 Fax
⊕ On the Web
✉ E-mail
🎫 Admission fee
☉ Open/closed times
► Start of walk/itinerary
Ⓜ Metro stations
▭ Credit cards

Outdoors

⅃ Golf
⚑ Camping

Hotels & Restaurants

🏨 Hotel
🛏 Number of rooms
⚷ Facilities
🍴 Meal plans
✗ Restaurant
⚵ Reservations
⟁ Dress code
⤱ Smoking
🍷 BYOB
✗🏨 Hotel with restaurant that warrants a visit

Other

☕ Family-friendly
🛈 Contact information
⇨ See also
⊠ Branch address
☞ Take note

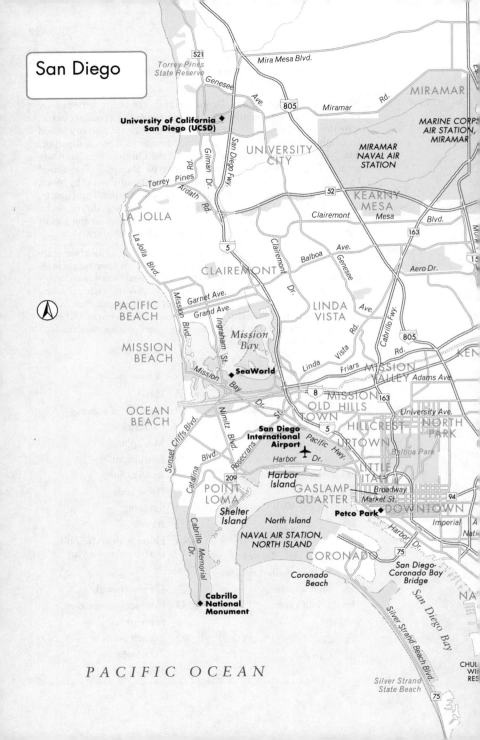

San Diego Trolley System

A trip takes you out of yourself. Concerns of life at home completely disappear, driven away by more immediate thoughts—about, say, what marvels will beguile the next day, or where you'll have dinner. That's where Fodor's comes in. We make sure that you know all your options, so that you don't miss something that's around the next bend just because you didn't know it was there. Because the best memories of your trip might well have nothing to do with what you came to San Diego to see, we guide you to sights large and small all over the region. You might set out to see every animal in the San Diego Zoo, but back at home you find yourself unable to forget peering into tide pools in La Jolla Cove and strolling around the colorful streets of Old Town. With Fodor's at your side, serendipitous discoveries are never far away.

Our success in showing you every corner of San Diego is a credit to our extraordinary writers. Although there's no substitute for travel advice from a good friend who knows your style, our contributors are the next best thing—the kind of people you would poll for travel advice if you knew them.

Rob Aikins has lived in the North Coast community of Leucadia for more than 17 years. In that time he has produced and managed surf, skate and music events, filmed a documentary on border life and written about music, art, action sports and travel for numerous publications and Web sites. The former editor of San Diego's *SLAMM music magazine,* he has written for the *San Diego Reader, San Diego Union-Tribune,* and online at Spin.com, NYTimes.com, and MTV.com.

Lenore Greiner grew up in San Francisco but transplanted herself to San Diego 14 years ago after vacationing in Coronado. Besides writing for other Fodor's guides, her travel articles have appeared in *Newsday,* the *San Francisco Examiner/ Chronicle,* Delta Airlines' *Sky,* Air New

Zealand's *Pacific Way, Woman,* and *Healing Retreats & Spas.*

Recipient of the prestigious Pluma de Plata award for writing on Mexico, **Maribeth Mellin** lives in San Diego near the Tijuana border in a home filled with folk art and photos from Latin America—including a snapshot of the 140-pound marlin she caught in the Sea of Cortez. She has authored travel books on Mexico, Costa Rica, Argentina, and Peru. She updated the Tijuana, Playas de Rosarito, and Ensenada chapter.

Dining writer **David Nelson** has known San Diego since childhood and has lived there for more than 20 years. Respected for his extensive knowledge of food lore, cooking techniques, and the restaurant industry, he was a columnist for the former San Diego edition of the *Los Angeles Times* for a dozen years. He now writes restaurant reviews and travel pieces for a number of southern California publications.

Longtime southern Californian **Bobbi Zane** makes her home in the mountain hamlet of Julian. Bobbi's byline has appeared in the *Los Angeles Times, Los Angeles Daily News,* and *Orange County Register.*

Like a giant conch shell, San Diego spirals around the bay, with Balboa Park at its center. The following neighborhoods are organized geographically, just as they are in Chapter 1, *Exploring,* starting with Balboa Park, continuing with the San Diego Bay shoreline, and ending with the San Diego North County communities.

Balboa Park

Straddling two mesas overlooking downtown and the Pacific Ocean, Balboa Park is set on 1,200 beautifully landscaped acres. Home to the majority of San Diego's museums and the world-famous zoo, the park serves as the cultural center of the city, as well as a lush green space for animal lovers, picnickers, and strollers. Most of the downtown thoroughfares lead north to the park (it's hard to miss). From the west side of downtown take any east–west street until you hit Park Boulevard, and drive north into the park. From Old Town take Interstate 5 south and use any of the well-marked exits.

Hillcrest

Northwest of Balboa Park is eclectic Hillcrest, the heart of San Diego's gay and lesbian community, where you'll find excellent restaurants tucked between independent boutiques, movie theaters, juice bars, and unusual bookstores. North Park is an extension of Hillcrest, directly above (you guessed it) Balboa Park. It's known for antiques, used-book stores, and vintage-clothing shops.

Downtown

San Diego's downtown and waterfront area is a bustling, colorful jumble of hotels, restaurants, shopping centers, gift shops, and seagoing vessels of every size and shape. The centerpiece is Horton Plaza, a shopping, dining, and entertainment complex that covers more than six city blocks. East of Horton Plaza is the Gaslamp Quarter, the city's hot dining and entertainment district with eateries, nightclubs, and boutiques housed in Victorian buildings and renovated warehouses. Downtown San Diego's main arteries are Harbor Drive, which runs along the Embarcadero; Broadway, which cuts through the center of downtown; and 6th Avenue as far as Balboa Park. South of the Embarcadero on Harbor Drive is Seaport Village, 14 acres of shopping plazas designed to reflect the architectural styles of early California. In 2004, Petco Park, on the waterfront and just east of the Gaslamp, replaced Qualcomm Stadium as the home of the Padres.

Coronado

Coronado, on an islandlike peninsula across the bay from San Diego's waterfront, is a historic Victorian village that grew up around the ornate Hotel Del Coronado, a celebrity hangout from the late 19th century and now a national historic site. Accessible from the San Diego–Coronado Bridge and the San Diego–Coronado Ferry, Coronado has wide, graceful streets, well-manicured neighborhood parks, and grand Victorian homes. By ordinance, no two houses here share the same building plan. Wealthy suburbanites and the Coronado Naval Base, which includes the North Island air station and amphibious base, also make their home here. Boutiques and restaurants line Orange Avenue, and you can catch some rays and splash in the surf at Silver Strand State Beach and Imperial Beach, which extend in a long arc to the south.

Harbor Island & Shelter Island
A man-made strip of land in the bay directly across from San Diego International Airport and a short drive from downtown, Harbor Island has several hotels and restaurants and makes a good base for a visit to San Diego. Shelter Island, known for its yacht-building and sport fishing industries, is just west of Harbor Island, also a short drive from downtown.

Point Loma
Standing as a buffer against the temperamental Pacific Ocean, Point Loma curves along San Diego Bay and extends south into the sea. Beyond its main streets, which are cluttered with fast-food restaurants and motels, Point Loma is made up of well-to-do neighborhoods and bay-side estates (it's a favorite retirement spot for naval officers). From the bay side you can enjoy a terrific view of downtown San Diego, and for an incomparable view of the Pacific head to Sunset Cliffs, between Point Loma and Ocean Beach, among the most dramatic places in San Diego to watch the sunset.

La Jolla
Spanish for "the jewel," La Jolla lives up to its name in both beauty and expense with its dramatic beachfront, spectacular views, and huge designer homes. Boutiques and restaurants cater to the affluent local gentry, but the largely unspoiled scenery of its coast, coves, and verdant hillsides is still free. North of Mission Bay, La Jolla can be approached on the meandering coastal road (Mission and La Jolla boulevards) or via Interstate 5.

Mission Bay & SeaWorld
The coastal Mission Bay area, located west of Interstate 5 and north of Interstate 8, is San Diego's monument to sports and fitness, where locals and visitors interested in boating, running, sunning, or jet skiing spend their days. Portions of the amorphous 4,600-acre aquatic park, which has numerous coves and inlets, 27 mi of bay front, and 17 mi of beachfront, are specifically designated for swimming, waterskiing, and sailing. Terrestrial types can jog, bike, rollerblade, play basketball, or fly a kite on the bay's peninsulas and two main islands, Vacation Island

and Fiesta Island. SeaWorld, easily the most popular attraction in Mission Bay (and for some, in all of San Diego), displays fish and captive marine mammals, including sea otters, dolphins, seals, and the trademark killer whales.

Old Town

A few miles north of downtown and east of Interstate 5, Old Town is essentially a collection of remnants from the original San Diego, the first European settlement in California. The former pueblo of San Diego is now preserved as a state historic park and contains several original and reconstructed buildings. The historic sites are clustered around Old Town Plaza, which is bounded by Wallace Street, Calhoun Street, Mason Street, and San Diego Avenue.

Mission Valley

The business and commercial center of San Diego, Mission Valley is home to hundreds of shops in Fashion Valley Shopping Center, Hazard Center, and Westfield Shoppingtown Mission Valley. Hotel Circle is where many business people and sports fans stay; the Chargers play at Qualcomm Stadium. Mission Valley is north of downtown and Hillcrest, on the San Diego River.

San Diego North County & Environs

The seaside towns north of La Jolla developed separately from San Diego, and from one another. Del Mar is a seaside preserve with expensive lodging, exclusive boutiques, and fancy restaurants. Small Solana Beach, long known for its mellow ambience, is evolving into a trendy art and design center. Encinitas is justly famous for its fabulous fields of flowers and gardens, which extend inland from excellent surfing waters. Carlsbad, once known for its healing waters, now lures families to Legoland California, and Oceanside shows off its harbor and Mission San Luis Rey. The coastal portion of North County is best accessed via Interstate 5, but traveling along Route S21 (old Highway 101) once you reach the area will give you a better feel for the differences among the communities.

Even though the coast is only a short drive away, the North County beach communities seem far removed from the resort/retirement town of Rancho Bernardo, the quiet lakes of Escondido, the avocado-growing country surrounding Fallbrook, the former gold-mining town of Julian, or the vineyards of Temecula. Home to old missions, San Diego Wild Animal Park, the Welk Resort Center, and innumerable three-generation California families, the inland area of North County is the quiet, rural sister to the rest of San Diego County. The Cleveland National Forest and Anza-Borrego Desert State Park mark the county's eastern boundaries; the busiest international border in the United States is its southern line.

Tijuana, Playas de Rosarito & Ensenada

Tijuana, just 23 mi south of San Diego, has grown during the past 20 years from a border town of 700,000 to a city of almost 2 million inhabitants; it continues to attract hordes of "yanquis" with its designer boutiques, souvenir shops, sports events, and great Mexican dining. Laid-back Playas de Rosarito (Rosarito Beach), 18 mi farther south, has become something of a weekend hangout for southern Californians. Ensenada is one of Mexico's largest seaports as well as its third-largest city.

San Diego in 5 Days

Many folks spend their time in San Diego just lazing away on a beach—if you're thus inclined, you'll enjoy some of the best sand and surf in the country. But the more energetic will find sufficient outlets to satisfy their sightseeing urges. The following suggested itineraries will help you structure your visit efficiently. See the neighborhood tours in Chapter 1 for more information about individual sights.

Day 1 Start with the San Diego Zoo in Balboa Park in the morning. It would be easy to spend your entire visit to the park here—and if you're traveling with kids, you may have little choice in the matter—but at least walk down El Prado with its rows of architecturally interesting museums. It's an easy walk from the zoo, or a five-minute drive south of the zoo on Park Boulevard.

Day 2 Start downtown at Seaport Village; after browsing the shops catch a ferry from the Broadway Pier to Coronado. From Coronado's Ferry Landing Marketplace board a bus going down Orange Avenue to see the town's Victorian extravaganza, the Hotel Del Coronado. Back in San Diego after lunch, stroll north on the Embarcadero to Ash Street; if you've returned from Coronado early enough, you can view the Maritime Museum or the San Diego Aircraft Carrier Museum, if it's open. If it's whale-watching season, skip the trip to Coronado, tour the Embarcadero in the late morning, have lunch, and book an afternoon excursion boat from the Broadway Pier. Another option is to spend the entire day with Shamu and the gang at SeaWorld of California.

Day 3 If you set out early enough, you might get a parking spot near La Jolla Cove. Watch the sea lions lounging on the beach at the Children's Pool and then head inland one block to Prospect Street, where you'll see the pink La Valencia hotel and a clutch of tony shops and galleries; this is also a good spot for an ocean-view lunch. Walk east on Prospect for a spin through the Museum of Contemporary Art, and then retrieve your car and head back into town on Interstate 5 to the Gaslamp Quarter, where you can explore the historic streets and perhaps stop by the adjacent Horton Plaza shopping mall. Dine at one of the many restaurants in the area, and drop into a coffeehouse or a nightclub for some music.

Day 4 Begin with a morning visit to Cabrillo National Monument. Have lunch at one of the seafood restaurants on Scott Street, and then head over to Old Town (take Rosecrans Street north to San Diego Avenue) to see portions of San Diego's earliest history brought to life. If the daily schedule lists low tide for the afternoon, reverse the order to catch the tide pools at Cabrillo.

Day 5 If you're traveling with young children, make Legoland California in Carlsbad your main destination for Day Five. En route to North County stop off at Torrey Pines State Park. If you're not going to Legoland, take Interstate 5 north to Del Mar for lunch, shopping, and sea views. A visit to Mission San Luis Rey, slightly inland from Oceanside on Highway 76, will infuse some history and culture into the tour.

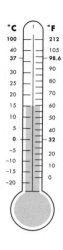

°C		°F
100		212
40		105
37		98.6
30		90
25		80
20		70
15		60
10		50
5		40
0		32
-5		20
-10		10
-15		0
-20		

For the most part, **any time of the year is the right time** for a trip to San Diego. The climate is generally close to perfect. Typical days are sunny and mild, with low humidity—ideal for sightseeing and for almost any sport that does not require snow and ice. From mid-December through mid-March gray whales can be seen migrating along the coast. In early spring wildflowers transform the mountainsides and desert into a rainbow of colors. In fall these same mountains present one of the most impressive displays of fall color to be found in southern California.

Climate

The annual high temperature averages 70°F with a low of 55°F, and the annual rainfall is usually less than 10 inches. Most of the rain occurs in January and February, but precipitation usually lasts for only part of the day or for a day or two at most.

What follows are average maximum and minimum temperatures for San Diego.

🔲 Forecasts **Weather Channel Connection** ⊕ www.weather.com.

SAN DIEGO

Jan.	62F	17C	May	66F	19C	Sept.	73F	23C
	46	8		55	13		62	17
Feb.	62F	17C	June	69F	21C	Oct.	71F	22C
	48	9		59	15		57	14
Mar.	64F	18C	July	73F	23C	Nov.	69F	21C
	50	10		62	17		51	11
Apr.	66F	19C	Aug.	73F	23C	Dec.	64F	18C
	53	12		64	18		48	9

While San Diego has obnoxiously perfect Southern California weather, it really does have seasons; with them come festivals and events that capture special moments throughout the city. Plan well in advance if you hope to be in town for any of these celebrations.

WINTER

Dec.

Balboa Park December Nights (☎ 619/239–0512 ⊕ www.balboapark. org) draws 100,000 guests on the first Friday and Saturday of December. Attractions include carolers, holiday food, music, dance, handmade crafts for sale, a visit from Saint Nick, a candlelight procession, and free admission to all the museums.

Old Fashioned Christmas Village in La Mesa (☎ 619/462–3000) features an outdoor market, caroling, horse-drawn carriage rides, and a visit from Santa Claus.

Old Town Holiday in the Park (☎ 619/220–5422) includes candlelight tours of historic homes and other buildings in Old Town by costumed docents; reservations are required.

The Wild Animal Park Festival of Lights (☎ 760/796–5615) includes free kid-oriented activities, Christmas caroling, live-animal presentations, and real snow.

The Port of San Diego Bay Parade of Lights (☎ 619/224–2240 ⊕ www.sdparadeoflights.org) fills the harbor with lighted boats cruising in a procession starting at Shelter Island and ending at the Navy carrier turning basin.

The Ocean Beach Parade and Tree Festival (☎ 619/226–8613) takes place on Newport Avenue, generally the second weekend in December. The Ocean Beach Geriatric Surf Club tops any entry in any parade, anywhere.

Feb.

The Borrego Springs Grapefruit Festival (☎ 760/767–5555) celebrates the ruby-red grapefruit, which is grown in the desert. Music, food, arts, crafts, and games are part of the event.

The Buick Invitational Golf Tournament (☎ 800/888–2842 ⊕ www. buickinvitational.com) attracts more than 100,000 people, including local and national celebrities, to the Torrey Pines Golf Course.

SPRING

Feb.–Mar.

Mardi Gras in the Gaslamp Quarter (☎ 619/233–5227 ⊕ www. gaslamp.org). This Fat Tuesday celebration features live music on severaloutdoor stages, traditional cajun food and drink.

Feb.–Apr.

Wildflowers in the desert (☎ 760/767–4684 ⊕ www.anzaborrego. statepark.org) bloom during a two- to six-week period in these months. The span and extent of the bloom is determined by the winter rainfall. Phone the Anza-Borrego Desert State Park visitor center for information.

Mar.	The Kiwanis Ocean Beach Kite Festival (☏ 619/531–1527) features a kite-making, decorating, and flying contest, plus a craft fair, food, and entertainment.
Mar. or Apr.	Tiptoe through fields of brilliantly colored ranunculuses. They're arranged rainbow-fashion on a hillside at Flower Fields at Carlsbad Ranch (✉ 5704 Paseo del Norte ☏ 760/431–0352) in Carlsbad.
Apr.	The San Diego Crew Classic (☏ 858/488–0700 ⊕ www.crewclassic.org) brings together more than 2,600 high school, college, and masters athletes from across the United States for a rowing competition at Crown Point Shores in Mission Bay.
	The ArtWalk Festival (☏ 619/615–1090 ⊕ www.artwalkinfo.com) showcases visual and performing artists in their studios and in staged areas; self-guided tours start downtown in Little Italy.
Apr.–May	The Del Mar National Horse Show (✉ 2260 Jimmy Durante Blvd. ☏ 858/792–4288 ⊕ www.sdfair.com) at the Del Mar Fairgrounds showcases international and national championship riders, draft horses, dressage, and western hunter–jumper competitions.
	Humming along for more than 30 years, the Adams Avenue Roots Festival (☏ 619/282–7329 ⊕ www.gothere.com/adamsave) is a free weekend festival of vintage blues, folk, jazz, country, and international music on six outdoor stages.
May	Balboa Park's Buds 'n Blooms is an event that lasts the month of May. It dazzles with colorful extravaganzas such as floral interpretations of 150 paintings housed at the San Diego Museum of Art.
	Fiesta Cinco de Mayo (☏ 619/296–3236 ⊕ www.fiestacincodemayo.com) commemorates Mexico's defeat of Napoleon's cavalry during the Battle of Puebla on May 5, 1862. In addition to an historic renactment, entertainment celebrates Latino culture in Old Town San Diego State Historic Park and the Bazaar del Mundo.
	Julian Wildflower Show (☏ 760/765–1857 ⊕ www.julianca.com) is an annual display of wildflowers gathered within a 15-mi radius of the mountain town, and usually includes desert blooms.

SUMMER

June	At the Threshing Bee & Antique Engine Show (☏ 760/941–1791 ⊕ www.agsem.com), which takes place at the Antique Gas & Steam Engine Museum in Vista, you can see demonstrations on early American crafts, farming, log sawing, and blacksmithing, plus an antique tractor parade.

A Taste of the Gaslamp (☎ 619/233–5227 ⊕ www.gaslamp.org) features a self-guided walking tour throughout the district where you can sample the best dishes prepared by Gaslamp Quarter chefs.

The Annual Inter-Tribal Pow Pow (☎ 760/724–8505), held at Mission San Luis Rey in Oceanside, draws participants from all over the United States and features dancing, Native American arts and crafts, food booths, and games.

June–July	The San Diego County Fair (☎ 858/793–5555 ⊕ www.delmar.fair.com) is a classic county fair, with live entertainment, flower and garden shows, a carnival, livestock shows, and Fourth of July fireworks.
June–Aug.	During the Summer Organ Festival (☎ 619/702–8138), enjoy free Sunday-afternoon and Monday-evening concerts at Balboa Park's Spreckels Organ Pavilion. Free concerts are also offered Tuesday, Wednesday, and Thursday evenings.
June–Sept.	The Nighttime Zoo (☎ 619/234–3153) at the San Diego Zoo and The Park at Dark (☎ 760/796–5621) at the San Diego Wild Animal Park are wild ways to spend the evening, with extended evening hours and additional entertainment through the beginning of September.
July	The Over-the-Line Tournament (☎ 619/688–0817 ⊕ www.ombac.org) is a rowdy party, with more than 1,000 three-person teams competing in a sport that's a cross between softball and stickball; it takes place during two weekends on Fiesta Island in Mission Bay.
	Patriots observe the July 4th Coronado Independence Day Celebration (☎ 619/437–8788) with a parade, U.S. Navy air–sea demonstrations, a concert in the park, and fireworks over Glorietta Bay.
	Julian Independence Day Celebration (☎ 760/765–1857 ⊕ www.julianca.com) is an old-fashioned, small-town July 4 celebration with a parade of animals, women dressed as floozies, and bands; there's also a Civil War reenactment, classic car show, a vintage airplane fly-over, old-west shoot-out, barbecue, and quilt show.
	U.S. Open Sandcastle Competition (☎ 619/424–6663) at Imperial Beach Pier brings together sand sculptors of all ages for one of the largest castle-building events in the United States.
	The annual Lesbian and Gay Pride Parade, Rally and Festival (☎ 619/297–7683 ⊕ www.sdpride.org) is a weekend of entertainment in Hillcrest and Balboa Park.
July–Sept.	In Balboa Park, the Old Globe Theatre (☎ 619/239–2255 ⊕ www.theoldglobe.org) features works of Shakespeare in repertory with other classic and contemporary plays.
	San Diego Symphony Summer Pops Series (☎ 619/235–0804 ⊕ www.sandiegosymphony.com) swings with occasional fireworks Friday and Saturday nights at Navy Pier.

Carlsbad Jazz-in-the-Park Series (☎ 760/434–2904) features free live performances at various parks in the Carlsbad area; call for a schedule.

Aug.

The World Body Surfing Championships (☎ 760/685–1992 ⊕ www.worldbodysurfing.org) pits more than 200 of California's top competitors against one another; viewing is from Oceanside Pier and Beach.

The Summerfest (☎ 858/459–3728 ⊕ www.lajollamusicsociety.org) chamber music festival at Sherwood Auditorium in La Jolla includes concerts, lectures, master classes, and open rehearsals.

FALL

Sept.

Street Scene (☎ 800/260–9985 ⊕ www.street-scene.com) transforms the historic Gaslamp Quarter into a rollicking three-day food and music festival, with 100 bands from around the world performing on 10 stages.

The Thunderboat Regatta Hydroplane Races (☎ 619/225–9160 ⊕ www.thunderboats.com) draws thunderboat enthusiasts to Mission Bay for an exhilarating, deafening weekend of racing.

The free annual Adams Avenue Street Fair (☎ 619/282–7329) attracts 50,000 jazz, blues, and rock fans to the Normal Heights neighborhood for concerts on five stages, food, games, and a carnival. The largest event of its type in southern California, it's popular with families.

Oct.

Octoberfest La Mesa (☎ 619/462–3000 ⊕ www.lamesavillage.com) is a traditional celebration featuring German sausages, Bavarian brass oompah bands, dancing, arts and crafts.

Admission to the San Diego Zoo is free on Founders Day (☎ 619/234–3153), the first Monday in October, and children get in free the entire month.

A series of events commemorates Juan Rodriquez Cabrillo's exploration of the West Coast at the Cabrillo National Monument (☎ 619/557–5450 ⊕ www.nps.gov/cabr) in Point Loma.

Nov.

El Cajon's Mother Goose Parade (☎ 619/444–8712 ⊕ www.mothergooseparade.com) is a two-hour nationally televised spectacular with 200 floats, bands, horses, and clowns. It takes place the Sunday before Thanksgiving.

Holiday of Lights (☎ 858/793–5555) showcases more than 350 animated and lighted holiday displays in a drive-through setting at the Del Mar Fairgrounds.

PLEASURES & PASTIMES

Beaches San Diego's coastline shimmers with crystalline Pacific waters rolling up to some of the prettiest beaches on the West Coast. Some, like the Silver Strand on Coronado, are wide and sandy; others, like Sunset Cliffs on Point Loma, are narrow and rocky. You can join the athletes and sun-worshipers on the beaches of Mission Bay, or wander the tiny, little-known coves of Point Loma and the North County community of Encinitas. Families with children love to explore the tidal pools at La Jolla Cove. Check the weather page of a local newspaper for information about tides and pollution before you head out.

Eating Well Striving to become one of the nation's premier "food cities" of the 21st century, sun-drenched San Diego has abandoned its former laid-back, laissez-faire attitude toward serious cooking and adopted the point of view that a region this blessed with gorgeous vegetables, fruits, herbs, and seafood should make a culinary statement. The result is a generation of chefs more eager to spend time in the kitchen than at the beach—a largely youthful group that likes to surprise, dazzle, and delight diners with inventive, California-colorful creations. A stroll down the 5th Avenue restaurant row reveals San Diego's preference for Italian cuisine above all others, but the selection nonetheless is cosmopolitan and extends to casual and *haute* French fare, Spanish tapas and paellas, traditional and contemporary Mexican cuisine, and all-American thick-cut steaks.

History As the site of California's earliest European settlement, San Diego occupies a special place in U.S. history. Well-preserved and reconstructed historic sites, such as Cabrillo National Monument, Old Town State Historic Park, and Mission San Luis Rey in Oceanside help you to imagine what the San Diego area was like when Spanish and Portuguese explorers and missionaries arrived, usually by sea, in the 16th and 17th centuries.

Shopping Horton Plaza, in the heart of downtown, is the place to go for department stores, mall shops, and one-of-a-kind boutiques; the adjoining Gaslamp Quarter is chock-full of art galleries, antiques shops, and specialty stores. Seaport Village on the waterfront is thick with theme shops and arts-and-crafts galleries. Coronado has a few blocks of fancy boutiques and galleries as well as Ferry Landing Marketplace, a waterfront shopping and dining center. Bazaar del Mundo in the historic Old Town district resembles a colorful Mexican marketplace, where you can browse in shops selling international goods, toys, souvenirs, and arts and crafts. Hillcrest is the place to go for vintage clothing, furnishings, and accessories. La Jolla has a collection of trendy designer boutiques and galleries along Prospect Street and Girard Avenue. Discounted designer fashions can also be found at the popular Carlsbad Company Stores.

FODOR'S CHOICE

The sights, restaurants, hotels, and other travel experiences on these pages are our editors' top picks—our Fodor's Choices. They're the best of their type in the area covered by the book—not to be missed and always worth your time. In the chapters that follow, you will find all the details.

LODGING

$$$$ **Four Seasons Resort Aviara,** Carlsbad. Atop a serene hill overlooking Batiquitos Lagoon and the Pacific beyond, this resort provides every luxury.

$$$$ **Hilton La Jolla Torrey Pines,** La Jolla. On a spectacular piece of Southern California coastline and the legendary Torrey Pines Golf Course, the Parterre Gardens of this hotel is a perfect setting for watching the sun set. It's also a favorite wedding spot.

$$$$ **Hotel Del Coronado,** Coronado. Red-roofed turrets and balconied walkways are the signature of this rambling Victorian confection. Whether it's a workout or a night out, all of your seaside holiday needs can be met here.

$$$$ **La Valencia,** La Jolla. An art deco landmark near the La Jolla village shops and restaurants, the venerable La Valencia has aged well and continues to attract repeat visitors enchanted by its setting.

$$$$ **Lodge at Torrey Pines,** La Jolla. Known for its fantastic Craftsman details, the Lodge delivers an old California experience starting with the timber, clinker brick, and stained glass entrance. The walls adorned with California Impressionist art can't compete with stunning views of the Torrey Pines Golf Course and the Pacific beyond.

$$$$ **Manchester Grand Hyatt San Diego,** Embarcadero. Within San Diego's largest hotel, the 40th-floor lounge is the city's most romantic spot to watch the sun set. But you don't need to leave your room to have sweeping vistas of bay, sea, and the islands beyond.

$$$$ **Rancho Valencia Resort,** Rancho Santa Fe. This contemporary resort caters to tennis players with its world-class tennis school, elegantly decorated individual casitas, a gracious restaurant, and impeccable service.

$$$$ **Westgate Hotel,** Gaslamp Quarter. Not your usual downtown business hotel, the Westgate offers European luxury and impeccable service. In a lobby decorated with Louis XIV gilded furnishings and crystal chandeliers, you can savor the best high tea in the city.

$$$–$$$$ **Catamaran Resort Hotel,** Mission Beach. The great beach location on Mission Bay means fun for families. The resort evokes Hawaii with the lobby's huge waterfall, plus tropical birds, exotic flowers, koi carp river, and palms everywhere. At night, mom and dad can party at the Cannibal Bar or take a romantic cruise on the resort's paddlewheel boat.

$$$–$$$$	**Grande Colonial.**, La Jolla. Exquisitely turned out with marble and French doors, this historic boutique hotel has had a privy spot in La Jolla village for over 90 years.
$$$–$$$$	**La Casa del Zorro**, Borrego Springs. This divine desert resort offers the ultimate in privacy, pampering, and personal service.
$–$$$	**Gaslamp Plaza Suites**, Gaslamp Quarter. This hotel has comfortable European-style accommodations and serves a complimentary Continental breakfast on the rooftop terrace.
$–$$$	**Heritage Park Inn**, Old Town. A beautiful restored Victorian home with a wraparound porch, a French toast breakfast, and old movies in the evening—what more could you want?

BUDGET LODGING

$–$$	**Surfer Motor Lodge**, Pacific Beach. Clean, cheap, on the beach, and a great value for its location in Mission Beach, the rooms are very basic but those on the top floor have a direct view of the ocean and the sunset.
¢–$$	**Comfort Inn Downtown**. The accommodations are simple but you can't beat the rates and the central location. You'll be close to Balboa Park and the zoo as well as the Gaslamp Quarter and the Embarcadero.

RESTAURANTS

$$$–$$$$	**El Bizcocho.**, Rancho Bernardo. A Spanish-style dining room is the setting for modern twists on classic cuisine.
$$$–$$$$	**George's at the Cove**, La Jolla. It's hard to say what's better here: the stunning view overlooking La Jolla Cove or the superb cooking.
$$$–$$$$	**Prince of Wales**, Coronado. Ocean views and inventive cooking drive this Hotel Del Cornado staple.
$$$–$$$$	**Star of the Sea**, Downtown. One of San Diego's top seafood restaurants has a terrace perfect for taking in the waterfront.
$$$–$$$$	**Tapenade**, La Jolla. This superb Provençal restaurant on a quiet side street serves brisk, earthy flavors in an intimate, bistro-like dining room or a spacious terrace.
¢–$$$$	**Baja Lobster**, Chula Vista. Meals of fried lobster, tortilla, rice, beans and salsa are every bit as savory as those served 60 mi south of the border in the famous "lobster village" of Puero Nuevo.

BUDGET RESTAURANTS

$–$$	**Region**, Hillcrest. Near-perfect entrées and fine sweets at reasonable prices invigorate this contemporary spot.

$-$$ Zocalo Grill, Old Town. Try to sit on the covered terrace, but the contemporary food tastes just as good anywhere in the spacious and handsome eatery.

¢-$$ Celadon Fine Thai Cuisine, Hillcrest. The menu is good enough to keep this small, well-furnished dining room jumping, even on Monday nights.

¢-$$ Sushi Ota, Pacific Beach. San Diego's best sushi is found in this unlikely space on Mission Bay Drive.

¢-$ Hodad's, Ocean Beach. Burgers are the thing, loaded with onions, pickles, tomatoes, and lettuce, and gloriously messy.

¢-$ The Tin Fish, Gaslamp Quarter. The quality of the food at this eatery less than 100 yards from the Petco Park routinely surpasses that at grander establishments.

MUSEUMS

Maritime Museum, Embarcadero. A collection of five restored sail- and steam-powered ships dating from the late 19th and early 20th centuries is a must for nautical history buffs.

Mingei International Museum, Balboa Park. All ages will enjoy the colorful and creative exhibits of toys, pottery, textiles, costumes, and gadgets from around the globe.

Reuben H. Fleet Science Center, Balboa Park. Clever interactive exhibits are sneakily educational. The IMAX Dome Theater screens exhilarating nature and science films.

San Diego Natural History Museum, Balboa Park. There are 7.5 million fossils, dinosaur models, and even live reptiles and other specimens here.

PARKS

Legoland California, Carlsbad. Thrill rides just big enough for little ones top the attractions here. Especially worth exploring is Miniland, created entirely of Lego blocks.

San Diego Wild Animal Park, Escondido. Civilized and wild at the same time, this is your best opportunity to experience the wilds of Africa without every leaving North America. You'll get up-close-and-personal with lions, cheetah, and giraffe.

SeaWorld of California, Mission Bay. Observe sharks and walruses in walk-through marine environments, or be entertained by killer whales, sea lions and otters in one of four arenas.

QUINTESSENTIAL SAN DIEGO

A Sunday picnic in Balboa Park. Forget about the park's museums (for one day, anyway) and settle down to your own custom-made meal on a grassy spot near one of the park's many gardens.

Hiking at Cabrillo National Monument on Point Loma. Perched at the end of the peninsula, this 144-acre preserve of rugged cliffs and shores and outstanding overlooks was set aside as a National Park Service site to commemorate Portuguese explorer Juan Rodríguez Cabrillo.

Following the Padres at Mission San Luis Rey. Walk in the steps of the Franciscan padres who founded California's 21 missions. Explore gardens, chapels, and everyday life at the largest and most prosperous of the missions.

Ferrying across San Diego Harbor. The ferry between San Diego and Coronado provides spectacular views of the harbor, downtown, and Coronado.

Exploring the San Diego Zoo. The mother of the modern "habitat" zoo, in Balboa Park, is a must-see if you venture anywhere near San Diego. By foot or by tram you can visit Malayan tapirs, Siberian reindeer, and giant pandas.

Unwinding on Silver Strand State Beach. Calm surf, plenty of lifeguards, and a generally quiet mood make this Coronado beach ideal for families.

Spotting a gray whale spouting during the winter migration. As many as 200 whales pass the San Diego coast each day on their way south to Mexico (starting in mid-December) or back north (until mid-March).

SHOPS WORTH A STOP

Bazaar Del Mundo, Old Town. This multi-colored Mexican *mercado* is aswirl with tiled fountains, flowers, and courtyard shops overflowing with handicrafts and other treasures. After shopping, have a margarita and terrific Mexican food.

Fashion Valley Center, Mission Valley. The best mall in San Diego, near Mission Valley hotels and a trolley station, has every chain shop and specialty store you'd want, plus valet parking.

Ferry Landing Marketplace, Coronado. For the quintessential San Diego shopping experience, take the ferry from the Embarcadero over to Coronado Island. The marketplace is full of gift shops, plus you get to savor the stunning backdrop of bay and downtown skyline.

VIEWS

Winter stargazing in Anza-Borrego Desert State Park. The absence of city lights in the clear winter sky provides a backdrop for a veritable cascade of stars, planets, constellations, meteor showers, and passing comets.

A morning stroll about La Jolla Cove. Palm-lined Ellen Browning Scripps Park on the cliffs overlooking the cove is one of the prettiest spots in the world. Try breakfast on the patio at Brockton Villa, which has a fantastic view of the cove.

Twilight Hot Air Ballooning over coastal North County. Several companies will fly you up to see incredible views of nearly the entire county from the ocean to the mountains.

Sunset from the Top of the Hyatt. Savor the most incredible views in the city while laying back in what feels like a private club lounge. Stop by around sunset for a drink and a view that will make you want to sell the house and move here.

Taking it in at Torrey Pines South Golf Course. The sweeping Pacific Ocean views and tournament quality links make it hard to believe you're playing on a municipal course.

Up on the roof at the W. The W hotel is the best indicator of the resurgence of cool in San Diego's nightlife. From the loungy Living Room bar to the rooftop Beach bar (complete with beach chairs and heated sand), it's no insider's secret that this is the hip spot to be. The blocks-long line to get in is proof.

SMART TRAVEL TIPS

Finding out about your destination before you leave home means you won't squander time organizing everyday minutiae once you've arrived. You'll be more streetwise when you hit the ground as well, better prepared to explore the aspects of San Diego that drew you here in the first place. The organizations in this section can provide information to supplement this guide; contact them for up-to-the-minute details, and consult the A to Z sections that end the North County chapter for facts on the various topics as they relate to the areas around San Diego. Happy landings!

ADDRESSES

Downtown San Diego streets are on a grid. Numbered avenues and streets run on the north–south axis. East–west streets are alphabetical. North of A Street, streets continue as Ash, Beech, Cedar, Date, through Upas Street. Below C Street are a few streets with names in place of letters.

AIR TRAVEL TO & FROM SAN DIEGO

BOOKING

When you book, look for nonstop flights and remember that "direct" flights stop at least once. Try to avoid connecting flights, which require a change of plane. Two airlines may operate a connecting flight jointly, so ask whether your airline operates every segment of the trip; you may find that the carrier you prefer flies you only part of the way. To find more booking tips and to check prices and make online flight reservations, log on to www.fodors.com.

CARRIERS

All major and some regional U.S. carriers serve San Diego International Airport. Aero Mexico is the only international carrier to San Diego. All others require a connecting flight, usually in Los Angeles. Other connection points are Chicago, Dallas, and San Francisco.

🛪 Major Airlines AeroMexico ☎ 800/237-6639 ⊕ www.aeromexico.com. American/American Eagle ☎ 800/433-7300, 0845/7789-789 in U.K. ⊕ www.aa.com. Continental ☎ 800/525-0280 ⊕ www.continental.com. Delta ☎ 800/221-1212,

0800/414767 in U.K. ⊕ www.delta.com. **Northwest** ☎ 800/225-2525 ⊕ www.nwa.com. **United/United Express** ☎ 800/538-2929, 0800/888555 in U.K. ⊕ www.united.com. **US Airways** ☎ 800/428-4322 ⊕ www.usairways.com.

🔝 Regional & Smaller Airlines **Alaska Airlines** ☎ 800/252-7522 ⊕ www.alaskaair.com. **America West** ☎ 800/235-9292 ⊕ www.americawest.com. **Frontier** ☎ 800/432-1359 ⊕ www.frontierairlines.com. **Hawaiian Airlines** ☎ 800/367-5320 ⊕ www.hawaiianair.com. **JetBlue** ☎ 800/538-2583 ⊕ www.jetblue.com. **Southwest** ☎ 800/435-9792 ⊕ www.iflyswa.com. **Sun Country** ☎ 800/359-6786 ⊕ www.suncountry.com.

CHECK-IN & BOARDING

Coastal fog can delay landings and take-offs, and a delayed flight or two can jam the small boarding areas. During inclement weather **call your airline** to see if there are delays.

Always **find out your carrier's check-in policy.** Plan to arrive at the airport about two hours before your scheduled departure time for domestic flights and 2½ to 3 hours before international flights. You may need to arrive earlier if you're flying from one of the busier airports or during peak air-traffic times. To avoid delays at airport-security checkpoints, try not to wear any metal. Jewelry, belt and other buckles, steel-toe shoes, barrettes, and underwire bras are among the items that can set off detectors.

Assuming that not everyone with a ticket will show up, airlines routinely overbook planes. When everyone does, airlines ask for volunteers to give up their seats. In return, these volunteers usually get a several-hundred-dollar flight voucher, which can be used toward the purchase of another ticket, and are rebooked on the next flight out. If there are not enough volunteers, the airline must choose who will be denied boarding. The first to get bumped are passengers who checked in late and those flying on discounted tickets, so get to the gate and check in as early as possible, especially during peak periods.

Always **bring a government-issued photo ID** to the airport; even when it's not required, a passport is best.

CUTTING COSTS

The least expensive airfares to San Diego are priced for round-trip travel and usually must be purchased in advance. Airlines generally allow you to change your return date for a fee; most low-fare tickets, however, are nonrefundable.

It's smart to call a number of airlines and check the Internet; when you are quoted a good price, book it on the spot—the same fare may not be available the next day, or even the next hour. Always check different routings and look into using alternate airports. Also, price off-peak flights, which may be significantly less expensive than others. Travel agents, especially low-fare specialists (⇨ Discounts & Deals), are helpful.

Consolidators are another good source. They buy tickets for scheduled flights at reduced rates from the airlines, then sell them at prices that beat the best fare available directly from the airlines. (Many also offer reduced car-rental and hotel rates.) Sometimes you can even get your money back if you need to return the ticket. Carefully read the fine print detailing penalties for changes and cancellations, purchase the ticket with a credit card, and confirm your consolidator reservation with the airline.

When you fly as a courier, you trade your checked-luggage space for a ticket deeply subsidized by a courier service. There are restrictions on when you can book and how long you can stay. Some courier companies list with membership organizations, such as the Air Courier Association and the International Association of Air Travel Couriers; these require you to become a member before you can book a flight.

🔝 Consolidators **AirlineConsolidator.com** ☎ 888/468-5385 ⊕ www.airlineconsolidator.com, for international tickets. **Best Fares** ☎ 800/880-1234 or 800/576-8255 ⊕ www.bestfares.com; $59.90 annual membership. **Cheap Tickets** ☎ 800/377-1000 or 800/652-4327 ⊕ www.cheaptickets.com. **Expedia** ☎ 800/397-3342 or 404/728-8787 ⊕ www.expedia.com. **Hotwire** ☎ 866/468-9473 or 920/330-9418 ⊕ www.hotwire.com. **Now Voyager Travel** ✉ 45 W. 21st St., Suite 5A, New York, NY 10010 ☎ 212/459-1616 📠 212/243-2711 ⊕ www.nowvoyagertravel.com.

Onetravel.com ⊕ www.onetravel.com. Orbitz ☎ 888/656–4546 ⊕ www.orbitz.com. Priceline.com ⊕ www.priceline.com. Travelocity ☎ 888/709–5983, 877/282–2925 in Canada, 0870/876–3876 in U.K. ⊕ www.travelocity.com.

🔝 Courier Resources Air Courier Association/Cheaptrips.com ☎ 800/280–5973 or 800/282–1202 ⊕ www.aircourier.org or www.cheaptrips.com; $34 annual membership. International Association of Air Travel Couriers ☎ 308/632–3273 ⊕ www.courier.org; $45 annual membership. Now Voyager Travel ✉ 45 W. 21st St., Suite 5A, New York, NY 10010 ☎ 212/459–1616 📠 212/243–2711 ⊕ www.nowvoyagertravel.com.

ENJOYING THE FLIGHT

State your seat preference when purchasing your ticket, and then repeat it when you confirm and when you check in. For more legroom, you can request one of the few emergency-aisle seats at check-in, if you're capable of moving obstacles comparable in weight to an airplane exit door (usually between 35 pounds and 60 pounds)—a Federal Aviation Administration requirement of passengers in these seats. Seats behind a bulkhead also offer more legroom, but they don't have under-seat storage. Don't sit in the row in front of the emergency aisle or in front of a bulkhead, where seats may not recline.

Ask the airline whether a snack or meal is served on the flight. If you have dietary concerns, request special meals when booking. These can be vegetarian, low-cholesterol, or kosher, for example. It's a good idea to pack some healthful snacks and a small (plastic) bottle of water in your carry-on bag. On long flights, try to maintain a normal routine, to help fight jet lag. At night, get some sleep. By day, eat light meals, drink water (not alcohol), and **move around the cabin** to stretch your legs. For additional jet-lag tips consult *Fodor's FYI: Travel Fit & Healthy* (available at bookstores everywhere).

Smoking policies vary from carrier to carrier. Many airlines prohibit smoking on all of their flights; others allow smoking only on certain routes or certain departures. Ask your carrier about its policy.

FLYING TIMES

Flying time to San Diego is 5 hours from New York, 3½ hours from Chicago, 3 ½ hours from Dallas, ¾ hour from Los Angeles, 10–11 hours from London. Travelers from London who transfer at Los Angeles's airport should expect to reach San Diego about two to three hours after landing in Los Angeles.

HOW TO COMPLAIN

If your baggage goes astray or your flight goes awry, complain right away. Most carriers require that you **file a claim immediately.** The Aviation Consumer Protection Division of the Department of Transportation publishes *Fly-Rights*, which discusses airlines and consumer issues and is available online. You can also find articles and information on mytravelrights.com, the Web site of the nonprofit Consumer Travel Rights Center.

🔝 Airline Complaints Aviation Consumer Protection Division ✉ U.S. Department of Transportation, Office of Aviation Enforcement and Proceedings, C-75, Room 4107, 400 7th St. SW, Washington, DC 20590 ☎ 202/366–2220 ⊕ www.airconsumer.ost.dot.gov. Federal Aviation Administration Consumer Hotline ✉ For inquiries: FAA, 800 Independence Ave. SW, Washington, DC 20591 ☎ 800/322–7873 ⊕ www.faa.gov.

RECONFIRMING

Check the status of your flight before you leave for the airport. You can do this on your carrier's Web site, by linking to a flight-status checker (many Web booking services offer these), or by calling your carrier or travel agent.

AIRPORTS & TRANSFERS

The major airport is **San Diego International Airport,** called Lindbergh Field locally. The airport's three-letter code is SAN. Major airlines depart and arrive at Terminal 1 and Terminal 2; commuter flights identified on your ticket with a 3000 sequence flight number depart from the commuter terminal. A red shuttle bus travels between terminals.

The San Diego International Airport remains too small to accommodate projected traffic. Small problems can cause congestion and delays. Delays of 20–30 minutes in baggage claim are not unusual. Most international flights depart from and arrive at the Los Angeles International Airport (LAX); both American Eagle and United Express have frequent flights between LAX and San Diego. Ground shuttle service is available between LAX and San Diego.

If you need travel assistance at the airport, Travelers Aid has two information booths, one in Terminal 1 (east) and one in Terminal 2 (west), open daily 8 AM–11 PM.

⛶ Airport Information **San Diego International Airport** ☎ 619/400-2400 ⊕ www.san.org.

AIRPORT TRANSFERS

The airport is three miles 3 mi from downtown. Ground transportation services include shuttle vans, buses, and taxis. All services operate from the Transportation Plaza, reached via the skybridges from Terminals 1 and 2. The cheapest and sometimes most convenient shuttle is San Diego Transit's Flyer route 922, red- and blue-stripe buses that serve the terminals at 10- to 15-minute intervals between 5 AM and 1 AM. These buses have luggage racks and make a loop from the airport to downtown along Broadway to 9th Avenue and back, stopping frequently within walking distance of many hotels; it also connects with the San Diego Trolley, Amtrak, and the Coaster. The fare is $2.25, including transfer to local transit buses and the trolley, and you should **have exact fare handy.** If you're heading to North County, the Flyer can drop you off at the Santa Fe Terminal, from which you can take the Coaster commuter train as far north as Oceanside for $3.75–$4.75. Of the various airport shuttles, only Cloud 9 can accommodate wheelchairs.

Limousine rates vary and are per hour, per mile, or both, with some minimums established. Most offer bilingual guide service.

Taxi fare is $10 plus tip to most downtown hotels. Fare to Coronado runs about $16 plus tip.

If you rent a car at the airport, take Harbor Drive east to reach downtown, or west to reach Shelter Island and Point Loma. To access I–5 and I–8, take Harbor Drive west to Nimitz Boulevard, then right on

Rosecrans Street. You can reach La Jolla and North County via I–5 North. Interstate 8 East leads to Hotel Circle, Fashion Valley, Mission Valley, and Qualcomm Stadium. To reach Mission Bay continue on Nimitz Boulevard, which intersects with Sunset Cliffs Boulevard. To get to Coronado, take Harbor Drive east and turn left on Grape Street to reach I–5 South. Take the Highway 75 exit to cross the San Diego–Coronado Bay Bridge.

⛶ Limousines & Shuttles **Cloud 9 Shuttle** ☎ 800/974-8885 ⊕ www.cloud9shuttle.com. **Five Star** ☎ 619/294-3000. **Premier Ride** ☎ 619/234-7433. **San Diego Transit** ☎ 619/233-3004 ⊕ www.sdcommute.com.

BOAT & FERRY TRAVEL

If you're arriving in San Diego by private boat, keep in mind that many hotels, marinas, and yacht clubs rent slips short-term. Call ahead as available space is limited. The San Diego and Southwestern yacht clubs have reciprocal arrangements with other yacht clubs.

The small Coronado ferry ($2 one-way fare and 50¢ per bicycle), is a reminder of the pre-Coronado Bridge days when ferries provided regular transportation between Coronado and downtown. Now it's a small excursion service that is fun to ride, but is not often used as a practical transportation method.

FARES & SCHEDULES

⛶ Boat & Ferry Information **San Diego-Coronado Ferry** ☎ 619/234-4111.

⛶ Marinas **Best Western Island Palms Hotel & Marina** ✉ 2051 Shelter Island Dr. ☎ 619/222-0561. **Dana Inn & Marina** ✉ 1710 W. Mission Bay Dr. ☎ 619/222-6440. **Hyatt Regency Islandia** ✉ 1441 Quivira Rd. ☎ 619/224-1234. **Shelter Pointe Hotel and Marina** ✉ 1551 Shelter Island Dr. ☎ 619/224-7547. **San Diego Marriott Hotel and Marina** ✉ 333 W. Harbor Dr. ☎ 619/234-1500. **San Diego Yacht Club** ✉ 1011 Anchorage La. ☎ 619/221-8400. **Southwestern Yacht Club** ✉ 2702 Qualtrough St. ☎ 619/222-0438.

BUSINESS HOURS

Most banks are open weekdays 10–6. Some open for several hours on Saturday. Most other businesses are open

Monday–Saturday 9 or 10 AM to 6 or 9 PM. Many others are also open Sunday from noon to 5 or 6.

MUSEUMS & SIGHTS

Most museums are open Tuesday through Sunday 10 to 5. Major attractions are open daily 9 to 5, later in summer and during the Christmas holidays.

PHARMACIES

Most pharmacies in malls are open daily from 8 or 9 AM to 9 PM; some may close at 6 PM on Sunday.

SHOPS

Mall and shopping center stores are open daily from 9 or 10 AM to 9 PM; some close at 6 PM on Sunday. Shops and boutiques in neighborhoods such as Hillcrest and La Jolla keep somewhat erratic hours, so it's a good idea to call first. Shops and restaurants in rural areas such as Julian and Descanso may close mid-week.

BUS TRAVEL TO & FROM SAN DIEGO

Greyhound operates 16 buses a day between San Diego and Los Angeles, connecting with buses to all major U.S. cities. Many buses are express or nonstop; others make stops at coastal towns en route.

Small bus companies connect San Diego to cities such as Chula Vista, National City, and Campo. Laidlaw Transit operates the Rural Bus that connects rural and backcountry communities such as Ramona, Jamul, Campo, Julian and Borrego Springs. Service and schedules vary.

FARES & SCHEDULES

One-way fare to Los Angeles is $15, round-trip is $25. You can buy Greyhound tickets at the depot or in advance by phone.

Community and rural bus routes charge from $1 to $3.75.

RESERVATIONS

Boarding is on a first-come, first-served basis.

▓ Bus Information **Chula Vista Transit** ☎ 619/233-3004 ⊕ www.sdcommute.com. **Greyhound** ✉ 120 W. Broadway ☎ 619/239-8082 or 800/231-2222. **National City Transit** ☎ 619/474-7505.

Northeast Rural Bus System ☎ 760/767-4287. **Rural Bus** ☎ 800/858-0291.

BUS TRAVEL WITHIN SAN DIEGO

Also see *Trolley Travel.*

San Diego County is served by a coordinated, efficient network of bus and rail routes that includes service to Oceanside in the north, the Mexican border at San Ysidro, and points east to the Anza-Borrego Desert. Under the umbrella of Metropolitan Transit District, there are two major transit agencies: San Diego Transit and North County Transit District (NCTD). The staff at the downtown Transit Store sells passes and can help plan your travel.

San Diego Transit Buses connect with the San Diego Trolley light rail system at the San Diego Zoo, Balboa Park, Lindbergh Field, Mission Beach, Pacific Beach, La Jolla, and regional shopping centers.

NCTD routes connect with Coaster commuter train routes between Oceanside and the Santa Fe Station in San Diego. They serve from Del Mar North to San Clemente, inland to Fallbrook, Pauma Valley, Valley Center, Ramona, and Escondido, with transfer points within the city of San Diego. NCTD also offers special express-bus service to Qualcomm Stadium for select major sporting events. In Coronado the ATV Van Co. operates a bus service.

FARES & SCHEDULES

San Diego Transit fares range $1–$2.25. NCTD fares are $1.50. Discounted fares of 75¢ are available for seniors and for people with disabilities. Most transfers are free; request one when boarding. Schedules are posted at each stop, and the buses usually are on time.

▓ Bus Information **North County Transit District** ☎ 800/266-6883 ⊕ www.sdcommute.com. **San Diego Transit** ☎ 619/233-3004, 619/234-5005 TTY, TDD ⊕ www.sdcommute.com. **Transit Store** ✉ 102 Broadway Downtown ☎ 619/234-1060.

PAYING

You must have exact change in coins and/or bills. Pay upon boarding.

CAMERAS & PHOTOGRAPHY

The most popular San Diego residents to capture on film are Shamu the whale at SeaWorld and the San Diego Zoo's giant pandas. The most dramatic views are the harbor from the Coronado Bridge and the ocean from the bluffs at La Jolla Cove. The *Kodak Guide to Shooting Great Travel Pictures* (available at bookstores everywhere) is loaded with tips.

🖪 Photo Help **Kodak Information Center** ☏ 800/242-2424 ⊕ www.kodak.com.

EQUIPMENT PRECAUTIONS

Don't pack film or equipment in checked luggage, where it is much more susceptible to damage. X-ray machines used to view checked luggage are extremely powerful and therefore are likely to ruin your film. Try to ask for hand inspection of film, which becomes clouded after repeated exposure to airport X-ray machines, and keep videotapes and computer disks away from metal detectors. Always keep film, tape, and computer disks out of the sun. Carry an extra supply of batteries, and be prepared to turn on your camera, camcorder, or laptop to prove to airport security personnel that the device is real.

CAR RENTAL

A car is essential for San Diego's sprawling freeway system and comes in handy for touring Baja California (though the trolley serves the border at Tijuana). Rates in San Diego fluctuate with seasons and demand, but generally begin at $39 a day and $250 a week for an economy car with air-conditioning, automatic transmission, and unlimited mileage. This does not include tax on car rentals, which is 7.5%.

🖪 Major Agencies **Alamo** ☏ 800/327-9633 ⊕ www.alamo.com. **Avis** ☏ 800/331-1212, 800/879-2847 or 800/272-5871 in Canada, 0870/606-0100 in U.K., 02/9353-9000 in Australia, 09/526-2847 in New Zealand ⊕ www.avis.com. **Budget** ☏ 800/527-0700, 0870/156-5656 in U.K. ⊕ www.budget.com. **Dollar** ☏ 800/800-4000, 0800/085-4578 in U.K. ⊕ www.dollar.com. **Hertz** ☏ 800/654-3131, 800/263-0600 in Canada, 0870/844-8844 in U.K., 02/9669-2444 in Australia, 09/256-8690 in New Zealand ⊕ www.hertz.com. **National Car Rental** ☏ 800/227-7368, 0870/600-6666 in U.K. ⊕ www.nationalcar.com.

CUTTING COSTS

For a good deal, book through a travel agent who will shop around. Also, price local car-rental companies—whose prices may be lower still, although their service and maintenance may not be as good as those of major rental agencies—and research rates on the Internet. Consolidators that specialize in air travel can offer good rates on cars as well (⇨ Air Travel). Remember to ask about required deposits, cancellation penalties, and drop-off charges if you're planning to pick up the car in one city and leave it in another. If you're traveling during a holiday period, also make sure that a confirmed reservation guarantees you a car.

Do look into wholesalers, companies that do not own fleets but rent in bulk from those that do and offer better rates than traditional car-rental operations. Prices are best during off-peak periods. Rentals booked through wholesalers often must be paid for before you leave home.

🖪 Local Agencies **Enterprise** ✉ 900 F St., 92101 ☏ 619/696-5000 picks up at area hotels.

INSURANCE

For about $9 to $25 a day, rental companies sell protection, known as a collision- or loss-damage waiver (CDW or LDW), that eliminates your liability for damage to the car; it's always optional and should never be automatically added to your bill. In most states you don't need a CDW if you have personal auto insurance or other liability insurance. Some states, including California, have capped the price of the CDW and LDW. However, **make sure you have enough coverage to pay for the car.** If you do not have auto insurance or an umbrella policy that covers damage to third parties, purchasing liability insurance and a CDW or LDW is highly recommended.

REQUIREMENTS & RESTRICTIONS

In California you must be 21 to rent a car, and rates may be higher if you're under 25. Some agencies will not rent to those under 25; check when you book. You'll pay extra for child seats (about $5 per day), which are compulsory for children under five. Children up to age six or 60 pounds must be placed in booster seats. There is no extra charge for an additional driver. Non–U.S. residents must have a license whose text is in the Roman alphabet, though it need not be in English. An international license is recommended but not required.

SURCHARGES

Before you pick up a car in one city and leave it in another, ask about drop-off charges or one-way service fees, which can be substantial. Also inquire about early-return policies; some rental agencies charge extra if you return the car before the time specified in your contract while others give you a refund for the days not used. To avoid a hefty refueling fee, fill the tank just before you turn in the car, but be aware that gas stations near the rental outlet may overcharge. It's almost never a deal to buy the tank of gas that's in the car when you rent it; the understanding is that you'll return it empty, but some fuel usually remains. Surcharges may apply if you're under 25 or if you take the car outside the area approved by the rental agency. You'll pay extra for child seats (about $8 a day), which are compulsory for children under five, and usually for additional drivers (up to $25 a day, depending on location).

CAR TRAVEL

When traveling in the San Diego area, it pays to consider the big picture to avoid getting lost. Water lies to the west of the city. On the east and north sides of the city, mountains separate the urban areas from the desert. Interstate 5 stretches from Canada to the Mexican border and bisects San Diego. Interstate 8 provides access from Yuma, Arizona, and points east. Drivers coming from Nevada and the mountain regions beyond can reach San Diego on I–15. During rush hour there are jams on I–5 and on I–15 between I–805 and Escondido.

EMERGENCY SERVICES

Dial 911 to report accidents on the road and to reach police, the highway patrol, or the fire department. Emergency phone boxes can be found along most Interstate highways.

GASOLINE

The cost of gas varies widely depending on location, oil company, and whether you use the full-serve or self-serve aisle. Prices on the West Coast tend to be higher than those in the rest of the country, and in San Diego prices run about 15% higher than in many other California cities. Regular unleaded gasoline at self-serve stations costs about $2.22 a gallon.

PARKING

Balboa Park, Cabrillo National Monument, and Mission Bay all have huge free parking lots and it's rare not to find a space, though it may seem as if you've parked miles from your destination. Lots downtown are plentiful and cost $3–$35 per day. Old Town has large lots off the Transit Center. Parking is more of a problem in La Jolla and Coronado, where you generally need to rely on hard-to-find street spots or expensive by-the-hour parking lots.

Parking at meters costs $2 an hour; enforcement is 8 AM–6 PM except Sunday. Be extra careful around rush hour, when certain street-parking areas become tow-away zones. In the evenings and during events it can be difficult to locate parking spaces downtown. Parking violations in congested areas can cost you $25 or more. Car renters are liable for parking tickets and towing charges incurred.

ROAD CONDITIONS

Highways are generally in good condition in the San Diego area. Traffic is particularly heavy on I–5, I–8, I–805, and I–15 during morning and afternoon rush hours 6–8:30 AM and 3:30–6 PM. Before venturing into the mountains, check on road conditions; mountain driving can be dangerous. Listen to radio traffic reports for information on the lines waiting to cross the border to Mexico.

Maps **AAA San Diego** ✉ 2365 Northside Dr., Suite 120 ☎ 619/233-1000.

RULES OF THE ROAD

Speed limits are 35 mph on city streets and 65 mph on freeways, unless otherwise indicated. Right turns are permitted at red lights after stopping unless otherwise indicated. In San Diego, be alert for one-way streets, "no left turn" intersections, and blocks closed to car traffic. Driving with a blood-alcohol level higher than 0.08 will result in arrest and seizure of driver's license. The law is strictly enforced, and fines are severe.

Seat belts are required at all times and tickets are given for failing to comply. Always **strap children age six and under, and weighing 60 pounds or less, into approved child-safety seats.** Children must wear seat belts regardless of where they're seated (studies show that children are safest in the rear rather than the front seats).

Many California freeways have High Occupancy Vehicle lanes, usually restricted to vehicles carrying two or more persons. Speed is checked by radar.

CHILDREN IN SAN DIEGO

San Diego is a family-oriented destination, with many attractions geared to kids. You'll find strollers for rent, diaper-changing facilities, kids' menus, and special activities for kids at most major attractions.

The monthly *San Diego Family Magazine* is filled with listings of events and resources; it's available by mail for $3.50, which covers postage and handling, or free in San Diego at Longs Drug Stores, Blockbuster, MacDonald's, and local libraries. If you're renting a car, don't forget to **arrange for a car seat** when you reserve. For general advice about traveling with children, consult *Fodor's FYI: Travel with Your Baby. Fodor's Around San Diego with Kids* can help you plan your days together.

🇮 Local Information **San Diego Family Magazine** 🗐 Box 23960, San Diego 92193 📠 619/685–6970 ⊕ www.sandiegofamily.com.

BABYSITTING

Many agencies specialize in on-and-off-site group and individual child care for conventions, tourists, and special events. They are licensed, bonded, and insured. Hotel concierges can usually recommend a reliable babysitting service.

🇮 Agencies **Panda Services** ✉ 4655 Ruffner St., No. 100, San Diego 92111 📠 858/292–5503 ⊕ www. sandiegobabysitters.com. **Marion's Child Care**

✉ 4328 60th St., San Diego 92115 📠 619/582–5029 ⊕ www.hotelchildcare.com.

FLYING

If your children are two or older, ask about children's airfares. As a general rule, infants under two not occupying a seat fly at greatly reduced fares or even for free. But if you want to guarantee a seat for an infant, you have to pay full fare. Consider flying during off-peak days and times; most airlines will grant an infant a seat without a ticket if there are available seats.

Experts agree that it's a good idea to use safety seats aloft for children weighing less than 40 pounds. Airlines set their own policies: if you use a safety seat, U.S. carriers usually require that the child be ticketed, even if he or she is young enough to ride free, because the seats must be strapped into regular seats. And even if you pay the full adult fare for the seat, it may be worth it, especially on longer trips. Do **check your airline's policy about using safety seats during takeoff and landing.** Safety seats are not allowed everywhere in the plane, so get your seat assignments as early as possible.

When reserving, request children's meals or a freestanding bassinet (not available at all airlines) if you need them. But note that bulkhead seats, where you must sit to use the bassinet, may lack an overhead bin or storage space on the floor.

FOOD

Most San Diego restaurants make at least some accommodation for kids: child-size portions, seats for children, amusements such as crayons and coloring paper, or, at a minimum, friendliness. The Gaslamp Quarter and La Jolla both have a Hard Rock Cafe, which is a big hit with kids and teenagers. Of the places reviewed in the Where to Eat chapter, the Cheesecake Factory, the Fish Market, Ghirardelli Soda Fountain & Chocolate Shop, Hob Nob Hill, Ricky's Family Restaurant, and Blumberg's are particularly suited to families; your children's din will blend right in.

LODGING

Most hotels in San Diego allow children under a certain age to stay in their parents' room at no extra charge, but others charge for them as extra adults; be sure to **find out the cutoff age for children's discounts.** Kids will find plenty to keep them busy at any of San Diego's waterfront hotels, including the Hotel Del Coronado, the Dana Inn, and Bahia Resort Hotel on Mission Bay.

▸ Best Choices **Bahia Resort Hotel** ✉ 998 W. Mission Bay Dr., Mission Bay ☎ 858/488-0551. **Dana Inn & Marina** ✉ 1710 W. Mission Bay Dr., Mission Bay ☎ 619/222-6440. **Hotel Del Coronado** ✉ 1500 Orange Ave., Coronado ☎ 619/435-6611.

SIGHTS & ATTRACTIONS

All of San Diego's top attractions are designed for family entertainment. Places that are especially appealing to children are indicated by a rubber-duckie icon (🐥) in the margin.

The San Diego Zoo has a Children's Zoo filled with pettable goats, lambs, bunnies, and guinea pigs; diapered baby primates are often the stars in the nursery. SeaWorld San Diego always makes a big splash with the kids, many of whom race for front-row seats at the Shamu show. Hands-on activities include Shamu's Happy Harbor, Forbidden Reef, and California Tide Pools.

At Legoland California colorful plastic building blocks are climb-on or crawl-through. Expect long lines at the driving school, the pedal boats, and for the Power Tower.

CONCIERGES

Concierges, found in many hotels, can help you with theater tickets and dinner reservations: a good one with connections may be able to get you seats for a hot show or prime-time dinner reservations at the restaurant of the moment. You can also turn to your hotel's concierge for help with travel arrangements, sightseeing plans, services ranging from aromatherapy to zipper repair, and emergencies. **Always tip** a concierge who has been of assistance (➪ Tipping).

CONSUMER PROTECTION

Whether you're shopping for gifts or purchasing travel services, **pay with a major credit card** whenever possible, so you can cancel payment or get reimbursed if there's

a problem (and you can provide documentation). If you're doing business with a particular company for the first time, contact your local Better Business Bureau and the attorney general's offices in your state and (for U.S. businesses) the company's home state as well. Have any complaints been filed? Finally, if you're buying a package or tour, always consider travel insurance that includes default coverage (➪ Insurance).

▸ BBBs **Council of Better Business Bureaus** ✉ 4200 Wilson Blvd., Suite 800, Arlington, VA 7505 3 ☎ 703/276-0100 🖶 703/525-8277 ⊕ www.bbb. org. **Better Business Bureau** ✉ 5050 Murphy Canyon Rd., Suite 110, San Diego, CA 92123 ☎ 858/ 637-6199 🖶 858/496-2141 ⊕ www.sandiegobbb.org.

CRUISE TRAVEL

Several cruise-ship lines make San Diego a port of call. Holland America and Royal Caribbean use San Diego as a regular point of embarkation for seasonal cruises to Alaska, the Mexican Riviera, and the Panama Canal. Other lines including Princess, Celebrity, and Norwegian Cruise Line originate repositioning cruises from San Diego throughout the year. The San Diego cruise ship terminal is on the downtown waterfront just steps from the San Diego Maritime Museum and Midway Museum. The terminal is a short taxi ride to Balboa Park, Little Italy, and the Gaslamp Quarter. To learn how to plan, choose, and book a cruise-ship voyage, check out Cruise How-to's on ⊕ www.fodors.com.

▸ Cruise Lines **Carnival** ☎ 800/327-95021 ⊕ www. carnival.com. **Celebrity** ☎ 800/437-3111 ⊕ www. celebrity.com. **Holland America** ☎ 800/426-0327 ⊕ www.hollandamerica.com. **Norwegian Cruise Line** ☎ 800/327-7030 ⊕ www.ncl.com. **Princess** ☎ 800/774-6237 ⊕ www.princess.com. **Radisson Seven Seas** ☎ 877/505-5370 ⊕ www.rssc.com. **Royal Caribbean International** ☎ 800/398-9819 ⊕ www.royalcaribbean.com. **Royal Olympic** ☎ 800/ 872-6400 ⊕ www.royalolympiccruises.com.

CUSTOMS & DUTIES

When shopping in Mexico, **keep receipts** for all purchases. Upon reentering the country, **be ready to show customs officials what you've bought.** If you feel a duty is incorrect, appeal the assessment. If you object to the way your clearance was handled, note the inspector's badge number. In either case, first ask to see a supervisor. If the problem isn't resolved, write to the appropriate authorities, beginning with the port director at your point of entry. Customs officers operate at the San Ysidro border crossing, San Diego International Airport, and in the bay at Shelter Island.

🄵 **San Ysidro Port of Entry** ✉ 720 E. San Ysidro Blvd., 92173 ☎ 619/690-8800 🖶 619/662-7374. **San Diego Customs Management Center** ✉ 610 W. Ash St., Suite 1200, San Diego 92101 ☎ 619/557-5455 🖶 619/557-5394 ⊕ www.customs.gov.

IN AUSTRALIA

Australian residents who are 18 or older may bring home A$400 worth of souvenirs and gifts (including jewelry), 250 cigarettes or 250 grams of cigars or other tobacco products, and 1,125 ml of alcohol (including wine, beer, and spirits). Residents under 18 may bring back A$200 worth of goods. Members of the same family traveling together may pool their allowances. Prohibited items include meat products. Seeds, plants, and fruits need to be declared upon arrival.

🄵 **Australian Customs Service** 🄳 Regional Director, Box 8, Sydney, NSW 2001 ☎ 02/9213-2000, 1300/363263, 02/9364-7222, or 1800/020-504 quarantine-inquiry line 🖶 02/9213-4043 ⊕ www.customs.gov.au.

IN CANADA

Canadian residents who have been out of Canada for at least seven days may bring in C$750 worth of goods duty-free. If you've been away fewer than seven days but more than 48 hours, the duty-free allowance drops to C$200. If your trip lasts 24 to 48 hours, the allowance is C$50. You may not pool allowances with family members. Goods claimed under the C$750 exemption may follow you by mail; those claimed under the lesser exemptions must accompany you. Alcohol and tobacco products may be included in the seven-day and 48-hour exemptions but not in the 24-hour exemption. If you meet the age requirements of the province or territory through which you reenter Canada, you may bring in, duty-free, 1.5 liters of wine

or 1.14 liters (40 imperial ounces) of liquor or 24 12-ounce cans or bottles of beer or ale. Also, if you meet the local age requirement for tobacco products, you may bring in, duty-free, 200 cigarettes and 50 cigars. Check ahead of time with the Canada Customs and Revenue Agency or the Department of Agriculture for policies regarding meat products, seeds, plants, and fruits.

You may send an unlimited number of gifts (only one gift per recipient, however) worth up to C$60 each duty-free to Canada. Label the package UNSOLICITED GIFT—VALUE UNDER $60. Alcohol and tobacco are excluded.

🄵 **Canada Customs and Revenue Agency** ✉ 2265 St. Laurent Blvd., Ottawa, Ontario K1G 4K3 ☎ 800/461-9999 in Canada, 204/983-3500, 506/636-5064 ⊕ www.ccra.gc.ca.

IN NEW ZEALAND

All homeward-bound residents may bring back NZ$700 worth of souvenirs and gifts; passengers may not pool their allowances, and children can claim only the concession on goods intended for their own use. For those 17 or older, the duty-free allowance also includes 4.5 liters of wine or beer; one 1,125-ml bottle of spirits; and either 200 cigarettes, 250 grams of tobacco, 50 cigars, or a combination of the three up to 250 grams. Meat products, seeds, plants, and fruits must be declared upon arrival to the Agricultural Services Department.

🄵 **New Zealand Customs** ✉ Head office: The Customhouse, 17-21 Whitmore St., Box 2218, Wellington ☎ 09/300-5399 or 0800/428-786 ⊕ www.customs.govt.nz.

IN THE U.K.

From countries outside the European Union, including the United States, you may bring home, duty-free, 200 cigarettes, 50 cigars, 100 cigarillos, or 250 grams of tobacco; 1 liter of spirits or 2 liters of fortified or sparkling wine or liqueurs; 2 liters of still table wine; 60 ml of perfume; 250 ml of toilet water; plus £145 worth of other goods, including gifts and souvenirs. Prohibited items include meat and dairy products, seeds, plants, and fruits.

⊠ HM Customs and Excise ⊠ Portcullis House, 21 Cowbridge Rd. E, Cardiff CF11 9SS ☎ 0845/010–9000, 0208/929–0152 advice service, 0208/929–6731, 0208/910–3602 complaints ⊕ www.hmce.gov.uk.

IN THE U.S.

U.S. residents who have been out of the country for at least 48 hours may bring home, for personal use, $800 worth of foreign goods duty-free, as long as they haven't used the $800 allowance or any part of it in the past 30 days. This exemption may include 1 liter of alcohol (for travelers 21 and older), 200 cigarettes, and 100 non-Cuban cigars. Family members from the same household who are traveling together may pool their $800 personal exemptions. For fewer than 48 hours, the duty-free allowance drops to $200, which may include 50 cigarettes, 10 non-Cuban cigars, and 150 ml of alcohol (or 150 ml of perfume containing alcohol). The $200 allowance cannot be combined with other individuals' exemptions, and if you exceed it, the full value of all the goods will be taxed. Antiques, which U.S. Customs and Border Protection defines as objects more than 100 years old, enter duty-free, as do original works of art done entirely by hand, including paintings, drawings, and sculptures. This doesn't apply to folk art or handicrafts, which are in general dutiable.

You may also send packages home duty-free, with a limit of one parcel per addressee per day (except alcohol or tobacco products or perfume worth more than $5). You can mail up to $200 worth of goods for personal use; label the package PER-SONAL USE and attach a list of its contents and their retail value. If the package contains your used personal belongings, mark it AMERICAN GOODS RETURNED to avoid paying duties. You may send up to $100 worth of goods as a gift; mark the package UNSO-LICITED GIFT. Mailed items do not affect your duty-free allowance on your return.

To avoid paying duty on foreign-made high-ticket items you already own and will take on your trip, register them with Customs before you leave the country. Consider filing a Certificate of Registration for laptops, cameras, watches, and other digital devices identified with serial numbers or other permanent markings; you can keep the certificate for other trips. Otherwise, bring a sales receipt or insurance form to show that you owned the item before you left the United States.

For more about duties, restricted items, and other information about international travel, check out U.S. Customs and Border Protection's online brochure, *Know Before You Go.*

⊠ U.S. Customs and Border Protection ⊠ For inquiries and equipment registration, 1300 Pennsylvania Ave. NW, Washington, DC 20229 ⊕ www.cbp. gov ☎ 877/287–8667 or 202/354–1000 ⊠ For complaints, Customer Satisfaction Unit, 1300 Pennsylvania Ave. NW, Room 5.2C, Washington, DC 20229.

DISABILITIES & ACCESSIBILITY

San Diego ranks as one of the most accessible cities in the United States for people using wheelchairs. Although the Old Town district has some moderately uneven streets, curb cuts and smooth sidewalks are decidedly the rule rather than the exception for the city as a whole. The extensive network of walkways in Balboa Park affords views that are both lovely and negotiable. Most major attractions, shopping malls, tour services and casinos are accessible. Special beach wheelchairs are available at the lifeguard station in Pacific Beach; make reservations 48 hours in advance. The Access Center of San Diego has a comprehensive guide to hotels, motels, attractions, and restaurants with access for people with disabilities. Accessible San Diego has a visitor information center and telephone hotline, makes hotel referrals, and provides guides to San Diego's attractions for visitors with mobility problems.

⊠ Local Resources Access Center of San Diego ⊠ Information and Referrals, 1295 University Ave., Suite 10, San Diego 92103 ☎ 619/293–3500, 619/293–7757 TDD ⊕ www.accesscentersd.org. **Accessible San Diego** ⊠ Executive Complex, 1010 2nd Ave., Suite 1700, San Diego 92101 ☎ 858/279–0704 ⊕ www.accessandiego.org. **MTS Access** ⊠ 4970 Market St., San Diego 92102 ☎ 888/517–9627 ⊕ www.sdcommute.com. **Pacific Beach Wheelchairs** ☎ 858/279–0704 ✐ beachpower-wheel@accessandiego.org.

LODGING

Despite the Americans with Disabilities Act, the definition of accessibility seems to differ from hotel to hotel. Some properties may be accessible by ADA standards for people with mobility problems but not for people with hearing or vision impairments, for example.

If you have mobility problems, ask for the lowest floor on which accessible services are offered. If you have a hearing impairment, check whether the hotel has devices to alert you visually to the ring of the telephone, a knock at the door, and a fire–emergency alarm. Some hotels provide these devices without charge. Discuss your needs with hotel personnel if this equipment isn't available, so that a staff member can personally alert you in the event of an emergency.

If you're bringing a guide dog, get authorization ahead of time and write down the name of the person with whom you spoke.

The downtown San Diego Marriott Hotel and Marina has 40 rooms designed for people who use wheelchairs. Comfort Inn and Suites in Mission Valley has 11 rooms with wheelchair-accessible showers, and rooms with text telephones and raised Braille signage. Holiday Inn San Diego on the Bay has 20 rooms with wheelchair-accessible showers, plus a lift-equipped airport shuttle, text telephones, and Braille signage.

▸ Best Choices Comfort Inn and Suites ✉ 7450 Hazard Center Dr. ☎ 619/297-5466 ⊕ www. choicehotels.com. **San Diego Marriott Hotel and Marina** ✉ 333 W. Harbor Dr. ☎ 619/234-1500 ⊕ www.marriotthotels.com/sandt. **Holiday Inn San Diego on the Bay** ✉ 1355 N. Harbor Dr. ☎ 619/232-3861 ⊕ www.holiday-inn.com.

RESERVATIONS

When discussing accessibility with an operator or reservations agent, ask hard questions. Are there any stairs, inside *or* out? Are there grab bars next to the toilet *and* in the shower–tub? How wide is the doorway to the room? To the bathroom? For the most extensive facilities meeting the latest legal specifications, opt for newer accommodations. If you reserve through a toll-free number, consider also calling the

hotel's local number to confirm the information from the central reservations office. Get confirmation in writing when you can.

SIGHTS & ATTRACTIONS

Most attractions have accessible restrooms, ramps, and parking spaces near the entrances reserved for people with disabilities. Travelers who use wheelchairs can see much of the San Diego Zoo via tram and get an overview of the Wild Animal Park from the monorail. SeaWorld San Diego has sign language interpreters, assistive listening devices, and wheelchairs for rent. Cabrillo National Monument waives admission fees for those with disability placards and has text telephones. Most attractions at Legoland have ramps and the park has wheelchairs for rent. Hornblower Cruises has an accessible gangway ramp and restroom.

TRANSPORTATION

Most public buses and the San Diego Trolley are equipped with lifts. About one-third of the bus lines are served by buses with elevator ramps. The San Diego Trolley has wheelchair lifts. Call San Diego Transit (⇨ Bus Travel within San Diego) for detailed information. MTS Access (⇨ Disabilities & Accessibility) provides curb-to-curb transportation for those with restricted mobility; advance reservations are required.

▸ Car Rental Avis Rental Cars at the Airport ✉ 3180 N. Harbor Dr. ☎ 619/231-7171, 800/852-4617 Ext. 5063.

▸ Complaints Aviation Consumer Protection Division (⇨ Air Travel) for airline-related problems. **Departmental Office of Civil Rights** ✉ For general inquiries, U.S. Department of Transportation, S-30, 400 7th St. SW, Room 10215, Washington, DC 20590 ☎ 202/366-4648 🖶 202/366-9371 ⊕ www.dot. gov/ost/docr/index.htm. **Disability Rights Section** ✉ NYAV, U.S. Department of Justice, Civil Rights Division, 950 Pennsylvania Ave. NW, Washington, DC 20530 ☎ ADA information line 202/514-0301, 800/514-0301, 202/514-0383 TTY, 800/514-0383 TTY ⊕ www.ada.gov. **U.S. Department of Transportation Hotline** ☎ For disability-related air-travel problems, 800/778-4838, 800/455-9880 TTY.

TRAVEL AGENCIES

In the United States, the Americans with Disabilities Act requires that travel firms serve the needs of all travelers. Some agencies specialize in working with people with disabilities.

Travelers with Mobility Problems **Access Adventures/B. Roberts Travel** ✉ 206 Chestnut Ridge Rd., Scottsville, NY 14624 ☎ 585/889–9096 ⊕ www.brobertstravel.com ⬧ dltravel@prodigy. net, run by a former physical-rehabilitation counselor. **Accessible Vans of America** ✉ 9 Spielman Rd., Fairfield, NJ 07004 ☎ 877/282–8267 or 888/282–8267, 973/808–9709 reservations ⎙ 973/808–9713 ⊕ www.accessiblevans.com. **CareVacations** ✉ No. 5, 5110–50 Ave., Leduc, Alberta, Canada, T9E 6V4 ☎ 780/986–6404 or 877/478–7827 ⎙ 780/986–8332 ⊕ www.carevacations.com, for group tours and cruise vacations. **Flying Wheels Travel** ✉ 143 W. Bridge St., Box 382, Owatonna, MN 55060 ☎ 507/451–5005 ⎙ 507/451–1685 ⊕ www. flyingwheelstravel.com.

Travelers with Developmental Disabilities **New Directions** ✉ 5276 Hollister Ave., Suite 207, Santa Barbara, CA 93111 ☎ 805/967–2841 or 888/967–2841 ⎙ 805/964–7344 ⊕ www.newdirectionstravel.com.

DISCOUNTS & DEALS

The International Visitor Information Center (⇨ Visitor Information) has a free coupon book, *San Diego Travel Values* that contains a list of 25 free activities in San Diego plus discount coupons to attractions, hotels, and restaurants. Multiday passes to SeaWorld and Legoland are available from some Mission Bay area hotels. Arts Tix sells half-price, same-day tickets for performances.

Some of the best San Diego attractions are free as the air. Balboa Park offers several free tours of historic buildings and gardens. Admission to most museums is free on Tuesday on a monthly rotating schedule. Free concerts are presented in the Spreckles Organ Pavilion on Sunday. You can see some of the best views without paying a cent; they include La Jolla Cove; waves crashing against more than 70 mi of public beaches; and spectacular sweeping city and ocean views from the tops of Mt. Soledad and Mt. Helix. Free tours include the Arco Olympic Training Center in Chula Vista, a walking tour of the Stuart Sculpture Collection at University of California at San Diego, and monthly sky-tours using

portable telescopes at the Ruben H. Fleet Science Center in Balboa Park.

The Passport to Balboa Park, available at the visitor center in the House of Hospitality and at many of the park's museums, grants admission to 13 museums for a reduced price. It can be used over a number of days. The Best of Balboa Park Combo includes the 13 museums and a deluxe tour of the San Diego Zoo including a 40-minute bus tour and aerial tram ride. The Zoo, SeaWorld, and Wild Animal Park offer a 3-for-1 Pass that is good for unlimited admission to these attractions for five consecutive days. A Two-Park Ticket, available from either the Zoo or Wild Animal Park, will get you into both places. During October, zoo admission is free for kids, so be prepared for crowds. Both SeaWorld and Legoland offer multiday tickets that may end up saving you money.

Be a smart shopper and compare all your options before making decisions. A plane ticket bought with a promotional coupon from travel clubs, coupon books, and direct-mail offers or purchased on the Internet may not be cheaper than the least expensive fare from a discount ticket agency. And always keep in mind that what you get is just as important as what you save.

Discount Arts Tickets **Arts Tix** ✉ Horton Plaza, Downtown ☎ 619/497–5000 ⊕ www. sandiegoperforms.com ⊙ Tues.–Thurs. 11–6, Fri. and Sat. 10–6, Sun. 10–5

DISCOUNT RESERVATIONS

To save money, look into discount reservations services with Web sites and toll-free numbers, which use their buying power to get a better price on hotels, airline tickets (⇨ Air Travel), even car rentals. When booking a room, always **call the hotel's local toll-free number** (if one is available) rather than the central reservations number—you'll often get a better price. Always ask about special packages or corporate rates.

Airline Tickets **Air 4 Less** ☎ 800/AIR4LESS; low-fare specialist.

Hotel Rooms **Accommodations Express** ☎ 800/444–7666 or 800/277–1064 ⊕ www.acex. net. **Hotels.com** ☎ 800/246–8357 ⊕ www.hotels.

com. **Quikbook** ☎ 800/789-9887 ⊕ www. quikbook.com. **Turbotrip.com** ☎ 800/473-7829 ⊕ www.turbotrip.com.

PACKAGE DEALS

Don't confuse packages and guided tours. When you buy a package, you travel on your own, just as though you had planned the trip yourself. Fly–drive packages, which combine airfare and car rental, are often a good deal.

Packages combining lodging, dining, theater tickets, and museum admission within San Diego County are available through San Diego Art + Sol. Packages vary and change frequently; you can order a brochure, but allow four to six weeks for delivery.

🎦 Packagers **San Diego Art + Sol** ☎ 800/270-9283 ⊕ www.sandiegoartandsol.com.

GAY & LESBIAN TRAVEL

With a large and visible gay community, San Diego is earning points as being one of the country's most gay-friendly destinations. Hillcrest is the main gay neighborhood and retail district, with many bars, cafés, and shops. *Update*, a weekly gay paper, is available in Hillcrest and at a few locations downtown. The lesbian–gay bookstore Obelisk is an excellent resource and hangout. The annual Lesbian and Gay Pride Parade, Rally, and Festival takes place during a weekend in July. For details about the gay and lesbian scene, consult *Fodor's Gay Guide to the USA* (available in bookstores everywhere).

🎦 Gay- & Lesbian-Friendly Travel Agencies **Different Roads Travel** ✉ 8383 Wilshire Blvd., Suite 520, Beverly Hills, CA 90211 ☎ 323/651-5557 or 800/429-8747 (Ext. 14 for both) 📠 323/651-5454 ✍ lgernert@tzell.com. **Kennedy Travel** ✉ 130 W. 42nd St., Suite 401, New York, NY 10036 ☎ 212/840-8659 or 800/237-7433 📠 212/730-2269 ⊕ www. kennedytravel.com. **Now, Voyager** ✉ 4406 18th St., San Francisco, CA 94114 ☎ 415/626-1169 or 800/255-6951 📠 415/626-8626 ⊕ www.nowvoyager. com. **Skylink Travel and Tour/Flying Dutchmen Travel** ✉ 1455 N. Dutton Ave., Suite A, Santa Rosa, CA 95401 ☎ 707/546-9888 or 800/225-5759 📠 707/636-0951; serving lesbian travelers.

🎦 Local Resources **Lesbian and Gay Men's Community Center** ✉ 3909 Centre St., San Diego 92103 ☎ 619/692-2077 ⊕ www.thecentersd.org. *Update*

☎ 619/299-0500 ⊕ www.sandiegogaynews.com. **Obelisk** ✉ 1029 University Ave., Hillcrest ☎ 619/297-4171.

HEALTH

DIVERS' ALERT

Do not fly within 24 hours of scuba diving.

HOLIDAYS

Major national holidays are New Year's Day (Jan. 1); Martin Luther King Day (3rd Mon. in Jan.); Presidents' Day (3rd Mon. in Feb.); Memorial Day (last Mon. in May); Independence Day (July 4); Labor Day (1st Mon. in Sept.); Columbus Day (2nd Mon. in Oct.); Thanksgiving Day (4th Thurs. in Nov.); Christmas Eve and Christmas Day (Dec. 24 and 25); and New Year's Eve (Dec. 31).

INSURANCE

The most useful travel-insurance plan is a comprehensive policy that includes coverage for trip cancellation and interruption, default, trip delay, and medical expenses (with a waiver for preexisting conditions).

Without insurance you'll lose all or most of your money if you cancel your trip, regardless of the reason. Default insurance covers you if your tour operator, airline, or cruise line goes out of business—the chances of which have been increasing. Trip-delay covers expenses that arise because of bad weather or mechanical delays. Study the fine print when comparing policies.

U.K. residents can buy a travel-insurance policy valid for most vacations taken during the year in which it's purchased (but check preexisting-condition coverage).

Always **buy travel policies directly from the insurance company**; if you buy them from a cruise line, airline, or tour operator that goes out of business you probably won't be covered for the agency or operator's default, a major risk. Before making any purchase, review your existing health and home-owner's policies to find what they cover away from home.

🎦 Travel Insurers In the U.S.: **Access America** ✉ 2805 N. Parham Rd., Richmond, VA 23294 ☎ 800/284-8300 📠 804/673-1491 or 800/346-9265 ⊕ www.accessamerica.com. **Travel Guard International** ✉ 1145 Clark St., Stevens Point, WI

54481 ☎ 715/345-0505 or 800/826-1300 🖷 800/ 955-8785 ⊕ www.travelguard.com.

FOR INTERNATIONAL TRAVELERS

For information on customs restrictions, see Customs & Duties.

CAR RENTAL

When picking up a rental car, non-U.S. residents need a reservation voucher for any prepaid reservations that were made in the traveler's home country, a passport, a driver's license, and a travel policy that covers each driver.

Your driver's license may not be recognized outside your home country. International driving permits (IDPs) are available from the American and Canadian automobile associations and, in the United Kingdom, from the Automobile Association and Royal Automobile Club. These international permits, valid only in conjunction with your regular driver's license, are universally recognized; having one may save you a problem with local authorities.

CAR TRAVEL

Gas stations in San Diego are plentiful. Most stay open late (24 hours along large highways and in big cities), except in rural areas, where Sunday hours are limited and where you may drive long stretches without a refueling opportunity. Highways are well paved. Interstate highways—limited-access, multilane highways whose numbers are prefixed by "I–"—are the fastest routes. Interstates with three-digit numbers encircle urban areas, which may have other limited-access expressways, freeways, and parkways as well. Tolls may be levied on limited-access highways. So-called U.S. highways and state highways are not necessarily limited-access but may have several lanes.

Along larger highways, roadside stops with restrooms, fast-food restaurants, and sundries stores are well spaced. State police and tow trucks patrol major highways and lend assistance. If your car breaks down on an interstate, pull onto the shoulder and wait for help, or have your passengers wait while you walk to an

emergency phone. If you carry a cell phone, dial *55, noting your location on the small green roadside mileage markers.

Driving in the United States is on the right. Do obey speed limits posted along roads and highways. Watch for lower limits in small towns and on back roads. On weekdays between 6 and 10 AM and again between 4 and 7 PM expect heavy traffic. To encourage carpooling, some freeways have special lanes for so-called high-occupancy vehicles (HOV)—cars carrying more than one passenger. There are Border Inspection stations along the major highways in San Diego County. For this reason, it's best to travel with your passport in case you are asked to pull into one.

Book stores, gas stations, convenience stores, and rest stops sell maps (about $3) and multiregion road atlases (about $10).

CONSULATES & EMBASSIES

🇨 Canada **Canada** ⊠ 300 S. Grand Ave., Los Angeles ☎ 213/346-2700.

🇳 New Zealand **Honorary Counsel** ⊠ Gray Cary, Ware & Freidenrich, 4365 Executive Dr., Suite 1100, San Diego ☎ 858/677-1485.

🇬 United Kingdom **United Kingdom** ⊠ 11766 Wilshire Blvd., No. 400, Los Angeles ☎ 310/477-3322.

CURRENCY

The dollar is the basic unit of U.S. currency. It has 100 cents. Coins are the copper penny (1¢); the silvery nickel (5¢), dime (10¢), quarter (25¢), and half-dollar (50¢); and the golden $1 coin, replacing a now-rare silver dollar. Bills are denominated $1, $5, $10, $20, $50, and $100, all mostly green and identical in size; designs and background tints vary. In addition, you may come across a $2 bill, but the chances are slim. The exchange rate at this writing is US$1.42 per British pound, 63¢ per Canadian dollar, 53¢ per Australian dollar, and 44¢ per New Zealand dollar.

ELECTRICITY

The U.S. standard is AC, 110 volts/60 cycles. Plugs have two flat pins set parallel to each other.

EMERGENCIES

For police, fire, or ambulance, **dial 911.**

INSURANCE

Britons and Australians need extra medical coverage when traveling overseas.
🛈 Insurance Information In the U.K.: **Association of British Insurers** ✉ 51 Gresham St., London EC2V 7HQ ☎ 020/7600-3333 🖶 020/7696-8999 ⊕ www. abi.org.uk. In Australia: **Insurance Council of Australia** ✉ Insurance Enquiries and Complaints, Level 12, Box 561, Collins St. W, Melbourne, VIC 8007 ☎ 1300/780808 or 03/9629-4109 🖶 03/9621-2060 ⊕ www.iecltd.com.au. In Canada: **RBC Insurance** ✉ 6880 Financial Dr., Mississauga, Ontario L5N 7Y5 ☎ 800/668-4342 or 905/816-2400 🖶 905/813-4704 ⊕ www.rbcinsurance.com. In New Zealand: **Insurance Council of New Zealand** ✉ Level 7, 111-115 Customhouse Quay, Box 474, Wellington ☎ 04/472-5230 🖶 04/473-3011 ⊕ www.icnz.org.nz.

MAIL & SHIPPING

You can buy stamps and aerograms and send letters and parcels in post offices. Stamp-dispensing machines can occasionally be found in airports, bus and train stations, office buildings, drugstores, and the like. You can also deposit mail in the stout, dark blue, steel bins at strategic locations everywhere and in the mail chutes of large buildings; pickup schedules are posted. You can deposit packages at public collection boxes as long as the parcels are affixed with proper postage and weigh less than one pound. Packages weighing one or more pounds must be taken to a post office or handed to a postal carrier.

For mail sent within the United States, you need a 37¢ stamp for first-class letters weighing up to 1 ounce (23¢ for each additional ounce) and 23¢ for postcards. You pay 80¢ for 1-ounce airmail letters and 70¢ for airmail postcards to most other countries; to Canada and Mexico, you need a 60¢ stamp for a 1-ounce letter and 50¢ for a postcard. An aerogram—a single sheet of lightweight blue paper that folds into its own envelope, stamped for overseas airmail—costs 70¢.

To receive mail on the road, have it sent c/o General Delivery at your destination's main post office (use the correct five-digit ZIP code). You must pick up mail in person within 30 days and show a driver's license or passport.

PASSPORTS & VISAS

When traveling internationally, carry your passport even if you don't need one (it's always the best form of ID) and **make two photocopies of the data page** (one for someone at home and another for you, carried separately from your passport). If you lose your passport, promptly call the nearest embassy or consulate and the local police.

Visitor visas aren't necessary for Canadian or European Union citizens, or for citizens of Australia who are staying fewer than 90 days.

🛈 Australian Citizens **Passports Australia** ☎ 131-232 ⊕ www.passports.gov.au. **United States Consulate General** ✉ MLC Centre, Level 59, 19-29 Martin Pl., Sydney, NSW 2000 ☎ 02/9373-9200, 1902/941-641 fee-based visa-inquiry line ⊕ www. usembassy-australia.state.gov/sydney.
🛈 Canadian Citizens **Passport Office** ✉ To mail in applications: 200 Promenade du Portage, Hull, Québec J8X 4B7 ☎ 819/994-3500, 800/567-6868, 866/255-7655 TTY ⊕ www.ppt.gc.ca.
🛈 New Zealand Citizens **New Zealand Passports Office** ✉ For applications and information, Level 3, Boulcott House, 47 Boulcott St., Wellington ☎ 0800/22-5050 or 04/474-8100 ⊕ www. passports.govt.nz. **Embassy of the United States** ✉ 29 Fitzherbert Terr., Thorndon, Wellington ☎ 04/462-6000 ⊕ www.usembassy.org.nz. **U.S. Consulate General** ✉ Citibank Bldg., 3rd fl., 23 Customs St. E, Auckland ☎ 09/303-2724 ⊕ www. usembassy.org.nz.
🛈 U.K. Citizens **U.K. Passport Service** ☎ 0870/521-0410 ⊕ www.passport.gov.uk. **American Consulate General** ✉ Danesfort House, 223 Stranmillis Rd., Belfast, Northern Ireland BT9 5GR ☎ 028/9032-8239 🖶 028/9024-8482 ⊕ www.usembassy.org.uk. **American Embassy** ✉ For visa and immigration information or to submit a visa application via mail (enclose an SASE), Consular Information Unit, 24 Grosvenor Sq., London W1 1AE ☎ 09055/444-546 for visa information, per-minute charges, 0207/499-9000 main switchboard ⊕ usembassy.org.uk.

TELEPHONES

All U.S. telephone numbers consist of a three-digit area code and a seven-digit local number. Within many local calling areas, you dial only the seven-digit number. Within some area codes, you must dial "1" first for calls outside the local area. To call between area-code regions, dial "1" then all 10 digits; the same goes for calls to numbers prefixed by "800," "888," "866," and "877"—all toll free. For calls to numbers preceded by "900" you must pay—usually dearly.

For international calls, dial "011" followed by the country code and the local number. For help, dial "0" and ask for an overseas operator. The country code is 61 for Australia, 64 for New Zealand, 44 for the United Kingdom. Calling Canada is the same as calling within the United States. Most local phone books list country codes and U.S. area codes. The country code for the United States is 1.

For operator assistance, dial "0." To obtain someone's phone number, call directory assistance at 555–1212 or occasionally 411 (free at many public phones). To have the person you're calling foot the bill, phone collect; dial "0" instead of "1" before the 10-digit number.

At pay phones, instructions often are posted. Usually you insert coins in a slot (usually 25¢–50¢ for local calls) and wait for a steady tone before dialing. When you call long-distance, the operator tells you how much to insert; prepaid phone cards, widely available in various denominations, are easier. Call the number on the back, punch in the card's personal identification number when prompted, then dial your number.

MAIL & SHIPPING
Staff at most U.S. Post Offices are efficient and helpful. Letters headed overseas take 10 days to two weeks to reach their destination. Private mailing services such as Mail Boxes, Etc. will pack and ship items for you. Most are authorized shippers for United Parcel Service (UPS), Federal Express (FedEx), and the U.S. Post Office.
🚹 Post Offices **San Diego Downtown** ✉ 815 E St. ☎ 619/232-8612 ⊙ Weekdays 8:30-5 ✉ **La Jolla Main** ✉ 1140 Wall St. ☎ 858/459-5476 ⊙ Mon. 7:30-5, Tues.-Fri. 8:30-5, Sat. 9-1 ✉ **Coronado Branch** ✉ 1320 Ynez Pl. ☎ 619/435-1160 ⊙ Weekdays 8:30-5, Sat. 8:30-noon.

OVERNIGHT SERVICES
Drop boxes for Federal Express and United Parcel Service can be found throughout the downtown area and at other locations in the county.
🚹 Major Services **Federal Express** ☎ 800/463-3339 ⊕ www.fedex.com. **United Parcel Service** ☎ 800/742-5877 ⊕ www.ups.com.

MEDIA

NEWSPAPERS & MAGAZINES
San Diego's major daily newspaper is the *San Diego Union-Tribune,* and locals also read the *Los Angeles Times.* The leading weekly newspaper is the *San Diego Reader,* available free in sidewalk racks around town. *San Diego Magazine* carries monthly entertainment listings.

RADIO & TELEVISION
All the major television networks have local affiliates in San Diego including **KGTV** Channel 10, ABC; **KFMB** Channel 8, CBS; **KNSD** Channel 39, NBC; and **KPBS** Channel 15, PBS. There are also local affiliates of UPN, WB, Fox, PAX, and the Spanish-language network. Check the *San Diego Union-Tribune* for listings. Los Angeles television and radio stations can be received in many areas of the county.

Major radio stations include **KOGO-AM** 600, news–talk; **KFMB-AM** 760, CBS talk–sports; **KSON-AM** 1240, Radio Disney; **KPBS-FM** 89.5, National Public Radio; **XLTN-FM** 104.5, Spanish; and **STAR-FM** 100.7, adult contemporary.

MEXICO
If you're planning a side trip to nearby Mexico, **note the travel requirements** detailed in Chapter 8 (⇨ Tijuana, Playas de Rosarito & Ensenada A to Z) and customs information under For International Travelers.

MONEY MATTERS
Average prices for accommodations, food, and in shops are comparable with those in Los Angeles. Expect to pay $1 to $2.50 for coffee, $6.95 for a sandwich, $4 for a beer, and $1.80 per mile for a taxi. Prices throughout this guide are given for adults. Substantially reduced fees are almost al-

ways available for children, students, and senior citizens. For information on taxes, *see* Taxes.

ATMS

Most ATMs in the San Diego area are linked to national networks that let you withdraw money from your checking account or take a cash advance from your credit card account for an additional fee. ATMs can be found at all banks and in many grocery and convenience stores. For more information on ATM locations that can be accessed with your particular account, call the phone number found on the back of your ATM or debit card.

CREDIT CARDS
Throughout this guide, the following abbreviations are used: **AE,** American Express; **D,** Discover; **DC,** Diners Club; **MC,** MasterCard; and **V,** Visa.

☑ Reporting Lost Cards **American Express** ☎ 800/992-3404. **Diners Club** ☎ 800/234-6377. **Discover** ☎ 800/347-2683. **MasterCard** ☎ 800/ 622-7747. **Visa** ☎ 800/ 847-2911.

NATIONAL PARKS
Look into discount passes to save money on park entrance fees. For $50, the National Parks Pass admits you (and any passengers in your private vehicle) to all national parks, monuments, and recreation areas, as well as other sites run by the National Park Service, for a year. (In parks that charge per person, the pass admits you, your spouse and children, and your parents, when you arrive together.) Camping and parking are extra. The $15 Golden Eagle Pass, a hologram you affix to your National Parks Pass, functions as an upgrade, granting entry to all sites run by the NPS, the U.S. Fish and Wildlife Service, the U.S. Forest Service, and the Bureau of Land Management. The upgrade, which expires with the parks pass, is sold by most national-park, Fish-and-Wildlife, and BLM fee stations. A major percentage of the proceeds from pass sales funds National Parks projects.

Both the Golden Age Passport ($10), for U.S. citizens or permanent residents who are 62 and older, and the Golden Access

Passport (free), for persons with disabilities, entitle holders (and any passengers in their private vehicles) to lifetime free entry to all national parks, plus 50% off fees for the use of many park facilities and services. (The discount doesn't always apply to companions.) To obtain them, you must show proof of age and of U.S. citizenship or permanent residency—such as a U.S. passport, driver's license, or birth certificate—and, if requesting Golden Access, proof of disability. The Golden Age and Golden Access passes are available only at NPS-run sites that charge an entrance fee. The National Parks Pass is also available by mail and via the Internet.

🛂 **National Park Foundation** ☑ 11 Dupont Circle NW, 6th fl., Washington, DC 20036 ☎ 202/238-4200 ⊕ www.nationalparks.org. **National Park Service** ☑ National Park Service–Department of Interior, 1849 C St. NW, Washington, DC 20240 ☎ 202/208-6843 ⊕ www.nps.gov. **National Parks Conservation Association** ☑ 1300 19th St. NW, Suite 300, Washington, DC 20036 ☎ 202/223-6722 ⊕ www.npca.org.

🛂 Passes by Mail & Online **National Park Foundation** ⊕ www.nationalparks.org. **National Parks Pass** National Park Foundation ⌂ Box 34108, Washington, DC 20043 ☎ 888/467-2757 ⊕ www. nationalparks.org; include a check or money order payable to the National Park Service, plus $3.95 for shipping and handling (allow 8 to 13 business days from date of receipt for pass delivery), or call for passes.

PACKING
San Diego's casual lifestyle and year-round mild climate set the parameters for what to pack. You can leave formal clothes and cold-weather gear behind.

Plan on warm weather at any time of the year. Cottons, walking shorts, jeans, and T-shirts are the norm. Pack bathing suits and shorts regardless of the season. Few restaurants require a jacket and tie for men. Women may want to bring something a little dressier than their sightseeing garb.

Evenings are cool, even in summer, so be sure to bring a sweater or a light jacket. Rainfall in San Diego is not usually heavy;

you won't need a raincoat except during the winter months, and even then, an umbrella may be sufficient protection. Be sure you **take comfortable walking shoes** with you. Even if you don't walk much at home, you'll find yourself covering miles while sightseeing on your vacation.

Sunglasses are a must in San Diego. Binoculars can also come in handy, especially if you're in town during whale-watching season from December through March.

In your carry-on luggage, pack an extra pair of eyeglasses or contact lenses and enough of any medication you take to last a few days longer than the entire trip. You may also ask your doctor to write a spare prescription using the drug's generic name, as brand names may vary from country to country. In luggage to be checked, **never pack prescription drugs, valuables, or undeveloped film.** And don't forget to carry with you the addresses of offices that handle refunds of lost traveler's checks. Check *Fodor's How to Pack* (available at online retailers and bookstores everywhere) for more tips.

To avoid customs and security delays, carry medications in their original packaging. Don't pack any sharp objects in your carry-on luggage, including knives of any size or material, scissors, nail clippers, and corkscrews, or anything else that might arouse suspicion.

To avoid having your checked luggage chosen for hand inspection, don't cram bags full. The U.S. Transportation Security Administration suggests packing shoes on top and placing personal items you don't want touched in clear plastic bags.

CHECKING LUGGAGE

You're allowed to carry aboard one bag and one personal article, such as a purse or a laptop computer. Make sure what you carry on fits under your seat or in the overhead bin. Get to the gate early, so you can board as soon as possible, before the overhead bins fill up.

Baggage allowances vary by carrier, destination, and ticket class. On international flights, you're usually allowed to check two

bags weighing up to 70 pounds (32 kilograms) each, although a few airlines allow checked bags of up to 88 pounds (40 kilograms) in first class. Some international carriers don't allow more than 66 pounds (30 kilograms) per bag in business class and 44 pounds (20 kilograms) in economy. On domestic flights, the limit is usually 50 to 70 pounds (23 to 32 kilograms) per bag. In general, carry-on bags shouldn't exceed 40 pounds (18 kilograms). Most airlines won't accept bags that weigh more than 100 pounds (45 kilograms) on domestic or international flights. Expect to pay a fee for baggage that exceeds weight limits. Check baggage restrictions with your carrier before you pack.

Airline liability for baggage is limited to $2,500 per person on flights within the United States. On international flights it amounts to $9.07 per pound or $20 per kilogram for checked baggage (roughly $640 per 70-pound bag), with a maximum of $634.90 per piece, and $400 per passenger for unchecked baggage. You can buy additional coverage at check-in for about $10 per $1,000 of coverage, but it often excludes a rather extensive list of items, shown on your airline ticket.

Before departure, itemize your bags' contents and their worth, and label the bags with your name, address, and phone number. (If you use your home address, cover it so potential thieves can't see it readily.) Include a label inside each bag and **pack a copy of your itinerary.** At check-in, make sure each bag is correctly tagged with the destination airport's three-letter code. Because some checked bags will be opened for hand inspection, the U.S. Transportation Security Administration recommends that you leave luggage unlocked or use the plastic locks offered at check-in. TSA screeners place an inspection notice inside searched bags, which are re-sealed with a special lock.

If your bag has been searched and contents are missing or damaged, file a claim with the TSA Consumer Response Center as soon as possible. If your bags arrive damaged or fail to arrive at all, file a written report with the airline before leaving the airport.

✸ Complaints **U.S. Transportation Security Administration Contact Center** ☎ 866/289–9673 ⊕ www.tsa.gov.

PASSPORTS & VISAS

When traveling internationally, carry your passport even if you don't need one (it's always the best form of ID) and **make two photocopies of the data page** (one for someone at home and another for you, carried separately from your passport). If you lose your passport, promptly call the nearest embassy or consulate and the local police.

U.S. passport applications for children under age 14 require consent from both parents or legal guardians; both parents must appear together to sign the application. If only one parent appears, he or she must submit a written statement from the other parent authorizing passport issuance for the child. A parent with sole authority must present evidence of it when applying; acceptable documentation includes the child's certified birth certificate listing only the applying parent, a court order specifically permitting this parent's travel with the child, or a death certificate for the nonapplying parent. Application forms and instructions are available on the Web site of the U.S. State Department's Bureau of Consular Affairs (⊕ www.travel.state.gov).

RESTROOMS

Major attractions and parks have public restrooms. In the downtown San Diego area, you can usually use the restrooms at major hotels and fast-food restaurants.

SAFETY

San Diego is generally a safe place for travelers who observe all normal precautions. Dress inconspicuously, remove badges when leaving convention areas, know the routes to your destination before you set out. At the beach check with lifeguards about any unsafe conditions such as dangerous rip tides or water pollution. San Diego Convention & Visitors Bureau publishes a Visitor Safety Tips brochure

listing normal precautions for many situations. It's available at the International Visitor Information Center.

SENIOR-CITIZEN TRAVEL

To qualify for age-related discounts, mention your senior-citizen status up front when booking hotel reservations (not when checking out) and before you're seated in restaurants (not when paying the bill). Be sure to have identification on hand. When renting a car, ask about promotional car-rental discounts, which can be cheaper than senior-citizen rates.

✸ Educational Programs **Elderhostel** ⊠ 11 Ave. de Lafayette, Boston, MA 02111–1746 ☎ 877/426–8056, 978/323–4141 international callers, 877/426–2167 TTY ☎ 877/426–2166 ⊕ www.elderhostel.org.

SIGHTSEEING TOURS

BALLOON TOURS

Weather permitting, hot-air balloons lift off from San Diego's North County and Temecula; the average cost is $140 per person. Most flights float at sunrise or sunset and are followed by a champagne toast.

✸ Fees & Schedules **A Balloon Adventure by California Dreamin'** ⊠ 33133 Vista Del Monte, Suite F35, Temecula ☎ 800/373–3359 ⊕ www. californiadreamin.com. **A Skysurfer Balloon Company** ⊠ 1221 Camino del Mar, Del Mar ☎ 858/481–6800 or 800/660–6809 ⊕ www. sandiegohotairballoons.com.

BOAT TOURS

Three companies operate one- and two-hour harbor cruises. San Diego Harbor Excursion and Hornblower Invader Cruises boats depart from the Broadway Pier. No reservations are necessary for the $13–$18 voyages, and both vessels have snack bars. Classic Sailing Adventures has morning and afternoon tours of the harbor and San Diego Bay and evening cruises in summer for $65 per person. These companies also operate during whale-watching season from mid-December to mid-March. Other fishing boats that do whale watches in season include H&M Landing and Seaforth Sportfishing.

✸ Fees & Schedules **Classic Sailing Adventures** ⊠ 1220 Rosecrans St., No. 137 ☎ 800/659–0141 ⊕ www.classicsailingadventures.com. **Hornblower**

Invader Cruises ✉ 1066 N. Harbor Dr. ☎ 619/234-8687 ⊕ www.hornblower.com. **San Diego Harbor Excursion** ✉ 1050 N. Harbor Dr. ☎ 619/234-4111 or 800/442-7847 ⊕ www.harborexcursion.com. **H&M Landing** ✉ 2803 Emerson St., Point Loma ☎ 619/222-1144 ⊕ www.hmlanding.com. **Seaforth Sportfishing** ✉ 1641 Quivira Rd. ☎ 619/223-1681 ⊕ www.seaforthboatrental.com.

BUS & TROLLEY TOURS

Free two-hour bus tours of the downtown redevelopment area, including the Gaslamp Quarter, are conducted by Centre City Development Corporation Downtown Information Center. Tours take place on the first and third Saturday of the month at 10 AM and noon. Advance reservations are necessary. The tour may be canceled if there aren't enough passengers.

Old Town Trolley Historic Tours take you to eight sites including Old Town, the Cruise Ship terminal, Seaport Village, the Marriott Hotel near the Convention Center, Horton Plaza near the Gaslamp Quarter, Coronado, the San Diego Zoo, and El Prado in Balboa Park. The tour is narrated, and you can get on and off as you please at any stop. An all-day pass costs $25 for adults and $13.50 for children 4–12; under 4, free. The trolley, which leaves every 30 minutes, operates daily. It takes the trolley two hours to make a full loop. The company also offers several special-interest tours, like Ghosts & Gravestones and Seal Tour, aboard an amphibious vehicle which cruises Mission Bay and the San Diego Harbor. The San Diego Passport is good for the trolley tour plus admission to the zoo, Maritime Museum, San Diego Museum of Art, one Hornblower cruise, and other goodies. The cost is $69.95 per person, and the passport is available at visitors centers and is good for one year.

🔝 Fees & Schedules **Centre City Development Corporation's Downtown Information Center** ✉ 225 Broadway, Suite 160 ☎ 619/235-2222 ⊕ www.ccdc.com. **Contactours** ✉ 1726 Wilson Ave., National City ☎ 619/477-8687 ⊕ www.contactours.com. **Old Town Trolley** ✉ 4010 Twiggs St. ☎ 619/298-8687 ⊕ www.trolleytours.com.

WALKING TOURS

Several fine walking tours are available on weekdays or weekends; upcoming walks are usually listed in the Thursday Night and Day section of the *San Diego Union-Tribune.* Coronado Walking Tours offers an easy 90-minute stroll ($8, Tuesday, Thursday, Saturday at 11) through Coronado's historic district with departures from the Glorietta Bay Inn. Make reservations. On Saturday at 10 AM and 11:30 AM, Offshoot Tours conducts free, hourlong walks through Balboa Park that focuses on history, palm trees, and desert vegetation. Long-time San Diego resident Patty Fares conducts Urban Safaris, two-hour Saturday walks ($10) through interesting neighborhoods such as Hillcrest, Ocean Beach, and Point Loma. Tours, which always depart from a neighborhood coffee house, focus on art, history, and ethnic eateries. Reservations are required. The Gaslamp Quarter Historical Foundation leads two-hour historical walking tours of the downtown historic district on Saturday at 11 AM ($8).

🔝 Fees & Schedules **Coronado Walking Tours** ✉ Glorietta Bay Inn Coronado ☎ 619/435-5993 **Offshoot Tours** ✉ Balboa Park Downtown ☎ 619/239-0512 ⊕ www.balboapark.org. **Urban Safaris** ☎ 619/944-9255 ⊕ www.walkingtoursofsandiego.com 💲 $10. **The Gaslamp Quarter Historical Foundation** ✉ 410 Island Ave. ☎ 619/233-4692 ⊕ www.gaslampquarter.org.

SMOKING

California has become distinctly hostile to smokers, even when they want to puff peacefully in the open air. The newest laws require those smoking outside office buildings to be at least 30 feet from the nearest entrance. Even in the seating area of outdoor stadiums, smoking is banned, but there are designated areas (generally outside the main structure) where it's possible to smoke without breaking the law. Note that some restaurant patios do permit cigarettes. But smoking indoors, other than in private residences and designated hotel rooms, is illegal, even in bars. The luxurious Westgate Hotel now bans smoking anywhere indoors, including guest rooms.

STUDENTS IN SAN DIEGO

San Diego State University (SDSU) is just east of Mission Bay, not to be confused with the University of California at San Diego (UCSD) in northern La Jolla. Most museums and other attractions have a discounted rate for students with identification.

🖪 IDs & Services **STA Travel** ☎ 212/627-3111 or 800/781-4040 🖷 212/627-3387 ⊕ www.sta.com. **Travel Cuts** ✉ 187 College St., Toronto, Ontario M5T 1P7, Canada ☎ 416/979-2406, 888/838-2887 in Canada 🖷 416/979-2406 ⊕ www.travelcuts.com.

TROLLEY TRAVEL

The San Diego Trolley light rail system connects with San Diego Transit buses. The bright-orange trolleys service downtown San Diego, Mission Valley, Old Town, South Bay, the U.S. Border, and East County. The trolleys operate seven days a week from about 5 AM to midnight, depending on the station, at intervals of about 15 minutes. Bus connections are posted at each station, and bicycle lockers are available at most. Trolleys can get crowded during morning and evening rush hours. On-time performance is excellent.

FARES & SCHEDULES

San Diego Trolley tickets are priced according to the number of stations traveled. Quick Tripper tickets good for two hours are $1 to $2.25; Round Tripper tickets good for a return trip on the date purchased are $2 to $4.50. Tickets are dispensed from self-service ticket machines at each stop; exact fare in coins is recommended, although some machines accept bills in $1, $5, $10, and $20 denominations. Transfers between buses and/or the trolley are free or require an upgrade if the second fare is higher.

Day Tripper Passes are available for one, two, three, or four days ($5, $9, $12, and $15, respectively), which give unlimited rides on regional buses and the San Diego Trolley. They may be purchased from most trolley vending machines, at the Transit Store, and at some hotels.

🖪 Trolley Information **San Diego Transit** ☎ 619/233-3004, 619/234-5005 TTY, TDD ⊕ www.sdcommute.com for city transit and San Diego Trolley.

TAXES

In San Diego County a sales tax of 7.75% is added to the price of all goods, except food purchased at a grocery store or as take-out from a restaurant. Hotel taxes are 9%–13%.

TAXIS

Taxis departing from the airport are subject to regulated fares—all companies charge the same rate (generally $1.80 for the first mile, $1.20 for each additional mile). Fares vary among companies on other routes, however, including the ride back to the airport. If you call ahead and ask for the flat rate ($8) you'll get it, otherwise you'll be charged by the mile (which works out to $9 or so). Taxi stands are located at shopping centers and hotels, otherwise you must call and reserve one. The Transportation Network comprises companies that serve the greater San Diego area including the airport. The companies listed below do not serve all areas of San Diego County. If you're going someplace other than downtown, **ask if the company serves that area.**

🖪 Taxi Companies **Crown City Cab** ☎ 619/437-8885 ⊕ www.driveu.com. **Orange Cab** ☎ 619/291-3333 ⊕ www.home.pacbell.net/orangesd.**Silver Cabs** ☎ 619/280-5555. **Yellow Cab** ☎ 619/234-6161 ⊕ www.driveu.com.

TIME

San Diego is in the Pacific time zone. Pacific Daylight Time is in effect from early April through late October; Pacific Standard Time, the rest of the year. Clocks are set ahead one hour when Daylight Time begins, back one hour when it ends.

TIPPING

At restaurants, a 15%–20% tip is standard for waiters, depending on the level of service provided. The same goes for taxi drivers, bartenders, and hairdressers. Coat-check operators usually expect $1; bellhops and porters should get 50¢ to $1 per bag; hotel maids should get about $1 per day of your stay—$2 in upscale hotels. A concierge typically receives a tip of $5 to $10, with an additional gratuity for special services or favors. On package tours, conductors and drivers usually get $10 per day from the group as a whole; check whether this has already been figured into your cost. For local sightseeing tours, you may individually tip the driver-guide $1 if he or she has been helpful or informative. Ushers in theaters do not expect tips.

TOURS & PACKAGES

Because everything is prearranged on a prepackaged tour or independent vacation, you spend less time planning—and often get it all at a good price.

BOOKING WITH AN AGENT

Travel agents are excellent resources. But it's a good idea to collect brochures from several agencies, as some agents' suggestions may be influenced by relationships with tour and package firms that reward them for volume sales. If you have a special interest, find an agent with expertise in that area; the American Society of Travel Agents (ASTA; ⇨ Travel Agencies) has a database of specialists worldwide. You can log on to the group's Web site to find an ASTA travel agent in your neighborhood.

Make sure your travel agent knows the accommodations and other services of the place being recommended. Ask about the hotel's location, room size, beds, and whether it has a pool, room service, or programs for children, if you care about these. Has your agent been there in person or sent others whom you can contact?

Do some homework on your own, too: local tourism boards can provide information about lesser-known and small-niche operators, some of which may sell only direct.

BUYER BEWARE

Each year consumers are stranded or lose their money when tour operators—even large ones with excellent reputations—go out of business. So check out the operator. Ask several travel agents about its reputation, and try to **book with a company that has a consumer-protection program.** (Look for information in the company's brochure.) In the United States, members of the United States Tour Operators Association are required to set aside funds ($1

million) to help eligible customers cover payments and travel arrangements in the event that the company defaults. It's also a good idea to choose a company that participates in the American Society of Travel Agents' Tour Operator Program; ASTA will act as mediator in any disputes between you and your tour operator.

Remember that the more your package or tour includes, the better you can predict the ultimate cost of your vacation. Make sure you know exactly what is covered, and beware of hidden costs. Are taxes, tips, and transfers included? Entertainment and excursions? These can add up.

🔁 Tour-Operator Recommendations American Society of Travel Agents (⇨ Travel Agencies). **National Tour Association (NTA)** ✉ 546 E. Main St., Lexington, KY 40508 ☎ 859/226–4444 or 800/682–8886 🖷 859/226–4404 ⊕ www.ntaonline.com. **United States Tour Operators Association (USTOA)** ✉ 275 Madison Ave., Suite 2014, New York, NY 10016 ☎ 212/599–6599 🖷 212/599–6744 ⊕ www.ustoa.com.

TRAIN TRAVEL TO & FROM SAN DIEGO

Amtrak serves downtown San Diego's Santa Fe Depot with daily trains to and from Los Angeles, Santa Barbara, and San Luis Obispo. Connecting service to Oakland, Seattle, Chicago, Texas, Florida, and points beyond is available in Los Angeles. Amtrak trains stop in San Diego North County at Solana Beach and Oceanside.

Coaster commuter trains, which run between Oceanside and San Diego Monday–Saturday and northbound on Friday night, stop at the same stations as Amtrak plus others. The Oceanside, Carlsbad, and Solana Beach stations have beach access. You can pick up Coaster flyers or brochures with detailed itineraries for each stop, including walking directions and connections to local bus service. Trains are typically on time.

Metrolink operates high-speed rail service between the Oceanside Transit Center and Union Station in Los Angeles.

CUTTING COSTS

Amtrak frequently offers discount passes that are good for travel within a specific geographic region of the United States, but you must book your schedule when buying the pass. If you want sleeping-car accommodations, in off-peak season you often can get a better price for a room by contacting the conductor after you board the train.

FARES & SCHEDULES

You can obtain Amtrak timetables at any Amtrak station, or by visiting the Amtrak Web site.

The Coaster runs between Oceanside and San Diego about every half hour during the rush hours on weekdays. There are four trains on Saturday, none on Sunday. One-way fares are $3.50 to $4.75, depending on the distance traveled.

Train Information Amtrak ☎ 800/872-7245 ⊕ www.amtrak.com. **Coaster** ☎ 800/266-6883 ⊕ www.sdcommute.com. **Metrolink** ☎ 800/371-5465. **Oceanside train station** ☎ 760/722-4622. **Santa Fe Depot** ✉ 1050 Kettner Blvd. ☎ 619/239-9021. **Solana Beach Amtrak station** ☎ 858/259-2697.

PAYING

Amtrak and the Coaster vending machines accept all major credit cards. Metrolink requires cash.

RESERVATIONS

Many Amtrak trains require advance reservations, especially for long-distance transcontinental routes. Advance reservations, which you can make online, are suggested for trains running on weekends between San Diego and Santa Barbara. For security reasons, Amtrak requires ticket purchasers to appear in person with photo ID.

TRANSPORTATION AROUND SAN DIEGO

Most of San Diego was laid out after the invention of the automobile; a car is a necessity for most visitors. Though public transportation serves most of the major attractions, getting from one place to another—from downtown to the beaches north of La Jolla, for instance—can take rather a long time. Two exceptions are the San Diego Trolley, which can save you time if you're heading from downtown to Old Town or Qualcomm Stadium, or to the Mexican border, and the Coronado

Ferry, the scenic route from the harbor to Coronado. Public transportation agencies have integrated their services in an effort to provide convenient connections between rail and bus travel throughout San Diego County. You can obtain an itinerary that will get you from one place to another by accessing the Web site ⊕ www.sdcommute.com or calling ☎ 800/266-6883.

Smoking is prohibited on all forms of public transport in California.

TRAVEL AGENCIES

A good travel agent puts your needs first. Look for an agency that has been in business at least five years, emphasizes customer service, and has someone on staff who specializes in your destination. In addition, **make sure the agency belongs to a professional trade organization.** The American Society of Travel Agents (ASTA)—the largest and most influential in the field with more than 20,000 members in some 140 countries—maintains and enforces a strict code of ethics and will step in to help mediate any agent-client disputes involving ASTA members if necessary. ASTA (whose motto is "Without a travel agent, you're on your own") also maintains a Web site that includes a directory of agents. (If a travel agency is also acting as your tour operator, *see* Buyer Beware *in* Tours & Packages.)

Local Agent Referrals American Society of Travel Agents (ASTA) ✉ 1101 King St., Suite 200, Alexandria, VA 22314 ☎ 703/739-2782, 800/965-2782 24-hr hotline ⊜ 703/684-8319 ⊕ www.astanet.com. **Association of British Travel Agents** ✉ 68-71 Newman St., London W1T 3AH ☎ 020/7637-2444 ⊜ 020/7637-0713 ⊕ www.abta.com. **Association of Canadian Travel Agencies** ✉ 130 Albert St., Suite 1705, Ottawa, Ontario K1P 5G4 ☎ 613/237-3657 ⊜ 613/237-7052 ⊕ www.acta.ca. **Australian Federation of Travel Agents** ✉ Level 3, 309 Pitt St., Sydney, NSW 2000 ☎ 02/9264-3299 or 1300/363-416 ⊜ 02/9264-1085 ⊕ www.afta.com. au. **Travel Agents' Association of New Zealand** ✉ Level 5, Tourism and Travel House, 79 Boulcott St., Box 1888, Wellington 6001 ☎ 04/499-0104 ⊜ 04/499-0786 ⊕ www.taanz.org.nz.

VISITOR INFORMATION

For general information and brochures before you go, contact the San Diego Convention & Visitors Bureau, which publishes the helpful *San Diego Official Visitors Guide* and *San Diego Visitors Pocket Guide*. When you arrive, stop by one of the local visitors centers for general information. Any written correspondence should me mailed to the B Street address.

Learn more about foreign destinations by checking government-issued travel advisories and country information. For a broader picture, consider information from more than one country.

🛈 City-Wide San Diego Convention & International Visitor Information Center ✉ 1040 1/3 W. Broadway at the Cruise Ship terminal, San Diego ☎ 619/232-3101 ⊕ www.sandiego.org ✉ Herschel Ave. at Prospect St. ☎ 619/236-1212 ⊕ www.sandiego.org ✉ 401 B St., Suite 1400, San Diego 92101.

🛈 Local Information Balboa Park Visitors Center ✉ 1549 El Prado ☎ 619/239-0512 ⊕ www.balboapark.org, open daily 9–4. **San Diego Visitor Information Center** ✉ 2688 E. Mission Bay Dr., off I-5 at the Clairemont Drive exit ☎ 619/275-8259, 619/276-8200 for recorded information ⊕ www.infosandiego.com, open daily 9–dusk.

🛈 San Diego County Borrego Springs Chamber of Commerce and Visitors Center ✉ 786 Palm Canyon Dr., 92004 ☎ 760/767-5555 ⊕ www.borregosprings.org. **Carlsbad Convention & Visitors Bureau** ✉ 400 Carlsbad Village Dr., 92008 ☎ 800/227-5722 ⊕ www.visitcarlsbad.com. **Chula Vista Convention & Visitors Bureau** ✉ 750 E. St., 91910 ☎ 619/426-2882 ⊕ www.chulavistaconvis.com. **Coronado Visitor Center** ✉ 1100 Orange Ave., 92118 ☎ 619/437-8788 ⊕ www.coronadovisitorcenter.org. **Del Mar Regional Chamber of Commerce** ✉ 1104 Camino del Mar, 92014 ☎ 858/793-5292 ⊕ www.delmarchamber.org. **Encinitas Chamber of Commerce** ✉ 138 Encinitas Blvd., 92024 ☎ 760/753-6041 ⊕ www.encinitaschamber.com. **Julian Chamber of Commerce** ✉ 2129 Main St., 92036 ☎ 760/765-1857 ⊕ www.julianca.com. **Promote La Jolla, Inc.** ✉ 1150 Silverado St., No. 202, 92037 ☎ 858/454-5718 ⊕ www.lajollabythesea.com. **California Welcome Center Oceanside** ✉ 928 N. Coast Hwy., 92054 ☎ 760/721-1011 or 800/350-7873 ⊕ www.oceansidechamber.com. **San Diego East Visitors**

Bureau ✉ 5005 Willows Rd., No. 208, Alpine 91901 ☎ 619/445-0180 or 800/463-0668 ⊕ www.visitsandiegoeast.com. **San Diego North Convention & Visitors Bureau** ✉ 360 N. Escondido Blvd., Escondido 92025 ☎ 760/745-4741 or 800/848-3336 ⊕ www.sandiegonorth.com.

🛈 Statewide California Division of Tourism ✉ 1102 Q St., Suite 6000, Sacramento, CA 95814 ☎ 916/444-4429 or 800/862-2543 ⊕ www.visitcalifornia.com.

🛈 In the U.K. California Tourist Office ⌨ ABC California, Box 35, Abingdon, Oxfordshire OX14 4TB ☎ 0891/200-278. Calls cost 50p per minute peak rate or 45p per minute cheap rate; send check for £3 for brochures.

🛈 Government Advisories Consular Affairs Bureau of Canada ☎ 800/267-6788 or 613/944-6788 ⊕ www.voyage.gc.ca. **U.K. Foreign and Commonwealth Office** ✉ Travel Advice Unit, Consular Division, Old Admiralty Bldg., London SW1A 2PA ☎ 0870/606-0290 or 020/7008-1500 ⊕ www.fco.gov.uk/travel. **Australian Department of Foreign Affairs and Trade** ☎ 300/139-281 travel advice, 02/6261-1299 Consular Travel Advice Faxback Service ⊕ www.dfat.gov.au. **New Zealand Ministry of Foreign Affairs and Trade** ☎ 04/439-8000 ⊕ www.mft.govt.nz.

WEB SITES

Do check out the World Wide Web when planning your trip. You'll find everything from weather forecasts to virtual tours of famous cities. Be sure to visit Fodors.com (⊕ www.fodors.com), a complete travel-planning site. You can research prices and book plane tickets, hotel rooms, rental cars, vacation packages, and more. In addition, you can post your pressing questions in the Travel Talk section. Other planning tools include a currency converter and weather reports, and there are loads of links to travel resources.

The California Parks Department site, ⊕ www.parks.ca.gov, has information about state-run parks in the San Diego area. The National Park Service site, ⊕ www.nps.gov, has listings about all San Diego–area parks and other lands administered by the park service. The Web site ⊕ www.sandiegohistory.org is a wonderful site covering San Diego's history, buildings, and personalities with articles, archival photos, links, and more. The San Diego Zoo and Wild Animal Park maintain the Web site ⊕ www.sandiegozoo.org, which has up-to-the-minute reports on new facilities, animal guests, and webcams on the giant pandas. Homeport San Diego's Web page, ⊕ www.homeport-sd.com, carries regional weather and other information. *San Diego Magazine*'s ⊕ www.sandiegomag.com carries feature stories about the city and capsule dining reviews. The site of the *San Diego Reader,* ⊕ www.sdreader.com, isn't visually impressive, but it provides a thorough guide to dining, nightlife, and the arts. The *San Diego Union-Tribune* operates the site ⊕ www.signonsandiego.com, which does a good job covering local shopping and dining.

EXPLORING
SAN DIEGO

1

WHERE REALITY LIVES UP TO THE HYPE
San Diego Zoo ➪*p.14*

MOST AWESOME PEARLY WHITES
SeaWorld's Shark Encounter ➪*p.47*

BEST SNEAKILY EDUCATIONAL OUTING
Reuben H. Fleet Science Center ➪*p.11*

GRANDEST HOTEL YOU OUGHT TO SEE
Hotel Del Coronado ➪*p.31*

BEST BET FOR HEARING A WHO
Horton Plaza ➪*p.24*

By Edie Jarolim

Updated by
Rob Aikins

EXPLORING SAN DIEGO MAY BE AN ENDLESS ADVENTURE, but there are limitations, especially if you don't have a car. San Diego is more a chain of separate communities than a cohesive city, and many of the major attractions are separated by some distance. Walking is good for getting an up-close look at how San Diegans live, but true southern Californians use the freeways that crisscross the county. Interstate 5 runs a direct north–south route through the coastal communities from Orange County in the north to the Mexican border. Interstates 805 and 15 do much the same inland, with I–8 as the main east–west route. Routes 163, 52, and 94 serve as connectors.

If you're going to drive around San Diego, study your maps before you hit the road. The freeways are convenient and fast most of the time, but if you miss your turnoff or get caught in commuter traffic, you'll experience a none-too-pleasurable hallmark of southern California living—freeway madness. Drivers rush around on a complex freeway system with the same fervor they use for jogging scores of marathons each year. They particularly enjoy speeding up at interchanges and entrance and exit ramps. Be sure you know where you're going before you join the chase.

Public transportation has improved a great deal in the past decade: the San Diego Trolley has expanded from Old Town to beyond Mission Valley; a commuter line called the *Coaster* runs from Oceanside into downtown; and the bus system covers almost all of the county. However, it's time-consuming to make the connections necessary to see the various sights. Fashion Valley Shopping Center in Mission Valley is one of the three major bus transfer points—downtown and Old Town are the others—but because many of the city's major attractions are along the coast, and because the coast is in itself a major attraction, you'll be best off staying there if you're carless. The bike-path system is extensive and well marked, the weather is almost always bicycle-friendly, and lots of buses have bike racks, so two-wheeling is a good option for the athletic. The large distances between sights render taxis prohibitively expensive for general transportation, although cabs are useful for getting around once you're in a given area. Old Town Trolley Historic Tours has a hop-on, hop-off route of eight popular spots around the city, but it takes so long to cover the route that you're unlikely to see more than two areas before having to catch the last trolley.

San Diego County's warm climate nurtures some amazing flora. Golden stalks of pampas grass grow in wild patches near SeaWorld. Bougainvilleas cover roofs and hillsides in La Jolla, spreading magenta blankets over whitewashed adobe walls. Towering palms and twisted junipers are far more common than maples or oaks, and fields of wild daisies and chamomile cover dry, dusty lots. Red-and-white poinsettias proliferate at Christmas, and candy-color pink- and yellow-flower ice plants edge the roads year-round. Jasmine blooms on bushes and vines in front yards and parking lots; birds-of-paradise poke up straight and tall, tropical testimonials to San Diego's temperate ways. Citrus groves pop up in unlikely places, along the freeways and back roads. When the orange, lemon, and lime trees bloom in spring, the fragrance of their tiny white

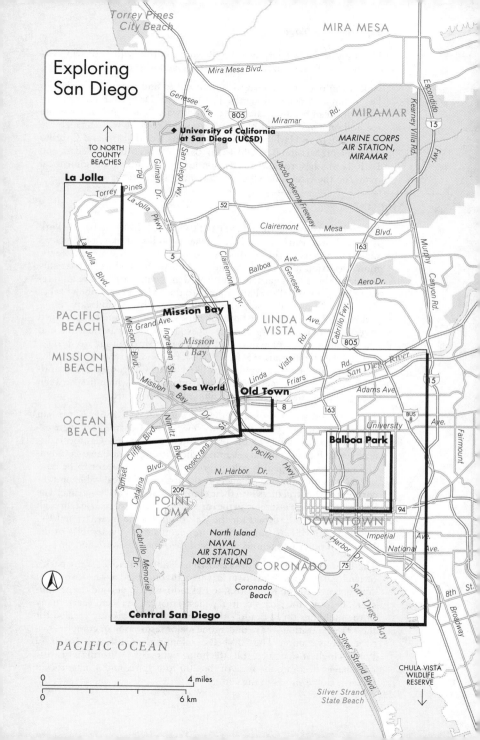

blossoms is nearly overpowering. Be sure to drive with your windows down—you'll be amazed at the sweet, hypnotic scent.

Unless you're on the freeway, it's hard *not* to find a scenic drive in San Diego, but an officially designated 52-mi Scenic Drive over much of central San Diego begins at the foot of Broadway. Road signs with a white sea gull on a yellow-and-blue background direct the way through the Embarcadero to Harbor and Shelter islands, Point Loma and Cabrillo Monument, Mission Bay, Old Town, Balboa Park, Mount Soledad, and La Jolla. It's best to take this three-hour drive, outlined on some local maps, on the weekend, when the commuters are off the road.

BALBOA PARK

Overlooking downtown and the Pacific Ocean, 1,200-acre Balboa Park is the cultural heart of San Diego, where you'll find most of the city's museums and its world-famous zoo. Most first-time visitors just see the museums strung along El Prado and the animals, but Balboa Park is really a series of botanical gardens. Cultivated and wild gardens are an integral part of all of Balboa Park, thanks to the "Mother of Balboa Park," Kate Sessions, who first suggested that the park hire a landscape architect in 1889. She made sure both the park's developed and undeveloped acreage bloomed with the purple blossoms of the jacaranda tree and planted thousands of palms and other trees throughout. (A bronze statue of Sessions stands at Sefton Plaza at the west entrance to the park.) Left alone, Balboa Park would look like Florida Canyon—an arid landscape of sagebrush, cactus, and a few small trees—which lies between the main park and Morley Field, along Park Boulevard.

The parkland was set aside by the city's founders in 1868. (Only San Francisco's Golden Gate Park and New York's Central Park were established earlier.) In 1915 the park hosted the Panama–California International Exposition that celebrated the opening of the Panama Canal, and gained some Spanish colonial revival buildings meant to be temporary exhibit halls. City leaders realized the buildings' value and incorporated the structures into their plans for Balboa Park's acreage. The Spanish theme first instituted in the early 1900s was in part carried through in new buildings designed for the California Pacific International Exposition of 1935–36, but architectural details from the temples of the Maya and other indigenous peoples of the Americas were added.

The Laurel Street Bridge, also known as Cabrillo Bridge, is the park's official gateway; it leads over a vast canyon, filled with downtown commuter traffic on Route 163, to El Prado, which, beyond the art museum, becomes the park's central pedestrian mall. In recent years, many of the buildings on El Prado—the courtyard and walkway created for the 1915 exposition—have undergone major restoration or complete historic reconstruction. The 100-bell carillon in the California Tower, El Prado's highest structure, tolls the hour; figures of California's historic personages decorate the base of the 200-foot spire, and a magnificent blue-tile dome shines in the sun.

The parkland across the Cabrillo Bridge, at the west end of El Prado, has been set aside for picnics and athletics. Rollerbladers zip along Balboa Drive, which leads to the highest spot in the park, Marston Point, overlooking downtown. A throwback to an earlier era, ladies and gents in all-white outfits meet regularly on summer afternoons for lawn-bowling tournaments at the green beside the bridge. Dirt trails lead into pine groves with secluded picnic areas. Southwest of the museums along Park Boulevard, the park's main north–south thoroughfare, Pepper Grove has lots of picnic tables as well as ADA-accessible play equipment.

East of Plaza de Panama, El Prado becomes a pedestrian mall and ends at a footbridge that crosses over Park Boulevard to the perfectly tended Rose Garden, which has more than 2,000 rosebushes. In the adjacent Cactus Garden, trails wind around prickly cacti and soft green succulents from around the world. Palm Canyon, north of the Spreckels Organ Pavilion, has more than 50 varieties of palms along a shady bridge.

The size, scope, and diversity of Balboa Park's attractions make it necessary to spend a few days time to adequately explore everything. For an in-depth look at the park's history and hidden treasures, consult *Discover Balboa Park: A Complete Guide to America's Greatest Urban Park* by Pamela Crooks, available at the visitor center in the House of Hospitality.

Parking near Balboa Park's museums is no small accomplishment, especially on sunny summer days, when the lots, which are all free, fill up quickly. If you're driving in via the Laurel Street Bridge, the first parking area you'll come to is off El Prado to the right, going toward Pan American Plaza. Don't despair if there are no spaces here; you'll see more lots as you continue down along the same road. If you end up parking a bit far from your destination, consider the stroll back through the greenery part of the day's recreational activities. Alternatively, you can just park at Inspiration Point on the east side of the park, off Presidents Way. Free trams run from there to the museums every 8–10 minutes, 9:30–5:30 daily.

Numbers in the text correspond to numbers in the margin and on the Balboa Park map.

Two Good Walks

It's impossible to cover all the park's museums in one day, so choose your focus before you head out. If your interests run to the aesthetic, the Museum of Photographic Arts, the San Diego Museum of Art, the Mingei International Museum of Folk Art, and the Timken Museum of Art should be on your list; architecture buffs will want to add the Marston House. Those with a penchant for natural and cultural history shouldn't miss the San Diego Natural History Museum and the Museum of Man; folks oriented toward space and technology should see the Reuben H. Fleet Science Center, the San Diego Aerospace Museum, and the San Diego Automotive Museum. If you're traveling with kids, the Mingei and Reuben H. Fleet are musts, as is catching a show at the Marie Hitchcock Puppet Theater.

On a nice day, you might just want to stroll outside and enjoy the architecture of the museum complex, with its wonderful Spanish and Mexican designs. A walk along El Prado is about 1 mi round-trip.

Enter via Cabrillo Bridge through the West Gate, which depicts the Panama Canal's linkage of the Atlantic and Pacific oceans. Park south of the **Alcazar Garden** ❶ ▶. It's a short stretch north across El Prado to the landmark California Building, modeled on a cathedral in Mexico and now home to the **San Diego Museum of Man** ❷. Look up to see busts and statues of heroes of the early days of the state. Next door are **The Globe Theatres** ❸, which adjoin the sculpture garden of the **San Diego Museum of Art** ❹, an ornate Plateresque-style structure built to resemble the 17th-century University of Salamanca in Spain.

Continuing east you'll come to the **Timken Museum of Art** ❺, the **Botanical Building** ❻, and the Spanish colonial revival–style Casa del Prado, where the San Diego Floral Association has its offices and a gift shop. At the end of the row is the **San Diego Natural History Museum** ❼; you'll have to detour a block north to visit the **Spanish Village Art Center** ❽. If you were to continue north, you would come to the **carousel** ❾, the **miniature railroad** ❿, and, finally, the entrance to the **San Diego Zoo** ⓫.

Return to the Natural History Museum and cross the Plaza de Balboa—its large central fountain is a popular meeting spot—to reach the **Reuben H. Fleet Science Center** ⓬. (Beyond the parking lot to the south lies the **Centro Cultural de la Raza** ⓭.) You're now on the opposite side of the Prado and heading west. You'll next pass **Casa de Balboa** ⓮; inside are the model-railroad and photography museums and the historical society. Next door in the **House of Hospitality** ⓯ is the Balboa Park Visitors Center, where you can buy a reduced-price pass to the museums, and the Prado restaurant. Across the Plaza de Panama, the Franciscan mission–style **House of Charm** ⓰ houses a folk art museum and a gallery for San Diego artists. Your starting point, the Alcazar Garden, is west of the House of Charm.

A second walk leads south from the Plaza de Panama, which doubles as a parking lot. The majority of the buildings along this route date to the 1935 fair, when the architecture of the Maya and native peoples of the Southwest was highlighted. The first sight you'll pass is the **Japanese Friendship Garden** ⓱. Next comes the ornate, crownlike **Spreckels Organ Pavilion** ⓲. The round seating area forms the base, with the stage as its diadem. The road forks here; veer to the left to reach the **House of Pacific Relations** ⓳, a Spanish mission–style cluster of cottages and one of the few structures on this route built for the earlier exposition. Another is the Balboa Park Club, which you'll pass next. Now used for park receptions and banquets, the building resembles a mission church; you might want to step inside to see the huge mural. Continue on beyond the Palisades Building, which hosts the **Marie Hitchcock Puppet Theater** ⓴, to reach the **San Diego Automotive Museum** ㉑, which, appropriately, is in the building that served as the Palace of Transportation in the 1935–36 exposition.

The road loops back at the spaceshiplike **San Diego Aerospace Museum and International Aerospace Hall of Fame** ㉒. As you head north again you'll notice the Starlight Bowl, an amphitheater on your right. Next comes perhaps the most impressive structure on this tour, the Federal Building, the home of the **San Diego Hall of Champions ㉓**. Its main entrance was modeled after the Palace of Governors in the ancient Mayan city of Uxmal, Mexico. You'll be back at the Spreckels Organ Pavilion after this, having walked a little less than a mile.

TIMING Unless you're pressed for time, you'll want to devote an entire day to the perpetually expanding zoo; there are more than enough exhibits to keep you occupied for five or more hours, and you're likely to be too tired for museum-hopping when you're through.

Although some of the park's museums are open on Monday, most are open Tuesday–Sunday 10–4; in summer a number have extended hours—phone ahead to ask. On Tuesday the museums have free admission to their permanent exhibits on a rotating basis; ⇨ *see* What's Free When box. Free architectural, historical, or nature tours depart from the visitor center every Saturday at 10, while park ranger–led tours start out from the visitor center at 1 PM every Wednesday and Sunday. Free concerts take place Sunday afternoons at 2 PM year-round and the House of Pacific Relations hosts Sunday-afternoon folk-dance performances.

Sights to See

❶ Alcazar Garden. The gardens surrounding the Alcazar Castle in Seville, Spain, inspired the landscaping here; you'll feel like royalty resting on the benches by the tiled fountains. The flower beds are ever-changing horticultural exhibits featuring more than 6,000 annuals for a nearly perpetual bloom. Bright orange-and-yellow poppies appear in spring and deep rust and crimson chrysanthemums arrive in fall. ⊠ *Off El Prado, Balboa Park.*

❻ Botanical Building. The graceful redwood-lathed structure, built for the 1915 Panama-California International Exposition, now houses more than 2,000 types of tropical and subtropical plants plus changing seasonal flower displays. Ceiling-high tree ferns shade fragile orchids and feathery bamboo. There are benches beside miniature waterfalls for resting in the shade. The rectangular pond outside, filled with lotuses and water lilies that bloom in the spring and fall, is popular with photographers. ⊠ *1550 El Prado, Balboa Park* ☎ *619/239–0512* 🎫 *Free* ☉ *Fri.–Wed. 10–4.*

❾ Carousel. Suspended an arm's-length away on this antique merry-go-round is the brass ring that could earn you an extra free ride (it's one of the few carousels in the world that continues this bonus tradition). Hand-carved in 1910, the bobbing animals include zebras, giraffes, and dragons; real horsehair was used for the tails. ⊠ *1889 Zoo Pl., behind zoo parking lot, Balboa Park* ☎ *619/460–9000* 🎫 *$1.75* ☉ *Mid–June–Labor Day, daily 11–6 during school year, only school holidays and weekends 11–5:30.*

⓮ Casa de Balboa. This building on El Prado's southeast corner houses three museums: the Museum of Photographic Arts, the San Diego Historical Society, and the San Diego Model Railroad Museum. ⊠ *1649 El Prado, Balboa Park.*

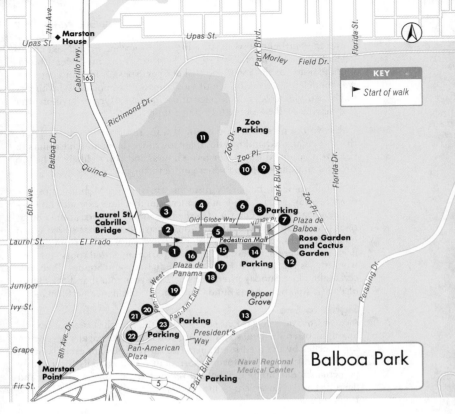

Balboa Park

⑬ Centro Cultural de la Raza. An old water tower was converted into this center for Mexican, Native American, and Chicano arts and culture. Attractions include a gallery with rotating exhibits and a theater, as well as a collection of mural art, a fine example of which may be seen on the tower's exterior. ⊠ *2004 Park Blvd., Balboa Park* ☎ *619/235–6135* ⊕ *www.centroraza.com* ✉ *Donation suggested* ⊙ *Thurs.–Sun. noon–5.*

off the beaten path

HILLCREST – Northwest of Balboa Park, Hillcrest is San Diego's center for the gay community and artists of all types. University, 4th, and 5th avenues are filled with cafés and interesting boutiques, including several indie new and used bookstores along 5th below University. Chain stores and eateries have been making strong inroads, however, and the self-contained residential-commercial Uptown District, on University Avenue at 8th Avenue, was built to resemble an inner-city neighborhood, with shops and restaurants within easy walking distance of high-price town houses. To the northeast, Adams Avenue, reached via Park Boulevard heading north off Washington Street, has many antiques stores. Adams Avenue leads east into Kensington, a handsome old neighborhood that overlooks Mission Valley.

➌ The Globe Theatres. Even if you're not attending a play, this complex, comprising the Cassius Carter Centre Stage, the Lowell Davies Festival Theatre, and the Old Globe Theatre, is a pleasant place to relax between museum visits. The theaters, done in a California version of Tudor style, sit between the Sculpture Garden of the San Diego Museum of Art and the California Tower. A gift shop (open Tuesday–Sunday noon–9:30 when there are performances, noon–5 other days) sells theater-related wares, including posters, cards, and brightly colored puppets. ⊠ *1363 Old Globe Way, Balboa Park* ☎ *619/239–2255* ⊕ *www.theglobetheatres.org.*

⑯ House of Charm. This structure was rebuilt in the mid-1990s from the ground up to replicate the Franciscan Mission style of the original expo building. Inside are the main branch of the Mingei International Museum of Folk Art and the San Diego Art Institute. ⊠ *1439 El Prado, Balboa Park.*

⑮ House of Hospitality. In the Balboa Park Visitors Center's building, you can pick up schedules and route maps for the free trams that operate around the park. You can also purchase the Best of Balboa Park Combo, which affords entry to 13 museums and the zoo for $55; it's worthwhile if you want to visit more than a few museums and aren't entitled to the discounts that most give to children, senior citizens, and military personnel. In addition, you can pick up a flyer that details the excellent free park tours that depart from here (or phone for a schedule). Stop by just to look at the beautiful new structure, which has won myriad awards for its painstaking attention to historical detail; 2,000 paint scrapes were taken, for example, to get the art deco colors exactly right. ⊠ *1549 El Prado, Balboa Park* ☎ *619/239–0512* ⊕ *www.balboapark.org* ⊙ *Daily 9–4.*

⑲ House of Pacific Relations. This is not really a house but a cluster of red tile–roof, stucco cottages representing some 30 foreign countries. And the word "pacific" refers not to the ocean—most of the nations represented are European, not Asian—but to the goal of maintaining peace. The cottages, decorated with crafts and pictures, hold open houses each Sunday afternoon, during which you can chat with transplanted natives and try out different ethnic foods. From the first Sunday in March through the last Sunday in October folk song and dance performances take place on the outdoor stage around 2 PM—check the schedule at the park visitor center. Across the road from the cottages but not affiliated with them is the Spanish colonial–style **United Nations Building.** Inside, the United Nations Association's International Gift Shop, open daily, has reasonably priced crafts, cards, and books. ⊠ *2160 Pan American Rd. W, Balboa Park* ☎ *619/234–0739* ⊕ *www.sdhpr.org* ✉ *Free, donations accepted* ☉ *Early Sept.–late May, Sun. noon–4; Memorial Day–Labor Day, Sun. noon–5.*

⑰ Japanese Friendship Garden. A koi pond with a cascading water wall, a 60-foot-long wisteria arbor, a large activity center, and a sushi bar are highlights of the park's authentic Japanese garden, designed to inspire contemplation. You can wander the various peaceful paths, meditate in the traditional stone-and-sand garden, or, at times, learn such arts as origami and flower arranging at the exhibit hall. Long-term plans are to develop an additional 9 acres with more attractions, including a teahouse, tea garden, and cherry orchard. ⊠ *2215 Pan American Rd., Balboa Park* ☎ *619/232–2721* ⊕ *www.niwa.org* ✉ *$3* ☉ *Tues.–Sun. 10–4.*

Marston House. George W. Marston (1850–1946), a San Diego pioneer and philanthropist who financed the architectural landscaping of Balboa Park—among his myriad other San Diego civic projects—was visited by such prominent people as President Teddy Roosevelt and Booker T. Washington. His 16-room home at the northwest edge of the park, now maintained by the San Diego Historical Society, was designed in 1905 by San Diego architects Irving Gill and William Hebbard. It's a classic example of the American Arts and Crafts style, which emphasizes simplicity and functionality of form, as are the furnishings, which include pieces by Tiffany, Roycroft, and Gustav Stickley. On the 5-acre grounds is a lovely English Romantic garden, as interpreted in California. Hour-long docent tours—the only way to see the house—illuminate many aspects of San Diego history in which the Marstons played a part. ⊠ *3525 7th Ave., Balboa Park* ☎ *619/298–3142* ✉ *$5* ☉ *Fri.–Sun. 10–4, last tour at 3:15.*

☙ ⑳ Marie Hitchcock Puppet Theater. One of the last of its kind, the theater has been presenting shows for more than 50 years and incorporates marionettes, hand puppets, rod puppets, shadow puppets, and ventriloquism. Stories range from traditional fairy tales to folk legends and contemporary puppet plays. Pantomime, comedy, and music round out the program. Kids will be wide-eyed at the short, energy-filled productions. Adults will be filled with nostalgia. ⊠ *2130 Pan American Plaza, Balboa Park* ☎ *619/685–5990* ⊕ *www.balboaparkpuppets.com* ✉ *$3* ☉ *Show-*

times mid-June–Labor Day, Wed.–Sun. 11, 1, 2:30; Sept.–mid-June, Wed., Thurs., and Fri. 10 and 11:30; weekends 11, 1, 2:30.

Mingei International Museum. All ages will enjoy the colorful and creative exhibits of toys, pottery, textiles, costumes, and gadgets from around the globe at the Mingei. Traveling and permanent exhibits in the high-ceiling, light-filled museum include everything from antique American carousel horses to the latest in Japanese ceramics. The name Mingei comes from the Japanese words *min*, meaning "all people," and *gei*, meaning "art." Thus, the museum's name describes what you'll find under its roof: "art of all people." It's hard to predict what you'll see, but you can depend on it being delightful. The gift shop has a great selection of Navajo, Hopi, and Huichol Indian artwork. ⊠ *House of Charm, 1439 El Prado, Balboa Park* ☎ *619/239–0003* ⊕ *www.mingei.org* ☞ *$6* ⊙ *Tues.–Sun. 10–4.*

Miniature railroad. Adjacent to the zoo parking lot and across from the carousel, a pint-size, 48-passenger train runs a ½-mi loop through four tree-filled acres of the park. The engine of this rare 1948 model train is a 1/5 scale version of a General Motors F-3 locomotive and is one of only 50 left in the world. ⊠ *2885 Zoo Pl., Balboa Park* ☎ *619/231–1515 Ext. 4219* ☞ *$1.25* ⊙ *June–Aug., daily 11–6:30; Sept.–May, weekends and school holidays 11–4:30.*

Morley Field Sports Complex. In addition to the 2-mi fitness course and ball diamonds, the park's athletic center has a flying-disc golf course, with challenging "holes"—wire baskets hung from metal poles—where players toss their Frisbees over canyons and treetops to reach their goal. Morley Field also has a public pool, a velodrome, an archery range, playgrounds, and boccie, badminton, and tennis courts. The complex is at the northeast corner of Balboa Park, across Park Boulevard and Florida Canyon. ⊠ *2221 Morley Field Dr., Balboa Park* ☎ *619/692–4919* ⊕ *www.morleyfield.com.*

Museum of Photographic Arts. World-renowned photographers such as Ansel Adams, Imogen Cunningham, Henri Cartier-Bresson, and Edward Weston are represented in the permanent collection, which includes everything from 19th-century daguerreotypes to contemporary photojournalism prints and Russian Constructivist images (with many by Alexander Rodchenko). The 28,000-square-foot facility has a state-of-the-art theater for screening cinema classics as well as a learning center. On Thursday nights, the museum is open late for movie presentations and the occasional jazz recital. ⊠ *Casa de Balboa, 1649 El Prado, Balboa Park* ☎ *619/238–7559* ⊕ *www.mopa.org* ☞ *$6 museum, $7 theater* ⊙ *Daily 10–5, 'til 9 on Thurs.*

Reuben H. Fleet Science Center. The Fleet Center's clever interactive exhibits are sneakily educational. You can reconfigure your face to have two left sides, or, by replaying an instant video clip, watch yourself coming and going at different speeds. The IMAX Dome Theater screens exhilarating nature and science films. The SciTours simulator is designed to take you on virtual voyages—stomach lurches and all. The Meteor Storm lets up to six players at a time have an interactive virtual-reality experience, this one sans motion sickness potential. A big hit is the Nierman Challenger Learning Center—a realistic mock mission-control and futuristic space station. ⊠ *1875 El Prado, Balboa Park* ☎ *619/238–1233* ⊕ *www.rhfleet.org* ⊠ *Gallery exhibits $6.75, gallery exhibits and 1 IMAX film $11.75* ⊙ *Mon.–Thurs. 9:30–5, Fri. and Sat. 9:30–8, Sun. 9:30–6; closing hrs vary, call ahead.*

★ ☾ ㉒ **San Diego Aerospace Museum and International Aerospace Hall of Fame.** The streamlined edifice commissioned by the Ford Motor Company for the 1935–36 exposition looks unlike any other structure in the park; at night, with a line of blue neon outlining it, the round building appears—appropriately enough—to be a landed UFO. Every available inch of space in the rotunda is filled with exhibits about aviation and aerospace pioneers, including examples of enemy planes during the world wars. All in all, there are 67 full-size aircraft on the floor and literally hanging from the rafters. Play with the interactive exhibits (kids love to pretend to fly in the DC-3 cockpit display). In addition to exhibits from eras including the golden age of flight and the jet age, the museum also displays a growing number of space-age exhibits, including the actual Apollo 9 space capsule. A collection of real and replicated aircraft fills the central courtyard. ⊠ *2001 Pan American Plaza, Balboa Park* ☎ *619/234–8291* ⊕ *www.aerospacemuseum.org* ⊠ *$8, behind-the-scenes restorations $3 extra* ⊙ *Daily 10–4:30, 5:30 in summer.*

⑯ **San Diego Art Institute.** Outside juries decide which works created by members of the Art Institute will be displayed in rotating shows, which change every six weeks. Painting, sculpture, watercolor—everything except crafts, reserved for the excellent small gift shop—are represented. The David Fleet Young Artists Gallery shows art executed by students at area schools. ⊠ *House of Charm, 1439 El Prado, Balboa Park* ☎ *619/236–0011* ⊕ *www.sandiego-art.org* ⊠ *$3* ⊙ *Tues.–Sat. 10–4, Sun. noon–4.*

㉑ **San Diego Automotive Museum.** Even if you don't know a choke from a chassis, you're bound to admire the sleek designs of the autos in this impressive museum. The core collection comprises vintage motorcycles and cars, ranging from an 1886 Benz to a De Lorean, as well as a series of rotating exhibits from collections around the world. There's an ongoing automobile restoration program, and the museum sponsors many outdoor automotive events; call to find out about any rallies or concours d'elegance that might be scheduled. ⊠ *2080 Pan American Plaza, Balboa Park* ☎ *619/231–2886* ⊕ *www.sdautomuseum.org* ⊠ *$7* ⊙ *Daily 10–5, last admission at 4:30.*

☾ ㉓ **San Diego Hall of Champions.** In a 70,000-square-foot building, this museum celebrates local jock heroes via a vast collection of memorabilia, uniforms, paintings, photographs, and computer and video displays. An amusing bloopers film is screened at the Sports Theater. The Center Court activity area hosts changing programs—everything from a Chargers mini-training camp to interactive bobsled races. In keeping with the progressive nature of the San Diego sports community, there are also exhibits of such extreme sports as skateboarding, surfing, and street luge.

✉ *Federal Bldg., 2131 Pan American Rd., Balboa Park* ☎ *619/234–2544* ⊕ *www.sandiegosports.org* ✏ *$6* ☉ *Daily 10–4.*

⑭ San Diego Historical Society Museum. The San Diego Historical Society maintains its research library in the Casa de Balboa's basement and organizes shows on the first floor. Permanent and rotating exhibits, which are often more lively than you might expect, survey local urban history after 1850, when California entered the Union. A 100-seat theater hosts public lectures, workshops, and educational programs, and a gift shop carries a good selection of books on local history as well as reproductions of old posters and other historical collectibles. ✉ *Casa de Balboa, 1649 El Prado, Balboa Park* ☎ *619/232–6203* ⊕ *www.sandiegohistory. org* ✏ *$6* ☉ *Fri.–Wed. 10–5, Thurs. 10–8.*

☾ ⑭ San Diego Model Railroad Museum. At 24,000 square feet, this is the largest indoor railroad display in the world. Elevated ramps allow great viewing of the displays that have terrain models of San Diego County. When the impressive, giant-scale exhibits of model trains of the Southwest are in operation, you'll hear the sounds of chugging engines, screeching brakes, and shrill whistles. If you come in through the back door on Tuesday and Friday evenings, 7:30–11, there's no charge to watch the model-train layouts being created. Children under 15 get in free with an adult. ✉ *Casa de Balboa, 1649 El Prado, Balboa Park* ☎ *619/696–0199* ⊕ *www.sdmodelrailroadm.com* ✏ *$5* ☉ *Tues.–Fri. 11–4, weekends 11–5.*

★ ④ San Diego Museum of Art. Known primarily for its Spanish Baroque and Renaissance paintings, including works by El Greco, Goya, Rubens, and van Ruisdael, San Diego's most comprehensive art museum also has strong holdings of South Asian art, Indian miniatures, and contemporary California paintings. The Baldwin M. Baldwin collection includes more than 100 pieces by Toulouse-Lautrec. If traveling shows from other cities come to San Diego, you can expect to see them here. An outdoor Sculpture Garden exhibits both traditional and modern pieces. The IMAGE (Interactive Multimedia Art Gallery Explorer) system allows you to call up the highlights of the museum's collection on a computer screen and custom-design a tour, call up historical information on the works and artists, and print color reproductions. The museum's goal is to "connect people to art and art to people," so they work to present exhibits with broad appeal. A good mix of American artists, international treasures, and shows with recognized masters is rounded out by lectures, concerts, and film events. Free docent tours are offered throughout the day. ✉ *Casa de Balboa, 1450 El Prado, Balboa Park* ☎ *619/232–7931* ⊕ *www.sdmart.org* ✏ *$8, $10–$12 for special exhibits* ☉ *Tues.–Sun. 10–6 'til 9 on Thurs.*

need a break? Take a respite from museum-hopping with a cup of coffee or a glass of California chardonnay in the San Diego Museum of Art's **Sculpture Garden Café** (☎ 619/696–1990), which also has a small selection of tasty sandwiches and salads Tuesday–Sunday 8:30–4 (it's often open for dinner, too, in summer). You can also get coffee and various noshes from a food cart outside the café.

San Diego Museum of Man. Exhibits at this highly respected anthropological museum focus on Southwestern, Mexican, and South American cultures. Carved monuments from the Mayan city of Quirigua in Guatemala, cast from the originals in 1914, are particularly impressive. Rotating shows might include examples of intricate beadwork from across the Americas, and demonstrations of such skills as weaving and tortilla-making are held regularly. Other great exhibits show the lifestyles of the Kumeyaay peoples who inhabited San Diego before Europeans arrived. Among the museum's more recent additions is the hands-on Children's Discovery Center. ✉ *California Bldg., 1350 El Prado, Balboa Park* ☏ *619/239–2001* ⊕ *www.museumofman.org* ✉ *$6* ☉ *Daily 10–4:30.*

★ **San Diego Natural History Museum.** There are 7.5 million fossils, dinosaur models, and even live reptiles and other specimens under this roof. Favorite exhibits include the Foucault pendulum, suspended on a 43-foot cable and designed to demonstrate the Earth's rotation; a full-size grey whale skeleton; and *Ocean Oasis,* the world's first large-format film about Baja California and the Sea of Cortéz. Traveling exhibits such as the Field Museum's exhibit on chocolate and photographic essays all make a stop here. The museum also sponsors community events. Call ahead for information on films, lectures, and free guided nature walks. ✉ *1788 El Prado, Balboa Park* ☏ *619/232–3821* ⊕ *www. sdnhm.org* ✉ *$8* ☉ *Daily 10–5.*

San Diego Zoo. Balboa Park's—and perhaps the city's—most famous attraction is its 100-acre zoo, and it deserves all the press it gets. Nearly 4,000 animals of some 800 diverse species roam in hospitable, expertly crafted habitats that replicate natural environments as closely as possible. The flora in the zoo, including many rare species, is even more costly than the fauna. Walkways wind over bridges and past waterfalls ringed with tropical ferns; elephants in a sandy plateau roam so close you're tempted to pet them.

Exploring the zoo fully requires the stamina of a healthy hiker, but open-air trams that run throughout the day let you zip through 80% of the exhibits on a 35-minute, 3-mi tour. The Kangaroo bus tours include the same informed and amusing narrations as the others, but for a few dollars more you can get on and off as you like at eight stops. The Skyfari ride, which soars 170 feet above the ground, gives a good overview of the zoo's layout and, on clear days, a panorama of the park, downtown San Diego, the bay, and the ocean, far past the Coronado–San Diego Bay Bridge. Unless you come early, however, expect to wait to be moved around. The line for the regular tram, and especially for the top tier, can take more than 45 minutes; if you come at midday on a weekend or school holiday, you'll be doing the in-line shuffle for a while.

In any case, the zoo is at its best when you wander the paths, such as the one that climbs through the huge, enclosed **Scripps Aviary,** where brightly colored tropical birds swoop between branches just inches from your face, and into the neighboring **Gorilla Tropics,** among the zoo's latest ventures into bioclimatic zone exhibits. Here animals live in enclosed environments modeled on their native habitats. These zones may look natural, but they're helped a lot by modern technology: the sounds of the tropical rain forest emerge from a 144-speaker sound system that plays CDs recorded in Africa.

The zoo's simulated Asian rain forest, **Tiger River,** has 10 exhibits with more than 35 species of animals; tigers, Malayan tapirs, and Argus pheasants wander among the collection of exotic trees and plants. The mist-shrouded trails winding down a canyon into Tiger River pass by fragrant jasmine, ginger lilies, and orchids, giving you the feeling of descending into an Asian jungle. In **Sun Bear Forest** playful beasts constantly claw apart the trees and shrubs that serve as a natural playground for climbing, jumping, and general merrymaking. At the popular **Polar Bear Plunge,** where you can watch the featured animals take a chilly dive, Siberian reindeer, white foxes, and other Arctic creatures are separated from their predatory neighbors by a series of camouflaged moats. **Ituri Forest**—a 4-acre African rain forest at the base of Tiger River—lets you glimpse huge but surprisingly graceful hippos frolicking underwater, and buffalo cavorting with monkeys on dry land. The zoo's newest tropical environment is **Absolutely Apes,** a lush, naturalistic environment where orangutans and siamangs climb, swing, and generally live almost as they would in the wild. Lined with 110-foot-long and 12-foot-high viewing windows, the exhibit offers a unique opportunity to view these endangered apes close up.

The San Diego Zoo houses the largest number of koalas outside Australia, and they remain major crowd pleasers, but these and other zoo locals are always overshadowed by the babies. Following the success with Hua Mei, the first panda cub born in the U.S to survive past four days, the zoo's Center for the Reproduction of Endangered Species again were able to successfully impregnate Bai Yun. Mei Sheng, a male Giant panda cub, was born in September 2003. He and his mother are generally available for viewing from 10:30 to 3:45 each day, but that can sometimes change. Call the panda hotline for up to date information.

For a hands-on experience there's the **Children's Zoo,** where goats, sheep, bunnies, and guinea pigs beg to be petted. There are two viewer-friendly nurseries where you may see various baby animals bottle feed and sleep peacefully in large-size baby cribs. Children can see entertaining creatures of all sorts at the Wegeforth National Park Sea Lion Show and the Wild Ones Show. Both are put on daily in a 3,000-seat outdoor amphitheater.

The zoo rents strollers, wheelchairs, and cameras; it also has a first-aid office, a lost and found, and an ATM. It's best to avert your eyes from the zoo's two main gift shops until the end of your visit; you can spend a half day just poking through the wonderful animal-related posters, crafts, dishes, clothing, and toys. One guilt-alleviating fact if you buy too much: some of the profits of your purchases go to zoo programs. Audio tours, behind-the-scenes tours, walking tours, tours in Spanish, and tours for people with hearing or vision impairments are available; inquire at the entrance. ⊠ *2920 Zoo Dr., Balboa Park* ☎ *619/234–3153, 888/697–2632 Giant panda hotline* ⊕ *www.sandiegozoo.org* ⊠ *$21 includes zoo, Children's Zoo, and animal shows; $32 includes above,* *plus 40-min guided bus tour and round-trip Skyfari ride; Kangaroo bus tour $12 additional, only $3 additional for purchasers of $32 ticket; zoo free for children under 12 in Oct. and for all 1st Mon. in Oct.; $52.65 pass good for admission to zoo and San Diego Wild Animal Park within 5 days ⊟ AE, D, MC, V ☉ July–Sept., daily 9–9; Sept.–May, daily 9–4; Children's Zoo and Skyfari ride generally close one hour earlier.*

need a break?

Plenty of **food stands** sell popcorn, pizza, and enormous ice-cream cones at the zoo. If you want to eat among strolling peacocks—who will try to cadge your food—consider the **Flamingo Café**, inside the main entrance, serving sandwiches, salads, and light meals. Of the zoo's indoor restaurants, the best is **Albert's**, part of a three-tier dining complex near Gorilla Tropics. Grilled fish, homemade pizza, and fresh pasta are among the offerings, and this is the only place where wine and beer are sold.

⑧ Spanish Village Art Center. Glassblowers, enamel workers, wood-carvers, sculptors, painters, jewelers, photographers, and other artists rent space in the 35 red tile–roof studio-galleries that were set up for the 1935–36 exposition in the style of an ancient Spanish village. The artists give demonstrations of their work on a rotating basis, aware, no doubt, that it's fun to buy wares that you've watched being created. ☒ *1770 Village Pl., Balboa Park* ☎ *619/233–9050* ⊕ *www.spanishvillageart.com* ☒ *Free* ☉ *Daily 11–4.*

⑱ Spreckels Organ Pavilion. The 2,000-seat pavilion, dedicated in 1915 by sugar magnates John D. and Adolph B. Spreckels, holds the 4,445-pipe Spreckels Organ, the largest outdoor pipe organ in the world. You can hear this impressive instrument at one of the year-round, 2 PM Sunday concerts, regularly performed by civic organist Carol Williams. On Monday evenings in summer, military bands, gospel groups, and barbershop quartets also perform. At Christmastime the park's Christmas tree and life-size Nativity display turn the pavilion into a seasonal wonderland. ☒ *2211 Pan American Rd., Balboa Park* ☎ *619/702–8138.*

⑤ Timken Museum of Art. Somewhat out of place in the architectural scheme of the park, this modern structure is made of travertine marble imported from Italy. The small museum houses works by major European and American artists as well as a superb collection of Russian icons. ☒ *1500 El Prado, Balboa Park* ☎ *619/239–5548* ⊕ *www.timkenmuseum.org* ☒ *Free* ☉ *Tues.–Sat. 10–4:30, Sun. 1:30–4:30.*

DOWNTOWN

Downtown is San Diego's Lazarus. Written off as moribund by the 1970s, when few people willingly stayed in the area after dark, downtown is now one of the city's prime draws for tourists and real estate agents. Massive redevelopment started in the late 1970s, giving rise to the Gaslamp Quarter Historic District, Horton Plaza shopping center, and San Diego Convention Center, which have spurred an upsurge of elegant hotels, upscale condominium complexes, and swank, trendy cafés

WHAT'S FREE WHEN

WHILE BEACHCOMBING, sunbathing, or simply strolling along the beach and bay will always be San Diego's most popular free activities, there are many other options for those days when you want to shake the sand out of your shoes and see another side of the city. The downtown location of the Museum of Contemporary art is free every day except Wednesday, when it is closed. The La Jolla location is free the first Sunday and second Tuesday of each month. Old Town State Historic Park is free at all times, as are many of the museums within its boundaries. The most options for freebies can be found in Balboa Park, both on a weekly basis and at special times of the year. You can pick up a free garden tour map at the visitor's center and use that to explore the dozens of gardens covering the parks 1200 acres, but you aren't limited to just that. The San Diego

Zoo is free for kids under 13 the whole month of October, and everyone gets in free on Founder's Day, October 1st. The December Nights festival on the first Friday and Saturday of that month include free admission and later hours to most of the Balboa Park museums. The outdoor events during the festival make it something not to miss. The free concerts at the Spreckels Organ Pavilion take place Sunday afternoons at 2 PM year-round and summer Monday evenings. Come through the back door of the The San Diego Model Train Museum on Tuesday and Fridays evenings (7:30–11) and there's no charge to watch the train layouts being created. The Timken Museum of Art is always free. The Centro Cultural de la Raza and Veterans Memorial Center are free, but a donation is requested at each. The best deal is the Free Tuesdays in the Park, a rotating schedule of free admission to most all of Balboa Park's museums.

First Tuesday
San Diego Model Railroad Museum
San Diego Natural History Museum
Reuben H. Fleet Science Center

Second Tuesday
Museum of Photographic Arts
Museum of San Diego History

Third Tuesday
San Diego Art Institute
San Diego Museum of Art
San Diego Museum of Man
Japanese Friendship Garden
Mingei International Museum

Fourth Tuesday
San Diego Aerospace Museum
San Diego Automotive Museum
San Diego Hall of Champions
House of Pacific Relations International
   Cottages

Fifth Tuesday
Normal museum prices are in effect.

and restaurants that have people lingering downtown well into the night—if not also waking up there the next morning.

Downtown's natural attributes were easily evident to its original booster, Alonzo Horton (1813–1909), who arrived in San Diego in 1867. Horton looked at the bay and the acres of flatland surrounded by hills and canyons and knew he had found San Diego's heart. Although Old Town, under the Spanish fort at the Presidio, had been settled for years, Horton understood that it was too far away from the water to take hold as the commercial center of San Diego. He bought 960 acres along the bay at 27½¢ per acre and gave away the land to those who would develop it or build houses. Within months he had sold or given away 226 city blocks.

The transcontinental railroad arrived in 1885, and the land boom was on. Although the railroad's status as a cross-country route was short lived, the population soared from 5,000 to 35,000 in less than a decade— a foreshadowing of San Diego's future. In 1887 the Santa Fe Depot was constructed at the foot of Broadway, two blocks from the water. Freighters chugged in and out of the harbor, and by the early 1900s the U.S. Navy had moved in.

As downtown grew into San Diego's transportation and commercial hub, residential neighborhoods blossomed along the beaches and inland valleys. The business district gradually moved farther away from the original heart of downtown, at 5th Avenue and Market Street, past Broadway, up toward Balboa Park. Downtown's waterfront fell into bad times during World War I, when sailors, gamblers, and prostitutes were drawn to one another and the waterfront bars.

But Alonzo Horton's modern-day followers, city leaders intent on prospering while preserving San Diego's natural beauty, reclaimed the downtown area. The Centre City Development Corporation (CCDC), a public, nonprofit organization, spearheaded development of the Gaslamp District in 1975, which attracted a groundswell of investment after the adjacent Horton Plaza shopping complex opened to huge success in 1985. This in turn led the way for the hotels, restaurants, shopping centers, and housing developments that are now rising on every square inch of available space. Waterfront transformation also proceeded apace, as old shipyards and canneries were replaced by hotel towers and waterfront parks. The Martin Luther King Jr. Promenade project, which cost an estimated $25 million by the time it was completed in early 1999, put 14 acres of greenery, a pedestrian walkway, and lots of artwork along Harbor Drive from Seaport Village to the convention center, and landscaped the railroad right-of-way from the Santa Fe depot to 8th Avenue. The San Diego Convention Center, which hosted its first events in 1990, proved so successful with events like the 1996 Republican National Convention that it has doubled in size to about 1.7 million square feet.

Of the newest downtown projects—there are more than 100 in the works—the most ambitious is the 26-block Ballpark District, which occupies the East Village area that extends between the railroad tracks up to J Street, and from 6th Avenue east to around 10th Street. It includes

Petro Park, a new 42,000-seat baseball stadium for the San Diego Padres; a distinctively San Diego–style, 8-acre "Park at the Park" from which fans watch games while picnicking; a sports-related retail complex; at least 850 hotel rooms; and several apartment and condominium complexes. The stadium opened in March 2004, and anchors the already burgeoning district. On downtown's waterfront sits the *USS Midway*, the home of the San Diego Aircraft Carrier Museum, which also opened in 2004.

Downtown's main thoroughfares are Harbor Drive, running along the waterfront; Broadway, through the center of downtown; and 6th Avenue, between Harbor Drive and Balboa Park. The numbered streets run roughly north–south; the lettered and named streets—Broadway, Market, Island, and Ash—run east–west. Only Broadway, Market Street, Harbor Drive, and Island Avenue have two-way traffic. The rest alternate one-way directions.

There are reasonably priced ($4–$7 per day) parking lots along Harbor Drive, Pacific Highway, and lower Broadway and Market Street. The price of many downtown parking meters is $1 per hour, with a maximum stay of two hours (meters are in effect Monday–Saturday [except holidays], 8–6); unless you know for sure that your stay in the area will be short, you're better off in a lot.

Numbers in the text correspond to numbers in the margin and on the Central San Diego map.

Two Good Walks

Most people do a lot of parking-lot hopping when visiting downtown, but for the energetic, two distinct areas may be explored on foot.

To stay near the water, start a walk of the **Embarcadero** ❶ ▶ at the foot of Ash Street on Harbor Drive, where the *Berkeley,* headquarters of the **Maritime Museum** ❷, is moored. A cement pathway runs south from the *Star of India* along the waterfront to the pastel B Street Pier. If you're traveling with firehouse fans, detour inland six blocks and north two blocks to the **Firehouse Museum** ❹, at the corner of Cedar and Columbia in Little Italy. Otherwise, another two blocks south on Harbor Drive brings you to the foot of Broadway and the Broadway Pier, where you can catch harbor excursion boats and the ferry to Coronado. Approximately one block south of Broadway is the Navy Pier, home of the **San Diego Aircraft Carrier Museum** ❸. Take Broadway inland two long blocks to Kettner Boulevard to reach the **Transit Center** ❺—you'll see the mosaic-domed Santa Fe Depot and the tracks for the trolley to Tijuana out front—and, right next door, the downtown branch of the **Museum of Contemporary Art, San Diego** ❻. (If you've detoured to the Firehouse Museum, take Kettner Boulevard south to the Transit Center.) Return to Harbor Drive and continue south past Tuna Harbor to **Seaport Village** ❼.

A tour of the working heart of downtown can begin at the corner of 1st Avenue and Broadway, near Spreckels Theater, a grand old stage that presents pop concerts and touring plays. Two blocks east and across the street sits the historic **U. S. Grant Hotel** ❽. If you cross Broadway, you'll

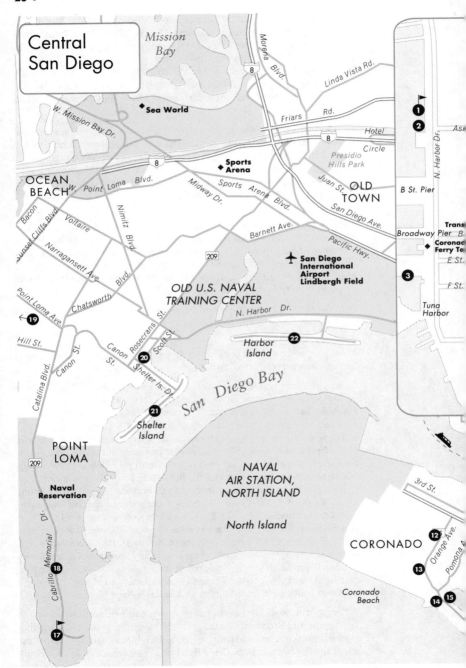

Central
San Diego

TO OLD TOWN, QUALCOMM STADIUM

DOWNTOWN

KEY

▶ Start of walk

Cedar St.

County Center/Little Italy Station

Beech St.

Ash St.

N. Harbor Dr.

Pacific Hwy.

Kettner Blvd.

India St.

Columbia St.

State St.

Union St.

Front St.

First Ave.

Second Ave.

Third Ave.

Fourth Ave.

Fifth Ave.

Beech St.

A St.

A St.

B St.

B St.

C St.

C St.

Civic Center Trolley Station

Amtrak/Transfer Center

Pier   Broadway

Coronado Ferry Terminal

American Plaza Station

Broadway

E St.

E St.

F St.

State St.

Union St.

F St.

First Ave.

Fourth Ave.

Fifth Ave.

G St.

TROLLEY LINE

rbor

G St.

Harbor Dr.

Seaport Trolley Station

Market St.

Market Pl.

Island Ave.

Second Ave.

William Heath Davis House

Harbor Dr.

J St.

Convention Center West Station

Petco Park

Embarcadero Marina Park North   South

San Diego Convention Center

Harbor   Dr.

Imperial Ave.

25th St.

32nd St.

National Ave.

75

Main St.

ange Ave.

Pomona Ave.

San Diego-Coronado Bay Bridge

NATIONAL CITY

Silver Strand Blvd.

0   1mile
0   1 km

be able to enter **Horton Plaza** ❾, San Diego's favorite retail playland. Fourth Avenue, the eastern boundary of Horton Plaza, doubles as the western boundary of the 16-block **Gaslamp Quarter** ❿. Head south to Island Avenue and 4th Avenue to the William Heath Davis House, where you can get a touring map of the district.

TIMING   The above walks take about an hour each, although there's enough to do in downtown San Diego to keep you busy for at least two days. Weather is a determining factor in any Embarcadero stroll, which is pretty much an outdoors endeavor, but San Diego rarely presents any problems along that line. Most of downtown's attractions are open daily, but the Museum of Contemporary Art is closed on Monday, and the Firehouse Museum is only open from Wednesday through Sunday. For a guided tour of the Gaslamp Quarter, plan to visit on Saturday. A boat trip on the harbor, or at least a hop over to Coronado on the ferry, is a must at any time of year, but from December through March, when the gray whales migrate between the Pacific Northwest and southern Baja, you should definitely consider booking a whale-watching excursion from the Broadway Pier.

Sights to See

▶ ❶ **Embarcadero.** The bustle along Harbor Drive's waterfront walkway comes less these days from the activities of fishing folk than from the throngs of tourists, but it remains the nautical soul of San Diego. People here still make a living from the sea. Seafood restaurants line the piers, as do sea vessels of every variety—cruise ships, ferries, tour boats, houseboats, and naval destroyers.

On the north end of the Embarcadero, at Ash Street, you'll find the Maritime Museum. South of it, the **B Street Pier** is used by ships from major cruise lines as both a port of call and a departure point. The cavernous pier building has a cruise-information center as well as a small bar—nice for cooling off on a hot day—and gift shop. Walk another block south and you can't miss the massive USS *Midway,* home of the San Diego Aircraft Carrier Museum.

Day-trippers getting ready to set sail gather at the **Broadway Pier,** also known as the excursion pier. Tickets for the harbor tours and whale-watching trips are sold here. The terminal for the Coronado Ferry lies just beyond the Broadway pier.

The U.S. Navy has control of the next few waterfront blocks to the south—**destroyers, submarines, and carriers** (☎ 619/437–2735 hours and types of ships, 619/545–1141 aircraft carriers) cruise in and out, some staying for weeks at a time. Unless the Navy is engaged in military maneuvers or activities, on weekends you can tour these floating cities. Check out the carrier USS *Constellation,* which docks across the harbor at North Island naval base when it's in port. **Tuna Harbor** is the former hub of one of San Diego's earliest and most successful industries, commercial tuna fishing. The tuna-fishing industry has gone south to Mexico, so these days there are more pleasure boats than tuna boats tied up at the adjoining G Street Pier, but the United States Tuna Foundation still has offices here. A pleasant park offers a great view across the bay of North Island, where aircraft carriers often dock.

The next bit of seafront greenery is a few blocks south along the paved promenade at **Embarcadero Marina Park North,** an 8-acre extension into the harbor from the center of Seaport Village. It's usually full of kite fliers, in-line skaters, and picnickers. Seasonal celebrations are held here and at the similar **Embarcadero Marina Park South.**

The **San Diego Convention Center,** on Harbor Drive between 1st and 5th avenues, was designed by Arthur Erickson. The backdrop of blue sky and sea complements the building's nautical lines. The center often holds trade shows that are open to the public, and tours of the building are available.

need a break? Those waiting for their boats at the Broadway Pier can enjoy some New England–style clam chowder in an edible sourdough bowl at the **Bay Café** (⊠ 1050 N. Harbor Dr., Embarcadero ☎ 619/595–1083).

☺ ❹ Firehouse Museum. Fire-fighting artifacts of all sorts fill this converted fire station, which at one time also served as the repair shop for all of San Diego's fire-fighting equipment. Three large rooms contain everything from 19th-century horse- and hand-drawn fire engines to 20th-century motorized trucks, the latest dating to 1942. Extinguishers, helmets, and other memorabilia from all over the world are also on display. Ages 12 and under are free. ⊠ *1572 Columbia St., Little Italy* ☎ *619/232–3473* ⊡ *$2* ☉ *Wed.–Fri. 10–2, weekends 10–4.*

❿ Gaslamp Quarter. The 16½-block national historic district contains most of San Diego's Victorian-style commercial buildings from the late 1800s, when Market Street was the center of early downtown. Businesses thrived in this area in the latter part of the 19th century, but at the turn of the 20th century downtown's commercial district moved west toward Broadway, and many of San Diego's first buildings fell into disrepair. During the early 1900s the quarter became known as the Stingaree district. Prostitutes picked up sailors in lively area taverns and dance halls, and crime flourished; the blocks between Market Street and the waterfront were best avoided.

As the move for downtown redevelopment emerged, there was talk of bulldozing the buildings in the quarter and starting from scratch. History buffs, developers, architects, and artists formed the Gaslamp Quarter Council in 1974. Bent on preserving the district, they gathered funds from the government and private benefactors and began cleaning up the quarter, restoring the finest old buildings, and attracting businesses and the public back to the heart of New Town. Their efforts have paid off. Former flophouses have become choice office buildings, and the area is filled with trendy shops, restaurants and nightclubs that draw crowds. ⊠ *Between 4th and 5th aves., from Broadway to Market St.*

William Heath Davis House (⊠ 410 Island Ave., at 4th Ave., Gaslamp Quarter ☎ 619/233–4692), one of the first residences in town, now serves as the information center for the historic district. Davis was a San Franciscan whose ill-fated attempt to develop the waterfront area preceded the more successful one of Alonzo Horton. In 1850 Davis had this prefab saltbox-style house shipped around Cape Horn and assembled in San Diego (it was originally located at State and Market streets). Docents give tours ($3) of the rest of the house during museum hours, which are Tuesday–Sunday 11–3. The place is staffed solely by volunteers, however, so be sure to phone ahead. Regularly scheduled two-hour walking tours of the historic district leave from the house on Saturday at 11; the cost for these is $8. The museum also sells detailed self-guided tour maps of the district for $2; guided tours can be arranged by calling ahead.

The Victorian **Horton Grand Hotel** (✉ 311 Island Ave., Gaslamp Quarter ☎ 619/544–1886) was created in the mid-1980s by joining together two historic hotels, the Kahle Saddlery and the Grand Hotel, built in the boom days of the 1880s; Wyatt Earp stayed at the Kahle Saddlery—then called the Brooklyn Hotel—while he was in town speculating on real estate ventures and opening gambling halls. The two hotels were dismantled and reconstructed about four blocks from their original locations. A small Chinese Museum serves as a tribute to the surrounding Chinatown district, a collection of modest structures that once housed Chinese laborers and their families.

The majority of the quarter's landmark buildings are on 4th and 5th avenues, between Island Avenue and Broadway. If you don't have much time, stroll down 5th Avenue, where highlights include the Backesto Building (No. 614), the Mercantile Building (No. 822), the Louis Bank of Commerce (No. 835), and the Watts-Robinson Building (No. 903). The Tudor-style **Keating Building** (✉ 432 F St., at 5th Ave., Gaslamp Quarter) was designed by the same firm that created the famous Hotel Del Coronado. Peer into the Hard Rock Cafe, at the corner of 4th Avenue and F Street, which occupies a restored turn-of-the-20th-century tavern with a 12-foot mahogany bar and a spectacular stained-glass domed ceiling.

The section of G Street between 6th and 9th avenues has become a haven for galleries; stop in one of them to pick up a map of the downtown arts district. Just to the north, on E and F streets from 6th to 12th avenues, the evolving Urban Art Trail has added pizzazz to drab city thoroughfares by transforming such things as trash cans and traffic controller boxes into canvases. For additional information about the historic area, call the **Gaslamp Quarter Association** (☎ 619/233–5227) or log on to their Web site www.gaslamp.org.

need a break? Fifth Avenue between F and G streets is lined with restaurants, many with outdoor patios. Hip coffeehouses have also sprung up in the Gaslamp Quarter. You can nurse a double espresso or imported beer at **Café LuLu** (✉ 419 F St., Gaslamp Quarter ☎ 619/238–0114).

★ ❾ **Horton Plaza.** Downtown's centerpiece is the shopping, dining, and entertainment mall that fronts Broadway and G Street from 1st to 4th avenues and covers more than six city blocks. Designed by Jon Jerde and completed in 1985, Horton Plaza is far from what one would imagine a shopping center—or city center—to be. A collage of pastels with elaborate, colorful tile work on benches and stairways, banners waving in the air, and modern sculptures marking the entrances, Horton Plaza rises in uneven, staggered levels to six floors; great views of downtown from the harbor to Balboa Park and beyond can be had here. The complex's architecture has strongly affected the rest of downtown's development—new apartment and condominium complexes along G and Market streets mimic its brightly colored towers and cupolas.

Horton Plaza has a multilevel parking garage, although lines to find a space can be long. The first three hours of parking are free with validation; after that it's $1 for every 20 minutes. If you use this notoriously confusing fruit-and-vegetable–theme garage, be sure to remember at which produce level you've left your car. If you're staying downtown, inquire at your hotel about the complimentary Horton Plaza shopping shuttle, which stops at the cruise ship terminal and the convention center in addition to several downtown lodgings.

Macy's, Nordstrom, and Mervyn's department stores anchor the plaza, with an eclectic assortment of more than 140 clothing, sporting-goods, jewelry, book, and gift shops flanking them. Other attractions include the country's largest Sam Goody music store and a Planet Hollywood. A movie complex, restaurants, and a long row of take-out ethnic food shops and dining patios line the uppermost tier. The respected San Diego Repertory Theatre has two stages below ground level. Most stores are open 10–9 weekdays, 10–6 Saturday, and 11–7 Sunday, but during the winter holidays and the summer many places stay open longer. ☎ 619/238–1596 ⊕ *www.hortonplaza.shoppingtown.com.*

The **International Visitors Information Center,** operated in the complex by the San Diego Convention and Visitors Bureau, is the best resource for information on the city. The staff members and volunteers who run the center speak many languages and are acquainted with myriad needs and requests of tourists. They dispense information (and discount coupons) on hotels, restaurants, and tourist attractions, including those in Tijuana. ✉ *Visitors center: 11 Horton Plaza, street level at corner of 1st Ave. and F St., Gaslamp Quarter* ☎ *619/236–1212* ⊕ *www.sandiego. org* 🕙 *Mon.–Sat. 8:30–5; June–Aug., also Sun. 11–5.*

need a break?

Hungry shoppers sit at the counters and tables outside the informal eateries on Horton Plaza's top level, where you can get everything from fresh hot cinnamon rolls to pizza and sushi. Just want a caffeine recharge? Coffee carts include the **Expresso Bar,** outside Nordstrom on level 1. **Starbucks** fans can get their fix inside stores on level 1 and on the street level, off Broadway Circle.

🐚 ❷ **Maritime Museum.** A must for anyone with an interest in nautical history—or who has ever read a Patrick O'Brian novel—this collection of five restored ships affords a fascinating glimpse of San Diego during its heyday as a commercial seaport. The museum's headquarters are the *Berkeley,* an 1898 ferryboat moored at the foot of Ash Street. The steam-driven ship, which served the Southern Pacific Railroad at San Francisco Bay until 1958, played its most important role during the great earthquake of 1906, when it carried thousands of passengers across San

Fodor'sChoice
★

Francisco Bay to Oakland in order to escape the fires that had engulfed San Francisco. Its ornate carved-wood paneling, stained-glass windows, and plate-glass mirrors have been restored, and its main deck serves as a floating museum, with permanent exhibits on West Coast maritime history and complementary rotating exhibits. Anchored next to the *Berkeley,* on the north side is the small Scottish steam yacht *Medea.* Launched in 1904, it may be boarded but has no interpretive displays. Another addition to the museum is the *Pilot,* which guided ships into and out of San Diego Bay for 82 years. Removed from service in 1996, it was refurbished and retrofitted for use as a floating classroom.

A large number of visitors are drawn to the museum's two sailing ships. The best known and most popular, often considered a symbol of the city, is the *Star of India,* an iron windjammer built in 1863, when iron ships were still a novelty. The ship's high wooden masts and white sails flapping in the wind have been a harbor landmark since 1927. The *Star of India* made 21 trips around the world in the late 1800s, when it traveled the East Indian trade route, shuttled immigrants from England to New Zealand, and served the Alaskan salmon trade. The ship languished after being retired to San Diego Harbor, virtually ignored until 1959, when volunteers organized by the Maritime Museum began the laborious task of stripping the wooden decks, polishing the figurehead, and mending the sails. The oldest active iron sailing ship in the world, it makes rare short excursions but for the most part stays moored at the pier and open to visitors. If you crave more than a dockside visit, take to the water in the *Californian,* a replica of a 19th-century Revenue Cutter that patrolled the shores of California. Designated the official tall ship of the State of California, the museum offers a variety of full and half-day sails (weather permitting). Typically, weekday cruises are reserved for schoolchildren, while weekend cruises are open to the general public. Tickets may only be purchased at the museum on day of sail. Full day sails leave at 10 AM and half-day sails leave at 1 PM. The sails are most popular on sunny days when it's recommended to show up at least one hour ahead of desired departure. ⊠ *1492 N. Harbor Dr., Embarcadero* ☎ *619/234–9153* ⊕ *www.sdmaritime.org* ⊠ *$8 includes entry to all 5 ships* ⊙ *Daily 9–8, until 9 PM in summer.*

❻ Museum of Contemporary Art, San Diego. The downtown branch of the city's modern art museum has taken on its own personality. Its post-modern, cutting-edge exhibitions are perfectly complemented by the steel-and-glass transportation complex of which it's a part. Four small galleries in the two-story building host rotating shows, some from the permanent collection in the older La Jolla branch, others loaned from far-flung international museums. If you get the chance, stop by TNT (Thursday Night Thing), an eclectic series of free events held at 7 PM the first Thursday of each month. Happenings include live bands, DJ lessons, films, or interpretive artists. ⊠ *1001 Kettner Blvd., Downtown* ☎ *619/234–1001* ⊠ *Free* ⊙ *Daily 11–5* ⊙ *Closed Wed.*

❸ San Diego Aircraft Carrier Museum. After 47 years of worldwide service, the retired USS *Midway* started its new tour of duty on the south side of the Navy pier in summer 2004. Launched just after the end of World

War II, the 1,001-foot-long ship was the largest in the world for the first 10 years of its existence. Now it serves as the most visible landmark on the north Embarcadero and as a floating interactive museum—an appropriate addition to the town that is home to one-third of the Pacific fleet and the birthplace of naval aviation. Start on the hangar deck, where an F-14 Tomcat jet fighter is just one of several aircraft displayed onboard. Through passageways and up and down ladderwells, you'll get to see how the *Midway's* 4,500 crew members lived and worked on this "city at sea." While the entire tour is impressive, you'll find yourself saying "wow" when you step out onto the four-acre flight deck for one of the most interesting vantage points of the bay and the city skyline. It's also the best place to get an idea of the ship's scale. The museum also includes changing displays of aircraft, a flight simulator, and interactive exhibits focusing on naval aviation. A restaurant, gift shop, and several areas for special events is planned. ⊠ *Navy Pier, 11A, Downtown* ☎ *619/702–7700* ⊕ *www.midway.org* ⊠ *$13* ☉ *Daily 10–5.*

★ ☺ ➐ **Seaport Village.** On a prime stretch of waterfront that spreads out across 14 acres connecting the harbor with hotel towers and the convention center, the village's three bustling shopping plazas are designed to reflect the architectural styles of early California, especially New England clapboard and Spanish mission. A ¼-mi wooden boardwalk that runs along the bay and 4 mi of paths lead to specialty shops—everything from a kite store and rubber-stamp emporium to a shop devoted to left-handed people—as well as snack bars and restaurants, many with harbor views; there are about 75 in all. Seaport Village's shops are open daily 10 to 9 (10 to 10 in summer); a few eateries open early for breakfast, and many have extended nighttime hours, especially in summer.

I. D. Looff crafted the hand-carved, hand-painted steeds on the **Broadway Flying Horses Carousel** for the Coney Island amusement park in 1890. The ride was moved from its next home, Salisbury Beach in Massachusetts, and faithfully restored for Seaport Village's West Plaza; tickets are $1. Strolling clowns, balloon sculptors, mimes, musicians, and magicians are also on hand throughout the village to entertain kids; those not impressed by such pretechnological displays can duck into the Time Out entertainment center near the carousel and play video games. ⊠ *Downtown* ☎ *619/235–4014, 619/234–6133 for carousel information, 619/235–4013 for events hotline* ⊕ *www.seaportvillage.com.*

need a break?

The food court near the carousel serves up fast Greek, Mexican, Italian, deli, and all-American fare—pretty much anything you can think of. You can sit at a table in a shaded courtyard, on a harborside patio, or perch on the nearby seawall. **Upstart Crow & Co.** (⊠ Seaport Village, Central Plaza, Embarcadero ☎ 619/232–4855), a combination bookstore and coffeehouse, serves good cappuccino and espresso with pastries and cakes.

➎ **Transit Center.** The Mission revival–style **Santa Fe Depot,** which replaced the original 1887 station on this site, serves Amtrak and Coaster passengers. A booth at the graceful, tile-domed depot has bus schedules, maps, and tourist brochures. Formerly an easily spotted area landmark, it's now overshadowed by **1 America Plaza** across the street. At the base of this 34-story office tower, designed by architect Helmut Jahn, is a center that links the train, trolley, and city bus systems. The building's signature crescent-shape, glass-and-steel canopy arches out over the trolley tracks. The Greyhound bus station (120 West Broadway) is a few blocks away. ✉ *Broadway and Kettner Blvd., Downtown.*

❽ U. S. Grant Hotel. Far more formal than most other hotels in San Diego, the doyenne of downtown lodgings has a marble lobby, gleaming chandeliers, attentive doormen, and other touches that hark back to the more gracious era when it was built (1910). Funded in part by the son of the president for whom it was named, the hotel was extremely opulent; 350 rooms of 437 had private baths, highly unusual for that time. Through the years it became noted for its famous guests—U.S. presidents from Woodrow Wilson to George Bush (the elder) have stayed here. Taking up a city block—it's bounded by 3rd and 4th avenues, C Street, and Broadway—the hotel occupies the site of San Diego's first hotel, constructed by Alonzo Horton in 1870. ✉ *326 Broadway, Gaslamp Quarter* ☎ *619/232–3121.*

off the
beaten
path

VILLA MONTEZUMA – The former residence of Jesse Shepard, a pianist, spiritualist, and novelist, adapts the elements of high Queen Anne style to Shepard's unique aesthetic interests. The 1887 house is filled with fascinating period and personal details: stained-glass windows depicting Shakespeare, Beethoven, Mozart, Sappho, and Goethe; redwood panels; tiled fireplaces; family portraits; and tributes from Shepard's famous admirers. Villa Montezuma was restored by the San Diego Historical Society, whose docents give continuous tours. Architecture buffs will enjoy combining a visit to this "Painted Lady," which is in a not-yet-gentrified area east of I–5, with one to the Marston House in Balboa Park, 10 minutes to the north and also operated by the Historical Society. ✉ *1925 K St., Downtown* ☎ *619/239–2211* 🎫 *$5* ⊙ *Fri.–Sun. 10–4:30, Dec. also open Thurs. 10–4:30; last tour at 3:45.*

CORONADO

Although it's actually an isthmus, easily reached from the mainland if you head north from Imperial Beach, Coronado has always seemed like an island—and is often referred to as such. The Spaniards called it Los Coronados, or "the Crowned Ones," in the late 1500s and the name stuck. Today's residents, many of whom live in grand Victorian homes handed down for generations, tend to consider their community to be a sort of royal encampment, safe from the hassles and hustle of San Diego proper.

North Island Naval Air Station was established in 1911 on Coronado's north end, across from Point Loma, and was the site of Charles Lindbergh's departure on the transcontinental flight that preceded his famous transatlantic voyage (a San Diego–area company manufactured the *Spirit of St. Louis*). Today high-tech aircraft and seacraft arrive and depart from North Island, providing a real-life education in military armament. Coronado's long relationship with the U.S. Navy and its desirable real estate have made it an enclave for wealthy military personnel; it's said to have the most retired admirals per capita in the United States.

The streets of Coronado are wide, quiet, and friendly, with lots of neighborhood parks where young families mingle with the area's many senior citizens. Grand old homes face the waterfront and the Coronado Municipal Golf Course, under the bridge at the north end of Glorietta Bay; it's the site of the annual Fourth of July fireworks display. Community celebrations and concerts take place in Spreckels Park on Orange Avenue.

Coronado is visible from downtown and Point Loma and accessible via the arching blue 2²/₁₀-mi-long Coronado–San Diego Bay Bridge, a landmark just beyond downtown's skyline. The bridge handles more than 67,000 cars each day, and rush hour tends to be slow, which is fine, because the view of the harbor, downtown, and the island is breathtaking, day and night.

Until the bridge was completed in 1969, visitors and residents relied on the Coronado Ferry, which ran across the harbor from downtown. When the bridge was opened, the ferry closed down, much to the dismay of those who were fond of traveling at a leisurely pace. In 1987 the ferry returned. Residents and commuting workers have quickly adapted to this traditional mode of transportation, and the ferry has become quite popular with bicyclists, who shuttle their bikes across the harbor and ride the wide, flat boulevards for hours.

San Diego's Metropolitan Transit System runs a shuttle bus, No. 904, around the island; you can pick it up where you disembark the ferry and ride it out as far as the Silver Strand State Beach. Buses start leaving from the ferry landing at 10:30 AM and run once an hour on the half hour until 6:30 PM.

You can board the ferry, operated by **San Diego Harbor Excursion** (☎ 619/234–4111, 800/442–7847 in CA), at downtown San Diego's Embarcadero from the excursion dock at Harbor Drive and Broadway; you'll arrive at the Ferry Landing Marketplace. Boats depart every hour on the hour from the Embarcadero and every hour on the half hour from Coronado, Sunday–Thursday 9–9, Friday and Saturday until 10; the fare is $2 each way, 50¢ extra for bicycles. San Diego Harbor Excursion also offers water taxi service Sunday–Thursday 2–10, and Friday and Saturday 11–11. The taxi can run between any two points in San Diego Bay and later hours can be arranged upon request. The fare is $5 per person. Call ☎ 619/235–8294 to book.

Numbers in the text correspond to numbers in the margin and on the Central San Diego map.

a good
tour

Coronado is easy to navigate without a car. When you depart the ferry, you can explore the shops at the **Ferry Landing Marketplace** ⑪ ▶ and from there rent a bicycle or catch the shuttle bus that runs down **Orange Avenue** ⑫, Coronado's main tourist drag. You might disembark the bus near the tourist information office, just off Orange, and pick up a map, return to Orange to visit the nearby **Coronado Museum of History and Art ⑬**, and then keep strolling along the boutiques-filled promenade until you reach the **Hotel Del Coronado ⑭** at the end of Orange Avenue. Right across the street from the Del is the **Glorietta Bay Inn ⑮**, another of the island's outstanding early structures. If you've brought your swimsuit, you might continue on to **Silver Strand State Beach ⑯**—just past the Hotel Del, Orange Avenue turns into Silver Strand Boulevard, which soon resumes its original across-the-bridge role as Route 75.

TIMING   A leisurely stroll through Coronado takes an hour or so, more if you shop or walk along the beach. If you're a history buff, you might want to visit on Tuesday, Thursday, or Saturday, when you can combine the tour of Coronado's historic homes that departs from the Glorietta Bay Inn at 11 AM with a visit to the Coronado Museum of History and Art, open Tuesday through Saturday. Whenever you come, if you're not staying overnight, remember to get back to the dock in time to catch the final ferry out. The last shuttle to the Ferry Landing Marketplace leaves from the Loews Coronado Bay Resort at 6:57.

Sights to See

⑬ **Coronado Museum of History and Art.** The neoclassical Historic First Bank building, constructed in 1910, holds the headquarters and archives of the Coronado Historical Society and a museum. The collection celebrates Coronado's history with photographs and displays of its formative events and major sights. Three galleries have permanent displays while a fourth hosts traveling exhibits; all offer interactive activities for children and adults. To check out the town's historic houses, pick up a copy of the inexpensive *Coronado California Centennial History & Tour Guide* at the gift shop. There's also a café and lecture hall. The museum also sponsors a 60-minute walking tour of the architecturally and historically significant buildings that surround the Museum. The tour departs from the museum lobby Wednesday at 2 PM and Friday at 10:30 AM and costs $8. ⊠ *1100 Orange Ave., Coronado* ☎ *619/435–7242* 🖅 *Donations accepted* ⊗ *Weekdays 9–5, Sat. 10–5, Sun. 11–4.*

★ ☾ ► ⑪ **Ferry Landing Marketplace.** This collection of shops at the point of disembarkation for the ferry is on a smaller—and generally less interesting—scale than Seaport Village, but you do get a great view of downtown's skyline from here. The little shops and restaurants resemble the gingerbread domes of the Hotel Del Coronado. If you want to rent a bike or in-line skates, stop in at **Bikes and Beyond** (⊠ *No. 122* ☎ *619/435–7180*). ⊠ *1201 1st St., at B Ave., Coronado* ☎ *619/435–8895.*

⑮ **Glorietta Bay Inn.** The former residence of John Spreckels, the original owner of North Island and the property on which the Hotel Del Coronado stands, is now a popular hotel. On Tuesday, Thursday, and Saturday mornings at 11 it's the departure point for a fun and informative 1½-hour walking tour of a few of the area's 86 officially designated historical homes. Sponsored by the Coronado Historical Association, the tour focuses on the Glorietta Bay Inn and the Hotel Del Coronado across the street. In addition, it includes—from the outside only—some spectacular mansions and the Meade House, where L. Frank Baum, author of *The Wizard of Oz,* wrote additional Oz stories. ✉ *1630 Glorietta Blvd., Coronado* ☎ *619/435–3101, 619/435–5892 for tour information* ✉ *$8 for historical tour.*

⑭ **Hotel Del Coronado.** One of San Diego's best known sites, the hotel has
Fodor's Choice been a national historic landmark in 1977. The hotel has a colorful his-
★ tory, integrally connected with that of Coronado itself. The Del, as natives call it, was the brainchild of financiers Elisha Spurr Babcock Jr.
and H. L. Story, who saw the potential of Coronado's virgin beaches
and its view of San Diego's emerging harbor. They purchased a 4,100-
acre parcel of land in 1885 for $110,000 and threw a lavish Fourth of
July bash for prospective investors in their hunting and fishing resort.
By the end of the year they had roused public interest—and had an ample
return on their investment. The hotel was opened in 1888, although it
wasn't actually completed for another six years.

The Del's distinctive red-tile peaks and Victorian gingerbread architecture has served as a set for many movies, political meetings, and extravagant social happenings. It's said that the Duke of Windsor first met
Wallis Simpson here. Fourteen presidents have been guests of the Del,
and the film *Some Like It Hot*—starring Marilyn Monroe, Jack Lemmon, and Tony Curtis—was filmed here.

Broad steps lead up to the main, balconied lobby, with grand oak pil-
lars and ceiling, which in turn opens out onto a central courtyard and
gazebo. To the right is the cavernous **Crown Room,** whose arched ceiling of notched sugar pine was constructed without nails. You can tell
by looking at this space that the hotel's architect, James Reed, had pre-
viously designed railroad stations. A lavish Sunday brunch is served here
9–2. To the left past the reception desk is the hotel's Signature Shop,
as well as a stairwell descending to the 22-shop Galleria level. Also on
this level is the History Gallery, which displays photos from the Del's
early days.

The patio surrounding the swimming pool is a great place for sitting
back and imagining what the bathers looked like during the 1920s,
when the hotel rocked with the good times. To its right, the new
Windsor Lawn provides a green oasis between the hotel and the beach.
To the pool's left are the two seven-story Ocean Tower accommodations. The gift shop sells books that elaborate on the hotel's history
and Kate Morgan, the Del's resident ghost. Guided tours are available for registered hotel guests. ✉ *1500 Orange Ave., Coronado*
☎ *619/435–6611* ⊕ *www.hoteldel.com.*

⑫ **Orange Avenue.** It's easy to imagine you're on a street in Cape Cod when
you stroll along this thoroughfare, Coronado's version of a downtown:
the clapboard houses, small restaurants, and boutiques—selling everything from upscale clothing to surfboards—are in some ways more
characteristic of New England than they are of California. But the East
Coast illusion tends to dissipate as quickly as a winter fog when you
catch sight of one of the avenue's many citrus trees—or realize it's
February and the sun is warming your face. Just off Orange Avenue,
the **Coronado Visitors Bureau** (✉ 1047 B Ave., Coronado ☎ 619/437–

8788 ⊕ www.coronadovisitors.com) is open weekdays 8–5, Saturday 10–5, and Sunday 11–4 year-round.

need a break?

There's an abundance of places to find a caffeine fix on Orange Avenue between 8th Street and the Hotel Del. At the hip **Cafe 1134** (⊠ 1134 Orange Ave., Coronado ☎ 619/437–1134) you can get a good curried tuna sandwich on French bread to accompany your espresso. Peruse the latest art magazine while sipping a latte at the sidewalk café of **Bay Books** (⊠ 1029 Orange Ave., Coronado ☎ 619/435–0070), San Diego's largest independent bookstore. For a deliciously sweet pick-me-up, check out the rich ice cream, frozen yogurt, and sorbet made fresh daily on the premises of **Mootime Creamery** (⊠ 1025 Orange Ave., Coronado ☎ 619/435–2422).

🅲 ⓰   **Silver Strand State Beach.** The stretch of sand that runs along Silver
Fodor'sChoice   Strand Boulevard from the Hotel Del Coronado to Imperial Beach dis-
★   pels the illusion that Coronado is an island. The beach is a perfect family gathering spot, with restrooms and lifeguards. Don't be surprised if you see groups exercising in military style along the beach; this is a training area for the U.S. Navy's SEAL teams. Across from the beach is the Coronado Cays, an exclusive community popular with yacht owners and celebrities, and the Loews Coronado Bay Resort.

en route

San Diego's Mexican-American community is centered in Barrio Logan, under the Coronado–San Diego Bay Bridge on the downtown side. **Chicano Park,** spread along National Avenue from Dewey to Crosby streets, is the barrio's recreational hub. It's worth taking a short detour to see the huge murals of Mexican history painted on the bridge supports at National Avenue and Dewey Street; they're among the best examples of folk art in the city.

HARBOR ISLAND, POINT LOMA & SHELTER ISLAND

The populated outcroppings that jut into the bay just west of downtown and the airport demonstrate the potential of human collaboration with nature. Point Loma, Mother Nature's contribution to San Diego's attractions, has always afforded protection to the center city from the Pacific's tides and waves. It's shared by military installations, funky motels and fast-food shacks, stately family homes, huge estates, and private marinas packed with sailboats and yachts. Newer to the scene, Harbor and Shelter islands are poster children for landfill. Created out of sand dredged from the San Diego Bay in the second half of the past century, they've become tourist hubs, their high-rise hotels, seafood restaurants, and boat-rental centers looking as solid as those anywhere else in the city.

Numbers in the text correspond to numbers in the margin and on the Central San Diego map.

a good tour

Take Catalina Boulevard all the way south to the tip of Point Loma to reach **Cabrillo National Monument** ⑰ ⌐; you'll be retracing the steps of the earliest European explorers if you use this as a jumping-off point for a tour. North of the monument, as you head back into the neighborhoods of Point Loma, you'll see the white headstones of **Fort Rosecrans National Cemetery** ⑱. Continue north on Catalina Boulevard to Hill Street and turn left to reach the dramatic **Sunset Cliffs** ⑲, at the western side of Point Loma near Ocean Beach. Return to Catalina Boulevard and backtrack south for a few blocks to find Canon Street, which leads toward the peninsula's eastern (bay) side. Almost at the shore you'll see **Scott Street** ⑳, Point Loma's main commercial drag. Scott Street is bisected by Shelter Island Drive, which leads to **Shelter Island** ㉑. For another example of what can be done with tons of material dredged from a bay, go back up Shelter Island Drive, turn right on Rosecrans Street, and make another right on North Harbor Drive to reach **Harbor Island** ㉒.

TIMING

If you're interested in seeing the tide pools at Cabrillo National Monument, call ahead or check the weather page of the *Union-Tribune* to find out when low tide will occur. Scott Street, with its Point Loma Seafoods, is a good place to find yourself at lunchtime, and Sunset Cliffs Park is where you might want to be when the daylight starts to wane. This drive takes about an hour if you stop briefly at each sight, but you'll want to devote at least an hour to Cabrillo National Monument.

Sights to See

★ ♻ ⌐ ⑰ **Cabrillo National Monument.** This 144-acre preserve marks the site of the first European visit to San Diego, made by 16th-century explorer Juan Rodríguez Cabrillo (circa 1498–1543)—historians have never conclusively determined whether he was Spanish or Portuguese. Cabrillo, who had earlier gone on voyages with Hernán Cortés, came to this spot, which he called San Miguel, in 1542. Government grounds were set aside to commemorate his discovery in 1913, and today the site, with its rugged cliffs and shores and outstanding overlooks, is one of the most frequently visited of all the national monuments.

The **visitor center** presents films and lectures about Cabrillo's voyage, the sea-level tide pools, and migrating gray whales. The center has an excellent shop with books about nature, San Diego, and the sea. Maps of the region, whale posters, flowers, shells, and the requisite postcards, slides, and film are also on sale. Restrooms and water fountains are plentiful along the paths that climb to the monument's various viewing points, but, except for a few vending machines at the visitor center, there's no food. Exploring the grounds consumes time and calories; bring a picnic and rest on a bench overlooking the sailboats.

Interpretive stations with recorded information in six languages—including, appropriately enough, Portuguese—have been installed along the walkways that edge the cliffs. Signs explain the views and wayside exhibits depict the various naval, fishing, and pleasure craft that sail into and fly over the bay. Directly south across the bay from the visitor center is the North Island Naval Air Station at the west end of Coronado. To the left on the shores of Point Loma is the Space and Naval Warfare

Systems Center; nuclear-powered submarines are now docked where Cabrillo's small ships anchored in 1542.

A **statue of Cabrillo** overlooks downtown from the next windy promontory, where people gather to admire the stunning panorama over the bay, from the snowcapped San Bernardino Mountains, 130 mi north, to the hills surrounding Tijuana to the south. The stone figure standing on the bluff looks rugged and dashing, but he is a creation of an artist's imagination—no portraits of Cabrillo are known to exist. The statue was donated by the Portuguese navy in 1957.

The moderately steep 2-mi **Bayside Trail** (☉ daily 9–4) winds through coastal sage scrub, curving under the cliff-top lookouts and bringing you ever closer to the bay-front scenery. You cannot reach the beach from this trail and must stick to the path to protect the cliffs from erosion and yourself from thorny plants and snakes—including rattlers. You'll see prickly pear cactus and yucca, black-eyed Susans, fragrant sage, and maybe a lizard or a hummingbird. The climb back is long but gradual, leading up to the old lighthouse.

The oil lamp of the **Old Point Loma Lighthouse** (☉ daily 9–5) was first lit in 1855. The light, sitting in a brass-and-iron housing above a white wooden house, shone through a state-of-the-art lens from France and was visible from the sea for 25 mi. Unfortunately, it was too high above the cliffs to guide navigators trapped in southern California's thick offshore fog and low clouds. In 1891 a new lighthouse was built 400 feet below. The old lighthouse, refitted with furnishings more accurate to the era when it was erected, is open to visitors. The U.S. Coast Guard still uses the newer lighthouse and a mighty foghorn to guide boaters through the narrow channel leading into the bay. On the edge of the hill near the lighthouse sits a refurbished radio room from World War I. It hosts displays of U.S. harbor defenses at Point Loma used during World War II.

The western and southern cliffs of Cabrillo National Monument are prime whale-watching territory. A sheltered **viewing station** has a tape-recorded lecture describing the great gray whales' migration from the Bering and Chukchi seas near Alaska to Baja California, and high-powered telescopes help you focus on the whales' water spouts. Whales are visible on clear days in January and February. Park rangers can help you spot whales during the annual Whale Watch Weekend, held the third weekend in January, which includes other interpretive programs and entertainment.

More accessible sea creatures can be seen in the **tide pools** (☉ daily 9–4:30) at the foot of the monument's western cliffs. Drive north from the visitor center to the first road on the left, which winds down to the coast guard station and the shore. When the tide is low you can walk on the rocks around saltwater pools filled with starfish, crabs, anemones, octopuses, and hundreds of other sea creatures and plants. ⊠ *1800 Cabrillo Memorial Dr., Point Loma* ☎ *619/222–8211 for visitor information line, 619/557–5450 for park headquarters* ⊕ *www.nps.gov/ cabr* ⊠ *$5 per car, $3 per person entering on foot or by bicycle, entrance pass allows unlimited admissions for 1 wk from date of purchase;*

free for Golden Age, Golden Access, and Golden Eagle passport holders ⊙ *Park daily 9–5:15 call for summer hrs.*

⑱ Fort Rosecrans National Cemetery. In 1934, 8 acres of the 1,000 set aside for a military reserve in 1852 were designated as a burial site. About 79,000 people are now interred here; it's impressive to see the rows upon rows of white headstones that overlook both sides of Point Loma just north of the Cabrillo National Monument. Some of those laid to rest at this place were killed in battles that predate California's statehood; the graves of the 17 soldiers and one civilian who died in the 1874 Battle of San Pasqual between troops from Mexico and the United States are marked by a large bronze plaque. Perhaps the most impressive structure in the cemetery is the 75-foot granite obelisk called the Bennington Monument, which commemorates the 66 crew members who died in a boiler explosion and fire on board the USS *Bennington* in 1905. The cemetery, visited by many veterans, is still used for burials. ⊠ *Rte. 209, Point Loma* ☎ *619/553–2084* ⊙ *Daily 9–5:30.*

㉒ Harbor Island. Following the success of nearby Shelter Island, the U.S. Navy decided to use the residue that resulted from digging berths deep enough to accommodate aircraft carriers to build another recreational island. In 1961 a 1½-mi-long peninsula was created adjacent to San Diego International Airport out of 12 million cubic yards of sand and mud dredged from San Diego Bay. Restaurants and high-rise hotels now line the inner shores of Harbor Island. The bay shore has pathways, gardens, and picnic spots for sightseeing or working off the calories from the various indoor or outdoor food fests. On the west point, Tom Ham's Lighthouse restaurant has a U.S. Coast Guard–approved beacon shining from its tower.

Across from the western end of Harbor Island, at the mainland's **Spanish Landing Park,** a bronze plaque marks the arrival in 1769 of a party from Spain that headed north from San Diego to conquer California. The group was a merger of the crew of two ships, the *San Carlos* and the *San Antonio,* and of a contingent that came overland from Baja California. No one knows exactly where the men landed and camped; we can only be certain it wasn't Harbor Island.

⑳ Scott Street. Running along Point Loma's waterfront from Shelter Island to the old Naval Training Center on Harbor Drive, this thoroughfare is lined with deep-sea fishing charters and whale-watching boats. It's a good spot from which to watch fishermen (and women) haul marlin, tuna, and puny mackerel off their boats.

need a break?

The freshest and tastiest fish to be found along Point Loma's shores—some would say anywhere in San Diego—comes from **Point Loma Seafoods** (⊠ 2805 Emerson St., Point Loma ☎ 619/223–1109), off Scott Street behind the Vagabond Inn. A fish market sells the catch of the day, and patrons crowd the adjacent take-out counter for seafood cocktails and salads, ceviche, and crab and shrimp sandwiches made with sourdough bread baked on the premises. There's outdoor and indoor seating, and you can expect crowds throughout the year. Park a few blocks away if you're coming on the weekend; the adjoining lot suffers from extreme gridlock.

㉑ Shelter Island. In 1950 San Diego's port director thought there should be some use for the sand and mud dredged by the Works Project Administration to deepen the ship channel in the 1930s and '40s. He decided it might be a good idea to raise the shoal that lay off the eastern shore of Point Loma above sea level, landscape it, and add a 2,000-foot causeway to make it accessible.

His hunch paid off. Shelter Island—actually a peninsula—now supports towering mature palms, a cluster of resorts, restaurants, and side-by-side marinas. It's the center of San Diego's yacht-building industry, and boats in every stage of construction are visible in the yacht yards. A long sidewalk runs from the landscaped lawns of the **San Diego Yacht Club** (tucked down Anchorage Street off Shelter Island Drive), past boat brokerages to the hotels and marinas, which line the inner shore, facing Point Loma. On the bay side, fishermen launch their boats or simply stand on shore and cast. Families relax at picnic tables along the grass, where there are fire rings and permanent barbecue grills. Within walking distance is the huge Friendship Bell, given to San Diegans by the people of Yokohama, Japan, in 1960.

⑲ Sunset Cliffs. As the name suggests, the 60-foot-high bluffs on the western side of Point Loma south of Ocean Beach are a perfect place to watch the sun descend over the sea. To view the tide pools along the shore, use the staircase off Sunset Cliffs Boulevard at the foot of Ladera Street.

The dramatic coastline here seems to have been carved out of ancient rock. The impact of the waves is very clear: each year more sections of the cliffs sport caution signs. Don't ignore these warnings—it's easy to lose your footing and slip in the crumbling sandstone, and the surf can be extremely rough. Small coves and beaches dot the coastline and are popular with surfers drawn to the pounding waves and locals from the neighborhood who name and claim their special spots. Needle's Eye is considered especially challenging. The homes along the boulevard are fine examples of southern California luxury, with pink stucco mansions beside shingled Cape Cod–style cottages. ⊠ *Sunset Cliffs Blvd., Point Loma.*

LA JOLLA

La Jollans have long considered their village to be the Monte Carlo of California, and with good cause. Its coastline curves into natural coves backed by verdant hillsides covered with homes worth millions. Although La Jolla is considered part of San Diego, it has its own postal zone and a coveted sense of class; it's gotten far more plebeian these days, but old-monied residents still mingle here with visiting film stars and royalty who frequent established hotels and private clubs. Development and construction have radically altered the once serene and private character of the village, but it has gained a cosmopolitan air that makes it a popular vacation resort.

The Native Americans called the site La Hoya, meaning "the cave," referring to the grottoes that dot the shoreline. The Spaniards changed the name to La Jolla (same pronunciation as La Hoya), "the jewel," and its residents have cherished the name and its allusions ever since.

To reach La Jolla from I–5, if you're traveling north, take the Ardath Road exit, which veers into Torrey Pines Road, and turn right onto Prospect Street. If you're heading south, get off at the La Jolla Village Drive exit, which will also lead into Torrey Pines Road. Traffic is virtually always congested in this popular area, which is dotted with four-way stop signs and clogged with drivers dropping off passengers and/or trolling for a parking spot. Drive carefully and be prepared to stop frequently when you get into the village.

For those who enjoy meandering, the best way to approach La Jolla from the south is to drive through Mission and Pacific beaches on Mission Boulevard, past the crowds of rollerbladers, bicyclists, and sunbathers. The clutter and congestion ease up as the street becomes La Jolla Boulevard. Road signs along La Jolla Boulevard and Camino de la Costa direct drivers and bicyclists past homes designed by such respected architects as Frank Lloyd Wright and Irving Gill. As you approach the village, La Jolla Boulevard turns into Prospect Street.

Prospect Street and Girard Avenue, the village's main drags, are lined with expensive shops and office buildings. Girard holds the village's only movie house, which tends to show indie films. Through the years the shopping and dining district has spread to Pearl and other side streets. Wall Street, a quiet tree-lined boulevard off Girard Avenue, was once the financial heart of La Jolla, but banks and investment houses can now be found throughout the village. La Jolla's nightlife scene is an active one, with jazz clubs, piano bars, and watering holes for the well-heeled younger set.

Numbers in the text correspond to numbers in the margin and on the La Jolla map.

a good tour

At the intersection of La Jolla Boulevard and Nautilus Street, turn toward the sea to reach **Windansea Beach** ❶ ▶, one of the best surfing spots in town. **Mount Soledad** ❷, about 1½-mi east on Nautilus Street, is La Jolla's highest spot. In the village itself you'll find the town's cultural center, the **Museum of Contemporary Art, San Diego** ❸, on the less trafficked southern end of Prospect. A bit farther north, at the intersection of Prospect Street and Girard Avenue, sits the pretty-in-pink **La Valencia** ❹; the hotel looks out onto the village's great natural attraction, **La Jolla Cove** ❺, which can be accessed from Coast Boulevard, one block to the west. Past the far northern point of the cove, a trail leads down to **La Jolla Caves** ❻.

The beaches along La Jolla Shores Drive north of the caves are some of the finest in the San Diego area, with long stretches allotted to surfers or swimmers. Nearby is the campus of the Scripps Institution of Oceanography. The institution's **Birch Aquarium at Scripps** ❼ is inland a bit, off Torrey Pines Road, across from the campus of University of California at San Diego.

La Jolla Shores Drive eventually curves onto Torrey Pines Road, off which you'll soon glimpse the world-famous **Salk Institute** ⑧, designed by Louis I. Kahn. The same road that leads to the institute ends at the cliffs used as the **Torrey Pines Glider Port** ⑨. The hard-to-reach stretch of sand at the foot of the cliffs is officially named **Torrey Pines City Park Beach** ⑩, but locals call it Black's Beach. At the intersection of Torrey Pines Road and Genesee Avenue you'll come to the northern entrance of the huge campus of the **University of California at San Diego** ⑪ and, a bit farther north, to the stretch of wilderness that marks the end of what most locals consider San Diego proper, **Torrey Pines State Beach and Reserve** ⑫.

TIMING   This tour makes for a leisurely day, although it can be driven in a couple of hours, including stops to take in the views and explore the village of La Jolla (though not to hit any of the beaches—or even a fraction of all the pricey boutiques). The Museum of Contemporary Art is closed Monday, and guided tours of the Salk Institute are given on weekdays only.

Sights to See

☺ ❼ **Birch Aquarium at Scripps.** The largest oceanographic exhibit in the United States, a program of the Scripps Institution of Oceanography, sits at the end of a signed drive leading off North Torrey Pines Road just north of La Jolla Village Drive. More than 30 tanks are filled with colorful saltwater fish, and a 70,000-gallon tank simulates a La Jolla kelp forest. Besides the fish themselves, attractions include a gallery with sea-theme exhibits, a simulated submarine ride, supermarket shelves stocked with products derived from the sea (including some surprisingly common ones), and other interactive educational exhibits. A concession sells food, and there are outdoor picnic tables. ⊠ *2300 Expedition Way, La Jolla* ☎ *858/534–3474* ⊕ *www.aquarium.ucsd.edu* ⊠ *$10, parking free for 3 hrs* ⊙ *Daily 9–5 last ticket sold at 4:30.*

Golden Triangle. La Jolla's newest enclave, spreading through the Sorrento Valley east of I–5, is a far cry from the beach communities with which the name La Jolla has long been associated. High-tech research-and-development companies, attracted to the Golden Triangle area in part by the facilities of the University of California at San Diego, the Scripps Institution of Oceanography, and the Salk Institute, have developed huge state-of-the-art compounds in areas that were populated solely by coyotes and jays not so long ago. The area along La Jolla Village Drive and Genesee Avenue has become an architectural proving ground for futuristic buildings. The most striking are those in the Michael Graves–designed Aventine complex, visible from I–5 at the La Jolla Village Drive exit. A bit south, near the Nobel exit, and eye-catching in another way, the huge, white Mormon Temple looks like a psychedelic medieval castle; completed in 1993, it still startles drivers heading up the freeway. ⊠ *La Jolla.*

☺ ❻ **La Jolla Caves.** It's a walk down 145 sometimes slippery steps to Sunny Jim Cave, the largest of the grottoes in La Jolla Cove. For many years the caves were entered via La Jolla Cave and Shell Shop, but in 1998 the shop moved to Seaport Village and the cave entrance came under the aegis of the Cave Store, a throwback to the 1902 shop that served as the underground portal. The Cave Store sells postcards, T-shirts, local

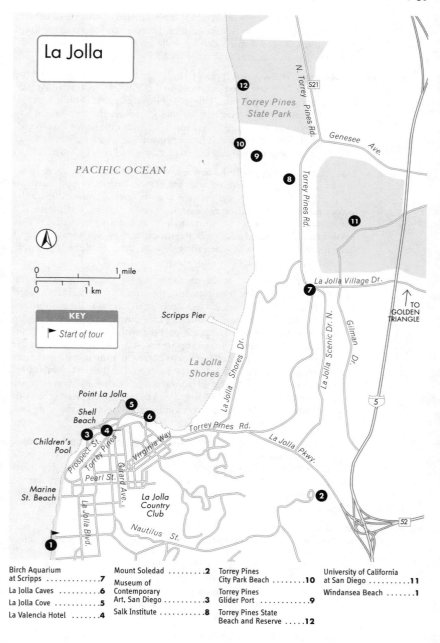

La Jolla

PACIFIC OCEAN

0 _____ 1 mile
0 _____ 1 km

KEY
► *Start of tour*

Torrey Pines State Park

S21
N. Torrey Pines Rd.

Genesee Ave.

Torrey Pines Rd.

La Jolla Village Dr.

Scripps Pier

La Jolla Shores

La Jolla Shores Dr.

Point La Jolla
Shell Beach
Children's Pool
Marine St. Beach

Prospect St.
Torrey Pines
Virginia Way
Girard Ave.
Pearl St.
La Jolla Blvd.

Torrey Pines Rd.

La Jolla Pkwy.

La Jolla Scenic Dr. N.
Gilman Dr.

5

TO GOLDEN TRIANGLE

La Jolla Country Club

Nautilus St.

52

Birch Aquarium
at Scripps **7**
La Jolla Caves **6**
La Jolla Cove **5**
La Valencia Hotel **4**

Mount Soledad **2**
Museum of
Contemporary
Art, San Diego **3**
Salk Institute **8**

Torrey Pines
City Park Beach **10**
Torrey Pines
Glider Port **9**
Torrey Pines State
Beach and Reserve **12**

University of California
at San Diego **11**
Windansea Beach **1**

landscape- and vintage watercolors; it also displays historic photos of La Jolla and collects cave admission fees. There's a coffee bar in the shop, and high tea is served in an English-style garden in the back. ⊠ *1325 Cave St., La Jolla* ☎ *858/459–0746* 🖃 *$3* ⊙ *Daily 9–5.*

★ ☪ ➎ **La Jolla Cove.** The wooded spread that looks out over a shimmering blue inlet is what first attracted everyone to La Jolla, from Native Americans to the glitterati; it's the village's enduring cachet. You'll find the cove—as locals always refer to it, as though it were the only one in San Diego—beyond where Girard Avenue dead-ends into Coast Boulevard, marked by towering palms that line a promenade where people strolling in drop-dead designer clothes are as common as Frisbee throwers.

Smaller beaches appear and disappear with the tides, which carve small private coves in cliffs covered with ice plants. Pathways lead down to the beaches. Keep an eye on the tide to avoid getting trapped once the waves come in. A long layer of sandstone stretching out above the waves provides a perfect sunset-watching spot, with plenty of tiny tide pools formed in eroded pockets in the rocks; starfish, sea anemones, and hermit crabs cluster here when the tide is in. Be careful, because these rocks can get slippery.

An underwater preserve at the north end of La Jolla Cove makes the adjoining beach the most popular one in the area. On summer days, when the water visibility reaches 20 feet deep or so, the sea seems to disappear under the mass of bodies floating face down, snorkels poking up out of the water. The small beach is covered with blankets, towels, and umbrellas, and the lawns at the top of the stairs leading down to the cove are staked out by groups of scuba divers, complete with wet suits and tanks. The **Children's Pool**, at the south end of the park, has a curving beach protected by a seawall from strong currents and waves. Since the pool and its beach have become home to an ever-growing colony of Harbor seals, it's no longer open to swimmers; however it's the best place on the coast to view these engaging creatures.

If you're not here by noon, forget about finding a parking spot or a small square of sand for your towel. But no matter what time you arrive, walk through **Ellen Browning Scripps Park**, past the groves of twisted junipers to the cliff's edge. Perhaps one of the open-air shelters overlooking the sea will be free, and you can spread your picnic out on a table and enjoy the scenery.

➍ **La Valencia.** The art deco–style La Valencia, which has operated as a luxury hotel since 1928, has long been a gathering spot for Hollywood celebrities; in the 1940s Gregory Peck would invite friends to La Valencia's Whaling Bar to try to persuade them to participate in one of his favorite projects, La Jolla Theater. Today the hotel's grand lobby, with floor-to-ceiling windows overlooking La Jolla Cove, is a popular wedding spot, and the Whaling Bar is still a favorite meeting place for power brokers. ⊠ *1132 Prospect St., La Jolla* ☎ *858/454–0771* ⊕ *www.lavalencia.com.*

➋ **Mount Soledad.** La Jolla's highest spot can be reached by taking Nautilus Street all the way east. The top of the mountain is an excellent vantage point from which to get a sense of San Diego's geography: looking down from here you can see the coast from the county's northern border to the south far beyond downtown—barring smog and haze. A half-acre on the summit is used to honor those killed in wars. The steel-and-concrete cross memorializes veterans, and services are held here on Memorial Day. ⊠ *La Jolla.*

★ ❸   **Museum of Contemporary Art, San Diego.** The oldest section of San Diego's modern art museum was a residence designed by Irving Gill (1870–1936) for philanthropist Ellen Browning Scripps in 1916. Robert Venturi and his colleagues at Venturi, Scott Brown and Associates updated and expanded the compound in the mid-1990s. The architects respected Gill's original geometric structure and clean, mission-style lines while adding their own distinctive touches. The result is a striking contemporary building that looks as though it's always been here.

The light-filled Axline Court serves as the entrance to the museum; it does triple duty as reception area, exhibition hall, and forum for special events. A patterned terrazzo floor leads to galleries where the museum's permanent collection and rotating exhibits are on display. The artwork inside gets major competition from the setting: you can look out from the top of a grand stairway onto a landscaped garden that contains permanent and temporary sculpture exhibits as well as rare 100-year-old California plant specimens and, beyond that, to the Pacific Ocean. The bookstore and the refurbished Sherwood Auditorium have separate outside entrances, so you don't have to enter the museum to browse the modern-art volumes and stylish design gifts or attend the auditorium's programs.

The permanent collection of post-1950s art naturally has a strong representation of California artists but also includes examples of every major art movement since that time—works by Andy Warhol, Robert Rauschenberg, Frank Stella, Joseph Cornell, and Jenny Holzer, to name a few. Important pieces by artists from San Diego and Tijuana were acquired in the 1990s. The museum also gets major visiting shows. The Museum Café serves soups, salads, and sandwiches as well as drinks. ⊠ *700 Prospect St., La Jolla* ☎ *858/454–3541* ⊕ *www.mcasandiego.org* ⊠ *$6, free 1st Sun. and 3rd Tues. of month* ☉ *Thurs. 11–7, Fri.–Tues. 11–5.*

❽   **Salk Institute.** The world-famous biological-research facility founded by polio vaccine inventor Jonas Salk sits on 26 cliff-top acres. For the original 1965 twin structures designed in consultation with Dr. Salk, modernist architect Louis I. Kahn used poured concrete and other low-maintenance materials to clever effect. The thrust of the laboratory–office complex is outward toward the Pacific Ocean, an orientation that is accentuated by a foot-wide "Stream of Life" that flows through the center of a travertine marble courtyard between the buildings. The courtyard and stream of water were inspired by architect Louis Barragán. Architects-to-be and building buffs enjoy the free tours of the property; call ahead to book, because the tours take place only when enough people express interest. ⊠ *10010 N. Torrey Pines Rd., La Jolla* ☎ *858/453–4100 Ext. 1200* ⊠ *Free* ☉ *Grounds weekdays 9–5; architectural tours*

Mon., Wed., and Fri. at noon, Thurs. at 12:30 and every other Tues. at 11. Reservations required, socall ahead.

10 **Torrey Pines City Park Beach.** Black's Beach—as locals call it—is one of the most beautiful and secluded stretches of sand in San Diego, backed by cliffs whose colors change with the angle of the sun. There are no restrooms, showers, or snack shops, although some hardy (and law-breaking) entrepreneurs lug ice chests filled with sodas and beer down the cliffs to sell to the unprepared. The paths leading down to the beach are steep, and the cliffs are unstable—pay attention to the safety signs and stick to the well-traveled trails. Black's Beach was clothing-optional for many years; although nudity is now prohibited by law, many people still shed their suits whenever the authorities are out of sight. ⊠ *La Jolla.*

9 **Torrey Pines Glider Port.** On days when the winds are just right, gliders line the cliffs, waiting for the perfect gust to carry them into the sky. Seasoned hang gliders with a good command of the current can soar over the sea for hours, then ride the winds back to the cliffs. Less-experienced fliers sometimes land on the beach below, to the cheers and applause of the sunbathers who scoot out of the way. If you're coming via the freeway, take the Genesee Avenue exit west from I–5 and follow the signs when you approach the coast. ⊠ *La Jolla.*

12 **Torrey Pines State Beach and Reserve.** *Pinus torreyana,* the rarest native pine tree in the United States, enjoys a 1,750-acre sanctuary at the northern edge of La Jolla. About 6,000 of these unusual trees, some as tall as 60 feet, grow on the cliffs here. The park is one of only two places in the world (the other is Santa Rosa Island, off Santa Barbara) where theTorrey pine grows naturally. The reserve has several hiking trails leading to the cliffs, 300 feet above the ocean; trail maps are available at the park station. Wildflowers grow profusely in spring, and the ocean panoramas are always spectacular. When in this upper part of the park, respect the various restrictions. Not permitted: picnicking, smoking, leaving the trails, or collecting plant specimens.

You can unwrap your sandwiches, however, at Torrey Pines State Beach, just below the reserve. When the tide is out, it's possible to walk south all the way past the lifeguard towers to Black's Beach over rocky promontories carved by the waves (avoid the bluffs, however; they're unstable). **Los Peñasquitos Lagoon** at the north end of the reserve is one of the many natural estuaries that flow inland between Del Mar and Oceanside. It's a good place to watch shorebirds. Volunteers lead guided nature walks at 11:30 and 1:30 on most weekends. ⊠ *N. Torrey Pines Rd. (Old Hwy. 101), La Jolla; exit I–5 onto Carmel Valley Rd. going west, then turn left (south) on Old Hwy. 101* ☎ *858/755–2063* ⌨ *Parking $6* ☉ *Daily 8–dusk.*

11 **University of California at San Diego.** The campus of San Diego's most prestigious research university spreads over 1,200 acres of coastal canyons and eucalyptus groves, where students and faculty jog, bike, and Rollerblade to class. If you're interested in contemporary art, ask at one of the two information booths for a campus map that shows the location of the Stuart Collection, 14 thought-provoking sculptures arrayed around campus; Nam June Paik, William Wegman, Niki de St. Phalle, and Jenny Holzer are among the artists whose works are displayed. UCSD's Price Center has a well-stocked, two-level bookstore—the largest in San Diego—and a good coffeehouse, Espresso Roma. Look for the postmodern Geisel Library (named for longtime La Jolla residents "Dr. Seuss" and his wife), which resembles a large spaceship. ⊠ *Exit I–5 onto La Jolla Village Dr. going west; take Gilman Dr. off-ramp to right and continue on to information kiosk at campus entrance on Gilman Dr., La Jolla* ☎ *858/534–4414 campus tour information* ⊗ *90-min campus tours Sun. at 2 from South Gilman Information Pavilion; reserve before 3 Fri.*

▶ **❶** **Windansea Beach.** Fans of pop satirist Tom Wolfe may recall *The Pump House Gang,* which pokes fun at the southern California surfing culture. Wolfe drew many of his barbs from observations he made at Windansea, the surfing beach west of La Jolla Boulevard near Nautilus Street. The wave action here is said to be as good as that in Hawai'i. ⊠ *La Jolla.*

need a break? A breakfast of the excellent buttery croissants or brioches at the **French Pastry Shop** (⊠ 5550 La Jolla Blvd., La Jolla ☎ 858/454–9094) is good preparation for time at Windansea Beach.

MISSION BAY & SEAWORLD

The 4,600-acre Mission Bay aquatic park is San Diego's monument to sports and fitness. Admission to its 27 mi of bay-shore beaches and 17 mi of ocean frontage is free. All you need for a perfect day is a bathing suit, shorts, and the right selection of playthings.

When explorer Juan Rodríguez Cabrillo first spotted the bay in 1542, he called it Bahía Falsa (False Bay) because the ocean-facing inlet led to acres of swampland that was inhospitable to boats and inhabitants. In the 1960s the city planners decided to dredge the swamp and build a bay with acres of beaches and lawns. Only 25% of the land was permitted to be commercially developed, and only a handful of resort hotels break up the striking natural landscape.

You don't have to go far from the freeway to experience the beach-party atmosphere of Mission Bay. A 5-mi-long pathway runs parallel to I–5 through the eastern section of the bay from a trailer park and miniature golf course, south past the high-rise Hilton Hotel to Sea World Drive. The sky above the lawns facing I–5 is flooded with the bright colors of huge, intricately made kites: the San Diego Kite Club meets on East Mission Bay Drive south of the Hilton, and on the weekends club members set loose their amazing creations.

Playgrounds and picnic areas abound on the beach and low grassy hills of the park. Group gatherings, company picnics, and birthday parties are common sights; huge parking lots accommodate swelling crowds on sunny days. On weekday evenings, joggers, bikers, and skaters take over. In the daytime, swimmers, water-skiers, anglers, and boaters—some in single-person kayaks, others in crowded powerboats—vie for space in the water. The San Diego Crew Classic, which takes place in late March or April, fills this area of the bay with teams from all over the country. College reunions, complete with flying school colors and keg beer, are popular at the event.

North of Belmont Park to Pacific Beach, Mission Boulevard runs along a narrow strip embraced by the Pacific Ocean on the west, called Mission Beach, and the bay on the east. The pathways in this area are lined with vacation homes, many of which can be rented by the week or month. Those who are fortunate enough to live here year-round have the bay as their front yard, with wide sandy beaches, volleyball courts, and—less of an advantage—an endless stream of sightseers on the sidewalk.

One Mission Bay caveat: swimmers should note signs warning about water pollution; certain areas of the bay are chronically polluted, and bathing is strongly discouraged.

Numbers in the text correspond to numbers in the margin and on the Mission Bay map.

a good
tour

If you're coming from I–5, the **San Diego Visitor Information Center ❶** ⌐ is just about at the end of the Clairemont Drive–East Mission Bay Drive exit (you'll see the prominent sign). At the point where East Mission Bay Drive turns into Sea World Drive you can detour left to **Fiesta Island ❷**, popular with jet skiers and speedboat racers. Continue around the curve to the west to reach **SeaWorld of California ❸**, the area's best-known attraction.

You'll next come to Ingraham Street, the central north–south drag through the bay. If you take it north, you'll shortly spot Vacation Road, which leads into the focal point of this part of the bay, the waterskiing hub of **Vacation Isle ❹**. At Ingraham, Sea World Drive turns into Sunset Cliffs Boulevard and intersects with West Mission Bay Drive. Past this intersection, Quivira Way leads west toward **Hospitality Point ❺**, where there are nice, quiet places to have a picnic.

If you continue west on West Mission Bay Drive, just before it meets Mission Boulevard, you'll come to the Bahia Resort Hotel, where you can catch the ***Bahia Belle ❻*** for a cruise around the bay. Ventura Cove, opposite the Bahia Hotel, is another good spot to unpack your cooler. Almost immediately south of where West Mission Bay Drive turns into Mission Boulevard is the resurrected **Belmont Park ❼**.

TIMING   It would take less than an hour to drive this tour. You may not find a visit to SeaWorld fulfilling unless you spend at least a half day; a full day is recommended. Belmont Park is open daily, but not all its attractions are open year-round.

Sights to See

❻ ***Bahia Belle.*** At the dock of the Bahia Resort Hotel, on the eastern shores of West Mission Bay Drive, you can board a restored stern-wheeler for a sunset cruise of the bay and party on until the wee hours. There's always music, mostly jazz, rock, and blues, and on Friday and Saturday

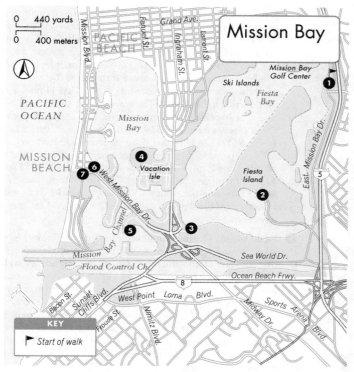

nights the bands are live. You can imbibe at the Belle's full bar, which opens at 9:30 PM, but many revelers like to disembark at the Bahia's sister hotel, the Catamaran, and have a few rounds at the Cannibal Bar before reboarding (the boat cruises between the two hotels, which co-own it, stopping to pick up passengers every half hour). The first cruise on Sunday is devoted to kids, but most cruises get a mixed crowd of families, couples, and singles. ⊠ *998 W. Mission Bay Dr., Mission Bay* ☎ *858/539-7779* ✆ *$6 for unlimited cruising; 9:30 PM or later, cruisers must be at least 21; free for guests of Bahia and Catamaran hotels* ⊗ *Sept.–Nov. and Jan.–June, Fri. and Sat. 6:30 PM–1 AM, departures every hr on the ½ hr; June, Wed.–Sun. 6:30 PM–1 AM; July and Aug., daily 6:30 PM–1 AM; closed in Dec.*

🐾 **❼** **Belmont Park.** The once-abandoned amusement park between the bay and Mission Beach boardwalk is now a shopping, dining, and recreation complex. Twinkling lights outline the **roller coaster** on which scream-ing thrill-seekers ride more than 2,600 feet of track and 13 hills (riders must be at least 4′2″). Created as the Giant Dipper in 1925 and listed on the National Register of Historic Places, this is one of the few old-time roller coasters left in the United States. **The Plunge,** an indoor swim-ming pool, also opened in 1925 as the largest—60 feet by 125 feet—saltwater pool in the world. It's had fresh water since 1951.

Johnny Weismuller and Esther Williams are among the stars who were captured on celluloid swimming across Belmont Park's favorite body of water. Other attractions include **Pirate's Cove,** a fantastic maze of brightly colored tunnels, slides, an obstacle course, and more, all with a pirate theme; a video arcade; a submarine ride; bumper cars; a tilt-a-whirl; an antique carousel; and a trampoline. Belmont Park also has the most consistent wave in the county at the **Wave House,** a stationary wave that opened in late 2004. The wave allows surfers and bodyboarders to ride a near perfect stationary wave. Plans to incorporate a skatepark are in place, as well. ⊠ *3146 Mission Blvd., Mission Bay* ☎ *858/488-1549, 858/488-3110 for pool* ⊕ *www.belmontpark.com* ⊠ *$4 for roller coaster, $3 for bumper cars, vertical plunge, and tilt-a-whirl, all other rides $2; full-day unlimited ride package $16.95 for 50″ and over, $13.95 for under 50″; all rides 75¢ June–Aug., Tues. 4 PM to closing; pool $5 for one-time entry* ⊙ *Park opens at 11 daily, ride hrs vary seasonally; pool open weekdays 5:30–8 AM, noon–1 PM, and 2:30–8 PM and weekends 8–4.*

❷ **Fiesta Island.** The most undeveloped area of Mission Bay Park is popular with bird-watchers (there's a large protected nesting site for the California tern at the northern tip of the island) as well as with dog owners—it's the only place in the park where pets can run free. Jet skiers and speedboat racers come here, too. At Christmas it provides an excellent vantage point for viewing the bay's Parade of Lights. In July the annual Over-the-Line Tournament, a competition involving a local version of softball, attracts thousands of players and oglers, drawn by the teams' raunchy names and outrageous behavior. When you drive onto Fiesta Island you can't immediately turn back, as the road leads one way around the perimeter.

❺ **Hospitality Point.** Enjoy lunch in this pretty, secluded spot, with a view of sailboats and yachts entering the open sea. At the entrance to Hospitality Point, the Mission Bay Park Headquarters supplies area maps and other recreational information. It's also the place to pick up a permit if you decide to throw a wedding in the park. ⊠ *2581 Quivira Ct., Mission Bay* ☎ *619/221–8901* ⊙ *Weekdays 9–5; closed city holidays.*

> **need a break?**
>
> **Sportsmen's Sea Foods** (⊠ 1617 Quivira Rd., Mission Bay ☎ 619/224–3551) serves good fish-and-chips to eat on the inelegant but scenic patio—by the marina, where sportfishing boats depart daily—or to take out to your chosen picnic spot.

▶ ❶ **San Diego Visitor Information Center.** In addition to being an excellent resource for San Diego tourists—it makes hotel and motel reservations, sells tickets to several attractions at a discount, offers various maps and guides, and has a small gift shop—the center is also a gathering spot for runners, walkers, and exercisers. For boaters it's the place to pick up a map detailing Mission Bay Park launch depths and speeds. ⊠ *2688 E. Mission Bay Dr., Mission Bay* ☎ *619/275–8259, 619/276–8200* ⊙ *Mon.–Sat. 9–5, until 6 in summer; Sun. 9:30–4:30, until 5:30 in summer.*

🐾 ❸ **SeaWorld of California.** One of the world's largest marine-life amusement
Fodor's Choice parks, SeaWorld is spread over 100 tropically landscaped bay-front
★ acres—and it seems to be expanding into every square inch of available
space with new exhibits, shows, and activities.

The majority of the exhibits are walk-through marine environments. In
a perpetual favorite, the **Penguin Encounter,** a moving sidewalk passes
through a glass-enclosed Arctic area where hundreds of emperor penguins slide over glaciers into icy waters. (The penguins like it cold, so
consider bringing a light sweater along for this one.) Kids get a particular kick out of the **Shark Encounter,** where they come face-to-face with
sandtiger, nurse, bonnethead, black-tipped, and white-tipped reef sharks
by walking through a 57-foot clear acrylic tube that passes through the
280,000-gallon shark habitat. The hands-on **California Tide Pool** exhibit gives you a chance to get to know San Diego's indigenous marine
life. At **Forbidden Reef** you can feed bat rays and go nose-to-nose with
creepy moray eels. At **Rocky Point Preserve** you can view bottlenose dolphins, as well as Alaskan sea otters. At **Wild Arctic,** which starts out
with a simulated helicopter ride to a research post at the North Pole,
beluga whales, walruses, and polar bears can be viewed in areas decked
out like the wrecked hulls of two 19th-century sailing ships. **Manatee
Rescue** lets you watch the gentle-giant marine mammals cavorting in a
215,000-gallon tank. Various **freshwater and saltwater aquariums** hold
underwater creatures from around the world. And for younger kids who
need to release lots of energy, **Shamu's Happy Harbor** is a hands-on fun
zone that features, among other attractions, a two-story ship, where pretend pirates aim water cannons at one another (be prepared with a change
of dry clothes).

SeaWorld's highlights are its four large-arena entertainments. You can
arrive 10 or 15 minutes in advance to get front-row seats, and the stadiums are large enough for everyone to get a seat even at the busiest
times. The traditional favorite is the **Shamu show,** with synchronized
killer whales bringing down the house, but the less publicized **Fools With
Tools** stars two California sea lions, Clyde and Seamore, as comic
handymen whose best-laid plans are foiled by a supporting cast of Asian
sea otters. Another favorite is the 3-D movie **R.L. Stine's Haunted Lighthouse,** a spine-tingling tale of a quest to find the secret of a lighthouse's
haunting. Haunted Lighthouse introduces a "fourth dimension," namely
special effects like sprays of water, blasts of air, and other wild surprises
designed to bring you into the scene. The film stars Christopher Lloyd
as Cap'n Jack.

Trainer For A Day, allows you to get a first-hand look at how Sea World's
trainers spend a work day. The $395 fee may seem hefty, but it buys a
once-in-a-lifetime opportunity. **Shipwreck Rapids,** SeaWorld of California's first adventure ride, offers plenty of excitement—but you may
end up getting soaked. For five minutes nine "shipwrecked" passengers careen down a river in a raftlike inner tube, encountering a series
of obstacles, including several waterfalls. There's no extra charge,
making this one of SeaWorld's great bargains—which means that you
should expect long lines.

Not all the exhibits are water-oriented. **Pets Rule!** showcases the antics of more common animals like dogs, cats, birds, and even a pig, all set to prove the supremacy of our four-legged (or feathered) friends. One segment of the show actually has regular house cats climbing ladders and hanging upside down as they cross a high-wire. The majority of the animals used in the show were adopted from shelters. Those who want to head to higher ground might consider the **Southwest Airlines Sky-tower,** a glass elevator that ascends 320 feet; the views of San Diego County from the ocean to the mountains are especially spectacular in early morning and late evening. The **Bayside Sky Ride,** a five-minute aerial tram ride that leaves from the same spot, travels across Mission Bay. Admission for the Skytower and the tram is $3 apiece. The fact that An-heuser-Busch is the park's parent company is evident in the presence of the beer company's signature Clydesdales, huge horses that you can visit in their "hamlet" when they're not putting on shows.

SeaWorld is chockablock with souvenir shops and refreshment stands (the only picnic grounds are outside the park entrance), so it's hard to come away from here without spending a lot of money on top of the hefty entrance fee (the children's admission is $37.95) and $7 parking tab. It's smart to take advantage of the two-day entry option, only $4 more than a single-day admission: if you try to get your money's worth by fitting everything in on a single day, you're all likely to end up tired and cranky. Many hotels, especially those in the Mission Bay area, also offer SeaWorld specials that may include rate reductions or two days' entry for the price of one. It's also a good idea to take a change of clothes along, especially when the weather is on the cool side and you sit in the first 10 rows at one of the marine shows, or ride Shipwreck Rapids; you can rent a locker to stow belongings. ✉ *1720 South Shores Rd., near west end of I–8, Mission Bay* ☎ *619/226–3815, 619/226–3901 recorded information* ⊕ *www.seaworld.com* ✆ *$46.95; parking $7 cars, $4 motorcycles, $9 RVs and campers; 90-min behind-the-scenes walk-ing tours $10 extra* ▤ *AE, D, MC, V* ⊙ *Daily 10–dusk; extended hrs in summer.*

need a
break?

One of the perks of visiting a theme park owned by a beer distributor is free samples of suds, a good way to wash down the corned-beef sandwiches and the like served at **The Deli,** in the Anheuser-Busch Hospitality Center near the park entrance. Healthier fare—grilled fish, vegetables, and salads, along with cheeseburgers and fries—are the order of the day at the huge **Shipwreck Reef Cafe,** where you're likely to be entertained by park animals and juggling castaways.

❹ **Vacation Isle.** Ingraham Street bisects the island, providing two distinct experiences for visitors. The west side is taken up by the San Diego Par-adise Point Resort, but you don't have to be a guest to enjoy the hotel's lushly landscaped grounds and bay-front restaurants. The water-ski clubs congregate at **Ski Beach** on the east side of the island, where there's a parking lot as well as picnic areas and restrooms. Ski Beach is the site of the Thunderboats Unlimited Hydroplane Championships, held in September. At a pond on the south side of the island children and

CALIFORNIA'S PADRE PRESIDENT

SAN DIEGO, the first European settlement in Southern California, was founded by Father Junípero Serra in July 1769. A member of the Franciscan order, Father Serra was part of a larger expedition that was headed by explorer Don Gaspar de Portola. King Charles III of Spain, responding to pressure from English and Russian explorers and traders moving down the West Coast, chartered the party to travel from outposts in Baja California north to explore and occupy the territory known then as Alta California.

When they arrived in San Diego, the Spaniards found about 20,000 Kumeyaay Indians living in a hundred or so villages along the coast and inland. To establish the foothold for the king, the missionaries attempted to convert the Kumeyaays to Christianity, and taught them agricultural and other skills so they could work what would become vast holdings of the missions.

Mission San Diego Alcalá, established on a hillside above what is now Mission Valley in San Diego, was the first of 21 that the Franciscans built along the coast of California. After establishing the mission and presidio in San Diego, Serra and Portola moved on, founding the Mission San Carlos Borromeo and presidio at Monterey. Mission San Carlos was later moved to Carmel, where Father Serra settled and maintained his headquarters until his death in 1784.

Father Serra, the padre president of California, established nine missions. These include: San Antonio de Padua, 1771; San Gabriel, 1771; San Luis Obispo, 1772; Mission Dolores, 1776; San Juan Capistrano, 1776; Santa Clara, 1777; and San Buenaventura, 1777. He personally oversaw the planning, construction, and staffing of each mission.

His work took him from Carmel to locations in northern and southern California, where he supervised the initial construction of the missions and conferred the sacraments. It's estimated that during this period he walked more than 24,000 mi in California to visit the other missions.

The missions, which became known as Serra's Beads, comprised millions of acres and were in fact small self-sufficient cities with the church as the centerpiece. In addition to converting the Indians to Christianity and teaching the Native Americans European ways, the padres managed farming, education, and industries such as candle making and tanning. San Diego is the southernmost mission, while the mission at Sonoma is the northernmost; each was established about 30 mi—or a day's walk—apart and was linked to the El Camino Highway. The missions were also the earliest form of lodging in the Golden State, known far and wide for the hospitality they afforded visitors.

Father Serra spent barely a year in San Diego before embarking on his journey to establish missions across California, but his presence left a lasting imprint on the city. You can see some of the history at the Serra Museum and at Mission San Diego Alcalá. And you can trace his footsteps along El Camino Real by driving U.S. 101, the historic route that traverses coastal California from south to north.

— Bobbi Zane

young-at-heart adults take part year-round in motorized miniature boat races. ✉ *Mission Bay.*

OLD TOWN

San Diego's Spanish and Mexican history and heritage are most evident in Old Town, north of downtown at Juan Street, near the intersection of Interstates 5 and 8. Old Town didn't become a state historic park until 1968, but private efforts kept the area's history alive until then, and a number of San Diego's oldest structures have been restored.

Old Town is the first European settlement in southern California, but the pueblo's true beginnings took place overlooking Old Town from atop Presidio Park, where Father Junípero Serra established the first of California's missions, San Diego de Alcalá, in 1769. Some of San Diego's original inhabitants, the Kumeyaay Indians—called the Diegueños by the Spaniards—were forced to abandon their seminomadic lifestyle and live at the mission. They were expected to follow Spanish customs and adopt Christianity as their religion, but they resisted fiercely; of all the California missions, San Diego de Alcalá was the least successful in carrying out conversions. For security reasons the mission was built on a hill, but it didn't have an adequate water supply, and food became scarce as the number of Kumeyaays and Spanish soldiers occupying the site increased.

In 1774 the hilltop was declared a Royal Presidio, or fortress, and the mission was moved 6 mi west to the San Diego River. The Kumeyaays, responding to the loss of their land as the mission expanded along the riverbed, attacked and burned it in 1775. A later assault on the presidio was less successful, and their revolt was short-lived. By 1800 about 1,500 Kumeyaays were living on the mission's grounds, receiving religious instruction and adapting to Spanish ways.

The pioneers living within the presidio's walls were mostly Spanish soldiers, poor Mexicans, and mestizos of Spanish and Native American ancestry, many of whom were unaccustomed to farming San Diego's arid land. When Mexico gained independence from Spain in 1821, it claimed its lands in California and flew the Mexican flag over the presidio. The Mexican government, centered some 2,000 mi away in Monterrey, stripped the missions of their landholdings, and an aristocracy of landholders began to emerge. At the same time, settlers were beginning to move down from the presidio to what is now Old Town.

A rectangular plaza was laid out along today's San Diego Avenue to serve as the settlement's center. In 1846, during the war between Mexico and the United States, a detachment of U.S. Marines raised the Stars and Stripes over the plaza. The flag was removed once or twice, but by early 1848 Mexico had surrendered California, and the U.S. flag remained. San Diego became an incorporated city in 1850, with Old Town as its center.

On San Diego Avenue, the district's main drag, art galleries and expensive gift shops are interspersed with tacky curios shops, restaurants, and open-air stands selling inexpensive Mexican pottery, jewelry, and blankets.

The Old Town Esplanade on San Diego Avenue between Harney and Conde streets is the best of several mall-like affairs constructed in mock Mexican-plaza style. Shops and restaurants also line Juan and Congress streets.

Access to Old Town is easy thanks to the nearby Transit Center. Ten bus lines stop here, as do the San Diego Trolley and the Coaster commuter rail line. Two large parking lots linked to the park by an underground pedestrian walkway ease some of the parking congestion, and signage leading from I–8 to the Transit Center is easy to follow. If you're not familiar with the area, however, avoid the "Old Town" exit from I–5, which leaves you floundering near Mission Bay without further directions.

Numbers in the text correspond to numbers in the margin and on the Old Town San Diego map.

a good tour

Because of the steep hills leading up to Heritage Park and Presidio Park, it's best to use a car to see all of Old Town's sights.

Visit the information center at Seeley Stable, just off Old Town Plaza, to orient yourself to the various sights in **Old Town San Diego State Historic Park** ❶ ☞. When you've had enough history, cross north on the west side of the plaza to **Bazaar del Mundo** ❷, where you can shop or munch nachos on the terrace of a Mexican restaurant. Walk down San Diego Avenue, which flanks the south side of Old Town's historic plaza, east to Harney Street and the **Thomas Whaley Museum** ❸. It's best to hop in a car at this point for the next sights. Continue east 2½ blocks on San Diego Avenue beyond Arista Street to the **El Campo Santo** ❹ cemetery. **Heritage Park** ❺ is perched on a hill above Juan Street, north of the museum and cemetery. Drive west on Juan Street and north on Taylor Street, which leads to Presidio Drive. This takes you up the hill on which **Presidio Park** ❻ and the **Junípero Serra Museum** ❼ sit.

TIMING Try to time your visit to coincide with the free daily tours of Old Town given at 11 AM and 2 PM by costumed park service employees at Seeley Stable. It takes about two hours to walk through Old Town. If you go to Presidio Park, definitely drive instead of walk, and allot another hour to explore the grounds and museum.

Sights to See

❷ **Bazaar del Mundo.** North of San Diego's Old Town Plaza lies the area's unofficial center, built to represent a colonial Mexican square. The central courtyard is always in blossom, with magenta bougainvillea, scarlet hibiscus, and irises, poppies, and petunias in season. Ballet Folklorico and flamenco dancers perform on weekend afternoons, and the bazaar frequently hosts arts-and-crafts exhibits and Mexican festivals. Sit on a patio at one of the five restaurants and soon enough, a strolling mariachi will come by. Colorful shops specializing in Latin American crafts and unusual gift items border the square. Although many of the shops here have high-quality wares, prices can be considerably higher than those at shops on the other side of Old Town Plaza; it's a good idea to do some comparative shopping before you make any purchases. ⊠ *2754 Calhoun*

Old Town
San Diego

St., Old Town ☎ 619/296–3161 ⊕ www.bazaardelmundo.com ☉ Shops
daily 10–9.

need a
break?

La Panadería (⊠ Southeast corner of the Bazaar del Mundo, Old
Town ☎ 619/291–7662) sells hot *churros*—long sticks of fried
dough coated with cinnamon and sugar. Get some to go and sit out
on one of the benches and enjoy the live music at the bandstand
(weekends only).

❹ **El Campo Santo.** The old adobe-walled cemetery established in 1849 was
the burial place for many members of Old Town's founding families, as
well as for some gamblers and bandits who passed through town until
1880. Antonio Garra, a chief who led an uprising of the San Luis Rey
Indians, was executed at El Campo Santo in front of the open grave he
was forced to dig for himself. These days the small cemetery is a peaceful stop for visitors to Old Town. Most of the markers give only ap-
proximations of where the people named on them are buried; some of
the early settlers laid to rest at El Campo Santo really reside under San
Diego Avenue. ⊠ *North side of San Diego Ave. S, between Arista and
Ampudia Sts., Old Town.*

❺ Heritage Park. A number of San Diego's important Victorian buildings are the focus of this 7⁸⁄₁₀-acre park, up the Juan Street hill near Harney Street. The buildings were moved here and restored by Save Our Heritage Organization, and include southern California's first synagogue, a one-room classic revival–style structure built in 1889 for Congregation Beth Israel. The most interesting of the six former residences might be the Sherman Gilbert House, which has a widow's walk and intricate carving on its decorative trim. It was built for real estate dealer John Sherman in 1887 at the then-exorbitant cost of $20,000—indicating just how profitable the booming housing market could be. Bronze plaques detail the history of all the houses, some of which may seem surprisingly colorful; they are in fact accurate representations of the bright tones of the era. The homes are now used for offices, shops, and, in one case, a bed-and-breakfast inn. The climb up to the park is a little steep, but the view of the harbor is great. Only the synagogue is open to visitors. ⊠ *County parks office: 2455 Heritage Park Row, Old Town* ☎ *858/ 694–3049.*

❼ Junípero Serra Museum. San Diego's original Spanish presidio (fortress) and California's first mission were perched atop the 160-foot hill overlooking Mission Valley. It's now the domain of a Spanish mission–style museum devoted to the history of the hill from the time it was occupied by the Kumeyaay Indians until 1929, when the museum was established, along with Presidio Park, by department store magnate and philanthropist George Marston. Artifacts include Kumeyaay baskets, Spanish riding gear, and a painting that Father Serra would have viewed in Mission San Diego de Alcalá. The education room has hands-on investigation stations where kids can grind acorns in *metates* (stones used for grinding grain), dig for buried artifacts with archaeology tools, or dress up in period costumes—one represents San Diego founding father Alonzo Horton. Ascend the tower to compare the view you'd have gotten before 1929 with the one you have today. The museum, now operated by the San Diego Historical Society, is at the north end of Presidio Park, near Taylor Street. ⊠ *2727 Presidio Dr., Old Town* ☎ *619/297–3258* ⊕ *www.sandiegohistory.org* ⧉ *$5* ⊗ *Fri.–Sun. 10–4:30.*

off the beaten path

MISSION SAN DIEGO DE ALCALÁ – It's hard to imagine how remote California's earliest mission once must have been; these days, it's accessible by a major freeway (I–15), and by the San Diego Trolley. Mission San Diego de Alcalá, the first of a chain of 21 missions stretching northward along the coast, was established by Father Junípero Serra in 1769 on Presidio Hill, and moved to its present location in 1774. There was no greater security from enemy attack here: Padre Luis Jayme, California's first Christian martyr, was clubbed to death by Kumeyaay Indians, whom he was trying to convert, in 1775. The present church is the fifth built on the site; it was reconstructed in 1931 following the outlines of the 1813 church. It's 150 feet long but only 35 feet wide because, without easy means of joining beams, the mission buildings were only as wide as the trees that served as their ceiling supports. Father Jayme is buried in the mission sanctuary; a small museum named for him documents the history of the mission and exhibits tools and artifacts from the early days. From the peaceful palm-bedecked gardens out back you can gaze at the 46-foot-high *campanario*, the mission's most distinctive feature; one of its five bells was cast in 1822. ⊠ *10818 San Diego Mission Rd., Mission Valley; from I–15, take Friars Rd. east and Rancho Mission Rd. south* ☎ *619/281–8449* ⊕ *www. missionsandiego.com* ⊠ *$3* ⊘ *Daily 9–4:45.*

★ ┌ ❶ **Old Town San Diego State Historic Park.** The six square blocks on the site of San Diego's original pueblo are the heart of Old Town. Most of the 20 historic buildings preserved or re-created by the park cluster around **Old Town Plaza,** bounded by Wallace Street on the west, Calhoun Street on the north, Mason Street on the east, and San Diego Avenue on the south. You can see the presidio from behind the cannon by the flagpole. The plaza is a pleasant place for resting and regrouping as you plan your tour of the park and watch passers-by. San Diego Avenue is closed to vehicle traffic here.

Some of Old Town's buildings were destroyed in a fire in 1872, but after the site became a state historic park in 1968, efforts were begun to reconstruct or restore the structures that remained. Seven of the original adobes are still intact. The tour pamphlet available at Seeley Stable gives details about all of the historic houses on the plaza and in its vicinity; a few of the more interesting ones are noted below. Several reconstructed buildings serve as restaurants or as shops purveying wares reminiscent of those that might have been available in the original Old Town; Racine & Laramie, a painstakingly reproduced version of San Diego's first (1868) cigar store, is especially interesting. The noncommercial houses are open daily 10–5; none charge admission, though donations are appreciated.

The **Robinson-Rose House** (☎ 619/220–5422) was the original commercial center of old San Diego, housing railroad offices, law offices, and the first newspaper press. In addition to serving as the park's visitor center and administrative center, it now hosts a model of Old Town as it looked in 1872, as well as various historic exhibits. Just behind the Robinson-Rose house is a replica of the Victorian-era Silvas-McCoy house, now an interpretive center.

On Mason Street, at the corner of Calhoun Street, **La Casa de Bandini** is one of the prettiest haciendas in San Diego. Built in 1829 by a Peruvian, Juan Bandini, the house served as Old Town's social center during Mexican rule. Albert Seeley, a stagecoach entrepreneur, purchased the home in 1869, built a second story, and turned it into the Cosmopolitan Hotel, a comfortable way station for travelers on the day-long trip south from Los Angeles. Today the hacienda's colorful gardens and main-floor dining rooms house a popular Mexican restaurant.

Seeley Stable (⊠ 2630 Calhoun St., Old Town ☎ 619/220–5427), next door to La Casa de Bandini, became San Diego's stagecoach stop in 1867 and was the transportation hub of Old Town until near the turn of the century, when trains became the favored mode of travel. The stable houses a collection of horse-drawn vehicles, some so elaborate that you can see where the term "carriage trade" came from. Also inside are western memorabilia, including an exhibit on the California *vaquero*, the original American cowboy, and a collection of Native American artifacts. An excellent free walking tour of the park leaves from here daily at 2.

La Casa de Estudillo (✉ 4001 Mason St., Old Town) was built on Mason Street in 1827 by the commander of the San Diego Presidio, Jose Maria Estudillo. The largest and most elaborate of the original adobe homes, it was occupied by members of the Estudillo family until 1887. It was purchased and restored in 1910 by sugar magnate and developer John D. Spreckels, who advertised it in bold lettering on the side as "Ramona's Marriage Place." Despite the meticulous attention to historical detail of the restoration, Spreckels' claim that the small chapel in the house was the site of the wedding in Helen Hunt Jackson's popular novel *Ramona* had no basis in fact; that didn't stop people from coming to see it, however.

The **San Diego Union Newspaper Historical Museum** (✉ Twigg St. and San Diego Ave., Old Town ☎ No phone) is in a New England–style, wood-frame house prefabricated in the eastern United States and shipped around Cape Horn in 1851. The building has been restored to replicate the newspaper's offices of 1868, when the first edition of the *San Diego Union* was printed.

Also worth exploring in the plaza area are the free **Dental Museum, Mason Street School, Wells Fargo Museum, San Diego Courthouse, Commercial Kitchen Museum, San Diego Sheriff's Museum** and the **Machado–Stewart Adobe Museum.** Ask at the visitor center for locations.

❻ Presidio Park. The hillsides of the 40-acre green space overlooking Old Town from the north end of Taylor Street are popular with picnickers, and many couples have taken their wedding vows on the park's long stretches of lawn, some of the greenest in San Diego. You may encounter enthusiasts of a Californian sport, grass skiing, gliding over the grass and down the hills on wheels. It's a nice walk to the summit from Old Town if you're in good shape and wearing the right shoes—it should take about half an hour. You can also drive to the top of the park via Presidio Drive, off Taylor Street. Presidio Park has a private canyon surrounded by palms at the bottom of the hill, off Taylor Street before it intersects with I–8.

If you do decide to walk, look in at the Presidio Hills Golf Course on Mason Street, which has an unusual clubhouse: it incorporates the ruins of Casa de Carrillo, the town's oldest adobe, constructed in 1820. At the end of Mason Street, veer left on Jackson Street to reach the **Presidio Ruins,** where adobe walls and a bastion have been built above the foundations of the original fortress and chapel. Archaeology students from San Diego State University who excavated the area have marked off the early chapel outlines, although they reburied the artifacts they uncovered in order to protect them. Also on-site are the 28-foot-high Serra Cross, built in 1913 out of brick tiles found in the ruins, and a bronze statue of Father Serra. Before you do much poking around here, however, it's a good idea to get some historical perspective at the

Junípero Serra Museum, just to the east. Take Presidio Drive southeast of the museum and you'll come to the site of Fort Stockton, built to protect Old Town and abandoned by the United States in 1848. Plaques and statues also commemorate the Mormon Battalion, which enlisted here to fight in the battle against Mexico. ⊠ *1 block north of Old Town.*

❸ **Thomas Whaley Museum.** Thomas Whaley was a New York entrepreneur who came to California during the gold rush. He wanted to provide his East Coast wife all the comforts of home, so in 1856 he had southern California's first two-story brick structure built. The house, which served as the county courthouse and government seat during the 1870s, stands in strong contrast to the Spanish-style adobe residences that surround the nearby historic plaza and marks an early stage of San Diego's "Americanization."

Period furnishings in the living quarters include a miniature dress dummy designed to look like Mary Todd Lincoln, a sofa from Andrew Jackson's White House, and a piano that belonged to singer Jenny Lind. Among the historical artifacts in the reconstructed courtroom is one of the six life masks of Abraham Lincoln. A garden out back includes many varieties of Old Garden roses from before 1867, when roses were first hybridized. The place is perhaps most famed, however, for the ghosts that are said to inhabit it; this is one of the few houses authenticated by the U.S. Department of Commerce as being haunted. ⊠ *2476 San Diego Ave., Old Town* ☎ *619/297–7511* ⊕ *www.whaleyhouse.org* ⊠ *$5* ⊙ *Wed–Mon. 10–4:30.*

WHERE TO EAT

2

By David
Nelson

SAN DIEGO'S STATUS AS A VACATIONER'S PARADISE and its growth into the seventh-largest city in the United States has made it a magnet for restaurateurs and chefs from around the globe. A good deal of the new talent also is homegrown, and it's not unusual for local youths to attend leading culinary academies and return home fired by the desire to remake San Diego cuisine. The city's growing corps of innovative and cutting-edge chefs includes Bernard Guillas at the Marine Room; Paul McHabe at Star of the Sea; Jesse Frost at Prince of Wales; Stephen Window at Roppongi; and Jean-Michel Diot at Tapenade. The new point of view is that a region this blessed with gorgeous vegetables, fruits, herbs, and seafood should make a culinary statement. An intriguing new restaurant in Hillcrest took the name Region to emphasize the delicious uses to which local products can be put.

As San Diego grows more serious about its cooking, it remains an informal city, and few other American cities yield so many dining options, indoors and out. Although the town as yet fails to offer a Tibetan eatery, it now takes for granted cuisines such as Cambodian, Ethiopian, Afghan, and Laotian. Many of these far-flung cuisines are served outside the center in the city's ever more diverse neighborhoods. Downtown, the dramatically restored Gaslamp Quarter offers vigorous nightlife and some 100 restaurants and can feel like the corner of Broadway and 42nd Street at times. The eateries range from down-at-the-heels holdouts from the days when this historic area had declined to Skid Row status, to stylish establishments priced for those doing business at the nearby San Diego Convention Center. In truth, Gaslamp is something of a victim of its own success, with difficult parking (valet parking is quite expensive) and more and more national chain feederies. But both locals and visitors identify it as San Diego's "party central," and the crowds come for lively fun. Definitely a family-friendly district, it has options for every group, and the sizeable number of nightclubs attract a clientele that steadily grows younger as the night wears on.

A stroll down the 5th Avenue restaurant row (which now extends both to 4th and 6th avenues) reveals San Diego's preference for Italian cuisine above all others, but the choice nonetheless is cosmopolitan and extends to casual, burgers and fries-type fare, Spanish tapas and paellas, traditional and nuevo Mexican cuisine, and all-American steaks cut thick enough to choke a horse. Fine, expensive steak houses are still the hot San Diego trend, thanks partly to prosperity in the local high-tech industries, and perhaps partly to boredom with the warnings of health mavens. Seafood abounds, and there's a whole lot of "fusion" going on, which is to say that many menus now present their chef's own rendition of contemporary cuisine, which borrows idiosyncratically from a mixture of culinary traditions. Sad to say, there's not a single fine Chinese restaurant downtown, but good Japanese cuisine is readily available.

Near the waterfront on the upper western edge of downtown, the rapidly gentrifying Little Italy district has become a center for excellent, affordable Italian dining, both traditional and more contemporary. The area has a few surprises to offer, too, such as an authentic English pub that is the unofficial headquarters for Commonwealth loyalists from around the globe and a Southwestern-style grill that is the ultimate in trendiness.

In addition to downtown, other areas of San Diego share in the keen sense of energy, fueled by a collective caffeine high acquired in the coffeehouses (some of which are listed in Chapter 4) springing up everywhere from the Gaslamp Quarter to the gas station on the corner. The uptown neighborhoods centered by Hillcrest—an urbane district with a hip San Francisco flavor—are marked by increasing culinary sophistication. Probably the best Thai and contemporary American restaurants in San Diego are located in this dynamic neighborhood. Mission Valley, the city's commercial heart, abounds in big restaurants of varying quality, interspersed by a few establishments devoted to superior fare. Just to the North, Convoy Street—the commercial spine of the busy Kearny Mesa area—is the unofficial Asian Restaurant Row of San Diego, and presents a comprehensive selection of Chinese, Korean and Vietnamese restaurants, a number of which qualify as "best in class." And rich, elegant La Jolla, with many of San Diego's most expensive restaurants, offers some of the best dining in the city. To be sure, great cooking blossoms beyond the city's official borders. In nearby Chula Vista, look for authentic, palate-pleasing Mexican fare, while Coronado—the peninsula city across San Diego Bay—has both casual, neighborhood-style eateries and grand hotel dining rooms with dramatic water views. And to the north in the plush suburbs of Del Mar, Solana Beach, and Rancho Santa Fe, elegant surroundings seem to demand good fare.

The proximity of Mexico and the city's many ties to Japan, China, Vietnam, and other Asian countries account for the influences that San Diego's chefs add to a local cuisine well grounded in classical French technique. The remarkably good local produce supplies ready inspiration to their talented hands.

Coronado & South Bay

Contemporary

$–$$ ✕ **Coronado Brewing Company.** The carefully crafted beers are good by themselves, but they also make a good accompaniment to beer-steamed bratwurst and beer-battered onion rings, served in mountainous portions. There's indoor seating, a pair of sidewalk terraces and, best of all, a walled garden that provides a quiet haven from the bustle of Orange Avenue. Simple choices are the wisest, from the Philadelphia-style steak sandwich to wood-fired pizzas to baby-back ribs basted with spicy, ginger-flavored barbecue sauce. It's a brewery, but popular with families with children. ⊠ *170 Orange Ave., Coronado* ☎ *619/437–4452* ⊟ *MC, V.*

¢–$$ ✕ **Tent City.** In a historic building in the heart of downtown Coronado, this vintage-2002 restaurant's eclectic cuisine emphasizes strong flavors and light effects, as in starters such as minced chicken with ponzu sauce and lettuce "wraps," and a "stacked" salad of crab, shrimp, and sliced yellow tomatoes. Main events include a grilled Portobello mushroom sandwich and, on the formal side, salmon baked in parchment. The name memorializes the waterside summer camp that San Diego residents frequented from 1900 to 1939. The dining room is pleasant, but the sidewalk terrace beckons in fine weather. ⊠ *1100 Orange Ave., Coronado* ☎ *619/435–4611* ▭ *MC, V.*

¢ ✕ **Aunt Emma's Pancakes.** The quintessential breakfast place, this decades-old Chula Vista landmark is 10 minutes south of downtown San Diego, and two blocks east of the E Street exit from I–5. Despite the motto "It's Always Pancake Time," Aunt Emma's serves from 6 AM to 3 PM only, when it bustles with people from every walk of life. The first menu item—fluffy, butter-drenched buttermilk pancakes—is as far as many guests read. Besides 20 pancake varieties, including mango crêpes, Aunt Emma's offers waffles, egg dishes, and Mexican specialties. The lunch menu includes burgers and sandwiches. ⊠ *700 E St., Chula Vista* ☎ *619/427–2722* ⚲ *Reservations not accepted* ▭ *MC, V* ⊘ *No dinner.*

¢ ✕ **Miracle Mile Delicatessen.** Nightly entrée specials that top out at $8.95 explains why Navy personnel, seniors, and guests of Coronado's many hotels arrive for hand-carved roast turkey, chicken noodle casserole, corned beef and cabbage and similar stick-to-the-ribs standards. The drawback is a somewhat sterile decor and a semi-self-service approach: order from the cooks at the steam table, and a runner delivers your food on a tray. Made-to-order sandwiches rise high with hot pastrami, rare roast beef, and other quality fillings. Cakes and other desserts easily serve two. ⊠ *980 Orange Ave., Coronado* ☎ *619/435–6655* ▭ *MC, V.*

French

$$–$$$ ✕ **Chez Loma.** This is widely considered one of the most romantic restaurants in Southern California, and it's a favorite with guests at nearby Hotel Del Coronado. Lots of windows, soft lighting, and an upstairs Victorian parlor for coffee and dessert are some of the charms. The more elaborate dishes among the carefully prepared meals are boeuf bourguignonne, pan-roasted lamb loin with vanilla-Merlot sauce, and New York steak au poivre. There's sidewalk dining and Sunday brunch. ⊠ *1132 Loma Ave., Coronado* ☎ *619/435–0661* ▭ *AE, DC, MC, V* ⊘ *No lunch.*

¢–$ ✕ **Tartine.** There's always a dish of water for canine pals on the terrace of this oh-so-French café a block from San Diego Bay. In France, a "tartine" is a toasted length of baguette, sometimes simply buttered, sometimes turned into a sandwich. At Tartine, these can be as hearty as a ham-and-Brie combo slathered with grain mustard, or as pinky-in-the-air as a layering of Gorgonzola cheese, walnuts, watercress and sliced pears. Other sandwiches, along with clever salads, the soup of the day, and a pâté plate round out the day-and-night menu. Continental breakfast commences at 6 AM, when just-baked, costly pastries silently command "Eat me!" ⊠ *1106 1st St., Coronado* ☎ *619/435–4323* ▭ *MC, V.*

Mexican

¢–$$ ✕ **Mexican Village Restaurant.** With lots of tile, a skylight, and a fountain, this restaurant achieves the south-of-the-border look, but it's not all tacos and burritos. There's also marinated grilled chicken and penne with tequila-tomato cream sauce. There's live music Thursday through Saturday night. Young people from the nearby North Island naval base fill the tables, but there's a kids' menu for families. Brunch is available

A fair number of San Diego restaurants offer "early-bird specials" before peak dining hours. There's no rule about the time for the specials, but they're generally offered between 5 PM and 6:30 PM on weekdays. Finer restaurants rarely offer such deals, yet there are some. La Jolla's oh-so-French Tapenade serves a set-price early-bird menu on weeknights before 6:30 PM.

With the boom of new apartments and condominiums in Little Italy, parking near one of the many restaurants well worth visiting has become a problem. However, the local San Diego Trolley stop is less than two blocks from Little Italy's India Street restaurant row. A plus, especially for those who lunch here, is the proximity of San Diego Bay, which is just a few streets to the west. It offers a superb promenade that both leads to interesting places and helps with the digestion of vast plates of pasta. If you use the trolley to get to downtown and Gaslamp Quarter restaurants, you can avoid parking fees that may exceed $10 and valets who expect healthy tips.

The advised attire at most of the restaurants listed below is casual. Only a handful of eateries discourage jeans, and only one or two still require jackets. The restaurants we list are the cream of the crop in each price category; they are grouped first by neighborhood, then by type of cuisine.

Children

San Diego rolls out the red carpet for everyone, including children, although some of the more formal establishments and large, expense account-oriented steak houses probably are inappropriate venues for junior citizens. Children's menus are neither unknown nor particularly common, but most establishments will cheerfully offer a few suggestions for the younger set if asked. Fast food is readily available in all quarters of the city, and you'll rarely be more than a pepperoni's toss from a pizza parlor. Hillcrest, while decidedly adult in nature, has the most popular "kid magnet" in town, Corvette Diner Bar & Grill, where birthday parties are a standard feature thanks to a 1950s menu and decor, and to servers who entertain with song and dance. Children are well received at the Convoy Street Chinese restaurants that specialize at lunch time in dim sum (myriad tiny pastries and dumplings). Youngsters who've never before seen such items sometimes develop quite a taste for egg rolls, fried pork dumplings, barbecued pork buns, and fried shrimp rolls. California-style Mexican cuisine that's usually a hit with kids for its messiness is not hard to find, especially in the bustling Old Town area. Fish tacos are all the rage, but if you're not sure what your kids will like, try a cheese quesadilla (melted cheese in a flour tortilla), chips and guacamole, or rolled tacos with guacamole. Always sample the salsa before offering it to your little ones, as it will be spicy more often than not.

Dress

San Diego restaurants have largely abandoned the battle to require stylish attire of their patrons, and while "Appropriate Dress Required" signs are sometimes displayed in the entrance, this generally means nothing more than clean and reasonably neat clothing. Some "dress-up" places remain, notably the Fontainebleau Room at the Westgate Hotel, Bertrand at Mister A's, and La Jolla institutions like Top of the Cove and George's at the Cove. Otherwise, a "come-as-you-are" attitude generally prevails. We mention dress only when men are required to wear a jacket or a jacket and tie.

Mealtimes
Unless otherwise noted, the restaurants listed in this guide are open daily for lunch and dinner. Lunch is typically served 11:30–2:30, and dinner service in most restaurants begins at 5:30 and ends at 10.

Prices
Meals still cost somewhat less in San Diego than in other major metropolitan areas. However, greatly increasing real estate prices and rents are reflected by more expensive entrées, especially in choice districts like La Jolla, the Gaslamp Quarter, and Little Italy. Some locals take advantage of the city's traditionally large portions by splitting any course they like, from appetizer to dessert. Most restaurants tolerate this, while several charge a few dollars extra for a shared plate. Choosing restaurants in less-expensive neighborhoods is one way to economize, and without question, diners can find reasonably priced meals along the Convoy Street Asian restaurant row, in Ocean Beach, and in other neighborhoods away from downtown. Even in the Gaslamp district, outposts of national chains (i.e., TGI Friday's) offer relatively affordable menus, although these do not feature the San Diego cuisine that the town's better chefs are currently inventing. As a rule, Mexican restaurants offer extremely good value, and in most cases will fill you up. The old-line pizza and spaghetti houses, such as the Filippi's chain, perform a similar service, although they are not the culinary equals of the new wave of Italian restaurants. These are operated by entrepreneurs who have come to San Diego as international businesspeople rather than immigrants.

WHAT IT COSTS				
$$$$	**$$$**	**$$**	**$**	**¢**
AT DINNER over $30	$23–$30	$16–$22	$10–$15	under $10

Prices are for a main course at dinner, excluding 7.75% tax.

Some restaurants listed are marked with a price range ($$–$$$, for example). This indicates one of two things: either the average cost straddles two categories, or if you order strategically, you can get out for less than most diners spend.

Reservations
Reservations are always a good idea; we mention them only when they're essential or not accepted. Book as far ahead as you can, and reconfirm as soon as you arrive. (Large parties should always call ahead to check the reservations policy.)

Smoking
Smoking is banned in restaurants but some permit cigarette smoking on their terraces.

Specialties
Because of its multiethnic population, you can find cuisine from nearly every part of the world in San Diego. A local specialty is the fish taco, filled with any sort of fish the restaurant chooses. These are sold at the chain restaurant Rubio's as well as at beach-side taco stands and in a few restaurants. During the local spiny lobster season, which runs roughly from late Oc-

tober to early March, restaurants serve these tasty beasts simply grilled, or lightly fried Baja California-style, or elaborately sauced and presented in the shell in good—and not so good—interpretations of lobster Thermidor. In addition to Mexican fare, San Diego has a couple of Hong Kong–style restaurants that specialize in this luxurious style of Chinese cooking. Both Emerald Chinese Seafood and Jasmine are on Convoy Street in the heavily commercial Kearny Mesa neighborhood, and the menus at both balance reasonably priced, generally delicious dishes with fresh-from-the-tank seafood that is priced according to the market and can be quite extravagant (i.e., a giant Australian king crab for $200). Beyond these, the city's better chefs are busy building a local cuisine, and the way to sample it is to seek out locally-owned, stand-alone establishments, such as Region, Marine Room, George's at the Cove, and Star of the Sea.

Tipping Most locals tip a standard 15% to 18%. But beware: many restaurants note on the menu that they automatically add an 18% tip to the check for parties sized six or more. Guests who don't pay attention when signing the credit card slip often add a standard tip themselves, and realize too late that they inadvertently and wildly over-tipped. A diner who feels the service was inadequate can decline to tip, and can decline the automatic tip added to checks for large parties.

Wine, Beer & Spirits Alcohol may be served between the hours of 6 AM and 2 AM. The legal age to buy alcoholic beverages in California is 21. Alcoholic beverages can be purchased in liquor stores, supermarkets, and virtually all convenience stores. As one of the wine capitals of the world, California produces an extraordinary selection of fine vintages in all price categories. San Diego restaurants generally present well-selected, reasonably priced lists, and a few attract national attention with their collections. Servers can often— but by no means always—assist in selecting a good accompaniment to dinner. In general, Asian and Mexican restaurants are weak in the wine category, but even here there are some shining stars. Note that several Mexican restaurants offer 100 or more kinds of tequila, many of them intriguingly flavored, and sometimes rather pricey. At the Gaslamp Quarter's Latin Room, chase a of shot of suave Herradura tequila with a small glass of house brewed "sangrita," a sweet-hot blend of juices and flavorings, including chiles.

Sunday. ⊠ *120 Orange Ave., Coronado* ☎ *619/435–1822* ⊟ *AE, D, DC, MC, V* ⊗ *No lunch.*

Seafood

$$$–$$$$ ✕ **Azzura Point.** Decorated in a romantic, 1930s style, Azzura Point is ideal for a leisurely and memorable meal. The view up San Diego Bay to the Coronado Bridge and the downtown skyline is unbeatable. Expect thoroughly contemporary preparations of first-class seasonal produce, such as sautéed foie gras with braised pineapple, pan-roasted ahi tuna with ginger-infused rice, and herb-crusted veal chop with polenta fritters. The herbs often come from the restaurant's extensive garden. Several choice, artisan cheeses are an alternative to the deftly executed desserts, and the wine list is written and served with particular skill.

✉ *Loews Coronado Bay Resort, 4000 Coronado Bay Rd., Coronado* ☎ *619/424–4477* ▭ *AE, DC, MC, V* ✆ *Closed Mon. No lunch.*

$$$–$$$$ ✕ **Prince of Wales.** The 1930s live on in the Hotel Del Coronado's restored
Fodor'sChoice   Prince of Wales, which affords sweeping ocean views from an elegant in-
★   door room and a breezy terrace. The inventive cooking includes such cre-
ations as a "Napoleon" of Hudson Valley foie gras with Port wine-fig
mousse, a pan-crisped filet of Hawaiian red snapper with cauliflower mousse,
and roasted duck breast with Port-braised short ribs and a toothsome "hash"
of root vegetables. After all this, the "trilogy" of a molten-centered cake,
a mousse, and a soup of white chocolate and walnuts concludes the af-
fair convincingly. ✉ *Hotel Del Coronado, 1500 Orange Ave., Coronado*
☎ *619/435–6611* ▭ *AE, D, DC, MC, V* ✆ *No lunch.*

$–$$$$ ✕ **Brigantine.** This home-grown chain takes a creative approach with
seafood, and sometimes dares itself to be more imaginative than neces-
sary. Swordfish, prime rib, and twin lobster tails are popular. There's
an outside lounge area for drinks. The young and old are catered to with
a kids' menu and early-bird suppers. ✉ *1333 Orange Ave., Coronado*
☎ *619/435–4166* ▭ *AE, DC, MC, V* ✆ *No lunch weekends.*

¢–$$$$ ✕ **Baja Lobster.** To experience something akin to dining in Puerto Nuevo,
Fodor'sChoice   Baja California—the famed lobstering village 20 mi south of the bor-
★   der—head to Baja Lobster. Its new location on Broadway, easily reached
from I–5, is more comfortable than their former pad, and offers full bar
service. Local lobsters are split and lightly fried, served with family-style
portions of fresh flour tortillas, creamy beans crammed with flavor, and
well-seasoned rice. While lobsters are the big catch, steak and chicken
options are on the menu, too. A pair of high-quality shrimp tacos costs
just $5.95. Note that a similarly named chain, Rockin' Baja Lobster, is
not related to Baja Lobster. ✉ *1060 Broadway, Chula Vista* ☎ *619/425–
2512* ▭ *MC, V.*

Downtown

American

¢–$$ ✕ **Hard Rock Cafe.** If you've been to one Hard Rock, you've been to them
all, but there's no denying that the mix of rock and roll memorabilia,
ear-splitting music, vivacious young staff, and generally satisfying, all-
American fare can be fun. A juicy, half-pound burger or high-rising, bacon-
rich chicken club will curb your appetite for a while. Best of all perhaps
are the "famous" grilled beef fajitas served with tortillas that let you
roll your own. As over-the-top as it may sound, a thick malted milk shake
goes well with any of these gut-busters. The bar hops at night. ✉ *801
4th Ave., Gaslamp Quarter* ☎ *619/615–7625* ▭ *AE, DC, MC, V.*

¢   ✕ **Ghirardelli Soda Fountain & Chocolate Shop.** This outpost of San Francisco's famed Ghirardelli chocolatier specializes in ice cream, served in
every size and form from a single scoop in a freshly baked waffle cone,
to elaborate sundaes and banana splits. Ambitious types can attempt
the Earthquake, a well of eight different ice creams, eight toppings, ba-
nanas, nuts, embarrassing quantities of whipped cream, and heaps of
glistening red cherries. This is the perfect "time out" place for families
with children, but in truth, adults usually are in the majority. ✉ *643
5th Ave., Gaslamp Quarter* ☎ *619/234–2449* ▭ *AE, MC, V.*

Brazilian

$$–$$$$ ✕ **Rei do Gado.** Bearing skewers of 14 different kinds of grilled meat, servers at this classic "churascarria" will encourage you to truly eat all you can. Choices include filet mignon, skirt steak, *linguica* sausage (a popular Portuguese sausage), pork loin, lamb leg, and even chicken hearts. The all-inclusive option extends to the salad, side dish, and dessert buffets and costs $29.95 weeknights, $34.95 on weekends and holidays. ⊠ *939 4th Ave., Gaslamp Quarter* ☎ *619/702–8464* ▤ *AE, DC, MC, V.*

Contemporary

$$–$$$ ✕ **Dobson's Bar & Restaurant.** As innovative today as when it opened in 1983, this "power" dining spot for downtown movers and shakers, socialites, and operagoers has never changed the recipe for its famous mussel bisque, baked in a deep crock covered with tender pastry. Owner Paul Dobson generally keeps a close eye on tables in both the downstairs room, where the bar frequently is packed, and in the upstairs mezzanine, which has a choice view of all the action. Specialties include chicken liver mousse; a salad of Stilton, pears, and baby spinach; pepper-crusted venison loin; and pan-roasted Chilean sea bass. ⊠ *956 Broadway Circle, Downtown* ☎ *619/231–6771* ☉ *Closed Sun. No lunch Sat.*

$$–$$$ ✕ **Rice.** Hotel W hit San Diego like a storm in 2003, and its trio of bars (including the roof-top Beach, with a sandy floor) became the top destinations for on-the-town singles. Amidst all the nightlife, the Rice dining room is a calm haven for serious contemporary dining, much of it in the "fusion" style that marries two or more cuisines. The menu changes, but expect satisfying appetizers such as sizzling vegetable tempura and lacquered spare ribs, and clever entrées like miso-glazed swordfish and honey-spice roasted chicken. Servers and decor are hip as the crowd. ⊠ *421 West B St., Downtown* ☎ *619/231–8220* ▤ *AE, D, MC, V.*

$–$$ ✕ **Cafe 828.** Off bustling 5th Avenue by one block, but still very much in the heart of the Gaslamp Quarter, this attractive dining room is a haven of quiet charm. Chef and proprietor Jay Greenfield's nightly specials, such as salmon in red wine sauce, are often the best choices. The standing menu pleases with colorful salads, slowly brewed soups, ravioli of the day, quality steaks, and seafood given interesting preparations. There's even a couple of well-made pizzas. The elegant bar was built for one of Joan Crawford's residences, and imprints from her high-heeled shoes memorialize what must have been a good party. ⊠ *828 6th Ave., Downtown* ☎ *619/231–8282* ▤ *AE, D, MC, V* ☉ *No lunch.*

★ ¢ ✕ **Bread on Market.** The baguettes at this artisan bakery near the Petco Park baseball stadium are every bit as good as in Paris. Baguettes, focaccia, and other superior loaves are the building blocks for solid, sometimes creative sandwiches, which range from the simple goodness of Genoa salami and sweet butter, to a vegan sandwich that includes locally grown avocado. The menu extends to a daily soup, a fruit-garnished cheese plate, and an appetizing Mediterranean salad. Snackers gravitate here for fudge-textured brownies, orange-almond biscotti, and other irresistible sweets. ⊠ *730 Market St., Downtown* ☎ *619/795–2730* ▤ *MC, V* ☉ *Closed Sun. No dinner.*

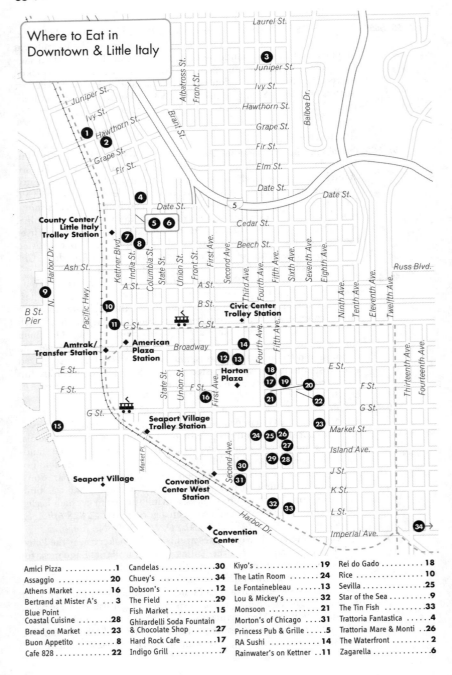

Where to Eat in Downtown & Little Italy

French

★ $$$-$$$$ ✕ **Le Fontainebleau.** The Westgate Hotel looks like an ordinary, 1960s mid-rise from outside, but inside is a wealth of exquisite French antiques in breathtaking public rooms. Le Fontainebleau, on the second floor, is worthy of the famous chateau for which it is named. Normandy-born chef Fabrice Hardel writes seasonal menus, but usually offers classics like French pepper steak (dramatically flambeed at table) and lobster Thermidor. Pairing the multicourse tasting menu with specially selected wines costs in excess of $100 per person, a price that seems not unreasonable when read to the accompaniment of the harp or piano music that is a Le Fontainebleau staple. ⊠ *1055 2nd Ave., Downtown* ☎ *619/557-3655* ⚐ *Jacket required* ☰ *AE, D, DC, MC, V.*

★ $$-$$$$ ✕ **Bertrand at Mister A's.** Restaurateur Bertrand Hug's sumptuous 12th-floor dining room has vanilla walls, contemporary paintings, and a view that stretches from the mountains to Mexico and San Diego Bay. You can watch the aerial ballet of jets descending upon nearby Lindbergh Field. Ideal for a special occasion, Bertrand at Mister A's serves luxurious seasonal dishes such sautéed foie gras with caramelized fruit and Dover sole in lemon butter. The dessert list encompasses a galaxy of sweets every bit as memorable as the view. ⊠ *2550 5th Ave., Middletown* ☎ *619/239-1377* ⚑ *Reservations essential* ⚐ *Jacket required* ☰ *AE, DC, MC, V* ☉ *No lunch weekends.*

Greek

$$-$$$ ✕ **Athens Market.** This cheerful eatery with an outdoor patio bustles with office workers and members of San Diego's small but active Greek community. Appetizers such as *taramasalata* (fish roe dip), hummus, and stuffed grape leaves are particularly tasty. Entrées include *arni psito* (roast leg of lamb), a very convincing rendition of moussaka, and the house Greek pasta, with garlic, onion, and cheese. The *galctobouriko* (a layering of crisp phyllo pastry, eggy custard, and clove-scented syrup) makes an excellent dessert. San Diego Chargers owner Alex Spanos has been a fan of Athens Market for years. ⊠ *109 W. F St., Downtown* ☎ *619/234-1955* ☰ *AE, D, DC, MC, V* ☉ *No lunch weekends.*

Indian

★ $-$$ ✕ **Monsoon.** An exceptionally attractive restaurant, Monsoon debuted in January 2004 with a room-centering waterfall that splashes like a cloudburst from a bower of hanging plants. Folding doors allow some tables to share the outdoor atmosphere of the terrace, but at a distance from the sidewalk. The menu offers many dishes not easily found at local Indian eateries, including a sweetly spiced mango soup, and "balti"-style pan-sautéed lamb. The dozens of curries and similar dishes are spiced to taste. ⊠ *729-733 4th Ave., Gaslamp Quarter* ☎ *619/234-5555* ☰ *AE, MC, V.*

Irish

$-$$ ✕ **The Field.** A family-run pub decorated with artifacts from an Irish farm, the Field has character to spare. The small sidewalk terrace is suitable for sipping a Guinness or Bass, but diners prefer the bric-a-brac–adorned, dark-wood walls indoors for solid meals of Irish stew, corned beef and cabbage, or, best of all, a *boxty*. Boxties are lacy but substantial potato pancakes, made to order and served crisp and hot with such fillings as sage-flavored chicken or Irish bacon and cheese. As the evening wears on, the crowd grows younger, livelier, louder, and sometimes rowdier. A traditional Irish breakfast is served Saturday and Sunday. ⊠ *544 5th Ave., Gaslamp Quarter* ☎ *619/232–9840* ▱ *MC, V.*

Italian

$$–$$$$ ✕ **Trattoria Mare & Monti.** The sea and mountains that contribute their special products to Italian cuisine are paid tribute in the name of this comfortable restaurant. The menu attempts to differentiate itself from those of other restaurants in the neighborhood, and is notable for a "Martini" of shellfish and tart limoncello liqueur, a stylish lobster salad, and pappardelle pasta in a red wine-rich lamb sauce. On the more affordable side, the kitchen turns out excellent pizzas baked in a wood-fired oven. Choose between a table on the narrow sidewalk terrace or in the spacious dining room. ⊠ *644 5th Ave., Gaslamp Quarter* ☎ *619/235–8144* ▱ *AE, DC, MC, V.*

¢–$ ✕ **Assaggio.** Assaggio coaxes diners away from the pricier 5th Avenue drag with old-world flavors at unbeatable prices. The small sidewalk terrace usually fills before the well-lighted dining room, but both are pleasant settings in which to enjoy a savory soup of homemade maltagliati pasta and cannellini beans, a caprese salad of buffalo mozzarella and tomatoes, or a richly stuffed lasagna. The oven is the source of both excellent, thinly crusted pizzas, and delicious cakes and cookies. ⊠ *835 4th Ave., Gaslamp Quarter* ☎ *619/234–6538* ▱ *MC, V.*

Japanese

$–$$$ ✕ **Kiyo's.** On quiet F Street, this restaurant and sushi bar seems an island of tranquillity buffered from the business of 5th Avenue. The menu is comprehensive, and the sushi chefs are renowned for their creativity. Sushi rolls delight or challenge: the "caterpillar" roll pairs local avocado with freshwater eel. Hot meals include gyoza dumplings, ginger-drenched *shoga* beef, a tasty pork *tonkatsu* cutlet, excellent shrimp tempura, or, perhaps, *una ju*, which is broiled eel basted with a sweet sauce. ⊠ *531 F St., Gaslamp Quarter* ☎ *619/238–1726* ▱ *AE, MC, V.*

¢–$$ ✕ **RA Sushi Bar Restaurant.** Servers in semi-sensational T-shirts (mottos include "Practice Safe Sushi") challenge a young clientele to strive for "attitude" in this small, intimate space carved out of a former department store. Two ultrahip bars—one for cocktails, one for sushi—fuel the popularity, bolstered by a dining room menu from which you can make a meal out of the many appetizers, such as coconut shrimp tempura and scallops in spicy "dynamite" sauce. Otherwise, choose sushi combination plates, spare ribs in smoked plum sauce, savory meat and seafood teriyaki specialties, and hearty noodle dishes. ⊠ *1014 5th Ave., entrance on Broadway, Downtown* ☎ *619/321–0021* ▱ *AE, DC, MC, V.*

Mexican

$$$–$$$$ ✕ **Candelas.** The scents and flavors of imaginative Mexican cuisine permeate this handsome, romantic little hideaway in the shadow of San Diego's tallest residential towers. Candles glow everywhere around the small, comfortable dining room and the bar. There isn't a burrito or taco in sight. Fine openers such as cream of black bean and beer soup, and salad of watercress with bacon and pistachios warm diners up for local lobster stuffed with mushrooms, jalapeño peppers, and aged tequila; or tequila-flamed jumbo prawns over creamy, seasoned goat cheese. The new, adjacent bar pours many elegant tequilas. ⊠ *416 3rd Ave., Gaslamp Quarter* ☎ *619/702–4455* ⊟ *MC, V* ☉ *Closed Sun. No lunch weekends.*

★ **$$–$$$** ✕ **The Latin Room.** A branch of Tijuana's stylish Cien Anos brings a hip salsa beat to the Gaslamp Quarter. As the night wears on, guests take to the dance floor and concentrate more on cocktails than dinner. The sound bounces off the brick walls, but before 9 PM you can count on a fairly quiet environment in which to enjoy expertly prepared appetizers like quesadillas *de cuitlacoche,* which wrap fragrant "corn fungus" mushrooms inside tender corn tortillas, and such entrées such as giant prawns in a tart, puckery tamarind sauce. Don't look for tacos or burritos, since the menu emphasizes sophisticated cuisine. ⊠ *560 4th Ave., Gaslamp Quarter* ☎ *619/237–7800* ⊟ *AE, D, MC, V* ☉ *No lunch.*

¢–$ ✕ **Chuey's Numero Uno.** You'll never come up one taco shy of a combination plate at this vintage-1956 eatery in a blue-collar neighborhood near downtown. Cops love it, Navy brass love it, guys who wear hard hats love it—in fact, just about everyone is enamored of the huge, Quonset hut setting, the cheerful servers, and the keep-you-going-all day meals. The only disappointment: Chuey's closes at 6 PM, so fill up on steak ranchero, *chile verde* (pork stewed in a very spicy green sauce) and chicken enchiladas before this hour, or return in the morning for huevos rancheros and other zesty egg dishes. ⊠ *1894 Main St., Barrio Logan* ☎ *619/234–6937* ⊟ *MC, V* ☉ *No dinner.*

Seafood

$$$–$$$$ ✕ **Star of the Sea.** The flagship of the Anthony's chain of seafood restaurants ensconces its patrons in its most formal dining room, making it
Fodor'sChoice an all-around favorite for location, cuisine, and design (although dress
★ is quite casual). The menu changes seasonally; you may find listings for exceptional oysters on the half shell, white-corn agnolotti pasta with shaved truffles, whole roasted snapper with Manila clams and marinated squid, and grilled escolar with a racy "tapenade" of sun-dried tomatoes. The baked-to-order soufflés are puffy, fragrant, and lovely on the palate. The outdoor patio takes full advantage of the choice waterfront location. ⊠ *1360 N. Harbor Dr., Downtown* ☎ *619/232–7408* ⊟ *AE, D, DC, MC, V* ☉ *No lunch.*

$$–$$$$ ✕ **Blue Point Coastal Cuisine.** If there's a convention in town, Blue Point gets jammed with diverse diners who share a taste for sophisticated seafood. The menu swims with international accents, so that the spicy calamari appetizer is served with Thai red chili sauce, and a ginger-soy butter sauce suavely finishes grilled ahi. Among choices from the land, Moroccan-spiced couscous cakes add a certain zing to grilled rack of lamb, and green peppercorn sauce livens a prime New York strip. The wine list is serious, and the service efficient and friendly. Allow room for desserts like the "harlequin" chocolate souffle. The airy dining room has gleaming woodwork and its two walls of windows look onto 5th Avenue and Market Street, probably the hottest corner in San Diego and prime for people-watching. ⊠ *565 5th Ave., Gaslamp Quarter* ☎ *619/233–6623* ⊟ *AE, D, DC, MC, V* ☉ *No lunch.*

$$-$$$$ ✕ **Fish Market.** Fresh mesquite-grilled fish is the specialty at this informal restaurant. There's also an excellent little sushi bar and good steamed clams and mussels. The view is stunning: enormous plate-glass windows look directly out onto the harbor. A more formal restaurant upstairs, the Top of the Market ($$$-$$$$), is expensive but worth the splurge, and is the place to find such rarities as true Dover sole, which the kitchen delicately browns in butter and finishes with a lemon-caper sauce. The Dungeness crab cocktail is well worth the cost. ⊠ *750 N. Harbor Dr., Downtown* ☎ *619/232–3474 Fish Market, 619/234–4867 Top of the Market* ⌣ *Reservations not accepted* ⊟ *AE, D, DC, MC, V.*

➤ ★ **¢-$** ✕ **The Tin Fish.** On the rare rainy day, the staff takes it easy at this eatery less than 100 yards from the Petco Park baseball stadium (its 100-odd seats are all outdoors). Musicians entertain some evenings, making this a lively spot for dinners of grilled and fried fish and shellfish, as well as Mexican-style seafood burritos and tacos. The quality here routinely surpasses that at grander establishments. The bread used for sandwiches stuffed with fried oysters and the like is baked fresh at the restaurant. For kids (or unadventurous grown-ups) there's an inexpensive peanut butter and jelly sandwich. ⊠ *170 6th Ave., Gaslamp Quarter* ☎ *619/ 238–8100* ⌣ *Reservations not accepted* ⊟ *MC, V.*

Spanish

$$-$$$ ✕ **Sevilla.** Increasingly a nightclub, Sevilla still offers a couple of experiences in one location. Lines form on weekend nights, when youthful throngs wait to crowd the ground-floor bar for drinks, tapas, and professional flamenco dancing. Others head to the downstairs club for classics from the Spanish kitchen and live music. There isn't a quiet corner to be found. The kitchen does a respectable job with the paella; try the paella Valenciana with shellfish, sausage, and chicken. It also makes highly flavorful baked rabbit and roasted pork tenderloin. Dinner shows take place Friday through Sunday, when a three-course meal is priced at $15.95. ⊠ *555 4th Ave., Gaslamp Quarter* ☎ *619/233–5979* ⊟ *AE, MC, V* ☉ *No lunch.*

Steak Houses

★ **$$$-$$$$** ✕ **Rainwater's on Kettner.** San Diego's premier homegrown steak house also ranks as the longest running of the pack, not least because it has the luxurious look and mood of an old-fashioned Eastern men's club. Settle back into the exceptionally deep banquettes and start with Rainwater's signature black bean soup with Madeira. Continue with the tender, expertly roasted prime rib. The menu branches out to encompass superb calves' liver with onions and bacon, broiled free-range chicken, fresh seafood, and amazingly succulent pork chops, all served in vast portions with plenty of hot-from-the-oven cornsticks on the side. The well-chosen wine list has pricey but superior selections. ⊠ *1202 Kettner Blvd., Downtown* ☎ *619/233–5757* ⊟ *AE, D, MC, V* ☉ *No lunch weekends.*

★ **$$-$$$$** ✕ **Morton's of Chicago.** Housed in the soaring Harbor Club towers near both the San Diego Convention Center and the Gaslamp Quarter, Morton's often teems with conventioneers out for a night on the town. Servers present the menu by wheeling up a cart laden with crimson prime steaks, behemoth veal and lamb chops, thick cuts of swordfish, and huge Maine lobsters that may wave their claws in alarm when they hear the prices (based on the market, but always astronomical) quoted. Expect a treat, since this restaurant knows how to put on a superb spread that takes the concept of indulgence to new heights. ⊠ *The Harbor Club, 285 J St., Downtown* ☎ *619/696–3369* ☐ *AE, D, MC, V* ☉ *No lunch.*

$–$$$$ ✕ **Lou & Mickey's.** The nearest restaurant to the San Diego Convention Center, this handsome, 1940s-style establishment (it opened in 2002) lures with thick steaks and chops, equally meaty seafood cuts such as the unusual T-bone of Alaskan halibut, richly sauced pastas, and chicken dishes of surprising flavor and sophistication. Be extravagant by opening with top-quality oysters and moving on to the $45 per-serving Alaskan king crab legs. Budgets can be met by investing in a filling and rather tasty garlic meat loaf "Po' Boy" sandwich, which costs just $8.95. Either way, plan on finishing with an impressive wedge of Key lime pie. ⊠ *224 5th Ave., Gaslamp Quarter* ☎ *619/237–4900* ☐ *AE, DC, MC, V* ☉ *No lunch.*

Little Italy

American

¢ ✕ **The Waterfront.** Not a destination for children, this historic bar and eatery, which opened in the 1930s and claims to be San Diego's oldest watering hole, is an attraction for any one in search of genuine atmosphere. The bar has supported the elbows of tuna fishermen and aviation workers in other eras, and now attracts lawyers, construction workers, and other souls hungry for a $5.25 bowl of really good chili, burgers that can't be beat, smoking-hot onion rings and french fries, and other great-tasting grub, including fish tacos. The Waterfront serves from early morning until midnight or later. ⊠ *2044 Kettner Blvd., Little Italy* ☎ *619/232–9656* ☐ *MC, V.*

British

$ ✕ **Princess Pub & Grille.** Packed to the rafters during any televised British football (soccer) championship, this cheerful neighborhood place is unofficial headquarters for transplanted Brits, Australians, and New Zealanders—but no matter where you're from, you can hoist a mug in good company. The selection of imported beers and ales, most of them from Merrie Olde, is quite impressive, and the menu complements them well with such offerings as sausage rolls, fish-and-chips, spicy chicken curry, and an elaborate Cheshire mixed grill of meats, sausage, egg, and mushrooms. The oversize buffalo burgers have a loyal following. The patrons seem equally fond of conversation and games of darts. ⊠ *1665 India St., Little Italy* ☎ *619/702–3021* ☐ *MC, V.*

Italian

★ $–$$$ ✕ **Buon Appetito.** Little Italy is booming again, and one charming arrival is Buon Appetito, which serves old-world–style cooking in a casual but decidedly sophisticated environment. The young Italian waiters' good humor makes the experience fun. Choose a table on the sidewalk, where the breeze blows brisk or balmy from San Diego Bay, or in an indoor room jammed with art and fellow diners. Baked eggplant all' Amalfitana is a dream of a dish, and in San Diego, tomato sauce doesn't get better than this. Consider also veal with tuna sauce, a hot chicken liver salad, fusilli pasta in savory duck ragu, and hearty seafood *cioppino.* ⊠ *1609 India St., Little Italy* ☎ *619/238–9880* ▤ *MC, V.*

$–$$ ✕ **Zagarella.** Take a seat in the small dining room or in the vast courtyard and relax to recorded opera music while studying a menu that suggests such appetizers as sautéed herbed shrimp on a bed of shoestring potatoes, or a plate of tender roasted peppers crowned with a whole school of anchovies. The Italian menu avoids clichés in favor of specialties like warm duck salad accented with pine nuts and golden raisins, baked eggplant timbale, ravioli tossed with radicchio braised in cream, and veal scallopini with artichokes and lemon sauce. Always study the daily specials board. ⊠ *1655 India St., Little Italy* ☎ *619/236–8764* ▤ *MC, V.*

$ ✕ **Trattoria Fantastica.** The shady, very private courtyard at the rear of this laid-back establishment is no secret, so reserve ahead if you want to score a table. Sicilian flavors abound on the menu, which is highlighted by such offerings as a salad of tomatoes, red onions, olive oil, and oregano; and the pasta Palermitana, rigatoni with spicy sausage, olives, capers, and marinara sauce. Many pastas come with cargoes of fresh seafood, and the pizzas baked in the wood-burning oven are robust and beautifully seasoned. Keep this in mind as a snack break for beautiful pastries, remarkable "gelato" ice creams, and freshly brewed Italian coffees. ⊠ *1735 India St., Little Italy* ☎ *619/234–1735* ▤ *AE, DC, MC, V.*

¢ ✕ **Amici Pizza & Deli.** This tiny restaurant is perfect for a quick, inexpensive lunch or early supper (served until 8 PM). Prices don't rise above $8 (the price of spaghetti with sausage) except in the case of the pizza pies. A large but inexpensive, bubbling-hot slice is as happy a lunch as can be found in Little Italy, especially when eaten on the terrace. Eggplant parmigiana, Philly cheese steak, and sausage-and-peppers "panini" sandwiches are equally convincing, but keep in mind that the hot meatball submarines may be the town's best. Friday's pasta special is linguini with red clam sauce. ⊠ *2034 Kettner Blvd., Little Italy* ☎ *619/239–4210* ▤ *No credit cards* ◷ *Closed weekends.*

Southwestern

$$–$$$ ✕ **Indigo Grill.** Chef–partner Deborah Scott uses inspirations from Mexico to Alaska to infuse her contemporary Southwestern cuisine. Indigo Grill has both a stone interior and a broad terrace whose cool breezes do nothing to moderate the chiles that heat such one-of-a-kind offerings as stacked beet salad, pecan-crusted trout, salmon roasted on a well-seasoned wooden plank, and beautifully flavored venison chops. Creative desserts are often so generous in size that they can satisfy two with ease. The crowd of young urban professionals enjoy the happening scene and cuisine in equal parts. ⊠ *1536 India St., Little Italy* ☎ *619/234–6802* ▤ *AE, D, DC, MC, V* ◷ *No lunch weekends.*

Uptown

American

★ **¢–$$** ✕ **Hob Nob Hill.** That Hob Nob never seems to change suits San Diego just fine. This is the type of place where regulars arrive on the same day of the week at the same time and order the same meal they've been ordering for 20 years. With its dark-wood booths and patterned carpets, Hob Nob Hill seems suspended in the 1950s, but you don't need to be a nostalgia buff to appreciate the bargain-price American home cooking—dishes such as oat-raisin French toast, fried chicken, and corned beef like your mother never really made. The crowds line up morning, noon, and night. Reservations are suggested for Sunday breakfast. ⊠ 2271 1st Ave., Middletown ☏ 619/239–8176 ⊟ AE, D, MC, V.

American–Casual

$–$$$ ✕ **Hash House A Go Go.** Expect to wait an hour for weekend breakfast at this trendy Hillcrest eatery, whose walls display photos of farm machinery and other icons of middle America, but whose menu takes an up-to-the-minute look at national favorites. At breakfast, huge platters carpeted with fluffy pancakes sail out of the kitchen and return empty in a matter of moments, while at noon, customers favor the overflowing chicken potpies crowned with flaky pastry. The parade of old-fashioned good eats continues at dinner with hearty meat and seafood dishes, characterized by a grand combination of sage-flavored fried chicken, bacon-flavored waffle, and hot maple syrup. ⊠ 3628 5th Ave., Hillcrest ☏ 619/298–4646 ⊟ MC, V.

¢–$ ✕ **Corvette Diner Bar & Grill.** The absolute San Diego County favorite for children's parties and other family occasions, Corvette Diner showcases a real Corvette (changed every two or three months) in a kitschy, 1950s-style dining room dominated by vintage movie posters and singing servers. The menu has what you'd expect—macaroni and cheddar, plump burgers, piled-high deli sandwiches, spaghetti and meatballs, greasy chile-cheese fries, and thick milk shakes. The daily "Blue Plate Specials" are well-priced classics like grilled pork chops and "picnic basket" fried chicken. ⊠ 3946 5th Ave., Hillcrest ☏ 619/542–1001 ⊟ AE, D, MC, V.

Contemporary

$$–$$$$ ✕ **Laurel.** Laurel is a premier dinner address, especially among those attending a performance at the Old Globe Theatre in Balboa Park. Polished service, a smart, contemporary design, and a notable wine list set the stage for an imaginative, expertly prepared seasonal menu that takes its inspiration from Mediterranean cuisine. Look for appetizers such as Pacific oysters on the half-shell with red wine "mignonette" sauce, and warm tart of Roquefort cheese and caramelized onions. Among the main courses, reliable choices include the chicken roasted in a clay pot, crisp duck confit, and pan-seared sea scallops. Leave time for a superb artisan cheese before curtain call. ⊠ 505 Laurel St., Middletown ☏ 619/239–2222 ⊟ AE, D, DC, MC, V ⊘ No lunch.

$–$$$ ✕ **The Prado.** This beautiful restaurant in the House of Hospitality on Balboa Park's museum row brings an inventive, contemporary menu to an area where picnic lunches are the only other option. The striking interior has elegantly painted ceilings and elaborate glass sculptures, and the bar is a fashionable pre- and post-theater destination for such light nibbles as crab cakes and steamed Manila clams. In the dining room, well-trained servers offer dishes that range from a dressy "farmer's

Where to Eat
in San Diego

KEARNY
MESA

Clairemont   Mesa   Blvd.

Balboa Ave.

Ave.

Aero Dr.

MISSION
VALLEY

San Diego R.

ashion
alley
enter

HILLCREST   Madison Ave.

Adams Ave.

El Cajon Blvd.

University   Ave.

Robinson

Balboa Park

**See Where to Eat
in Downtown &
Little Italy Map**

Broadway

Market St.

Imperial Ave.

San Diego-
Coronado Bay
Bridge

National   Ave.

NATIONAL
CITY

San Diego Bay

Silver Strand Blvd.

salad" to saffron linguine with shellfish of the day, marinated baby lamb rack, and steamed sea bass with mango-jalapeño salsa. ✉ *1549 El Prado, Balboa Park* ☎ *619/557–9441* ▭ *AE, D, MC, V.*

$–$$$ ✕ **Terra.** Catching the wave of special diets, this restaurant offers menus that have been a hit with diabetics and followers of the Atkins Diet. The grilled meats and seafood with light but savory, vegetable-based sauces are very good indeed. On the seasonal standing menu, chef–proprietor Jeff Rossman offers options like sage-roasted chicken with pumpkin purée and forest mushroom risotto, and grilled filet mignon in a racy, Argentine-style chimichurri sauce flavored with more than one dozen herbs. Filling the terrace in summer are the weekly barbecues accompanied by live jazz. ✉ *3900 Vermont St., Hillcrest* ☎ *619/293–7088* ▭ *AE, D, MC, V* ⊘ *No lunch weekends.*

$–$$ ✕ **Region.** Rich in talented owner–chefs who use the finest local produce **Fodor's**Choice to create traditional recipes, Region is one of the most intriguing restau-★ rants to open in San Diego recently (late 2003). The kitchen's approach nears perfection with dishes like veal osso buco, roast pork with sweet potatoes, and pan-gilded skate (a fish rarely encountered on local menus) that flakes at the touch of a fork. The menu changes daily, but count on fine sweets like cooked-to-order doughnuts with olive oil gelato. The dining room is somewhat spare, but the food and prices make this less important than it would be at other top establishments. A chalkboard is illustrated daily to highlight the special fruits and vegetables that evening. Reservations are strongly advised. ✉ *3671 5th Ave., Hillcrest* ☎ *619/ 299–6499* ▭ *AE, D, DC, MC, V* ⊘ *No lunch. No dinner Sun. and Mon.*

Eclectic

$$–$$$ ✕ **Parallel 33.** True to its name, Parallel 33 traces this imaginary line around the globe, serving dishes based on American, Moroccan, Middle Eastern, Chinese, and Japanese cuisines. Chef–proprietor Amiko Gubbins has a sure handle on everything she cooks. Her Moroccan-style chicken-and-egg pie hides a deliciously savory filling inside a flaky, phyllo crust, and the spiced vegetarian samosas are joined by contrasting, excitingly flavorful chutneys. Among other favorites are pan-seared, Goa-style shrimp curry, Moroccan lamb tajine, and grilled duck breast with sweet potato gnocchi. The lands of the 33rd parallel are represented with fascinating artworks built especially for the restaurant. ✉ *741 W. Washington St., Mission Hills* ☎ *619/260–0033* ▭ *AE, D, MC, V* ⊘ *Closed Sun. No lunch.*

Indian

★ $–$$ ✕ **Bombay Exotic Cuisine of India.** Notable for its elegant dining room, Bombay employs a chef whose generous hand with raw and cooked vegetables gives each course a colorful freshness reminiscent of California cuisine, though the flavors definitely hail from India. Try the tandoori lettuce wrap appetizer and any of the stuffed *nan* (a delectably chewy tandoori bread). The unusually large selection of curries may be ordered with meat, chicken, fish, or tofu. The curious should try the *dizzy noo shakk,* a sweet and spicy banana curry. Try a "thali," a plate that includes an entrée, traditional sides, nan, dessert, and tea. ✉ *Hillcrest Center, 3975 5th Ave., Suite 100, Hillcrest* ☎ *619/298–3155* ▭ *AE, D, DC, MC, V.*

Italian

$–$$$ ✕ **Busalacchi's Ristorante.** This long-running hit on the fringe of Hillcrest offers a romantic, low-key dining room and a stylish, sheltered patio that overlooks busy 5th Avenue. The lengthy menu zeroes in on elegant, fully flavored Sicilian specialties—it may be the only place in San Diego offering an "insalata de cetrioli" of beets, roasted pearl onions and Gorgonzola. The pasta dishes include familiar favorites, but classically Sicilian is the rigatoni in an aromatic sausage-caper sauce; the stuffed, breaded veal *spiedini* (on skewers) also is superb. ✉ *3683 5th Ave., Hillcrest* ☎ *619/298–0119* 🖃 *AE, DC, MC, V* ☾ *No lunch weekends.*

$ ✕ **La Pizzeria Arrivederci.** The wood-burning oven roars on what pass for cold nights in San Diego, sending the shadows of dancing flames across the cozy dining room. Out come pizzas topped with forest mushrooms and smoky Scamorza cheese, or perhaps "alla Messicana," a Mexican-style pie whose topping includes pork sausage, cilantro, and crushed red peppers. The list of imaginative pizzas is long (yes, you can get a pepperoni pizza, too), but there are also expertly made pastas such as penne in creamy vodka sauce with smoked salmon, and penne in pungent "puttanesca" sauce. Young waiters from Italy treat guests well. ✉ *3789 4th Ave., Hillcrest* ☎ *619/542–0293* 🖃 *MC, V* ☾ *No lunch weekends.*

Thai

★ ¢–$$ ✕ **Celadon Fine Thai Cuisine.** Talk to young proprietor Alex Thao if you want to try some of the specialties not listed on the menu, like the spicy, stir-fried cashew appetizer, or the tart, invigorating stir-fry of shredded dried beef and citrus sauce. These dishes are superb, but the everyday menu is good enough to keep the small, well-furnished dining room jumping, even on Monday nights. Start with "Celadon squares," small toasts covered with a paste of shrimp and pork, and move along to refreshing, if spicy, papaya salad, the excellent *tom kha* soup, and such entrées asdeep-fried whole striped bass with green mangoes. ✉ *540 University Ave., Hillcrest* ☎ *619/297–8424* 🖃 *MC, V.*

Kearny Mesa

Argentinian

$–$$$ ✕ **Pampas Argentine Grill.** It has been said that Argentinians like to eat a lot of food slowly, and you can test the pace at Pampas, which is a few blocks east of the Convoy Street Asian restaurant row. Meats, mostly cut in hefty portions, grilled and served with zesty, herb-rich chimichurri sauce, are the main thrust of the menu, and choices include rib eye, filet mignon, and strip steaks, along with marinated boneless chicken and the seafood of the day. The spacious restaurant is gently lighted and hung with paintings that strive for the romance of the tango. Live music is offered several evenings each week. ✉ *8690 Aero Dr., Kearny Mesa* ☎ *858/278–5971* 🖃 *AE, MC, V* ☾ *Closed Mon. No lunch.*

Chinese

★ $–$$$$ ✕ **Emerald Chinese Seafood Restaurant.** The first Hong Kong–style restaurant to open in San Diego, Emerald holds pride of place among fanciers of elaborate, carefully prepared, and sometimes costly seafood dishes. Even when the vast restaurant is full to capacity with 300 diners, the noise level is moderate and conversation flows easily between bites of some of the best Chinese cuisine in the area. The shrimp, prawns, lobsters, clams, and fish reside in tanks until the moment of cooking. Simple preparations flavored with scallions, black beans, and ginger are among the best. Other recommended dishes include beef with Singapore-style satay sauce, honey-walnut shrimp, baked chicken in five spices, Peking duck served in two savory courses, and, at lunch, the dim sum. ⊠ *3709 Convoy St., Kearny Mesa* ☎ *858/565–6888* ☐ *AE, MC, V.*

¢–$$$$ ✕ **Jasmine.** This cavernous, Hong Kong–style establishment seats no fewer than 800 people; even so, there frequently are lines outside during lunchtime on Saturday and Sunday, when groups arrive en masse to enjoy fragrant soups, steaming noodles, and dim sum pastries from carts that constantly circle the room. At dinner it's a hard choice between the seafood from the wall-mounted tanks and "Peking duck two ways"—the crisp skin sandwiched in tasty buns as a first course, the meat deliciously stir-fried for a savory follow-up. A supplementary menu of "special-priced dishes" offers bargains like one-half of a roasted chicken for $7.50. ⊠ *4609 Convoy St., Kearny Mesa* ☎ *858/268–0888* ☐ *AE, MC, V.*

★ ¢–$ ✕ **Dumpling Inn.** Modest, family-style, and absolutely wonderful, this tiny establishment loads its tables with bottles of aromatic and spicy condiments for the boiled, steamed, and fried dumplings that are the house specialty. These delicately flavored, hefty mouthfuls preface a meal that may continue simply, with hearty pork and pickled cabbage soup, or elaborately, with Shanghai-style braised pork shank. Ask about daily specials, such as shredded pork in plum sauce served on a sea of crispy noodles. You may bring your own wine or beer; the house serves only tea and soft drinks. ⊠ *4619 Convoy St., #F, Kearny Mesa* ☎ *858/268–9638* ⚅ *Reservations not accepted* ☐ *MC, V* ☢ *Closed Mon.*

Korean

¢–$$$ ✕ **Buga Korean B.B.Q. Restaurant.** The cook-it-yourself fun of Korean barbecue and Japanese-style shabu shabu focuses attention on your table's built-in cooking unit, not on the modest decor. Suspended exhaust fan hoods create something of a draft when the restaurant is full of guests barbecuing sharply marinated cuts of meat and seafood. *Shabu shabu,* a multicourse meal of paper-thin meats, vegetables, and noodles, is cooked in iron pots of boiling liquid that provides a final course of tasty broth. Pleasant servers explain the cooking procedures. The restaurant is a few blocks west of the Convoy Street corridor. ⊠ *5580 Clairemont Mesa Blvd., Clairemont* ☎ *858/560–1010* ☐ *MC, V.*

Vietnamese

¢–$$ ✕ **Phuong Trang.** Widely considered the leading Vietnamese restaurant in San Diego, Phuong Trang cooks up no fewer than 248 appetizers, soups, noodle dishes, and main courses, which can make choosing a meal a bewildering process. Waiters tend to steer you toward tasty offerings like fried egg rolls, char-grilled shrimp paste wrapped around sugarcane, beef in grape leaves, and fresh spring rolls filled with pork and shrimp. Noodles topped with a grilled pork chop makes a satisfying meal. The large, relatively spare dining room gets packed to the rafters, but ser-

WHERE TO REFUEL AROUND TOWN

SAN DIEGO HAS A FEW HOME-GROWN CHAINS as well as many stand-alone eateries that will amiably fill you up without demanding too much in return.

The three locations of the Mission are in Mission Beach, North Park, and the Petco ballpark district. The latter location holds the newest Mission within a vintage-1870 building originally known as Rosario Hall. Called the Mission SoMa (short for "South of Market Street"), it fulfills its mission as a breakfast-and-lunch destination (as at all Missions, there's no service after 3 PM). The diverse menu spans from banana-blackberry pancakes to a Zen breakfast complete with tofu and brown rice, to creative black bean burritos and a smoked turkey sandwich.

There's something for everyone, a statement equally true of San Diego's enormously popular Sammy's Woodfired Pizza chain. With convenient outlets in La Jolla, Mission Valley, and the Gaslamp Quarter, Sammy's makes friends with oversize salads, a vast selection of pizzas, entrées and pastas, and the fun "messy sundae," which lives up to its name.

Filippi's Pizza Grottos (best locations are on India Street in Little Italy and in Pacific Beach) please crowds with vast platters of spaghetti and meatballs, as well as very good pizzas.

Also home-grown and from the same post-World War II era as Filippi's, Anthony's Fish Grotto enjoys considerable renown for batter-fried fish filets and shellfish, as well as chowders, char-broiled fish, and other simple, well-prepared offerings. Anthony's on the Embarcadero in downtown is built over the water and often has a line at the door; the Chula Vista branch is at freeway Exit 10, minutes south of downtown.

If you can't leave San Diego without downing a fish taco, the nation-spanning Rubio's chain was founded here and has multiple locations.

Besides chains, keep these streets or neighborhoods in mind for refueling: funky Ocean Beach, famed for its easy-going breakfast places; Little Italy (India Street), with endless Italian options; Hillcrest in the vicinity of the Fifth Avenue–University Avenue intersection, a buffet of international cuisines; and, if you want Asian, Convoy Street is the place to go.

— David Nelson

vice is speedy, if sometimes curt. ⊠ *4170 Convoy St., Kearny Mesa* ☎ *858/ 565–6750* ▤ *MC, V.*

Beaches

American–Casual

★ ¢–$ ✕ **Hodad's.** No, it's not a flashback, the 1960s live on at this fabulously funky burger joint founded in that era. An unrepentant hippy crowd sees to it. Walls are covered with license plates, and the amiable servers with tattoos. Very much a family place, Hodad's clientele often includes toddlers and octogenarians. Burgers are the thing, loaded with onions, pickles, tomatoes, lettuce, and condiments, and so gloriously messy that you might wear a swimsuit so you can stroll to the beach for a bath afterwards. The mini-hamburger is good, the double bacon cheeseburger absolutely awesome. ⊠ *5010 Newport Ave., Ocean Beach* ☎ *619/224–4623* ▤ *AE, MC, V.*

¢–$ ✕ **Mardi Gras Cafe & Market Place.** The taste of New Orleans comes packed into weighty muffaletta sandwiches (round loaves piled with cold cuts, cheeses, and olive salad), po' boy sandwiches filled with batter-fried shellfish, seafood gumbo, crawfish étouffée, and a steaming bowl of red beans and rice fleshed out with chunks of smoked sausage. Not far from Ocean Beach, this market-cum-eatery sets its tables next to shelves crammed with canned goods, a remarkable selection of hot sauces, as well as a range of New Orleans culinary necessities. Portions are vast, and the prices low. ⊠ *3185 Midway Dr.* ☎ *619/223–5501* ▤ *AE, MC, V.*

Contemporary

$$–$$$ ✕ **Thee Bungalow.** Two generations of San Diegans have developed a taste for roast duck with a variety of sauces (orange, black cherry, green peppercorn, pepper-rum) at this old-style Continental restaurant in Ocean Beach that's as comfortable as an old shoe. Decorated with flowers, eye-pleasing paintings, and tables set with crisp linens, Thee Bungalow ambles along amiably as a purveyor of such favorites as garlic-herb-crusted lamb rack with sauce Bearnaise, pepper steak in brandy-rich Bordelaise sauce, crab-stuffed salmon baked in puff pastry, and a classic bouillabaisse. The cooking gets more adventurous at periodic wine dinners, when startlingly superior vintages flow. The wine list is always remarkable and reservations for any night are suggested. ⊠ *4996 W. Point Loma Blvd., Ocean Beach* ☎ *619/224–2884* ▤ *AE, D, DC, MC, V* ☾ *No lunch.*

$–$$$ ✕ **3rd Corner.** Ed Moore, the owner of Thee Bungalow across the street, offers his local clientele comfortable banquettes under soft lighting or a seat at the bar, where you can order an appetizer to go with that good glass of wine. Service is personable and the well-prepared menu is characterized by such starters as artisan goat cheese baked until bubbling with sautéed forest mushrooms. Mussels steamed in a white wine-based broth and an elegant prosciutto salad are attractive prefaces to such entrées as seared, pastry-wrapped ahi in cilantro sauce, grilled marinated pork rack chop with creamy polenta, and oven-roasted chicken with crisply perfect pommes frites. The well-chosen wine list includes excellent bargains. ⊠ *2265 Bacon St., Ocean Beach* ☎ *619/223–2700* ▤ *AE, DC, MC, V* ☾ *No lunch.*

Cuban

¢–$ ✕ **Andre's Restaurant.** For more than two decades, Andre's was San Diego's sole outpost for solid, savory Cuban cuisine. In a nondescript building in the Morena Boulevard home furnishings district near Pacific Beach, Andre's is not much to look at, although the enclosed-patio dining room is comfortable, and servers smile as they place heaped-high plates of breaded steak, roast pork, and grilled marinated fish in front of impressed diners. For Cuban home cooking at its best, order the *picadillo*, a meat hash with bold and piquant flavors. Like all entrées, it's accompanied by oceans of delicious black beans and mountains of rice. ✉ *1235 Morena Blvd., Morena District* ☎ *619/274–4114* 🖃 *MC, V* ☉ *Closed Sun.*

German

★ $$–$$$ ✕ **Kaiserhof.** Without question this is the best German restaurant in San Diego County, and the lively bar and beer garden work to inspire a sense of *Gemutlichkeit* (happy well-being). Tourist board-style posters of Germany's romantic destinations hang on the wall, Warsteiner and St. Pauli Girl flow from the tap. Since the gigantic portions are accompanied by such side dishes as potato pancakes, bread dumplings, red cabbage, and spaetzle noodles, only the truly famished should attempt starters. Entrées include sauerbraten, Wiener schnitzel, goulash, and smoked pork chops, plus excellent daily specials such as venison medallions in green peppercorn sauce. Reservations are a good idea. ✉ *2253 Sunset Cliffs Blvd., Ocean Beach* ☎ *619/224–0606* 🖃 *MC, V* ☉ *Closed Mon. No lunch Tues.–Thurs.*

Italian

¢–$$$ ✕ **Caffe Bella Italia.** Contemporary Italian cooking as prepared in Italy— an important point in fusion-mad San Diego—is the rule at this simple restaurant near one of the principle intersections in Pacific Beach. The menu presents Neapolitan-style macaroni with sausage and artichoke hearts in spicy tomato sauce, *pappardelle* (wide ribbons of pasta) with a creamy Gorgonzola and walnut sauce, plus formal entrées like chicken breast sautéed with balsamic vinegar, and slices of rare filet mignon tossed with herbs and topped with arugula and Parmesan shavings. Impressive daily specials include beet-stuffed ravioli in creamy saffron sauce. ✉ *1525 Garnet Ave., Pacific Beach* ☎ *858/273–1224* 🖃 *MC, V* ☉ *Closed Mon.*

$–$$ ✕ **The Venetian.** The spacious back room of this neighborhood eatery is actually a sheltered garden that you can enjoy in all weather. The menu takes a personal view of Italian cuisine with house specialties like seafood pasta in tangy marinara sauce, and bow-tie pasta tossed with prosciutto, peas, mushrooms, and a rose-tinted cream sauce. The well-priced selection of veal, chicken, and seafood dishes is excellent, but many regulars settle for the lavishly garnished antipasto salad and one of the tender-crusted pizzas. ✉ *3663 Voltaire St., Ocean Beach* ☎ *619/223–8197* 🖃 *MC, V.*

$–$$ ✕ **Old Venice.** This long-running favorite near Shelter Island is treasured for its casual, welcoming atmosphere and for a menu that has both well-made pizzas and familiar Italian dishes like cannelloni baked in a rich meat sauce, generously stuffed lasagna, and eggplant parmigiana. A creamy pesto sauce adds glamour and a pungent flavor to the baked, spinach-stuffed chicken breast Florentine. Request a table on the semi-enclosed terrace behind the restaurant. ⊠ *2910 Canon St., Point Loma* ☎ *619/ 222–5888* ▭ *MC, V* ◌ *No lunch Sun.*

Japanese

★ ¢–$$ ✕ **Sushi Ota.** Wedged into a minimall between a convenience store and a looming medical building, Sushi Ota initially seems less than prepossessing. Still, San Diego–bound Japanese business people frequently call for reservations before boarding their trans-Pacific flights. Look closely at the expressions on customers' faces as they stream in and out of the doors, and you'll see eager anticipation and satisfied glows due to San Diego's best sushi. Besides the usual California roll and tuna and shrimp sushi, sample the sea urchin or surf clam sushi, and the soft-shell crab roll. Sushi Ota offers the cooked as well as the raw. There's additional parking behind the mall. ⊠ *4529 Mission Bay Dr., Pacific Beach* ☎ *619/270–5670* ⌖ *Reservations essential* ▭ *AE, D, MC, V* ◌ *No lunch Sat.–Mon.*

Mexican

$–$$ ✕ **Gringo's.** About a stone's throw from the ocean in the heart of lively Pacific Beach, this sizeable restaurant often seems like party central. A good variety of margaritas help fuel the atmosphere, but so does a menu cleverly divided between "Cali-Mex" favorites like quesadillas, enchiladas, burritos and fajitas, and authentic regional specialties from the Mexican heartland. The latter includes dishes like *chiles en nogada* (meat-stuffed chilies in a walnut-cream sauce) and oven-roasted pork chops in Oaxacan-style molé sauce. Make reservations, because this joint jumps. ⊠ *4474 Mission Blvd., Pacific Beach* ☎ *858/490–2877* ▭ *AE, D, DC, MC, V.*

¢–$$ ✕ **Cantina Panaderia.** You'll find Asian accents on the menu at this family destination a few blocks from the blue Pacific, but South-of-the-Border flavors prevail at the "Bakery Cantina," so named because the premises housed a neighborhood bakery for decades. Appetizers like steak-filled lettuce wraps and plantains dressed with sour cream and caviar are fun; expect to be filled up by such entrées as the wood-fired rotisserie chicken with black beans, rice, and crisp plantains, or green chile tamales with tofu. The coconut flan finishes the meal nicely. A small selection of Mexican artworks reinforce the theme of the cuisine. ⊠ *966 Felspar St., Pacific Beach* ☎ *858/272–8400* ▭ *AE, DC, MC, V.*

Seafood

★ ¢–$ ✕ **Hudson Bay Seafood.** Part of the pleasure in this small, friendly, waterside fish house is watching the day-charter boats arrive at the adjacent dock and discharge their passengers, some seasoned fishermen and some first-timers grateful to be back on dry land. More than a few march up the wooden walkway to Hudson Bay, which bakes the sourdough rolls in which it places delicately fried fish fillets or shellfish. The french fries are freshly cut, the fish tacos taste of Mexico, and even the tartar sauce is homemade. There are salads and excellent breakfasts, too, and even the burgers are exceptional. ⊠ *1403 Scott St., Shelter Island* ☎ *619/222–8787* ▭ *MC, V.*

La Jolla

¢ ✕**Chicago On A Bun.** Hot dog! Fans of Chicago-style hot dogs know where to go when they get a craving for Windy City sidewalk cuisine. The decor—mostly built around Chicago Cubs memorabilia—is imported from the City of the Broad Shoulders, as are the Vienna-brand beef hot dogs, and even the steamed poppy seed buns. Garnish a dog your way, or take it Chicago-style, which means piled with mustard, onion, relish, chopped tomatoes, tiny hot peppers, celery salt and dill pickles. A basket of fried-to-order potato chips is almost obligatory with hot dogs, juicy Italian beef sandwiches, and chili cheeseburgers. ✉ *8935 Towne Centre Dr., Golden Triangle–La Jolla* ☏ *858/622–0222* ▤ *MC, V.*

Contemporary

★ **$$$–$$$$** ✕ **Marine Room.** Gaze at the ocean from this venerable La Jolla Shores mainstay and, if you're lucky, watch the grunion run or the waves race across the sand and beat against the glass. Creative seasonal menus score with "trilogy" plates that combine three meats, sometimes including game, in distinct preparations. Disparate elements like candied chestnuts, apple curry sauce, and green beans contribute to the success of such entrées as gooseberry-glazed chicken breast. Watercress salad and a limoncello liqueur–chervil emulsion add sparkle to the taste of butter-basted lobster tail. Sunday brunch is lavish; in winter call for information about the high-tide breakfasts. ✉ *2000 Spindrift Dr., La Jolla* ☏ *858/ 459–7222* ▤ *AE, D, DC, MC, V.*

$$$–$$$$ ✕ **Top o' the Cove.** Although flashier newcomers rival this once peerless La Jolla institution, the elegant but comfortable Top o' the Cove still receives high marks from San Diegans for the romantic ocean view from its cottage windows and its fine European-American cuisine. The menu provides plenty for the thoughtful diner to consider, such as roasted Cornish game hen with chestnut gnocchi, and a thick, succulent prime New York steak with cream cheese–rich mashed potatoes. Subtle flavors pervade these simple-sounding preparations. The service is attentive but not overbearing and the wine list leaves nothing to be desired. ✉ *1216 Prospect St., La Jolla* ☏ *858/454–7779* ▤ *AE, DC, MC, V.*

$$–$$$$ ✕ **Cafe Japengo.** Framed by marbled walls and accented with bamboo trees and unusual black-iron sculptures, this Pacific Rim restaurant serves Asian-inspired cuisine with many North and South American touches. The curry-fried calamari and the Japengo pot sticker appetizers are guaranteed to wake up your mouth. There's also a selection of grilled, wood-roasted, and wok-fried entrées; try the 10-ingredient fried rice, or the crispy whole striped bass. The sushi bar is always very fresh. Service can be slow, but the pace in the bar, crowded with young locals, is fast and lively. If you savor quiet, avoid weekend evenings. ✉ *Aventine Center, 8960 University Center La., Golden Triangle, La Jolla* ☏ *858/450–3355* ▤ *AE, D, DC, MC, V* ☾ *No lunch weekends.*

★ **$$–$$$$** ✕ **Roppongi.** A hit from the moment it opened, Roppongi serves global cuisine with strong Asian notes. The contemporary dining room done in wood tones and accented with Asian statuary has a row of comfortable booths along one wall. It can get noisy when crowded; tables near the bar are generally quieter. Order the imaginative Euro-Asian tapas as appetizers or combine them for a full meal. Try the barbecued mini lamb chops, seafood pot stickers with caviar sauce, and the high-rising Polynesian crab stack. Good entrées are boneless beef shortribs with honey-mustard glaze, and fresh seafood. ⊠ *875 Prospect St., La Jolla* ☎ *858/551–5252* ⊟ *AE, D, DC, MC, V.*

Deli

¢–$ ✕ **Elijah's.** Formerly known as Blumberg's, this large, somewhat sterile-looking, brightly-lit delicatessen is in the La Jolla Village area near Interstate 5. Prominent are towering sandwiches, blintzes, smoked fish plates, and specialties like "mish-mosh" soup, which combines noodles, matzo balls, and shredded crêpes in a big bowl of steaming chicken broth. Count on reliable chopped liver, hearty breakfasts, and dinners like chicken-in-the-pot and savory beef brisket. The restaurant prides itself on Reuben sandwiches, which do impress. Friendly servers keep their arms in shape with the over-laden plates. ⊠ *8861 Villa La Jolla Dr., La Jolla* ☎ *858/455–1462* ⊟ *AE, D, MC, V.*

French

$$$–$$$$ ✕ **Tapenade.** Inspired by the south of France, celebrated Tapenade (named after the delicious Provençal black olive–and–anchovy paste that accompanies the bread) has shed some of the cuisine's weight in the cross-Atlantic delivery. In an unpretentious, light, and airy room lined with 1960s French movie posters, it serves cuisine to match. Very fresh ingredients, a delicate touch with sauces, and an emphasis on seafood characterize the menu. It changes frequently, but with good fortune may include pan-gilded sea scallops in fragrant curry sauce, veal with morel mushrooms, and desserts like crisp, pear-stuffed spring rolls with caramel sauce. ⊠ *7612 Fay Ave., La Jolla* ☎ *858/551–7500* ⊟ *AE, D, DC, MC, V.*

FodorśChoice
★

★ ¢–$$$ ✕ **Michele Coulon Dessertier.** A "dessertier" confects desserts, a job that Michele Coulon does exceedingly well in the back of a small, charming shop in the heart of La Jolla's "village." Colorful raspberry pinwheel *bombe* (a molded dessert of cake, jam, and creamy filling), Amareno cherry torte, and a tri-color mousse of chocolate and coffee creams are a few treats. Weekday lunches and Thursday-through-Saturday dinners are prepared by son Nathan Coulon, whose evening specialties include chicken breast in Normandy-style cream sauce, halibut in an artichoke-enriched butter sauce, and a meltingly tender pepper steak. Make reservations for dinner, which is served at oak tables set with roses fresh from a family member's garden. ⊠ *7556 Fay Ave., La Jolla* ☎ *858/456–5098* ⌂ *Reservations essential* ⊟ *AE, D, MC, V* ☉ *Closed Sun. No dinner Mon.–Wed.*

Italian

$–$$$ ✕ **Sofia's Italian Table.** Michael and Victoria McGeath, owners of the long-running and popular Trattoria Acqua, ushered in a younger sister in 2003. Its marble bar attracts a younger crowd "just picking" on thin-crusted pizzas and sizeable salads. In a dining room furnished with marble tables and Venetian carnival masks you can enjoy the same items, or baked pasta shells with eggplant "ragu" and smoked mozzarella, amazingly crisp and light veal milanese, and filet mignon with Gorgonzola. The beer-battered shrimp in orange-mustard sauce comes in a giant's portion, Tuscan-style bread salad and butternut squash ravioli in sage butter. ⊠ *8990 University Center La., Golden Triangle–La Jolla* ☎ *858/ 546–8797* ⊟ *AE, DC, MC, V* ⊘ *Closed Sun. No lunch Sat.*

$–$$$ ╳ **Trattoria Acqua.** Reservations are a good idea for this Mediterranean-inspired bistro above La Jolla Cove. On the lower level of Coast Walk center, this romantic eatery has dining rooms that are semi-open to the weather and the view, yet sufficiently sheltered for comfort. Choose from stuffed, deep-fried zucchini blossoms, lobster-filled ravioli in a lobster-scented *beurre blanc* (white-wine and butter sauce), and stuffed roasted quail flavored with bacon. The superb wine list earns kudos from aficionados. ⊠ *1298 Prospect St., La Jolla* ☎ *858/454–0709* ⊟ *AE, DC, MC, V.*

¢–$$$ ╳ **Barolo.** This cozy, candlelit restaurant in the Golden Triangle's Renaissance Towne Center uses its namesake to sauce the house specialty, Gorgonzola-topped beef filet in a Barolo reduction. This filling dish joins other specialties like veal scallops with pesto and goat cheese, and polenta-crusted salmon in horseradish sauce on a menu that opens encouragingly with a crisp "fritto misto" of fired squid, shrimp, and zucchini. The salad of chopped tomato and red onion with blue cheese dressing nicely kicks off a meal that may go on simply to a sausage pizza, or to the enjoyable pear-stuffed ravioli. The banquettes that line the wall are the preferred tables. Service is suave and eager-to-please. ⊠ *8953 Towne Center Dr., Golden Triangle–La Jolla* ☎ *858/622–1202* ⊟ *AE, D, MC, V* ⊘ *No lunch weekends.*

Mexican

$–$$ ╳ **Alfonso's of La Jolla.** Some things never change, and laid-back Alfonso's is one of them. From the sidewalk terrace on busy Prospect Street, you can review the passing parade while downing sizeable margaritas and plates laden with *carne asada*. This marinated, grilled steak is a house specialty and arrives both garnished *tampiquena*-style with a cheese enchilada, rice, and beans; or chopped as a filling for tacos and quesadillas. The menu extends to typical enchiladas and burritos, as well as to a couple of piquant shrimp preparations. The continuity of quality cuisine guarantees this landmark's popularity. ⊠ *1251 Prospect St., La Jolla* ☎ *858/454–2232* ⊟ *AE, MC, V.*

Seafood

$$$–$$$$ ╳ **George's at the Cove.** Hollywood types and other visiting celebrities
Fodor'sChoice can be spotted in the elegant main dining room, where a wall-length window overlooks La Jolla Cove. Renowned for fresh seafood and fine preparations of beef and lamb, this also is the place to taste the wonders chef Trey Foshee works with seasonal produce from local specialty growers. Give special consideration to imaginatively garnished, wild California salmon, or choice cuts of beef and pork from the state's celebrated Niman Ranch. For more informal dining and a sweeping view of the coast try the rooftop Ocean Terrace ($–$$). ⊠ *1250 Prospect St., La Jolla* ☎ *858/ 454–4244* ⟐ *Reservations essential* ⊟ *AE, D, DC, MC, V.*

$$–$$$ ╳ **Fresh.** By all means request a patio table when reserving at this hip, very popular eatery that doubles as a fashion show of some of La Jolla's ladies-who-lunch. Plants partially screen the covered patio from the street, and in cool weather, heaters keep the chill at bay. The food can be very good indeed, from ultrafresh oysters on the half-shell with green apple-

TALKING TACOS

A CITY OF TRANSPLANTS—FROM AROUND THE UNITED STATES, from south of the border, from Asia, and from everywhere else—San Diego introduces newcomers to local topics such as surfing, sunblock, and how to beat rush hour on the freeways (you can't). Even though terms like tacos, burritos, enchiladas, and tostadas are as common as macaroni and cheese to San Diegans, don't count on widespread agreement among residents as to what they mean. Authentic cuisine brought from Mexico is quite at odds with Southern California's home-grown "Cal-Mex" style of cooking, although both can be delicious.

An authentic taco never takes the form of a folded, fried-hard shell piled high with ground beef, sour cream, and chopped lettuce and tomatoes. Even so, this is the version many novices encounter the first time around, and as San Diegans say, finding one is "no problemo." If you meet a soft tortilla (more authentically made with corn masa dough rather than from white flour) rolled around a filling and served fresh, fragrant, and hot, it's the real thing. Fillings can be shredded beef or chicken, or slowly simmered tongue in green sauce, or grilled or deep-fried fish or seafood, or just about any savory tidbit. Garnishes usually include a drizzle of salsa and often a squeeze of tart Mexican lime (a citrus different from that raised in the States), along with cilantro sprigs, sliced radishes, chopped onion and whatever else the cook is in the mood for. Some San Diego entrepreneurs identify the city as the fish taco capital of the planet, but the title really belongs to Ensenada, a port city about 60 mi south of the California border. Arranged cheek-by-jowl near the sizeable, attractively-stocked and decidedly aromatic waterside fish market, a good 100 stands offer a kaleidoscope of tacos, each slightly different from the others, and accompanied by a slightly varied selection of condiments.

In San Diego, to be "one taco shy of a combination plate" is to be, shall we say, rather divorced from reality. A combination plate is anchored by such constants as delicately flavored rice, and frijoles refritos, smooth, creamy, well-cooked beans that must be draped with melted shredded cheese, and usually support a small raft of shredded lettuce dabbed with a bit of sour cream. Any empty spaces (you shouldn't see more of the plate than the rim) will be hidden by the preferred combination of tacos, tortillas, chiles rellenos, and burritos. What are those? Tortillas can be filled with cheese, chicken, or beef and topped with savory enchilada sauce. Chiles rellenos are mild, deep-fried peppers stuffed with cheese. Burritos are tortillas filled with beans and shredded meat. A platter might even include a mini-tostada, a sort of salad-buffet arranged on a crisply fried tortilla. It's good, filling food, and you'll enjoy it. And that's the whole enchilada.

cucumber "mignonette" sauce to prosciutto-wrapped pork tenderloin and crisp roast chicken in red wine sauce. Seafood stars in all courses, starting with a Maine lobster "Napoleon" appetizer, and continuing with a poached seafood salad, coriander-crusted mahi mahi and shellfish-stuffed rainbow trout. ⊠ *1044 Wall St., La Jolla* ☎ *858/551–7575* ⊟ *AE, D, DC, MC, V.*

Mission Valley

American

$–$$ ✕ **Cheesecake Factory.** This cavernous eatery in San Diego's leading shopping mall, Fashion Valley, can be relied upon to have a line at the door at peak meal hours. Part of the patronage is drawn by the huge, creamy cheesecakes, and more by the multipage menu featuring innovative pizzas, gigantic salads, pastas, and such house specialties as chicken with biscuits, mashed potatoes, and country gravy. When the crowd is in full cry the noise can be deafening, but the friendly and eager-to-please servers handle the crush well. ⊠ *Fashion Valley Center, 7067 Friars Rd., Mission Valley* ☎ *619/683–2800* ⊟ *AE, D, MC, V.*

¢–$ ✕ **Ricky's Family Restaurant.** Chain feederies haven't driven out San Diego's old-line family restaurants, and this unpretentious place on the quiet fringe of Mission Valley remains dear to the city's heart. A traditional three-meals-daily restaurant, Ricky's serves big portions of unassuming, well-prepared, all-American cooking, but is famed for its breakfasts, when savory corned-beef hash and fluffy, strawberry-crowned Belgian waffles are the rule. The spectacular apple pancake, a soufflé-like creation that takes 20 minutes to bake, arrives burning hot and is irresistible to the last molecule of molten cinnamon sugar. ⊠ *2181 Hotel Circle S, Mission Valley* ☎ *619/291–4498* ⊟ *MC, V.*

Italian

$–$$ ✕ **Prego Ristorante.** Since the late 1980s, this Tuscan-style villa in bustling Hazard Center has been a magnet for diners on a quest for good Italian fare in Mission Valley. Scents waft from the open kitchen and the cases laden with fresh-baked pastries. Possessed of an unusually good service staff, Prego greets the budget-conscious with excellent pizzas, including an unusual pie topped with meaty Portobello mushrooms and goat cheese. More formal meals might consist of linguine sauced with prawns and Manila clams, lobster-filled agnolotti pasta, plump mesquite-grilled pork chops, and the day's meats and poultry from the rotisserie. The restaurant also offers one of the most comfortable bars in the valley. ⊠ *1370 Frazee Rd., Mission Valley* ☎ *619/294–4700* ⊟ *AE, D, DC, MC, V.*

Japanese

$–$$ ✕ **Oki Ton Japanese Bistro.** The best Japanese fare in Mission Valley is found in Oki Ton, a good-looking but informal eatery in the imposing Fenton Marketplace center just off busy Friars Road. The sushi chefs acquit themselves well with specialty rolls like the "inside-out" dragon roll of eel, avocado, shrimp tempura and crab. For its part, the kitchen does equally well with a katsu platter of crisply breaded pork, chicken breast and prawns, grilled salmon with ginger sauce, and excellent chicken teriyaki. The filling meals include Japanese pickles, rice, salad and the special house miso soup. ⊠ *2408 Northside Dr., Mission Valley* ☎ *619/284–8036* ▤ *AE, DC, MC, V.*

Seafood

¢–$$$$ ✕ **King's Seafood Co.** This warehouse-size restaurant remains wildly popular with shoppers at Mission Valley's many malls, owing to extremely friendly and efficient service, tanks filled with lively lobsters and Dungeness crabs, and a daily-changing menu with a fine selection of fresh-shucked oysters. Specialties include New Orleans–style barbecued shrimp, and a full-size New England clambake complete with red potatoes and sweet corn on the cob. Fish and shellfish are char-grilled, deep-fried, sautéed, steamed, and skewered, and the menu obliges meat-eaters with a convincing cheeseburger, roasted chicken, and grilled sirloin. ⊠ *825 Camino de la Reina N, Mission Valley* ☎ *619/574–1230* ▤ *AE, DC, MC, V.*

¢–$$ ✕ **The Little Fish Market.** This spin-off of downtown's Fish Market is custom-designed for the restaurant row at the Fenton Marketplace near Qualcomm Stadium. It's billed a "quick service restaurant" because you order at the counter, but it still has table service. The menu includes shellfish cocktails, smoked fish plates, sushi, and chowder served in a bread bowl, and more significant meals of deep-fried and char-broiled fish and shellfish. ⊠ *1401 Fenton Pkwy., Mission Valley* ☎ *619/280–2277* ⚠ *Reservations not accepted* ▤ *MC, V.*

Old Town

Mexican

★ $–$$ ✕ **Zocalo Grill.** Try for a table by the fireplace on the covered terrace, but the contemporary cuisine tastes just as good anywhere in the spacious and handsome eatery. Instead of traditionally simmering the *carnitas* (pork chunks) in well-seasoned lard, Zocalo braises them in a mixture of honey and Porter beer and serves the dish with mango salsa and avocado salad. Recommended starters include artichoke fritters and crisp shrimp skewers with pineapple-mango relish. The Seattle surf & turf roasts wild salmon and forest mushrooms on a cedar plank. ⊠ *2444 San Diego Ave., Old Town* ☎ *619/298–9840* ▤ *AE, D, DC, MC, V.*

Seafood

$$–$$$ ✕ **Cafe Pacifica.** The airy Cafe Pacifica serves eclectic contemporary cuisine with an emphasis on seafood. Fresh fish is grilled with your choice of savory sauces. Other good bets include the griddle-fried mustard catfish, sole stuffed with rock shrimp and Dungeness crab, and grilled, line-caught salmon. The crème brûlée is worth blowing any diet for. Cafe Pacifica's wine list has received kudos from *Wine Spectator* magazine, but also consider the pomegranate-flavored margarita. ⊠ *2414 San Diego Ave., Old Town* ☎ *619/291–6666* ▤ *AE, D, DC, MC, V* ☺ *No lunch.*

Thai

¢–$ ✕ **Saffron Noodles and Sate.** Comfortable outdoor tables on a narrow sidewalk and inexpensive prices make this and the neighboring Saffron

Thai Chicken take-out worth a short detour from Old Town. The simple menu has spicy and mild noodle soups; stir-fried noodles with chicken, beef, pork, or turkey; a couple of uncommon Vietnamese and Thai-Indian noodle dishes bathed with aromatic sauces; and grilled sate skewers. The latter are served with jasmine rice, tart-sweet cucumber salad, and savory peanut sauce. ⊠ *3737 India St., Old Town* ☎ *619/ 574–7737* ▭ *MC, V.*

WHERE TO STAY

3

By Lenore
Greiner

SAN DIEGO IS SPREAD OUT, so the first thing to consider when selecting lodging is location. If you choose a hotel with a waterfront setting and extensive outdoor sports facilities, you may find yourself choosing to shorten your sightseeing agenda. But if you plan to sightsee, take into account a hotel's proximity to attractions. There are plenty of hotel-resorts for families in Mission Valley and Mission Bay, which are convenient to the San Diego Zoo, SeaWorld, or a day at the beach.

The downtown center has hipster boutique hotels and preserved Victorian-era hostelries in the Gaslamp Quarter. For true luxe, you'll find high-end hotels from the downtown up to La Jolla, which also has a landmark 1920s Spanish-style hotel. Staying on the water isn't only for wealthy leisure travelers: surfers make themselves at home at Banana Bungalow in Pacific Beach and conventioneers pack themselves into towers on San Diego Bay.

Die-hard aficionados of California's Craftsman architectural tradition can book themselves into a 1,500-square-foot suite at the Lodge at Torrey Pines; there, they cuddle in front of a fire in Stickley chairsto enjoy sweeping ocean and golf course views. For a downtown skyline, settle into a window seat at the stylish WOW Presidential Suite at the W San Diego Hotel, decorated to reflect local beach culture.

The latest news in San Diego lodging are the medium-range hotels slated for revitalized East Village, where San Diego's brand new Petco Park baseball stadium stands alongside the bay.

Coronado

Quiet, out-of-the-way Coronado feels like something out of an earlier, more gracious era. With boutiques and restaurants lining Orange Avenue—the main street—and its fine beaches, Coronado is great for a getaway. But if you plan to see many of San Diego's attractions, you'll probably spend a lot of time commuting across the bridge or riding the ferry.

$$$$ ⊞ **Coronado Island Marriott Resort.** Near San Diego Bay, this snazzy hotel has many rooms with great views of downtown's skyline. Large rooms and suites in low-slung buildings are done in a cheerful California–country French fashion, with colorful impressionist prints; all rooms have separate showers and tubs and come with plush robes. The spa facilities are top-notch, but the service can be somewhat uncouth. ⊠ *2000 2nd St., Coronado 92118* 🕾 *619/435–3000 or 800/543–4300* 🖹 *619/ 435–3032* ⊕ *www.marriotthotels.com/sanci* ⚟ *273 rooms, 27 suites* ♨ *4 restaurants, room service, in-room data ports, cable TV with movies, 6 tennis courts, 3 pools, aerobics, health club, hair salon, 2 outdoor hot tubs, massage, sauna, spa, beach, snorkeling, windsurfing, boating, jet skiing, waterskiing, bicycles, bar, shops, laundry service, concierge, business services, convention center, meeting rooms, parking (fee); no smoking* ⊟ *AE, D, DC, MC, V.*

$$$$ ⊞ **Hotel Del Coronado.** "The Del" stands as a social and historic landmark, its whimsical red turrets and balconied walkways taking you as far back as 1888, the year it was built. U.S. presidents, European royalty, and movie stars have stayed in the Victorian rooms and suites, all

FodorsChoice
★

renovated with the necessities of modern-day life. Public areas always bustle with activity; for quieter quarters, consider staying in the contemporary, seven-story Ocean Towers building or in one of the eight beachfront cottages. Rates are defined largely by room views. ✉ *1500 Orange Ave., Coronado 92118* ☎ *619/435–6611 or 800/468–3533* 🖷 *619/ 522–8262* ⊕ *www.hoteldel.com* ➰ *676 rooms* ⚷ *2 restaurants, coffee shop, room service, in-room data ports, cable TV with movies, 3 tennis courts, 2 pools, gym, hair salon, outdoor hot tub, massage, sauna, spa, steam room, beach, bicycles, 4 bars, piano bar, shops, children's programs (ages 3–17), laundry service, concierge, business services, convention center, meeting rooms, parking (fee); no smoking* ▤ *AE, D, DC, MC, V.*

$$$$ ⌘ **Loews Coronado Bay Resort.** You can park your boat at the 80-slip marina of this elegant resort, set on a secluded 15-acre peninsula on the Silver Strand. Rooms are tastefully decorated, and all have furnished balconies with views of water—either bay, ocean, or marina. New in 2004 is the 10,000-square-foot Zen-like spa with a garden with alfresco showers. The Azzura Point restaurant specializes in seafood. ✉ *4000 Coronado Bay Rd., Coronado 92118* ☎ *619/424–4000 or 800/815– 6397* 🖷 *619/424–4400* ⊕ *www.loewshotels.com/coronado.html* ➰ *403 rooms, 37 suites* ⚷ *3 restaurants, room service, in-room data ports, minibars, cable TV with movies, 5 tennis courts, 3 pools, health club, hair salon, spa, 3 hot tubs, beach, windsurfing, boating, jet skiing, waterskiing, bicycles, 3 bars, shop, children's programs (ages 4–12), laundry service, concierge, business services, convention center, meeting rooms, parking (fee); no smoking* ▤ *AE, D, DC, MC, V.*

$$–$$$$ ⌘ **Glorietta Bay Inn.** The main building of this property was built in 1908 for sugar baron John D. Spreckels, who once owned much of downtown San Diego. Rooms in this Edwardian-style mansion and in the newer motel-style buildings are attractively furnished. Some rooms have patios or balconies. The inn is adjacent to the Coronado harbor and near many restaurants and shops, but is much smaller and quieter than the Hotel Del across the street. Tours ($8) of the island's historical buildings depart from the inn three mornings a week. Ginger snaps and lemonade are served daily from 3 to 5. ✉ *1630 Glorietta Blvd., Coronado 92118* ☎ *619/435–3101 or 800/283–9383* 🖷 *619/435–6182* ⊕ *www.gloriettabayinn.com* ➰ *100 rooms* ⚷ *Dining room, in-room data ports, some kitchenettes, refrigerators, cable TV with movies, pool, outdoor hot tub, bicycles, library, laundry service, concierge, business services, free parking; no smoking* ▤ *AE, MC, V.*

$$–$$$$ ⌘ **La Avenida Inn.** An old-school motor lodge surrounding a pool landscaped with palms and tropical flowers, this inn caters to a budget crowd in a tony area. It's the most economical choice on this half of the island. The big plus here is the convenient location one-half block from historic Hotel Del Coronado and one block to the beach. Continental breakfast is served daily and double-paned windows with plantation shutters in the rooms reduce the street noise. ✉ *1315 Orange Ave., Coronado 92118* ☎ *619/435–3191 or 800/437–0162* 🖷 *619/435–5024* ⊕ *www.laavenidainn.com* ➰ *27 rooms, 2 suites* ⚷ *Cable TV, pool, free parking* ⊙ *CP* ▤ *AE, DC, MC, V.*

3

San Diego has hotels in abundance, and several on the drawing boards could add more than 3,000 rooms in the next few years. All this means lower prices for those who shop around. When you make reservations, ask about specials. Hotel packages are your best bet; deals range from arts and culture escapes to relaxing spa weekends to special event getaways. Check hotel Web sites for Internet specials and try to call a property directly; sometimes doing this results in a lower rate. Several properties in the Hotel Circle area of Mission Valley offer special rates and free tickets to local attractions, the San Diego Zoo, Wild Animal Park, SeaWorld, or Legoland. Many hotels promote lower-price weekend packages to fill rooms after convention and business customers leave town. Book well in advance, especially if you plan to visit in summer. Since the weather is great year-round, don't expect substantial discounts in winter. You can save on hotels and attractions by visiting the San Diego Convention & Visitors Bureau Web site (www.sandiego.org) for a free Vacation Planning Kit with a Travel Value Coupon booklet.

As for rates, expect to pay around $80 for a simple room in a central area near a freeway or two. After that, the sky's the limit in terms of prices since San Diego, like her California counterparts Los Angeles and San Francisco, is not a bargain destination.

The lodgings we list in each price category run from bare bones basic to lavishly upscale. We always list the facilities that are available, but we don't specify whether they cost extra; when pricing accommodations, always ask what's included and what costs extra. Properties are assigned price categories based on the range from their least-expensive standard double room at high season (excluding holidays) to the most expensive. Assume that hotels operate on the **European Plan** (EP, with no meals) unless we specify otherwise.

Children A great year-round family destination, virtually all tourist-oriented areas of San Diego have hotels suited to a family's budget and/or recreational needs, and many allow kids under 18 to stay free with their parents. You'll find the most choices and diversity in and around Mission Bay, which is close to SeaWorld, beaches, parks, and Old Town. Many Mission Bay hotels offer SeaWorld packages or discounts. Another central choice is Mission Valley, which has San Diego Trolley stations and malls. The resort Rancho Bernardo Inn has full- and half-day programs for kids ages 5–17 that include swimming, arts and crafts, and, for kids over 12, golf and tennis. The programs run during the major spring and summer holidays and the month of August. Within the italicized service information below each lodging review, look for "children's programs" if these services are important to you.

Prices In terms of price, even the most expensive areas have some reasonably priced rooms. High season is summer, and rates are lowest in the fall. If an ocean view is important, request it when booking, but be aware the cost will be significantly more than a non-ocean view room. Properties are assigned price categories based on the range from their least expensive standard double room at high season (excluding holidays) to the most expensive. We always list the facilities that are available—but we don't specify whether they cost extra: when pricing accommodations, always ask what's included.

	WHAT IT COSTS				
	$$$$	$$$	$$	$	¢
FOR 2 PEOPLE	over $250	$176–$250	$121–$175	$90–$120	under $90

Prices are for a standard double room in high (summer) season, excluding 10.5% tax.

Reservations Summer is the busy season for most hotels, and spring and fall conventions can fill every downtown hotel room. Also, special sports events such as golf or tennis tournaments mean fully booked host resorts and nearby hotels.

Services You can assume that all rooms have private baths, phones, TVs, and air-conditioning unless otherwise noted. Downtown hotels cater primarily to business travelers, while those at Mission Bay, in coastal locations such as Carlsbad and Encinitas, and at inland resorts offer luxury, golf, spa services, children's activities, and more.

$$–$$$$ 🏨 **Villa Capri By The Sea.** Look for the world-famous "Diving Lady" neon sign outside this hotel. The classic 1950s architecture is fitting for its frequent brushes with fame—ask innkeeper John Miller about the hotel's storied history. ⊠ *1417 Orange Ave., Coronado 92118* 🕾 *619/435–4137* 🖷 *619/435–3383* ⊕ *www.villacapribythesea.com* ⇨ *7 rooms, 7 suites* ⟁ *Microwaves, refrigerators, in-room VCRs, pool* ⊟ *AE, D, DC, MC, V.*

$–$$$$ 🏨 **El Cordova Hotel.** Built as a countryside mansion in 1902, this two-story Spanish-style building was converted into a hotel in 1930. Its quaint Old Mexico courtyard is populated with shops and cafés. Most rooms are suites, and you can walk to the beach from here. ⊠ *1351 Orange Ave., Coronado 92118* 🕾 *619/435–4131* 🖷 *619/435–0632* ⇨ *8 rooms, 32 suites* ⟁ *BBQs, picnic area, some kitchenettes, cable TV, pool, business services* ⊟ *AE, D, DC, MC, V.*

$–$$$ 🏨 **Cherokee Lodge.** This small inn, brought across the bay more than a century ago by barge, exudes elegance and charm with armoires, embroidered couches, polished headboards and beautiful woodwork. ⊠ *964 D Ave., Coronado 92118* 🕾 *877/743–6213 or 619/437–1967* 🖷 *619/437–1012* ⊕ *www.cherokeelodge.com* ⇨ *12 rooms* ⟁ *In-room data ports, cable TV with movies, laundry facilities, refrigerators; no smoking, no a/c.*

$–$$$ 🏨 **Crown City Inn & Bistro.** On Coronado's main drag, the Crown City Inn is close to shops, restaurants, and the beach. For the price, it's easily one of the best deals on the island. However, this two-story motor inn lacks the amenities and prestige of Coronado's bigger and better-known lodgings. A public park is across the street. ⊠ *520 Orange Ave., Coronado 92118* 🕾 *619/435–3116 or 800/422–1173* 🖷 *619/435–6750* ⊕ *www.crowncityinn.com* ⇨ *33 rooms* ⟁ *Restaurant, room service, in-room data ports, minibars, microwaves, refrigerators, cable TV* *with movies, pool, bicycles, laundry facilities, parking (fee); no smoking* ▤ *AE, D, DC, MC, V.*

Downtown

A lively, continuously revitalized downtown has helped make the city center the hotel hub of San Diego. Hotel types range from budget chains to boutique hotels to business accommodations and major high-rises. Much to see is within walking distance—Seaport Village, the Embarcadero, the Gaslamp Quarter, theaters and nightspots, galleries and coffeehouses, and the Horton Plaza shopping center. The zoo and Balboa Park are also nearby. Downtown has plenty of good restaurants, especially along 4th and 5th avenues south of Broadway in the Gaslamp Quarter.

$$$$

Fodor'sChoice

★

🏨 **Manchester Grand Hyatt San Diego.** The 34- and 40-story towers adjacent to Seaport Village make the Manchester the West Coast's tallest waterfront building. The interior combines old-world opulence with California airiness; palm trees pose next to ornate tapestry couches in the light-filled lobby. All of the British Regency–style guest rooms have water views and windows open to catch fresh bay breezes. The hotel's proximity to the convention center attracts a large business trade. The Business Plan includes access to an area with desks and office supplies. A trolley station is one block away and the Gaslamp's clubs and restaurants are also within walking distance. ⊠ *1 Market Pl., Embarcadero 92101* 🕾 *619/232–1234 or 800/233–1234* 🖷 *619/233–6464* ⊕ *www.manchestergrand.hyatt.com* ↶ *1,625 rooms, 95 suites* ♻ *3 restaurants, room service, in-room data ports, cable TV, minibars, 4 tennis courts, pool, health club, outdoor hot tub, sauna, steam room, boating, bicycles, 2 bars, shops, dry cleaning, laundry service, concierge, concierge floor, business services, meeting rooms, airport shuttle, car rental, parking (fee); no smoking* ▤ *AE, D, DC, MC, V.*

$$$$

🏨 **San Diego Marriott Hotel and Marina.** This 25-story twin tower next to the San Diego Convention Center has everything a businessperson—or leisure traveler—could want. As a major site for conventions, the complex can be hectic and impersonal, and the hallways can be noisy. Lending some tranquillity are the lagoon-style pools nestled between cascading waterfalls. The standard rooms are smallish, but pay a bit extra for a room with a balcony overlooking the bay and you'll have a serene, sparkling world spread out before you. Seaport Village and a trolley station are nearby. ⊠ *333 W. Harbor Dr., Embarcadero 92101* 🕾 *619/234–1500 or 800/228–9290* 🖷 *619/234–8678* ⊕ *www.marriotthotels.com/sandt* ↶ *1,300 rooms, 54 suites* ♻ *3 restaurants, room service, in-room data ports, cable TV with movies, 6 tennis courts, 2 pools, aerobics, health club, hair salon, outdoor hot tub, massage, sauna, boating, bicycles, basketball, 3 bars, recreation room, video game room, shops, laundry facilities, concierge, concierge floor, business services, convention center, meeting rooms, airport shuttle, car rental, parking (fee); no smoking* ▤ *AE, D, DC, MC, V.*

$$$$

Fodor'sChoice

★

🏨 **Westgate Hotel.** A nondescript, modern high-rise across from Horton Plaza hides what must be the most opulent hotel in San Diego. The lobby, modeled after the anteroom at Versailles, has hand-cut Bac-

CloseUp

HOTEL DEL CORONADO

THIS STATELY WHITE CLAPBOARD BUILDING IS A MUST-SEE for anyone in the San Diego area. "The Hotel Del," as it's known, was made famous by its legions of celebrated guests, and by its role in the 1959 movie Some Like it Hot. Stars Jack Lemmon and Tony Curtis pose as women in an all-girl band—with Marilyn Monroe as the band's singer and ukulele player—and hop a train south to Florida. Where they really end up is the Hotel Del Coronado. Set on 26 acres of Pacific Ocean beachfront, this Victorian jewel still charms and delights.

In the late 1800s, two businessmen from the Midwest, Elisha Babcock and H. L. Story, dreamed of building a resort hotel that would become the "talk of the Western world." They imported lumber and labor from San Francisco, had a mahogany bar built in Pennsylvania, then had the bar transported by ship (fully assembled) around the tip of South

America. An electrical powerplant and a kiln to fire the bricks were built on site. Even back then, the hotel cost the astronomical sum of $1 million to construct and furnish.

In 1891 Benjamin Harrison became the first of many U.S. Presidents to stay at the Del. Charles Lindbergh was honored at the Del after his legendary trans-Atlantic flight in 1927. L. Frank Baum, the author of The Wonderful Wizard of Oz, is said to have based his vision of the Emerald City on the turret-design of the hotel. And many think that Edward (the then Prince of Wales) first met Wallis Spencer Simpson, the divorcée for whom he gave up the English throne, at the Del when he visited in 1920.

carat chandeliers. Rooms are individually furnished with antiques, Italian marble counters, and bath fixtures with 24-karat-gold overlays. From the ninth floor up the views of the harbor and city are breathtaking. Afternoon high tea is served in the lobby to the accompaniment of piano and harp music. The San Diego Trolley stops right outside the door. ⊠ 1055 2nd Ave., Gaslamp Quarter 92101 ☎ 619/238–1818 or 800/221–3802, 800/522–1564 in CA ⌸ 619/557–3737 ⊕ www. westgatehotel.com ⇒ 223 rooms ᐃ 2 restaurants, room service, in-room data ports, cable TV with movies, health club, hair salon, spa, bicycles, bar, concierge, business services, meeting rooms, airport shuttle, parking (fee); no smoking ⊟ AE, D, DC, MC, V.

$$$–$$$$ ⌸ **Embassy Suites–San Diego Bay.** The front door of each spacious, contemporary suite opens out onto a 12-story atrium, and rooms facing the harbor have spectacular views. A cooked-to-order breakfast and afternoon cocktails are complimentary, as are airport transfers and a daily newspaper. Room rates vary greatly depending upon occupancy. The convention center, the Embarcadero, Seaport Village, and a trolley station are nearby. ⊠ 601 Pacific Hwy., Embarcadero 92101 ☎ 619/239–2400 or 800/362–2779 ⌸ 619/239–1520 ⊕ www.embassy-suites.com ⇒ 337 suites ᐃ Restaurant, room service, in-room data ports, mi-

crowaves, refrigerators, cable TV with movies and video games, tennis court, pool, health club, hair salon, outdoor hot tub, sauna, bicycles, bar, shops, laundry facilities, laundry service, concierge, business services, meeting rooms, airport shuttle, car rental, parking (fee); no smoking ▤ AE, D, DC, MC, V.

$$$–$$$$ ▦ **Holiday Inn San Diego on the Bay.** On the Embarcadero and overlooking San Diego Bay, this twin high-rise hotel has unsurprising but spacious rooms and views from the balconies are hard to beat. Although the hotel grounds are nice if fairly sterile, the bay is just across the street and offers boat rides, restaurants, and picturesque walking areas. The hotel is very close to the airport and Amtrak station. The English-style Elephant and Castle Pub is a great place for food, drink, and meeting people. ▧ *1355 N. Harbor Dr., Embarcadero 92101* ▨ *619/232–3861 or 800/877–8920* ▨ *619/232–4924* ⊕ *www.holiday-inn.com* ✑ *600 rooms, 17 suites* ◔ *3 restaurants, in-room data ports, cable TV, 2 pools, gym, outdoor hot tub, sauna, bar, shops, laundry facilities, concierge, business services, meeting rooms, airport shuttle, car rental, parking (fee); no smoking* ▤ *AE, D, DC, MC, V.*

$$$–$$$$ ▦ **Residence Inn San Diego Downtown.** This all-suite hotel is near the harbor; it's a short, refreshing walk to the bayfront, where you can watch cruise ships set sail. The suites have full kitchens, but if you don't want to cook, the hotel serves a convenient, buffet-style, full breakfast accompanied by a morning paper. ▧ *1747 Pacific Hwy., Little Italy 92101* ▨ *619/338–8200 or 800/331–3131* ▨ *619/338–8219* ⊕ *www.marriott.com* ✑ *121 suites* ◔ *Dining room, in-room data ports, kitchens, refrigerator, cable TV with movies, pool, gym, outdoor hot tub, babysitting, laundry facilities, laundry service, concierge, Internet, business services, meeting room, car rental, travel services, parking (fee), some pets allowed (fee); no smoking* ▤ *AE, D, DC, MC, V.*

$$$–$$$$ ▦ **U. S. Grant Hotel.** Across the street from the Horton Plaza shopping center, this 1910 San Diego classic was built by President Ulysses S. Grant's grandson. Crystal chandeliers, polished marble floors, and mahogany furnishings in the stately rooms recall when President Franklin D. Roosevelt and Charles Lindbergh stayed here. High-power business types gather at the hotel's clubby Grant Grill, and English high tea is served in the lobby 2 PM–6 PM Friday and Saturday. ▧ *326 Broadway, Gaslamp Quarter 92101* ▨ *619/232–3121* ▨ *619/232–3626* ✑ *225 rooms, 60 suites* ◔ *2 restaurants, café, room service, in-room data ports, cable TV with movies, gym, bar, shops, concierge, Internet, business services, meeting rooms, airport shuttle, parking (fee); no smoking* ▤ *AE, D, MC, V.*

★ $$$–$$$$ ▦ **W Hotel.** The W chain's urban finesse adapts to San Diego with nautical blue-and-white rooms with beach-ball pillows and goose-down comforters atop the beds. The Beach bar has a heated sand floor and fire pit, but the pool is tiny by San Diego standards. The lobby doubles as the futuristic Living Room lounge, a local hipster nightspot where non-hotel guests have to wait behind a velvet rope. Be sure to get a room on an upper floor—the leather- and black-clad crowd parties into the night. The hotel restaurant, Rice, serves stylish Asian and Latin cuisine. The

Where to Stay Downtown

Laurel St.
Juniper St.
Ivy St.
Hawthorn St.
Grape St.
Fir St.
Elm St.
Date St.
Date St.

Juniper St.
Ivy St.
Hawthorn St.
Grape St.
Fir St.

Albatross St.
Front St.
Brant St.
Balboa Dr.

County Center/ Little Italy ◆Trolley Station

Cedar St.
Beech St.
Russ Blvd.

Harbor Dr.
Ash St.

Kettner Blvd.
India St.
Columbia St.
State St.
Union St.
Front St.
First Ave.
Second Ave.
Third Ave.
Fourth Ave.
Fifth Ave.
Sixth Ave.
Seventh Ave.
Eighth Ave.
Ninth Ave.
Tenth Ave.
Eleventh Ave.
Twelfth Ave.

Pacific Hwy.

A St.
A St.
B St.
Civic Center Trolley Station

B St.
Pier

C St.
C St.

Amtrak/ Transfer Station ◆
American Plaza Station
Broadway

E St.
E St.
F St.
F St.

Horton Plaza

G St.
G St.
Seaport Village Trolley Station

State St.
Union St.
First Ave.
Second Ave.
Fourth Ave.
Fifth Ave.

Market St.
Island Ave.
J St.
K St.
L St.

Thirteenth Ave.
Fourteenth Ave.

Market Pl.

Seaport Village ◆
Convention Center West Station

◆ Convention Center

Harbor Dr.
Imperial Ave.

spa, Away, opened in 2004. ⊠ *421 West B St., Downtown 92101* 🕾*619/ 231–8220 or 877/946–8357* 🖴 *619/232–3626* ⊕ *www.whotels.com/ sandiego* ⟨⟩ *277 rooms, 16 suites* ⚹ *Restaurant, room service, in-room data ports, cable TV with video games, in-room VCRs, gym, bars, spa, concierge, business services, meeting rooms, airport shuttle, parking (fee); no smoking* ⊟ *AE, D, MC, V.*

$$$–$$$$ ⊡ **Westin Hotel San Diego–Horton Plaza.** You know you're there when you see the startling lighted blue obelisk fronting this high-rise hotel. Inside, it's all understated cream-color marble and curved staircases. This hotel will complete an $8 million guest room redecoration in a stylish urban design by April 2004. The lobby lounge is packed every night with business travelers and weary shoppers back from the adjacent Horton Plaza. ⊠ *910 Broadway Circle, Gaslamp Quarter 92101* 🕾 *619/239– 2200 or 888/625–5144* 🖴 *619/239–0509* ⊕ *www.westin.com* ⟨⟩ *450 rooms, 14 suites* ⚹ *2 restaurants, room service, in-room data ports, cable TV with movies, 2 tennis courts, pool, health club, hot tub, basketball, lounge, sports bar, shops, dry cleaning, laundry service, concierge, business services, meeting rooms, airport shuttle, car rental, parking (fee); no smoking* ⊟ *AE, D, DC, MC, V.*

$$–$$$$ ⊡ **Radisson Hotel–Harbor View.** This 22-story hotel dwarfs the many two-story Victorian homes in the area, providing many rooms with unobstructed views of San Diego Bay and the downtown skyline. The art deco–inspired rooms are ordinary, but most have balconies. Although the hotel is practically adjacent to a freeway offramp, the noise level is tolerable. The airport and eateries and coffeehouses of Little Italy are nearby. ⊠ *1646 Front St., Downtown 92101* 🕾 *619/239–6800 or 800/ 333–3333* 🖴 *619/238–9561* ⊕ *www.radisson.com* ⟨⟩ *313 rooms, 20 suites* ⚹ *2 restaurants, in-room data ports, cable TV with video games, pool, gym, hot tub, sauna, bar, lounge, business services, airport shuttle* ⊟ *AE, D, DC, MC, V.*

$$$ ⊡ **Harbour Lights Resort.** A good choice if you have children, this hotel furnishes each suite with a king-size bed and a queen-size pull-out. All the suites have kitchens, including a dishwasher. You can rent videos from the hotel's library. It's a short walk to the stores and cinemas of Horton Plaza and the carousel at Seaport Village. ⊠ *911 5th St., Gaslamp Quarter 92101* 🕾*619/233–3300* 🖴*619/233–0340* ⟨⟩*56 suites* ⚹ *Restaurant, kitchens, refrigerators, cable TV with movies, in-room VCRs, gym, massage, sauna, laundry facilities, parking (fee); no smoking* ⊟ *AE, D, DC, MC, V.*

$$–$$$$ ⊡ **Horton Grand Hotel & Suites.** A Victorian confection, the Horton Grand comprises two 1880s hotels moved brick by brick from nearby locations and fit together. The delightfully retro rooms are furnished with period antiques, ceiling fans, and gas-burning fireplaces. The choicest rooms overlook a garden courtyard that twinkles with miniature lights. The hotel is a charmer, but service can be erratic. ⊠ *311 Island Ave., Gaslamp Quarter 92101* 🕾 *619/544–1886 or 800/542–1886* 🖴 *619/ 239–3823* ⊕ *www.hortongrand.com* ⟨⟩ *132 rooms, 24 suites* ⚹ *Restaurant, kitchenettes, microwaves, refrigerators, piano bar, theater, business services, meeting rooms, airport shuttle, parking (fee); no smoking* ⊟ *AE, D, DC, MC, V.*

$$–$$$$ 🏨 **Ramada Inn & Suites–Downtown.** Found on the northern end of the Gaslamp, this historic, 12-story building was San Diego's tallest when it opened in 1913. Now a boutique hotel, it's conveniently close to many restaurants, nightclubs, and shops but away from the hustle and bustle on 4th and 5th avenues. Good value and location make up for small rooms. The suites come with robes, coffeemakers, and in some cases hot tubs, big-screen TVs, and breakfast nooks. ⊠ *830 6th Ave., Gaslamp Quarter 92101* 🕿 *619/531–8877 or 800/664–4400* 🖷 *619/231–8307* ⊕ *www.ramada.com* ⤜ *87 rooms, 12 suites* ⚇ *Restaurant, room service, in-room data ports, minibars, cable TV with movies, meeting rooms, parking (fee); no smoking* ⊟ *AE, D, DC, MC, V.*

$$–$$$ 🏨 **Super 8 Bayview.** This motel's location is less noisy than those of the chain's other low-cost establishments in the area. The accommodations are nondescript but clean. Continental breakfast is complimentary. ⊠ *1835 Columbia St., Little Italy 92101* 🕿 *619/544–0164 or 800/800–8000* 🖷 *619/237–9940* ⊕ *www.super8.com* ⤜ *101 rooms* ⚇ *Some refrigerators, cable TV with movies, pool, gym, hot tub, laundry facilities, laundry service, airport shuttle, car rental, free parking; no smoking* ⊟ *AE, D, DC, MC, V* ⍾⦿ *CP.*

$$–$$$ 🏨 **Wyndham San Diego at Emerald Plaza.** This property's office and conference facilities draw many business travelers. Still, the Wyndham is also fine for vacationers who want to be near downtown shopping and restaurants. The beige-dominated standard rooms are rather bland and not large, but many of the upper-floor rooms have panoramic views. The health club is fully equipped and rarely crowded. ⊠ *400 W. Broadway, Gaslamp Quarter 92101* 🕿 *619/239–4500 or 800/996–3426* 🖷 *619/239–4527* ⊕ *www.wyndham.com* ⤜ *416 rooms, 20 suites* ⚇ *Restaurant, in-room data ports, minibars, cable TV with movies, pool, health club, outdoor hot tub, sauna, steam room, bar, shops, laundry service, concierge, Internet, business services, meeting rooms, airport shuttle, parking (fee); no smoking* ⊟ *AE, D, DC, MC, V.*

$–$$$ 🏨 **The Bristol.** Pop Art on the walls by Peter Max and Andy Warhol marks the style of this splashy boutique hotel. Rooms are decorated in fearless red, yellow, orange, and bright blue and come with bathrobes and CD players. A nice perk is complimentary high-speed Internet access and free wireless Internet in the lobby, bar, and restaurant. The Trolley stops right outside on First and Broadway. ⊠ *1055 1st Ave., Downtown 92101* 🕿 *619/232–6141 or 800/622–4477* 🖷 *619/232–0118* ⊕ *www.thebristolsandiego.com* ⤜ *102 rooms* ⚇ *Restaurant, in-room data ports, gym, bar, concierge, business services, Internet, meeting rooms, parking (fee)* ⊟ *AE, D, DC, MC, V.*

$–$$$ 🏨 **Gaslamp Plaza Suites.** On the National Registry of Historic Places, this 11-story structure a block from Horton Plaza was built in 1913 as one of San Diego's first "skyscrapers." Appealing public areas have old marble, brass, and mosaics. Although most rooms are rather small, they are well decorated with dark-wood furnishings that give the hotel an elegant flair. You can enjoy the view and a complimentary Continental breakfast on the rooftop terrace. Book ahead if you're visiting in summer. ⊠ *520 E St., Gaslamp Quarter 92101* 🕿 *619/232–9500 or 800/874–8770* 🖷 *619/238–9945* ⊕ *www.gaslampplaza.com* ⤜ *52 suites*

FodorsChoice
★

LET YOUR HOST BE A GHOST

SAN DIEGO'S FOUNDING DATES TO 1769, and with its rich history comes a fair share of ghost stories. Two of these tales revolve around local hostelries.

One of the most infamous concerns a woman named Kate Morgan, who checked into the Hotel del Coronado in November 1892. She eventually checked out of the hotel, and soon after checked out for good. The story goes that Morgan, who was pregnant at the time, had been anticipating the arrival of her estranged husband, but he never showed. She was found dead along the hotel beachfront of a gunshot wound to the head. Investigators ruled her death a suicide, but rumors have long circulated to the contrary.

Kate's spirit is said to haunt Room 3312 of the hotel, but there have been reports of ghostly occurrences in Room 3502 as well. Hotel guests and employees report having heard strange, unexplained noises and observed curtains billowing when windows are closed.

The Horton Grand Hotel is also said to have its phantoms in residence. Most famous of the hotel's spooks is a gambler from the 1880s named Roger Whitaker who is said to occupy Room 309. A number of peculiar occurrences here have ensured the hotel's reputation as being haunted by Whitaker, and maybe some other ghosts, too. According to legend, Roger was caught cheating at cards one night at the hotel. He tried to hide in Room 309 but was found and shot and killed.

To find out more about San Diego's best haunts, take the **Ghosts and Gravestones Tour of San Diego** (☎ 619/298–8687 or 800/868–7482 ⊕ www.ghostsandgravestones.com).

⚓ Cable TV with VCR, restaurant, microwaves, refrigerators, hot tub, bar, nightclub, parking (fee); no a/c ⊟ AE, D, DC, MC, V ⧫⧫ CP.

$–$$ 🏨 **Days Inn.** On one of downtown's quieter streets, this chain property in Cortez Hill is clean, comfortable, and pleasantly decorated. Continental breakfast is complimentary. The hotel is near Balboa Park, the zoo, and freeways. ⊠ 833 Ash St., Downtown 92101 ☎ 619/239–2285 or 800/424–6423, 800/522–1528 in CA ⊠ 619/235–6951 ⊕ www.rodeway.com ⇆ 44 rooms ⚓ In-room data ports, refrigerators, cable TV with movies, hot tub, sauna, laundry facilities, business services, meeting rooms, free parking; no smoking ⊟ AE, D, DC, MC, V ⧫⧫ CP.

¢–$$ 🏨 **Comfort Inn Downtown.** This three-story, stucco property surrounds a parking lot and courtyard. There's nothing fancy about the accommodations, but some rooms on the south side of the hotel have good views of the city skyline. It's close to downtown hot spots as well as the attractions of Balboa Park. ⊠ 719 Ash St., Downtown 92101 ☎ 619/232–2525 or 800/404–6835 ⊠ 619/687–3024 ⊕ www.comfortinn.com ⇆ 45 rooms ⚓ In-room data ports, microwave, cable TV with movies, hot tub, business services, airport shuttle, car rental, free parking; no smoking ⊟ AE, D, DC, MC, V.

Fodor'sChoice
★

¢ ⌑ **HI–San Diego Downtown.** In the center of the Gaslamp, this two-story hostel has basic, modern furnishings and facilities. A special event—from pizza and movie parties to discussions on traveling in Mexico—is scheduled every evening. There are 150 beds, a large common kitchen, and a TV room. Most rooms are dorm style with four bunks each. There are a few doubles, coed dorms, and group rooms (with 10 beds). ⊠ *521 Market St., Gaslamp Quarter 92101* ☎ *619/525–1531 or 800/909–4776* 🖷 *619/338–0129* ⅊ *Bicycles, billiards, laundry facilities; no room phones, no room TVs, no smoking, no a/c* ▭ *MC, V.*

¢ ⌑ **USA Hostels.** This bright, clean hostel is friendly and communal, but strictly for the independent backpacker (any nationality, any age) with a valid passport showing international travel. It makes its home in an 1887 Victorian hotel in the heart of the Gaslamp Quarter. There are 60 beds and five private rooms (two doubles and a triple). A variety of tours and parties are hosted weekly including beach and Tijuana trips. Continental breakfast is complimentary and there's a kitchen for guest use, but you are asked to clean up after yourself. ⊠ *726 5th Ave., Gaslamp Quarter 92101* ☎ *619/232–3100 or 800/438–8622* 🖷 *619/232–3106* ⊕ *www.usahostels.com* ⅊ *Recreation room, laundry facilities, airport shuttle, travel services; no room phones, no room TVs, no smoking, no a/c* ▭ *MC, V* ⏍| *CP.*

Harbor Island, Shelter Island & Point Loma

Harbor Island and Shelter Island, two man-made peninsulas between downtown and the community of Point Loma, both have grassy parks, tree-lined paths, lavish hotels, and good restaurants. Harbor Island is closest to downtown and less than five minutes from the airport. Narrower Shelter Island is nearer to Point Loma. Both locations command views of the bay and the downtown skyline. Not all the lodgings listed here are on the islands themselves, but all are in the vicinity.

$$$$ ⌑ **Sheraton San Diego Hotel & Marina.** Of this property's two high-rises, the smaller, more intimate West Tower has larger rooms with separate areas suitable for business entertaining. The East Tower has better sports facilities. Rooms throughout are decorated with plush, contemporary furnishings. Views from the upper floors of both sections are superb, but because the West Tower is closer to the water it has fine outlooks from the lower floors, too. ⊠ *1380 Harbor Island Dr., Harbor Island 92101* ☎ *619/291–2900 or 888/625–5144* 🖷 *619/ 692–2337* ⊕ *www.sheraton.com* ⏎ *1,044 rooms, 50 suites* ⅊ *3 restaurants, patisserie, room service, in-room data ports, minibars, cable TV with movies, 4 tennis courts, 3 pools, wading pool, health club, 2 outdoor hot tubs, massage, sauna, beach, boating, marina, bicycles, 2 bars, shop, dry cleaning, laundry service, concierge, business services, meeting rooms, airport shuttle, parking (fee); no smoking* ▭ *AE, D, DC, MC, V.*

$$–$$$$ ⌑ **Humphrey's Half Moon Inn & Suites.** This sprawling South Seas–style resort has grassy open areas with palms and tiki torches. Rooms, some with kitchens and some with harbor or marine views, have modern furnishings. Locals throng to Humphrey's, the hotel's seafood restaurant,

and to the jazz lounge; the hotel also hosts outdoor jazz and pop concerts from June through October. ⊠ *2303 Shelter Island Dr., Shelter Island 92106* ☎ *619/224–3411 or 800/542–7400* 🖷 *619/224–3478* ⊕ *www.halfmooninn.com* ↳ *128 rooms, 54 suites* ⚥ *Restaurant, room service, in-room data ports, kitchenettes, minibars, refrigerators, cable TV with movies and video games, putting green, pool, pond, health club, hot tub, boating, bicycles, croquet, Ping-Pong, bar, concert hall, laundry facilities, business services, meeting rooms, airport shuttle, free parking; no smoking* ▤ *AE, D, DC, MC, V.*

$$–$$$ 🖭 **Bay Club Hotel & Marina.** Rooms in this appealing low-rise Shelter Island property are large, light, and furnished with rattan tables and chairs and Polynesian tapestries; all have views of either the bay or the marina from outside terraces. A buffet breakfast and limo service to and from the airport or Amtrak station are included. ⊠ *2131 Shelter Island Dr., Shelter Island 92106* ☎ *619/224–8888 or 800/672–0800* 🖷 *619/225–1604* ⊕ *www.bayclubhotel.com* ↳ *95 rooms, 10 suites* ⚥ *Restaurant, room service, in-room data ports, refrigerators, cable TV with movies, pool, gym, outdoor hot tub, bar, shop, concierge, business services, meeting rooms, airport shuttle, free parking; no smoking* ▤ *AE, D, DC, MC, V* ⱐ⚌ *BP.*

$$–$$$ 🖭 **Best Western Island Palms Hotel & Marina.** This waterfront inn, with an airy lobby brightened by skylights, is a good choice if you have a boat to dock; the adjacent marina has guest slips. Both harbor- and marina-view rooms are available. Standard accommodations are fairly small; if you're traveling with family or more than one friend, the two-bedroom suites with kitchens are a good deal. ⊠ *2051 Shelter Island Dr., Shelter Island 92106* ☎ *619/222–0561 or 800/345–9995* 🖷 *619/222–9760* ⊕ *www.islandpalms.com* ↳ *68 rooms, 29 suites* ⚥ *Restaurant, fans, in-room data ports, kitchenettes, refrigerator, cable TV with movies and video games, pool, gym, outdoor hot tub, boating, bar, laundry service, business services, meeting rooms, free parking; no smoking* ▤ *AE, D, DC, MC, V.*

$$–$$$ 🖭 **Shelter Pointe Hotel & Marina.** This 11-acre property blends Mexican and Mediterranean styles. The spacious and light-filled lobby, with its Mayan sculptures and terra-cotta tiles, opens onto a lush esplanade that overlooks the hotel's marina. The rooms are well appointed, if a bit small, and most look out onto either the marina or San Diego Bay. The attractive hotel is popular for business meetings. ⊠ *1551 Shelter Island Dr., Shelter Island 92106* ☎ *619/221–8000 or 800/566–2524* 🖷 *619/221–5953* ⊕ *www.shelterpointe.com* ↳ *206 rooms, 31 suites* ⚥ *Restaurant, room service, kitchenettes, cable TV with movies and video games, 2 tennis courts, 2 pools, health club, 2 hot tubs, 2 saunas, beach, boating, marina, bicycles, volleyball, bar, meeting rooms, airport shuttle, free parking; no smoking* ▤ *AE, D, DC, MC, V.*

★ $$ 🖭 **Holiday Inn Express.** In Point Loma near the West Mission Bay exit off I–8, this Holiday Inn Express is a surprisingly quiet lodging despite proximity to bustling traffic. The three-story building is only about a half mile from both SeaWorld and Mission Bay. Continental breakfast is included. ⊠ *3950 Jupiter St., Sports Arena 92110* ☎ *619/226–8000 or 800/320–0208* 🖷 *619/226–1409* ⊕ *www.basshotels.com/holiday-inn*

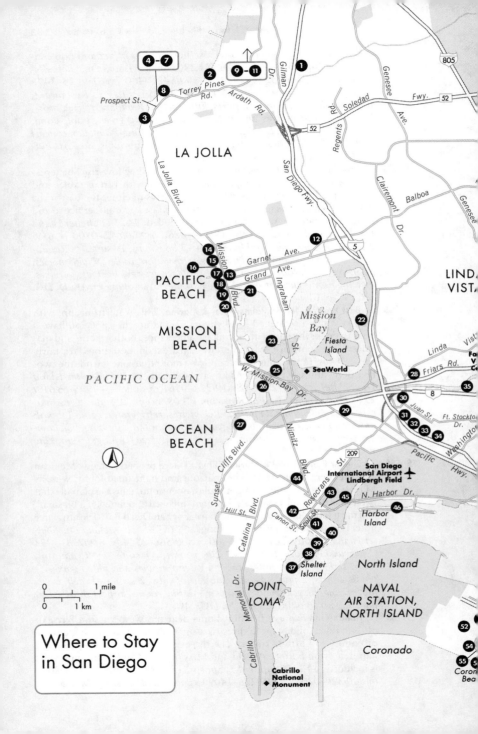

Where to Stay
in San Diego

Map labels:

15

52

KEARNY MESA

Clairemont

Conway St.

Mesa Blvd.

15

163

Balboa Ave.

Ave.

Aero Dr.

Jacob Dekema Fwy.

Cabrillo Fwy.

Mission Center Rd.

Ave.

MISSION VALLEY

Rd.

48

San Diego R.

47

15

ashion alley enter ◆

36

Adams Ave.

HILLCREST Madison Ave.

El Cajon Blvd.

Alabama St. Texas St. 28th

University Ave.

Robinson

Richmond Park Blvd.

49

163

Laurel St.

Balboa Park

See Downtown Lodging Map

1st Ave. 4th Ave. 6th Ave.

Broadway

94

Market St.

Imperial Ave.

50

Harbor Dr.

San Diego-Coronado Bay Bridge

National Ave.

National City Blvd.

1

53

75

56

San Diego Bay

58

NATIONAL CITY

do h

Silver Strand Blvd.

Legend:

Bahia Resort Hotel **24**
Balboa Park Inn **49**
Banana Bungalow
San Diego **18**
Bay Club
Hotel & Marina **39**
Beach Haven Inn **16**
Best Western
Blue Sea Lodge **20**
Best Western
Hacienda Suites–
Old Town **31**
Best Western Island Palms
Hotel & Marina **38**
Best Western
Posada Inn at the
Yacht Harbor **45**
Catamaran
Resort Hotel **21**
Cherokee Lodge **52**
Comfort Inn
at the Harbor **43**
Coronado Island
Marriott Resort **50**
Courtyard San Diego
Old Town **32**
Crown City
Inn & Bistro **51**
Crystal Pier Hotel **17**
Dana Inn & Marina **25**
Days Inn Mission Bay . . .**12**
Diamond Head Inn **13**
Doubletree Hotel
San Diego
Mission Valley **47**
El Cordova Hotel **55**
Glorietta Bay Inn **56**
The Grande Colonial **4**
Handlery Hotel
& Resort **36**
Heritage Park Inn **30**
HI–San Diego Point
Loma **44**
Hilton La Jolla
Torrey Pines **9**
Hilton San Diego
Resort **22**
Holiday Inn Express **29**
Holiday Inn Express–
La Jolla **10**
Holiday Inn Express–
Old Town **33**
Hotel Del Coronado **57**
Hotel Parisi **6**
Humphrey's Half Moon
Inn & Suites **40**
Hyatt Islandia **26**
Hyatt Regency
La Jolla **1**
La Avenida Inn **54**
La Jolla Cove Suites **8**

La Jolla Inn **7**
La Valencia **5**
Lodge at Torrey Pines . . .**11**
Loews Coronado
Bay Resort **58**
Ocean Beach International
Backpackers Hostel **27**
Pacific Shores Inn **15**
Pacific Terrace Hotel **14**
Ramada Limited
San Diego Airport **42**
Red Lion Hanalei
Hotel **35**
San Diego Marriott
Mission Valley **48**
San Diego Paradise
Point Resort & Spa **23**
Scripps Inn **3**
Sea Lodge **2**
Shelter Pointe
Hotel & Marina **37**
Sheraton San Diego
Hotel & Marina **46**
Super 8 Motel **28**
Surfer Motor Lodge **19**
Vagabond Inn–
Point Loma **41**
Villa Capri By The Sea . . .**53**
Western Inn–
Old Town **34**

↪ *70 rooms, 2 suites & In-room data ports, refrigerator, cable TV with movies, pool, hot tub, laundry service, concierge, business services, free parking; no smoking ☰ AE, D, DC, MC, V ⎮◯⎮ CP.*

$–$$ ▦ **Best Western Posada Inn at the Yacht Harbor.** Many of the rooms at this comfortable if plain inn have harbor views. Some rooms have microwaves, mini-refrigerators, and video players. Point Loma's seafood restaurants are within walking distance. Weekly rates, package plans, and senior discounts are available. Continental breakfast is included. ✉ *5005 N. Harbor Dr., Point Loma 92106* ☎ *619/224–3254 or 800/ 231–3811* ⎙ *619/224–2186* ⊕ *www.bestwestern.com* ↪ *112 rooms & Restaurant, in-room data ports, cable TV with movies, pool, gym, outdoor hot tub, bar, laundry service, meeting rooms, airport shuttle, free parking; no smoking ☰ AE, D, DC, MC, V ⎮◯⎮ CP.*

$–$$ ▦ **Vagabond Inn–Point Loma.** This two-story budget motel is safe, clean, and comfortable, close to the airport, yacht clubs, and Cabrillo National Monument—and the popular and excellent Point Loma Seafoods restaurant is next door. A daily newspaper and Continental breakfast are included. ✉ *1325 Scott St., Point Loma 92106* ☎ *619/224–3371* ⎙ *619/ 223–0646* ⊕ *www.vagabondinn.com* ↪ *40 rooms & Restaurant, in-room safes, some kitchens, some refrigerators, cable TV with movies, pool, bar, airport shuttle, free parking; no smoking ☰ AE, D, DC, MC, V.*

$ ▦ **Comfort Inn at the Harbor.** You'll get the same view here as at the higher-price hotels—for far less money. Of course, there are fewer amenities and the neighborhood isn't as serene, but the rooms—all with coffeemakers—are adequate and clean. ✉ *5102 N. Harbor Dr., Point Loma 92106* ☎ *619/223–8171 or 800/578–7878* ⎙ *619/222–7330* ⊕ *www. comfortinn.com* ↪ *45 rooms & In-room data ports, cable TV, refrigerators, pool, free parking; no smoking ☰ AE, D, DC, MC, V.*

$ ▦ **Ramada Limited San Diego Airport.** The location is convenient, although on a busy street, and the rooms with bay views are quite a deal. Continental breakfast, daily newspaper, and local calls are complimentary. There's a heated pool and a bay-view bar with billiards, and there's a free shuttle to area attractions. ✉ *1403 Rosecrans St., Point Loma 92106* ☎ *619/225–9461 or 888/298–2054* ⎙ *619/225–1163* ⊕ *www. ramada.com* ↪ *83 rooms & Restaurant, dining room, cable TV, pool, bar, meeting rooms, airport shuttle, free parking, some pets allowed (fee); no smoking ☰ AE, D, DC, MC, V ⎮◯⎮ CP.*

¢ ▦ **HI–San Diego Point Loma.** This hostel is in a large converted house, in a quiet area straddling the Ocean Beach and Point Loma neighborhoods. Though it's far from San Diego's attractions and nightlife, there's a bus stop nearby. Special events are scheduled weekly. The hostel has a large kitchen, a large patio, and a TV room. Rates include linens and a free pancake breakfast. ✉ *3790 Udall St., Ocean Beach 92107* ☎ *619/ 223–4778 or 800/909–4779 Ext. 44* ⎙ *619/223–1883* ↪ *61 beds & Bicycles, laundry service, free parking; no room phones, no room TVs, no smoking, no a/c ☰ MC, V ⎮◯⎮ BP.*

Old Town & Vicinity

Staying in Old Town affords easy access to SeaWorld and the beaches to the west, downtown and Mexico to the south, and Mission Valley and the zoo to the east. But most important, it puts you smack in the middle of the most popular park in the California state system, the Old Town San Diego State Historical Park. Old Town has a few picturesque lodgings and some modestly priced chain hotels near I–5; when you're making reservations, request a room that doesn't face the freeway. West of the freeway is the Midway District, with a few budget hotels near the San Diego Sports Arena.

$$–$$$ ▦ **Courtyard San Diego Old Town.** This hacienda-style hotel has Spanish colonial–style fountains and courtyards, and painted tiles and Southwestern decor in the rooms. A breakfast buffet and transfers to the airport, bus, and Amtrak stations are complimentary. ⊠ *2435 Jefferson St., Old Town 92110* ☎ *619/260–8500 or 800/255–3544* 🖷 *619/297–2078* ⊕ *www.marriott.com* ⇌ *174 rooms, 19 suites* ⚒ *Restaurant, in-room data ports, cable TV with movies and video games, pool, gym, outdoor hot tub, bar, shop, laundry service, concierge, Internet, business services, meeting rooms, airport shuttle, free parking; no smoking* ⊟ *AE, D, DC, MC, V* ❙⊙❙ *BP.*

★ **$$–$$$** ▦ **Holiday Inn Express–Old Town.** Already an excellent value for Old Town, this cheerful property throws in such perks as garage parking, Continental breakfast, and afternoon snacks. Rooms have a European look. If you've had enough of the heated pool off the shaded courtyard, the historic park's attractions and restaurants are nearby. ⊠ *3900 Old Town Ave., Old Town 92110* ☎ *619/299–7400 or 800/272–6232* 🖷 *619/299–1619* ⊕ *www.basshotels.com/holiday-inn* ⇌ *125 rooms, 4 suites* ⚒ *Restaurant, room service, in-room data ports, microwaves, refrigerators, cable TV, pool, outdoor hot tub, shops, laundry service, concierge, business services, meeting rooms, airport shuttle, free parking; no smoking* ⊟ *AE, D, DC, MC, V* ❙⊙❙ *CP.*

$–$$$ ▦ **Heritage Park Inn.** The beautifully restored mansions in Heritage Park
Fodor'sChoice   include this romantic 1889 Queen Anne–style B&B. Rooms range from
★   smallish to ample, and most are bright and cheery. A two-bedroom suite is decorated with period antiques, and there's also a minisuite. A full breakfast and afternoon tea are included. There is a two-night minimum stay on weekends, and weekly and monthly rates are available. Some rooms share a bath. Classic vintage films are shown nightly in the parlor on a small film screen. ⊠ *2470 Heritage Park Row, Old Town 92110* ☎ *619/299–6832 or 800/995–2470* 🖷 *619/299–9465* ⊕ *www. heritageparkinn.com* ⇌ *10 rooms, 2 suites* ⚒ *In-room data ports, cable TV, library, meeting rooms; no smoking* ⊟ *AE, MC, V* ❙⊙❙ *BP.*

$$ ▦ **Best Western Hacienda Suites–Old Town.** Pretty and white, with balconies and Spanish-tile roofs, the Hacienda is in a quiet part of Old Town, away from the freeway and the main retail bustle. The layout is somewhat confusing, and accommodations are not large enough to earn the "suite" label the hotel gives them, but they're decorated in tasteful Southwestern style and are well-equipped. ⊠ *4041 Harney St., Old Town 92110* ☎ *619/298–4707 or 800/888–1991* 🖷 *619/298–4771* ⊕ *www. bestwestern.com* ⇌ *169 rooms* ⚒ *Restaurant, room service, microwaves, refrigerators, cable TV, in-room VCRs, pool, gym, outdoor hot tub, bar, laundry service, concierge, business services, meeting rooms, airport shut-*

LODGING ALTERNATIVES

Apartment Rentals

If you're planning an extended stay or need lodgings for four or more people, consider an apartment rental. Oakwood Apartments rents comfortable furnished apartments in the Mission Valley, La Jolla Colony, and Coronado areas with maid service and linens; there's a one-week to 30-day minimum stay depending on locations. Several hotels also offer special weekly and monthly rates, especially in the beach communities. Rental apartments and condominiums are also available through realtors who specialize in Mission Beach, Pacific Beach, La Jolla's Golden Triangle–University City area, Carlsbad, and Escondido. In addition, there are three Residence Inns by Marriott in San Diego; these sometimes offer good value for families traveling on weekends.

Hideaways International ✉ *767 Islington St., Portsmouth, NH 03801* ☎ *603/430–4433 or 800/843–4433* 🖷 *603/430–4444* ⊕ *www.hideaways.com, annual membership $145.* **Vacation Home Rentals Worldwide** ✉ *235 Kensington Ave., Norwood, NJ 07648* ☎ *201/767–9393 or 800/633–3284* 🖷 *201/767–5510* ⊕ *www.vhrww.com.*

Oakwood Apartments ☎ *800/888–0808* ⊕ *www.oakwood.com* **Penny Realty** ☎ *800/748–6704* ⊕ *www.missionbeach.com* and **San Diego Vacation Rentals** ☎ *800/222–8281* ⊕ *www.sdvr.com* handle rentals in the Mission Bay and La Jolla areas.

Bed & Breakfasts

San Diego is known more for its resorts and solid chain properties, but the city has several bed-and-breakfasts, most of which are very well maintained and accommodating. Most of these are in private homes. Historic Julian, in the mountains east of San Diego, has many bed-and-breakfasts. The Bed and Breakfast Guild of San Diego lists a number of high-quality member inns. The Bed & Breakfast Directory for San Diego covers San Diego County.

Bed & Breakfast Directory for San Diego ☎ *619/297–3130 or 800/619–7666* ⊕ *www.sandiegobandb.com.* **Bed and Breakfast Guild of San Diego** ☎ *619/523–1300* ⊕ *www.bandbguildsandiego.org.* **Julian Bed and Breakfast Guild** ☎ *888/765–4333* ⊕ *www.julianbnbguild.com.*

Chains

Best Western ☎ *800/528–1234* ⊕ *www.bestwestern.com.* **Choice** ☎ *800/424–6423* ⊕ *www.choicehotels.com.* **Clarion** ☎ *800/424–6423* ⊕ *www.choicehotels.com.* **Comfort Inn** ☎ *800/424–6423* ⊕ *www.choicehotels.com.* **Days Inn** ☎ *800/325–2525* ⊕ *www.daysinn.com.* **Doubletree Hotels** ☎ *800/222–8733* ⊕ *www.doubletree.com.* **Embassy Suites** ☎ *800/362–2779* ⊕ *www.embassysuites.com.* **Fairfield Inn** ☎ *800/228–2800* ⊕ *www.marriott.com.* **Four Seasons** ☎ *800/332–3442* ⊕ *www.fourseasons.com.* **Hilton** ☎ *800/445–8667* ⊕ *www.hilton.com.* **Holiday Inn** ☎ *800/465–4329* ⊕ *www.ichotelsgroup.com.* **Howard Johnson** ☎ *800/446–4656* ⊕ *www.hojo.com.* **Hyatt Hotels & Resorts** ☎ *800/233–1234* ⊕ *www.hyatt.com.* **La Quinta** ☎ *800/531–5900* ⊕ *www.lq.com.* **Marriott** ☎ *800/228–9290* ⊕ *www.marriott.com.* **Quality Inn** ☎ *800/424–6423* ⊕ *www.choicehotels.com.* **Radisson** ☎ *800/333–3333* ⊕ *www.radisson.com.* **Ramada** ☎ *800/228–2828, 800/854–7854* international reservations ⊕ *www.ramada.com or www.ramadahotels.com.* **Red Lion and WestCoast Hotels and Inns** ☎ *800/733–5466* ⊕ *www.redlion.com.* **Sheraton** ☎ *800/325–3535* ⊕ *www.starwood.com/sheraton.* **Sleep Inn** ☎ *800/424–6423* ⊕ *www.choicehotels.com.* **Westin Hotels & Resorts** ☎ *800/228–*

3000 ⊕ www.starwood.com/westin.
Wyndham Hotels & Resorts ☎ 800/822–4200 ⊕ www.wyndham.com.

Home Exchanges

If you would like to exchange your home for someone else's, join a home-exchange organization, which will send you its updated listings of available exchanges for a year and will include your own listing in at least one of them. It's up to you to make specific arrangements.

HomeLink International ✆ Box 47747, Tampa, FL 33647 ☎ 813/975–9825 or 800/638–3841 🖷 813/910–8144 ⊕ www.homelink.org; $110 yearly for a listing, online access, and catalog; $70 without catalog. **Intervac U.S.** ⊠ 30 Corte San Fernando, Tiburon, CA 94920 ☎ 800/756–4663 🖷 415/435–7440 ⊕ www.intervacus.com; $125 yearly for a listing, online access, and a catalog; $65 without catalog.

Hostels

No matter what your age, you can save on lodging costs by staying at hostels. Throughout San Diego, Hostelling International (HI), a worldwide umbrella group for a number of national youth-hostel associations, offers single-sex, dorm-style beds. They cater to college students and budget backpackers, and most require an international passport to check in. Rooms usually have four to six bunks; however, some hostels have a few private or double rooms.

Membership in any HI national hostel association, open to travelers of all ages, allows you to stay in HI-affiliated hostels at member rates; one-year membership is about $28 for adults (C$35 for a two-year minimum membership in Canada, £14 in the U.K., A$52 in Australia, and NZ$40 in New Zealand); hostels charge about $10–$30 per night. Members have priority if the hostel is full; they're also eligible for discounts around the world, even on rail and bus travel in some countries.

Hostelling International–USA ⊠ 8401 Colesville Rd., Suite 600, Silver Spring, MD 20910 ☎ 301/495–1240 🖷 301/495–6697 ⊕ www.hiusa.org. **Hostelling International–Canada** ⊠ 205 Catherine St., Suite 400, Ottawa, Ontario K2P 1C3 ☎ 613/237–7884 or 800/663–5777 🖷 613/237–7868 ⊕ www.hihostels.ca. **YHA England and Wales** ⊠ Trevelyan House, Dimple Rd., Matlock, Derbyshire DE4 3YH, U.K. ☎ 0870/870–8808, 0870/770–8868, 0162/959–2600 🖷 0870/770–6127 ⊕ www.yha.org.uk. **YHA Australia** ⊠ 422 Kent St., Sydney, NSW 2001 ☎ 02/9261–1111 🖷 02/9261–1969 ⊕ www.yha.com.au. **YHA New Zealand** ⊠ Level 1, Moorhouse City, 166 Moorhouse Ave., Box 436, Christchurch ☎ 03/379–9970 or 0800/278–299 🖷 03/365–4476 ⊕ www.yha.org.nz.

tle, car rental, travel services, free parking; no smoking, no a/c ▭ AE, D, DC, MC, V.

★ ¢-$ ⌧ **Western Inn–Old Town.** The three-story Western Inn is decorated in a Spanish motif and is close to shops and restaurants, but far enough away from the main tourist drag that you don't have to worry about noise and congestion. There's a free Continental breakfast, and a barbecue area where you can cook for yourself. A bus, trolley, and Coaster station is a few blocks away. ✉ 3889 Arista St., Old Town 92110 ☎ 619/298–6888 or 888/475–2353 🖷 619/692–4497 ⊕ www. westerninn.com ⇨ 29 rooms, 6 suites ⚴ In-room data ports, refrigerators, cable TV, airport shuttle, free parking; no smoking ▭ AE, D, DC, MC, V ⫟❑ CP.

Mission Valley & Hotel Circle

Mission Valley once thrived as a dairy farm area, a history you'd never guess from its appearance today. Beginning in the late 1950s, hotels started popping up along what is now called Hotel Circle, in the western end of the valley. Today the area is paved over with shopping centers, car lots, Qualcomm Stadium, and hotels except for a narrow greenbelt lining the San Diego River. Most of the 20 hotels along Hotel Circle are reasonably priced, their quality ranging from a bit haggard and dated to brand new. A little farther east you'll find a selection of bigger and pricier properties, although this puts you farther from major attractions and the beaches.

$$$ ⌧ **Doubletree Hotel San Diego Mission Valley.** Near Fashion Valley Center and adjacent to the Hazard Center—which has a seven-screen movie theater, four major restaurants, a food pavilion, and more than 20 shops—the Doubletree is also convenient to Route 163 and I–8. A San Diego Trolley station is within walking distance. Public areas are bright and comfortable, well suited to this hotel's large business clientele. Spacious rooms have ample desk space; complimentary coffee, irons, and ironing boards are also provided. ✉ 7450 Hazard Center Dr., Mission Valley 92108 ☎ 619/297–5466 or 800/222–8733 🖷 619/297–5499 ⊕ www.doubletree.com ⇨ 294 rooms, 6 suites ⚴ Restaurant, room service, in-room data ports, minibars, cable TV with movies, 2 tennis courts, 2 pools, gym, outdoor hot tub, sauna, 2 bars, shops, laundry facilities, laundry service, concierge, business services, meeting rooms, airport shuttle, free parking; no smoking ▭ AE, D, DC, MC, V.

★ $$-$$$ ⌧ **San Diego Marriott Mission Valley.** This 17-floor high-rise is well equipped for business travelers—the front desk provides 24-hour fax and photocopy services, and rooms come with desks and private voice mail. The hotel is in the middle of the San Diego River valley near Qualcomm Stadium and the Rio Vista Plaza shopping center, minutes from the Mission Valley and Fashion Valley malls. There's free transportation to the malls and the San Diego Trolley stops across the street. Rooms are comfortable (with individual balconies) and the staff is friendly. ✉ 8757 Rio San Diego Dr., Mission Valley 92108 ☎ 619/692–3800 or 800/228–9290 🖷 619/692–0769 ⊕ www.marriott.com ⇨ 350 rooms, 5 suites ⚴ Restaurant, room service, in-room data ports, mini-

bars, cable TV with movies, tennis court, pool, gym, health club, out-door hot tub, sauna, sports bar, nightclub, shops, laundry service, con-cierge, concierge floor, Internet, business services, meeting rooms, airport shuttle, parking (fee); no smoking ⊟ *AE, D, DC, MC, V.*

$–$$ ⊡ **Handlery Hotel & Resort.** Well-managed and pleasant, this moderate hotel within walking distance of the Fashion Valley shopping mall has free shuttle service to area attractions. The Riverwalk Golf Club next door offers guests reduced rates to tee off. The heated pool areas are pleasing and an on-site shop covers necessities as well as souvenirs. ⊠ *950 Hotel Circle N, Mission Valley 92108* ☎ *619/298–0511 or 800/843–4343* 🖷 *619/298–9793* ⊕ *www.handlery.com* ↩ *217 rooms, 3 suites* ♨ *Restaurant, room service, in-room data ports, cable TV with movies, refrigerators, 2 pools, gym, outdoor hot tub, shop, laundry facilities, laundry service, concierge, beauty salon, car rental, business services, meeting rooms, airport shuttle, parking (fee); no smoking* ⊟ *AE, D, DC, MC, V.*

$–$$ ⊡ **Red Lion Hanalei Hotel.** As the name suggests, the theme of this friendly property is Hawaiian: palms, waterfalls, koi ponds, and tiki torches abound. Rooms are decorated in tropical prints. What used to be a golf course next door has been restored to a bird sanctuary. Free trans-portation is provided to local malls and Old Town. The hotel is virtu-ally surrounded by heavy traffic, which can make for a noisy stay. ⊠ *2270 Hotel Circle N, Hotel Circle 92108* ☎ *619/297–1101 or 800/882–0858* 🖷 *619/297–6049* ⊕ *www.hanaleihotel.com* ↩ *402 rooms, 14 suites* ♨ *2 restaurants, room service, in-room data ports, cable TV, pool, gym, hot tub, bar, laundry service, business services, meeting rooms, car rental, travel services, parking (fee); no smoking* ⊟ *AE, D, DC, MC, V.*

¢–$ ⊡ **Super 8 Motel.** Simple, clean rooms are available here in the same area of as Mission Valley's pricier hotels. ⊠ *445 Hotel Circle S, Mission Valley 92108* ☎ *619/692–1288 or 800/800–8000* 🖷 *619/298–0668* ⊕ *www.super8.com* ↩ *144 rooms* ♨ *In-room data ports, cable TV with movies, laundry, some refrigerators, pool, gym, free parking* ⊟ *AE, D, DC, MC, V.*

La Jolla

Million-dollar homes line the beaches and hillsides of beautiful and pres-tigious La Jolla. Its exclusiveness and seclusion make it easy to forget that La Jolla is part of the city of San Diego and not a separate town. The village—the heart of La Jolla—is chockablock with expensive bou-tiques, galleries, and restaurants. Don't despair, however, if you're not old money or nouveau riche; this popular vacation spot has sufficient lodging choices for every purse.

$$$$ ⊡ **Hilton La Jolla Torrey Pines.** The hotel blends discreetly into the Tor-
Fodor'sChoice rey Pines cliff top, overlooking the Pacific Ocean and the 18th hole of
★ the Torrey Pines Municipal Golf Course, site of the 2008 U.S. Open. Oversize accommodations are simple but elegant; most have balconies or terraces. Torreyana Grille's menu changes with the seasons. Caesar salad and filet mignon are menu stalwarts, but you're likely to find lob-

ster pot stickers and coffee-lacquered duck breast as well. ✉ *10950 N. Torrey Pines Rd., La Jolla 92037* ☎ *858/558–1500 or 800/774–1500* 🖷 *858/450–4584* ⊕ *www.hilton.com* 🖙 *377 rooms, 17 suites* ⟆ *3 restaurants, room service, in-room data ports, in-room safes, minibars, cable TV with movies, putting green, 3 tennis courts, pool, gym, outdoor hot tub, sauna, bicycles, 3 bars, babysitting, laundry service, concierge, business services, meeting rooms, airport shuttle, car rental, parking (fee); no smoking* ☰ *AE, D, DC, MC, V.*

★ **$$$$** 🏨 **Hotel Parisi.** A Zen-like peace welcomes you in the lobby with its skylit waterfall and Asian art. The suites are decorated using the principles of Feng-shui; you can order a massage, a yoga session, or the on-staff psychologist from room service. Favored by celebrities, each hushed, earth-tone suite has granite bathrooms, fluffy robes, and ergonomic tubs. The rooms are set back enough from the street noise, but in the ocean-view suites you have to look over buildings across the street to view the Pacific. Continental breakfast is served daily in a breakfast room off the lobby. ✉ *1111 Prospect St., La Jolla 92037* ☎ *858/454–1511* 🖷 *858/ 454–1531* ⊕ *www.hotelparisi.com* 🖙 *20 suites* ⟆ *Room service, in-room data ports, in-room safes, minibar, cable TV with movies, in-room VCR, massage, business services, meeting rooms, free parking; no smoking* שׂ⚊ *CP* ☰ *AE, D, MC, V.*

$$$$ 🏨 **La Valencia.** This pink Spanish-Mediterranean confection drew Hollywood film stars in the 1930s and '40s with its setting and views of La Jolla Cove. Many rooms have a genteel European look, with antique pieces and richly-colored rugs. The personal attention provided by the staff, as well as the plush robes and grand bathrooms, make the stay even more pleasurable. The hotel is near the shops and restaurants of La Jolla Village. Rates are lower if you're willing to look out on the village. Be sure to stroll the tiered gardens in back. ✉ *1132 Prospect St., La Jolla 92037* ☎ *858/454–0771 or 800/451–0772* 🖷 *858/456–3921* ⊕ *www.lavalencia.com* 🖙 *117 rooms, 15 villas* ⟆ *3 restaurants, room service, in-room safes, minibars, cable TV with movies and video games, in-room VCRs, pool, health club, outdoor hot tub, massage, sauna, beach, bicycles, Ping-Pong, shuffleboard, bar, lounge, laundry facilities, concierge, business services, meeting rooms, airport shuttle, parking (fee); no smoking* ☰ *AE, D, MC, V.*

Fodor'sChoice
★

$$$$ 🏨 **Lodge at Torrey Pines.** This beautiful Craftsman-style lodge sits on a bluff between La Jolla and Del Mar and commands a view of miles of coastline. You know you're in for a different sort of experience when you see the Scottish kilted doorman. Rooms, though dim, are roomy and furnished with antiques and reproduction turn-of-the-20th-century pieces. The service is excellent and the restaurant, A. R. Valentin, serves fine California cuisine. Beyond the 6-acre grounds are the Torrey Pines Municipal Golf Course and scenic trails that lead to the Torrey Pines State Beach and Reserve. The village of La Jolla is a 10-minute drive away. ✉ *11480 N. Torrey Pines Rd., La Jolla 92037* ☎ *858/453–4420 or 800/995–4507* 🖷 *858/453–7464* ⊕ *www.lodgetorreypines.com* 🖙 *175 rooms* ⟆ *2 restaurants, in-room data ports, in-room safes, kitchenettes, cable TV, 18-hole golf course, pool, gym, hot tub, massage, spa, 2 bars, Internet, meeting rooms, free parking; no smoking* ☰ *AE, D, DC, MC, V.*

Fodor'sChoice
★

$$$$ 🖭 **Sea Lodge.** One of few hotels actually on the beach, the Sea Lodge is at La Jolla Shores Beach and Tennis Club. Palms, fountains, red-tile roofs, and Mexican tile work lend character to the low-lying compound. Rooms have rattan furniture, floral-print bedspreads, and wood balconies overlooking the ocean. Hair dryers, coffeemakers, and irons are included. Tennis lessons are available. ⊠ *8110 Camino del Oro, La Jolla 92037* ☎ *858/459–8271 or 800/237–5211* 🖷 *858/456–9346* ⊕ *www.sealodge. com* ➷ *127 rooms, 1 suite* ♿ *Restaurant, room service, in-room data ports, some kitchenettes, refrigerators, cable TV, 2 tennis courts, pool, health club, outdoor hot tub, massage, sauna, beach, volleyball, bar, laundry service, business services, meeting rooms, free parking; no smoking* ⊟ *AE, D, DC, MC, V.*

$$$–$$$$ 🖭 **The Grande Colonial.** This white wedding-cake–style hotel has ocean
FodorśChoice views and is in central La Jolla village. Built in 1913 and expanded and
★ redesigned in 1925–26, the Colonial is graced with charming European details: chandeliers, a marble hearth, mahogany railings, oak furnishings, and French doors. The hotel's restaurant, NINE-TEN, is run by chef Michael Stebner and is well liked by locals for its fresh, seasonal California cuisine. ⊠ *910 Prospect St., La Jolla 92037* ☎ *858/454–2181 or 800/826–1278* 🖷 *858/454–5679* ⊕ *www.thegrandecolonial.com* ➷ *58 rooms, 17 suites* ♿ *Restaurant, room service, in-room data ports, cable TV with movies and video games, pool, bar, meeting rooms, parking (fee); no smoking* ⊟ *AE, D, DC, MC, V.*

$$$–$$$$ 🖭 **Scripps Inn.** You'd be wise to make reservations well in advance for this small, quiet inn tucked away on Coast Boulevard; its popularity with repeat visitors ensures that it's booked year-round. Lower weekly and monthly rates (not available in summer) make it attractive to long-term guests. Rooms are done with Mexican and Spanish decor, with wood floors, and all have ocean views; some have fireplaces. Continental breakfast is served in the lobby each morning. ⊠ *555 S. Coast Blvd., La Jolla 92037* ☎ *858/454–3391 or 800/439–7529* 🖷 *858/456–0389* ⊕ *www.jcresorts.com* ➷ *14 rooms* ♿ *In-room safes, cable TV, some kitchens, free parking; no smoking* ⊟ *AE, D, MC, V* ⊺◎⊢ *CP.*

★ $$–$$$$ 🖭 **Hyatt Regency La Jolla.** The Hyatt is in the Golden Triangle area, about 10 minutes from the beach and the village of La Jolla. The postmodern design of architect Michael Graves' striking lobby continues in the spacious rooms, where warm cherry-wood furnishings contrast with austere gray closets. Fluffy down comforters and cushy chairs and couches make you feel right at home, though, and business travelers will appreciate the endless array of office and in-room services. The hotel's four trendy restaurants include Cafe Japengo. Rates are lowest on weekends. ⊠ *Aventine Center, 3777 La Jolla Village Dr., La Jolla 92122* ☎ *858/552–1234 or 800/233–1234* 🖷 *858/552–6066* ⊕ *www.hyatt.com* ➷ *419 rooms, 20 suites* ♿ *4 restaurants, room service, minibar, cable TV with movies, 2 tennis courts, pool, health club, hair salon, outdoor hot tub, massage, basketball, bar, dry cleaning, laundry service, concierge, business services, meeting rooms, parking (fee); no smoking* ⊟ *AE, D, DC, MC, V.*

$$–$$$ 🖭 **La Jolla Cove Suites.** It may lack the charm of some of the older properties of this exclusive area, but this motel with studios and suites (some with spacious oceanfront balconies) gives its guests the same first-class

views of La Jolla Cove at lower rates. The beach is across the street and down a short cliff, and snorkelers and divers can take advantage of lockers and outdoor showers. Continental breakfast is served in the sunroom. The free underground lot is also a bonus in a section of town where a parking spot is a prime commodity. ☒ *1155 S. Coast Blvd., La Jolla 92037* ☎ *858/459–2621 or 800/248–2683* 🖷 *858/454–3522* ⊕ *www. lajollacove.com* 🖙 *96 rooms* ⚓ *In-room safes, kitchenettes, cable TV with movies, putting green, pool, hot tub, bicycles, laundry service, business services, meeting rooms, airport shuttle, free parking; no smoking* ▭ *AE, D, DC, MC, V.*

$$–$$$ 🏨 **La Jolla Inn.** One block from the beach and near some of the best shops and restaurants, this European-style inn with a delightful staff sits in a prime spot in La Jolla Village. Many rooms have sweeping ocean views from their balconies; one spectacular penthouse suite faces the ocean, another the village. Enjoy the delicious complimentary Continental breakfast on the upstairs sundeck. ☒ *1110 Prospect St., La Jolla 92037* ☎ *858/454–0133 or 800/433–1609* 🖷 *858/454–2056* ⊕ *www.lajollainn. com* 🖙 *21 rooms, 2 suites* ⚓ *Room service, in-room data ports, some kitchenettes, some refrigerators, cable TV with movies, library, shop, dry cleaning, laundry facilities, concierge, business services, free parking; no smoking* ▭ *AE, D, DC, MC, V* ⦿ *CP.*

$–$$$ 🏨 **Holiday Inn Express–La Jolla.** Many rooms at this modest property in the southern section of La Jolla are remarkably large, with huge closets. The decor is nothing to write home about, but this is a good value for families who want to stay in La Jolla and still have a few dollars left over for shopping and dining. Continental breakfast is included. ☒ *6705 La Jolla Blvd., La Jolla 92037* ☎ *858/454–7101 or 800/451–0358* 🖷 *858/454–6957* ⊕ *www.basshotels.com/holiday-inn* 🖙 *61 rooms, 11 suites* ⚓ *In-room data ports, some kitchenettes, refrigerator, cable TV, pool, gym, outdoor hot tub, sauna, laundry service, business services, meeting rooms, airport shuttle, free parking; no smoking* ▭ *AE, D, DC, MC, V* ⦿ *CP.*

Mission Bay & the Beaches

Mission Bay Park, with its beaches, bike trails, boat-launching ramps, golf course, and grassy parks—not to mention SeaWorld—is a hotel haven. Mission Beach and Pacific Beach have many small hotels, motels, and hostels. The coastal areas have a casual atmosphere and busy thoroughfares that provide endless shopping, dining, and nightlife possibilities. You can't go wrong with any of these locations, as long as the frenzy of crowds at play doesn't bother you.

$$$$ 🏨 **Crystal Pier Hotel.** A landmark since 1927, the cottages of the Crystal Pier Hotel are rustic little oases with a charm all their own. True, they lack some of the amenities of comparably priced hotels, but you're paying for character and proximity to the ocean—the blue-and-white cottages here are literally on the pier. The units sleep four but cost the same no matter what the occupancy; only one has air-conditioning. Call four to six weeks in advance for reservations. The minimum stay permitted is three nights from mid-June through mid-September, two nights

KID-FRIENDLY HOTELS

GOT KIDS IN TOW? *San Diego is designed for family fun; the year-round sunny, warm weather ensures lots of play days. The focus is on outdoor activities, such as surfing or swimming, but be sure to spend a day at Balboa Park's gardens, museums, and IMAX theater. Many hotels let kids under 18 stay free—just ask. And check into kids' activity programs, family-size suites, in-room Nintendo or kitchenettes. Shop around for hotel packages, which often include tickets to local attractions, SeaWorld, San Diego Zoo, Wild Animal Park, and Legoland.*

Some of the high-end properties give kids the special treatment with children's programs; most occur during the summer, some year-round. The famous **Hotel Del Coronado** *has tons of activities from surfing lessons, treasure hunts, and kayak tours to making sand candles on the resort's white-sand beach. They also offer a "kid's nite out" so Mom and Dad can enjoy a couple's night out. The* **Loews Coronado Bay Resort** *has welcome gifts for children, a kids-only pool, a game library, and special menus. Some recreational fun is offered seasonally, such as sunset sails and gondola rides. And kids can bring their pets.*

Across the bay, resorts on family-friendly Mission Bay cater to moppets. The **Hilton San Diego Resort** *holds a summer Kid's Kamp (ages 5–12, $7 per child per hour) with koi fish feeding, sand-castle building, and scavenger hunts. There's a special children's wading pool, a lawn croquet course, a sand volleyball court, and plenty of water-sport rentals, paddle boats, and Jet Skis. Teddy bears await the kids arriving at the* **Catamaran Resort Hotel***; just let reservations know you have young ones in your party. At the resort's library, kids over age 12 can play pool or watch movies borrowed from the concierge; it's*

open from 8:00 AM until 11:00 PM. And kids will enjoy the macaws and Black Australian swans that live on the property. The **Hyatt Islandia** *has kids menus, free Disney Channel, and a game room open from 7 AM 'til midnight.*

— Lenore Greiner

the rest of the year. The cottages are a bargain in off-season. ✉ *4500 Ocean Blvd., Pacific Beach, 92109* ☎ *858/483–6983 or 800/748–5894* 🖶 *858/483–6811* ⊕ *www.crystalpier.com* ⇱ *29 cottages* ⚬ *Kitchenettes, cable TV, beach, fishing, free parking; no smoking, no a/c in some rooms* ▭ *D, MC, V.*

$$$$ ▣ **Pacific Terrace Hotel.** This terrific hotel, overlooking the beach, offers great ocean views from most rooms. It's the perfect place for watching sunsets over the Pacific. Private balconies (or patios) and coffeemakers come with every room. Eight of the suites have indoor hot tubs. Continental breakfast is complimentary, as is the daily delivery of the *San Diego Union-Tribune*. Even the smallest room is fairly large. The friendly, casual staff makes for a comfortable stay. ✉ *610 Diamond St., Pacific Beach 92109* ☎ *858/581–3500 or 800/344–3370* 🖶 *858/274–3341* ⊕ *www.pacificterrace.com* ⇱ *73 rooms, 12 suites* ⚬ *In-room data ports, in-room safe, some kitchenettes, minibars, cable TV with movies and video games, pool, outdoor hot tub, laundry service, Internet, meeting rooms, parking (fee); no smoking* ▭ *AE, D, DC, MC, V* ⧍ *CP.*

★ **$$$$** ▣ **San Diego Paradise Point Resort &Spa.** The beautiful landscape at this 44-acre resort on Vacation Isle has been the setting for a number of movies. The botanical gardens have ponds, waterfalls, footbridges, waterfowl, and more than 600 varieties of tropical plants. It makes a convincing backdrop for the Balinese spa. Many recreation activities are offered and there's access to a marina. The room's bright fabrics and plush carpets are cheery; unfortunately, the walls here are motel-thin. ✉ *1404 W. Vacation Rd., Mission Bay 92109* ☎ *858/274–4630 or 800/344–2626* 🖶 *858/581–5929* ⊕ *www.paradisepoint.com* ⇱ *462 cottages* ⚬ *3 restaurants, room service, in-room data ports, refrigerators, cable TV with movies, putting green, 6 tennis courts, 6 pools, pond, fitness classes, gym, outdoor hot tub, massage, sauna, spa, beach, boating, jet skiing, bicycles, croquet, shuffleboard, volleyball, 2 bars, concierge, business services, meeting rooms, airport shuttle, free parking; no smoking* ▭ *AE, D, DC, MC, V.*

$$$–$$$$ ▣ **Bahia Resort Hotel.** This huge complex on a 14-acre peninsula in Mission Bay Park has studios and suites with kitchens; many have wood-beam ceilings and a tropical theme. The hotel's *Bahia Belle* offers complimentary cruises on the bay at sunset and also has a Blues Cruise on Saturday night and live entertainment on Friday night. Rates are reasonable for a place so well located—within walking distance of the ocean—and with so many amenities, including use of the facilities at its sister hotel, the nearby Catamaran. ✉ *998 W. Mission Bay Dr., Mission Bay 92109* ☎ *858/488–0551 or 800/576–4229* 🖶 *858/488–1387* ⊕ *www.bahiahotel.com* ⇱ *321 rooms* ⚬ *Restaurant, room service, in-room data ports, kitchenettes, cable TV with movies, 2 tennis courts, pool, gym, outdoor hot tub, boating, bicycles, 2 bars, shops, business services, meeting rooms, free parking; no smoking* ▭ *AE, D, DC, MC, V.*

$$$–$$$$ ▣ **Catamaran Resort Hotel.** Exotic birds perch in the lush lobby of this
FodorśChoice appealing hotel on Mission Bay. Tiki torches light the way through
★ grounds thick with tropical foliage to the six two-story buildings and the 14-story high-rise. The room design continues the Hawaiian theme. The popular Cannibal Bar hosts rock bands; a classical or jazz pianist tick-

les the ivories nightly at the Moray Bar. The resort's many water-oriented activities include free cruises on Mission Bay aboard a stern-wheeler. ✉ *3999 Mission Blvd., Mission Beach 92109* ☎ *858/488–1081 or 800/ 422–8386* 🖷 *858/488–1387* ⊕ *www.catamaranresort.com* ⟿ *313 rooms* ⚲ *Restaurant, room service, in-room data ports, kitchenettes, refrigerators, cable TV with movies, pool, gym, outdoor hot tub, beach, boating, jet skiing, bicycles, volleyball, 2 bars, nightclub, shops, business services, meeting rooms, parking (fee); no smoking* ▭ *AE, D, DC, MC, V.*

$$$–$$$$ ▦ **Hilton San Diego Resort.** Trees, Japanese bridges, and ponds surround the bungalows at this deluxe resort; rooms and suites in the high-rise have views of Mission Bay. The well-appointed rooms have wet bars, coffeemakers, and spacious bathrooms; all have patios or balconies. Children stay free, and there's complimentary day care for children over five (daily in summer, on weekends the rest of the year). The sports facilities are excellent and aquatic sports equipment is available for rent at their own boat dock on the resort beach. The Bayside Terrace Grill serves California coastal cuisine and has fire pits for sunset viewing. Villa Di Lusso spa is a full service European-style spa, specializing in sports and therapeutic massages. ✉ *1775 E. Mission Bay Dr., Mission Bay 92109* ☎ *619/276–4010 or 800/445–8667* 🖷 *619/275–8944* ⊕ *www.hilton. com* ⟿ *337 rooms, 20 suites* ⚲ *2 restaurants, room service, in-room data ports, minibars, refrigerators, cable TV with movies, 4 putting greens, 5 tennis courts, pool, wading pool, gym, hair salon, 4 outdoor hot tubs, massage, spa, beach, boating, waterskiing, bicycles, basketball, Ping-Pong, 2 bars, children's programs (ages 5–12), playground, laundry service, concierge, business services, meeting rooms, car rental, travel services, free parking; no smoking* ▭ *AE, D, DC, MC, V.*

$$$–$$$$ ▦ **Hyatt Islandia.** This property has rooms in several low-level, lanai-style units, as well as marina suites and rooms in a high-rise building, all in Mission Bay Park. Many rooms overlook the hotel's gardens and koi fish pond; others have dramatic views of the bay area. This hotel is famous for its lavish Sunday champagne brunch. Whale-watching expeditions depart from the Islandia's marina in winter. ✉ *1441 Quivira Rd., Mission Bay 92109* ☎ *619/224–1234 or 800/233–1234* 🖷 *858/ 224–0348* ⊕ *www.hyatt.com* ⟿ *346 rooms, 76 suites* ⚲ *2 restaurants, room service, in-room data ports, some kitchenettes, cable TV with movies, pool, gym, outdoor hot tub, boating, fishing, bar, shops, dry cleaning, laundry service, concierge, business services, meeting rooms, car rental, free parking; no smoking* ▭ *AE, D, DC, MC, V.*

$$–$$$$ ▦ **Best Western Blue Sea Lodge.** All rooms in this low-rise have patios or balconies, and many have ocean views. Suites have kitchenettes, and many of them front the ocean. A shopping center with restaurants and boutiques is nearby. ✉ *707 Pacific Beach Dr., Pacific Beach 92109* ☎ *858/ 488–4700 or 800/258–3732* 🖷 *858/488–7276* ⊕ *www.bestwestern-bluesea.com* ⟿ *128 rooms, 10 suites* ⚲ *Café, in-room safes, some kitchenettes, cable TV with movies, pool, outdoor hot tub, fishing, bicycles, laundry service, concierge, travel services, parking (fee); no smoking* ▭ *AE, D, DC, MC, V.*

$$–$$$ ▦ **Dana Inn & Marina.** This hotel with an adjoining marina has a fun aquarium in its lobby. Rooms are done in bright pastels and those on the second floor have high ceilings, and in some a view of the inn's marina. Scheduled for completion in May 2004 are two new buildings, a pool, a spa, and a fitness center. SeaWorld and the beach are within walking distance. The Marina Village Conference Center next door offers meeting and banquet rooms with bay views. ⊠ *1710 W. Mission Bay Dr., Mission Bay 92109* ☎ *619/222–6440 or 800/326–2466* 🖷 *619/222–5916* ⊕ *www.danainn.com* ⇨ *196 rooms* ⚓ *Restaurant, room service, cable TV with movies, 2 tennis courts, pool, outdoor hot tub, boating, waterskiing, fishing, bicycles, Ping-Pong, shuffleboard, bar, laundry service, business services, meeting rooms, airport shuttle, car rental, free parking; no smoking* ⊟ *AE, D, DC, MC, V.*

$$ 🏨 **Beach Haven Inn.** This pleasant little hotel resembles an apartment building—rooms have exterior entrances and are situated around the pool and courtyard. It's on Mission Boulevard, the main beach drag, but on a fairly quiet stretch. Within two minutes you can sink your feet into the sand of Pacific Beach, and grassy Palisades Park, famous for its sunsets, is approximately three blocks away. Continental breakfast and a daily newspaper are included. ⊠ *4740 Mission Blvd., Pacific Beach 92109* ☎ *858/272–3812 or 800/831–6323* 🖷 *858/272–3532* ⊕ *www.beachhaveninn.com* ⇨ *23 rooms* ⚓ *Kitchenettes, refrigerators, cable TV with movies, pool, outdoor hot tub, laundry service, free parking; no smoking* ⊟ *AE, D, DC, MC, V* �|◯| *CP.*

$$ 🏨 **Diamond Head Inn.** Directly on the boardwalk facing Pacific Beach, many rooms overlook the beach and classic California sunsets. It's also within three blocks of Pacific Beach's main drag or restaurants and nightspots—Garnet Avenue—and the Pacific Beach Pier. Continental breakfast is complimentary. ⊠ *605 Diamond St., Pacific Beach 92109* ☎ *858/273–1900* 🖷 *858/274–3341* ⇨ *21 rooms* ⚓ *Kitchenettes, cable TV with movies, beach, free parking, some pets allowed (fee); no smoking, no a/c* ⊟ *AE, D, MC, V* �|◯| *CP.*

$$ 🏨 **Pacific Shores Inn.** This property is less than a half block from the beach. Rooms, some of them spacious, have a simple contemporary style. Kitchen units with multiple beds are available at reasonable rates. Continental breakfast is included. ⊠ *4802 Mission Blvd., Pacific Beach 92109* ☎ *858/483–6300 or 800/826–0715* 🖷 *858/483–9276* ⊕ *www.pacificshoresinn.com* ⇨ *56 rooms, 3 suites* ⚓ *Kitchenettes, refrigerators, cable TV with movies, pool, laundry service, free parking, some pets allowed (fee); no smoking* ⊟ *AE, D, DC, MC, V* �|◯| *CP.*

$–$$ 🏨 **Surfer Motor Lodge.** This four-story building is right on the beach and
Fodor'sChoice   directly behind a shopping center with restaurants and boutiques. Rooms
★   are plain, but those on the upper floors have good views. ⊠ *711 Pacific Beach Dr., Pacific Beach 92109* ☎ *858/483–7070 or 800/787–3373* 🖷 *858/274–1670* ⊕ *www.surfermotorlodge.com* ⇨ *52 rooms* ⚓ *Restaurant, kitchenettes, pool, beach, bicycles, laundry service, free parking; no smoking, no a/c* ⊟ *AE, DC, MC, V.*

¢–$ 🏨 **Days Inn Mission Bay.** This modest, three-story hotel is near freeways and Mission Bay, and the price is right for its simple but clean rooms. Continental breakfast is complimentary. There's no elevator. ⊠ *4540 Mission Bay Dr., Mission Bay 92109* ☎ *858/274–7888 or 800/329–7466* ⊕ *www.daysinn.com* ⇨ *116 rooms* ⚓ *Cable TV, in-room safes, pool,* *laundry service, airport shuttle, free parking, some pets allowed (fee); no smoking* ⊟ *AE, D, DC, MC, V* ⏋⃝⏊ *CP.*

¢ ⊞ **Banana Bungalow San Diego.** Literally a few feet from the beach, this hostel's location is its greatest asset. However, dampness and sand take their toll, and some parts of the hostel are in need of repair. All dorm rooms are coed and there are a total of 70 beds. Keg and movie-night parties are held weekly, as are various organized events. Complimentary Continental breakfast is served on the sundeck. There are lockers and a small TV room. ⊠ *707 Reed Ave., Pacific Beach 92109* ☏ *858/ 273–3060 or 800/546–7835* ⊞ *858/273–1440* ⊕ *www.bananabungalow. com* ⚓ *Beach, bicycles, volleyball, airport shuttle, travel services; no room phones, no room TVs, no smoking, no a/c* ⊟ *MC, V.*

¢ ⊞ **Ocean Beach International Backpackers Hostel.** This converted 1920s hotel is two blocks from the beach and offers free use of surfboards and boogie boards. There are 100 beds. Private rooms with private baths are available. Continental breakfast is complimentary, and dinner is free on Tuesday and Friday. The hostel, which is close to many Ocean Beach restaurants and nightspots, has kitchen facilities, a storage area, vending machines, a TV room, a recreation room, and a patio. Weekly rates are available. ⊠ *4961 Newport Ave., Ocean Beach 92107* ☏ *619/223–7873 or 800/339–7263* ⊞ *619/223–7881* ⊕ *members.aol.com/obihostel/hostel* ⚓ *Bicycles, recreation room, laundry service, Internet, airport shuttle; no room TVs, no smoking, no a/c* ⊟ *MC, V* ⏋⃝⏊ *CP.*

North Park

San Diego's North Park area is close to the zoo and Balboa Park and melds into the neighborhoods of Hillcrest, Mission Hills, and University Heights. There are not a lot of hotels to choose from—quality or otherwise—but these neighborhoods offer pedestrian-friendly shopping districts and great restaurants.

$$–$$$ ⊞ **Balboa Park Inn.** This all-suites B&B stands in four Spanish colonial–style 1915 residences connected by courtyards. Prices are reasonable for romantic one- and two-bedroom suites, done in either Italian, French, Spanish, or early Californian style. Some rooms have fireplaces, whirlpool tubs, patios, and kitchens. A generous, complimentary Continental breakfast is delivered to your room on Monday–Saturday mornings; you also get a newspaper. The lack of off-street parking is inconvenient, but the San Diego Zoo is a 10-minute walk away. ⊠ *3402 Park Blvd., North Park 92103* ☏ *619/298–0823 or 800/938–8181* ⊞ *619/294–8070* ⊕ *www.balboaparkinn.com* ⌑ *26 suites* ⚓ *Some kitchenettes, some microwaves, refrigerators, cable TV with movies; no smoking, no a/c* ⊟ *AE, D, DC, MC, V* ⏋⃝⏊ *CP.*

NIGHTLIFE &
THE ARTS

BEST BOHO COFFEE HOUSE
Twiggs ⇨*p.125*

BEST NIGHTLIFE INNOVATION
Karl Strauss's beer by the gallon ⇨*p.123*

HIPPEST CABANA
The Beach Bar at W Hotel ⇨*p.124*

MOST ROMANTIC RENDEZVOUS
Swanky piano bar Top of the Hyatt ⇨*p.130*

SOMETHING FOR EVERYONE
Three floors of dancing and a
diverse crowd at Club Montage ⇨*p.128*

BEST ESCAPE FROM HOLLYWOOD
An art house flick at Ken Cinema ⇨*p.133*

BEST USE OF A QUONSET HUT
Music mecca Belly Up Tavern ⇨*p.130*

NIGHTLIFE

Updated by
Rob Aikins

SAN DIEGO MAY BE CLOSE TO LOS ANGELES, but it can seem worlds away. Indeed, weekend freeway traffic heading south to San Diego can slow considerably with all the Angeleños heading to town to get away from the L.A. scene. Celebrity sightings in San Diego are not frequent. People come to San Diego for the beach, and out-of-towners will find they're the only ones populating the clubs during the week. Crowds come out on the weekend, syphoning off into the various nightlife districts of the city. Downtown is where the majority of cultural events—symphony, theater, and opera—happen. Just down the street is the Gaslamp Quarter, home to dozens of dance clubs, martini bars, and the most expensive drinks and cover charges in the city. Most are only open on Friday and Saturday. The beach areas offer a more casual atmosphere. The dance clubs and bars of Pacific Beach and Mission Beach appeal to a casually dressed, college-age crowd. Ocean Beach has no dance clubs and is preferred by bikers, drinkers, and patchouli-scented fans of reggae and Grateful Dead–style jam bands.

The Uptown district around Hillcrest is the heart of San Diego's gay nightlife and home to a few coffeehouses where conversation is the entertainment. Coffeehouse culture is still prevalent throughout the county and there's usually someone playing an acoustic set any given night.

San Diego's music scene centers around rock. Hard rock, alternative rock, and indie rock dominate the music listings. Despite that fact, some of the county's best known musical artists play a softer style of music: Jewel got her start in the city's coffeehouses and Grammy-winning gospel group Nickel Creek calls San Diego home. Nevertheless, local boys Ratt, Blink-182, and hard rockers P.O.D give testament to the fact that rockers can make it out of San Diego.

Check the *Reader* (it comes out every Thursday)—San Diego's free alternative newsweekly—for the 411 on nightlife, or *San Diego* magazine's "Restaurant & Nightlife Guide" for further ideas. Also, the *San Diego-Union Tribune* publishes a weekly (Thursday) entertainment insert, *Night and Day.*

State law prohibits the sale of alcoholic beverages after 2 AM; last call is usually at about 1:40. You must be 21 to purchase and consume alcohol—be prepared to show ID. California also has some of the most stringent drunken-driving laws in the country; sobriety checkpoints are not an uncommon sight. Also, unless operated exclusively for private members, all bars, nightclubs, and restaurants are smoke-free—although many have patios or decks where smoking is permitted.

Bars & Nightclubs

Aero Club (✉ 3365 India St., Middletown ☎ 619/297–7211) is a square cinderblock building named for its proximity to the airport. Local aerospace workers have long used it as a hangout. Formerly a dive, it's now a beer, wine, and pool bar popular with hipply dressed indie rockers who stop in for cheap drinks and low-key atmosphere. The rather dominant mural showing a historical progression of fighting warplanes is true to the club's roots.

Bitter End (✉ 770 5th Ave., Gaslamp Quarter ☎ 619/338–9300) is a tri-level martini bar and dance club that draws a crowd any night of the week. With its dark, molded wood paneling and a few overstuffed armchairs, at times you get the feel of being in your rich uncle's study. Except your uncle probably wouldn't make you stand in the long lines that form here on weekends. The martinis are potent and a stylish upscale crowd keeps the night interesting.

Blind Melons (✉ 710 Garnet Ave., Pacific Beach ☎ 858/483–7844), a small, dark space, hosts well-known local and, occasionally, national bands playing rock, blues, and reggae. This is a good place to enjoy a drink before or after a nice walk on the boardwalk or on Crystal Pier, literally just steps away.

Blue Tattoo (✉ 835 5th Ave., Gaslamp Quarter ☎ 619/231–7041) pulls in crowds of hip-hop-loving young professionals. The club is open Thursday through Sunday with a strict dress code (no jeans, T-shirts, hats, sweatshirts, or tennis shoes) on Friday and Saturday nights. Entertainment consists of a variety of DJs and there is a nominal cover charge.

'Canes Bar and Grill (✉ 3105 Ocean Front Walk, Mission Beach ☎ 858/488–1780) is closer to the ocean than any other music venue in town. Step outside for a walk on the beach where the sounds of the national rock, reggae, and hip-hop acts onstage create a cacophony with the crashing waves. Step back inside to enjoy some of the best cutting edge tunes in town.

Cannibal Bar (✉ 3999 Mission Blvd., Pacific Beach ☎ 858/488–1081) offers an eclectic lineup of live music acts. Swing, jazz, rock, and reggae are possibilities, and some nights a DJ spins tunes—usually Top 40 or classic rock. Because of its beach location, the tropical-theme nightclub in the Catamaran Resort Hotel attracts locals and visitors of all ages.

Dave & Buster's (✉ 2931 Camino Del Rio N, Mission Valley ☎ 619/275–1515) comprises a restaurant, two bars, billiards, shuffleboard, and a midway packed with arcade games. It's a place to let your inner wild child loose—real kids must be accompanied by an adult and are banished from 10 PM on.

Hard Rock Cafe (✉ 801 4th Ave., Gaslamp Quarter ☎ 619/615–7625 ✉ 909 Prospect St., La Jolla ☎ 858/456–7625), the ubiquitous theme restaurant chain, has a pair of locales in greater San Diego, both filled with the usual house-blend of rock-and-roll memorabilia and costumes. Check out the restored stained-glass dome just above the Gaslamp bar. La Jolla's location is a great place to stop either before or after a stroll on the beach.

Jimmy Love's (✉ 672 5th Ave., Gaslamp Quarter ☎ 619/595–0123) combines a dance club, a sports bar, and a restaurant on two levels. Upstairs, rock, funk, reggae, and jazz bands alternate nightly. Downstairs, hang at the bar or play a game of pool. Expect lines, though—Jimmy's is loved by many.

Karl Strauss' Old Columbia Brewery & Grill (✉ 1157 Columbia St., Downtown ☎ 619/234-2739 ✉ 1044 Wall St., La Jolla ☎ 858/551-2739) was the first microbrewery in San Diego. The original locale draws an after-work downtown crowd and later fills with beer connoisseurs from all walks of life; the newer La Jolla version draws a mix of locals and tourists. Beer-to-go by the gallon is a very popular choice.

Live Wire (✉ 2103 El Cajon Blvd., North Park ☎ 619/291-7450) is an underground hole-in-the-wall popular with the twentysomething pierced and tattooed set. DJs spin during the week and on occasional weekends. A well-stocked jukebox is the only other entertainment in this hip dive.

Maloney's on 5th (✉ 777 5th Ave., Gaslamp Quarter ☎ 619/232-6000) is down a flight of stairs. Inside, big-screen TVs broadcast ball games to this crowd of sports nuts, nine-to-fivers, and regular joes. Grab a seat in one of the comfy booths and make yourself at home.

Martini Ranch (✉ 528 F St., Gaslamp Quarter ☎ 619/235-6100) mixes more than 30 varieties of its namesake. Actually two clubs in one, the original Martini Ranch hosts jazz groups on weekdays and a DJ spining an eclectic mix on Friday and Saturday. Next door in the larger Shaker Room, local and traveling DJs spin all-star dance beats. In either room the bartenders might show you one of their tricks, like mixing a martini on their forehead or pouring five drinks at one time, if you ask nicely.

Moondoggies (✉ 832 Garnet Ave., Pacific Beach ☎ 858/483-6550) is not just for Gidget anymore, but is home to a mixed, laid-back crowd of people who don't mind bumping into each other or minor beer spills. A large, airy sports bar feel is heightened by the dozens of TVs in every available spot. Many TVs show surf and skate videos that remind you the beach is only two blocks away. A large, heated outdoor patio draws smokers. Occasionally, local rock, funk, or reggae bands play here.

O'Hungrys (✉ 2547 San Diego Ave., Old Town ☎ 619/298-0133) is famous for its yard-long beers and sing-alongs. The seafaring decor stands in juxtaposition to the Mexican-theme Old Town State Historic Park—just outside the doors. Be sure to drink up quickly, though—this landmark saloon closes at midnight.

Onyx Room/Thin (✉ 852 5th Ave., Gaslamp Quarter ☎ 619/235-6699) is the hippest split-level in town. Although both Onyx and Thin are separate clubs, the fact that they share the same owners and building makes for many options as you move back and forth between the two, sampling each bar's unique decor and ambience. Onyx is downstairs and feels like two bars in one. In front there's a mood-lit cocktail lounge, and in the next room acid jazz bands and DJs keep the crowds dancing on the tiny dance floor. Thin, the upstairs venue, has a stainless-steel–heavy interior that could be the inside of an UFO. Thin is more conducive to the conversation-minded, although a DJ spins down-tempo acid jazz and funk tunes on weekends. Weekend cover charges allow entrance to both clubs.

Pacific Beach Bar & Grill (✉ 860 Garnet Ave., Pacific Beach ☎ 858/272–1242) is a stumbling block away from the beach. The popular nightspot has a huge outdoor patio so you can enjoy star-filled skies as you party. The lines here on the weekends are generally the longest of any club in Pacific Beach. There's plenty to see and do, from billiards and satellite TV sports to an interactive trivia game. The grill takes orders until 1 AM so it's a great place for a late-night snack.

The purple-neon-streaked **Tavern at the Beach** (✉ 1200 Garnet Ave., Pacific Beach ☎ 858/272–6066) draws fun-loving college students. Drink specials and socializing are the main attractions, although if you get bored you can always watch one of the 30 TVs.

Turf Supper Club (✉ 1116 25th St., Uptown ☎ 619/234–6363) attracts musicians and local music industry types who come here for its divey feel and the self-serve grill where you can cook or burn your steak or burger to your liking. The neighborhood may seem a little rough around the edges, but the scene inside is relaxed and friendly with red vinyl booths and many lively conversations.

The Waterfront (✉ 2044 Kettner Blvd., Downtown ☎ 619/232–9656) is San Diego's oldest neighborhood bar. It's not actually on the waterfront, but has been the workingman's refuge in Little Italy since the days when the area was the Italian fishing community. Now considered a local landmark, developers actually constructed an apartment building around it rather than tear it down. It's also famous for its bar burgers and it's still the hangout for working-class heroes, even if most of the collars are now white.

Fodor'sChoice There are three bars at the **W Hotel** (✉ 421 W. B St., Downtown ☎ 619/231–8220), and together they've become the trendiest places to be for the young bar-hopping set. Start at the ground floor Living Room, where cozy chairs and couches in alcoves give a true lounge feel. You can take your drink from bar to bar, so move next to Magnet, a restaurant bar where you can grab a bite to eat before heading to the beach. Or more accurately, Beach, the W's open-air rooftop with private beach cabanas, firepits, and tons of heated sand covering the floor. Dump the sand out of your shoes later—California has just as strict footwear laws as its no-smoking ones. Get here before 9 PM on weekends to avoid a line.

Coffeehouses

Like the rest of the country, San Diego has gotten into cafés and coffeehouses in a big way. If you're up for caffeine-hopping, the Hillcrest–North Park area on University Avenue is abuzz with options—all of them grinding a variety of elixirs and proffering everything from full meals to light pastries. Many offer live entertainment on weekends. Most open their doors by 7 AM and continue serving until midnight or later. The crowds are diverse, ranging from lesbian and gay fashion plates to bookish college students to yuppies.

★ **Brockton Villa Restaurant** (✉ 1235 Coast Blvd., La Jolla ☎ 858/454–7393), a palatial café overlooking La Jolla Cove, has indoor and outdoor seating, as well as scrumptious desserts and coffee drinks; the beans are roasted in San Diego. It closes at 9 most nights, earlier on Sunday and Monday.

Café Crema (✉ 1001 Garnet Ave., Pacific Beach ☎ 858/273–3558) is a meeting spot for the pre- and post-bar crowd. Its industrial-style decor is anathema to the rest of beachy Pacific Beach. It's easy to lose track of time here as you watch all the college-age singles come and go.

Claire de Lune (✉ 2906 University Ave., North Park ☎ 619/688–9845), on a corner in artsy North Park, won an award for its redesign of the historic Oddfellows building. High ceilings and huge arched windows give it a funky charm. The wood-floor hangout has sofas and armchairs for lounging as well as tables for studying. Local musicians and poets take the stage on various nights, and San Diego's most popular, and longest running, open-mike poetry night takes place every Tuesday.

★ The name, **Extraordinary Desserts** (✉ 2929 5th Ave., Hillcrest ☎ 619/294–7001), explains the line at a café even with 90 seats. Paris-trained Karen Krasne turns out award-winning cakes, tortes, and pastries of exceptional beauty (many are decorated with fresh flowers). The Japanese-theme patio invites you to linger over yet another coffee drink. The offerings change daily so it's worth stopping in more than once.

Gelato Vero Caffe (✉ 3753 India St., Middletown ☎ 619/295–9269) is where a mostly young crowd gathers for some fine desserts and a second-floor view of the downtown skyline. The place is usually occupied by regulars who stay for hours at a time.

Javanican (✉ 4338 Cass St., Pacific Beach ☎ 858/483–8035) serves the young beach-community set. Aside from a good cup of joe, live acoustic entertainment is a draw. Adventurous musicians can sign up to play at the open mike Monday night. Other local musicians headline throughout the week.

Living Room (✉ 1018 Rosecrans St., Point Loma ☎ 619/222–6852) is in an old house not far from the water. The wooden floors creak and there are plenty of cubbyholes for the studious college students who frequent here. It's a great place to catch a caffeine buzz before walking along Shelter Island.

Pannikin (✉ 7467 Girard Ave., La Jolla ☎ 858/454–5453) is a bright coffeehouse with indoor and outdoor seating. Amidst the regulars are folks who've been shopping and sightseeing in La Jolla's village. Several locations are scattered throughout the county.

Twiggs (✉ 4590 Park Blvd., University Heights ☎ 619/296–0616) is full of the din of conversation when music isn't playing. Poetry readings and musicians playing their acoustic originals make this venue the picture of a true bohemian experience. Open mike night on Wednesday is always popular.

Upstart Crow (✉ 835 West Harbor Dr., Seaport Village ☎ 619/232–4855) is a bookstore and coffeehouse in one. The secluded upstairs space contains the java joint and is ideal for chatting or perusing the book that you just bought. Funky gifts are sold, too.

Zanzibar Coffee Bar and Gallery (✉ 976 Garnet Ave., Pacific Beach ☎ 858/272–4762), a cozy, dimly lit spot along Pacific Beach's main strip, is a great place to mellow out and eavesdrop, or to just watch the club-hopping singles make their way down the street.

Comedy & Cabaret

Comedy Store La Jolla (✉ 916 Pearl St., La Jolla ☎ 858/454–9176), like its sister establishment in Hollywood, hosts some of the best national touring and local talent. Cover charges range from nothing on open mike nights to $20 or more for national acts. A two-drink minimum applies for all shows. Seating is at bistro-style tables.

Lips (✉ 2770 5th Ave., Hillcrest ☎ 619/295–7900) serves you dinner while female impersonators entertain. Their motto, "where the men are men and so are the girls," says it all.

At the **Shouthouse** (✉ 655 4th Ave., Gaslamp Quarter ☎ 619/231–6700), dueling pianos and rock-and-roll sing-alongs make for a festive, even boisterous, ambience. It's open only on Thursday, Friday, and Saturday so make reservations or come early to get a good seat.

Country–Western

In Cahoots (✉ 5373 Mission Center Rd., Mission Valley ☎ 619/291–1184), with its great sound system, large dance floor, and DJ, is the destination of choice for cowgirls, cowboys, and city slickers alike. Free dance lessons are given every day except Wednesday, when seasoned two-steppers strut their stuff. Happy hour seven days a week is one of this bar's many lures.

Magnolia Mulvaney's (✉ 8861 N. Magnolia Ave., Santee ☎ 619/448–8550) serves as country-music headquarters for East County residents. Line dancers kick up their heels when local bands play on Friday and Saturday nights.

Tio Leo's (✉ 5302 Napa St., Bay Park ☎ 619/542–1462) is a throwback to the days when lounges were dark and vinyl-filled. The crowd is retro-attired as well. The lounge is within a Mexican restaurant, and an incredible variety of country, rockabilly, and swing acts grace the small stage.

Dance Clubs

★ **Deco's** (✉ 721 5th Ave., Gaslamp Quarter ☎ 619/696–3326) is another popular high-end martini–dance bar in the Gaslamp Quarter. Fashionably dressed urbanites line up outside for a chance to dance in one of two main areas. The indoor room plays house while the packed open-air area in the back plays hip-hop mixes. Loungy seating, wipsy white drapes, and floor-to-ceiling windows give you the feel that you're in a friend's ritzy loft apartment for the best house party ever.

E Street Alley (✉ 919 4th Ave., Gaslamp Quarter ☎ 619/231–9200), or "Club E," is one of the city's hotspots below street level. The smartly designed, spacious club is a treat for the senses, with a good light show on the dance floor and an exquisite restaurant and sushi bar, Chino's.

The menu features American cuisine with Southeast Asian touches. DJs spin Top 40 and club tunes Thursday through Saturday.

5ifth Quarter (✉ 600 5th Ave., Gaslamp Quarter ☎ 619/236–1616) is popular with the happy-hour sports crowd due to its 32 flat-screen and two big-screen TVs. Later in the evening, bands play retro disco, R & B, and '80s music. This locale has long been a major stop on the bachelorette party circuit.

L5 (✉ 203 5th Ave., Gaslamp Quarter ☎ 619/858–2100) runs until 4 AM, making it a good after-hours dance option. However, the alcohol is pulled from the floor before 2 AM. The best local and traveling DJs regularly spin underground house, breakbeat, and hip-hop cuts.

Olé Madrid (✉ 751 5th Ave., Gaslamp Quarter ☎ 619/557–0146) is not for the meek or mild. Leave the squares at street level and head straight to the basement for deep house grooves and tribal rhythms spun by celebrated DJs from near and far. Between songs, sip a tangy sangria. Friday and Saturday the groove goes on until 4 AM.

★ **On Broadway** (✉ 615 Broadway, Gaslamp Quarter ☎ 619/231–0011). A long line of wannabe patrons points the way to the trendiest dance club in town. Even the $20 cover charge does little to discourage San Diego's best-dressed young professionals from waiting hours to spend their hard-earned money inside. The club gets crowded early and stays that way until closing, making it hard to get a drink from the sometimes unfriendly staff. The huge club in a former bank building is only open Friday and Saturday. The marble floors, Greek columns, and original vault doors mix well with the modern decor, computerized light show, and 90,000-watt sound system.

Plan B (✉ 945 Garnet Ave., Pacific Beach ☎ 858/483–9921) has a stainless-steel dance floor and numerous places from which to view it, making the interior of this club a standout among the other beach clubs. DJs play a variety of high-energy dance music most nights. The crowd is more upscale than usually found at the beach. Plan B has the only permanent laser show in San Diego.

Rox (✉ 901 5th Ave., Gaslamp Quarter ☎ 619/234–5554), underneath the Dakota Grill restaurant, spins house and Top 40 mix dance tunes Friday and Saturday only. A state-of-the-art, 100-inch plasma screen provides eclectic visuals.

Sevilla (✉ 555 4th Ave., Gaslamp Quarter ☎ 619/233–5979) brings a Latin flavor to the Gaslamp Quarter with its mix of contemporary and traditional Spanish and Latin American music. Get fueled up at the tapas bar before venturing downstairs for dancing. This is the best place in San Diego to take lessons in salsa and lambada.

Gay & Lesbian Nightlife

Men's Bars

Bourbon Street (✉ 4612 Park Blvd., University Heights ☎ 619/291–0173) is one of the popular places to meet old friends or make new ones. Several scenes exist in this one bar. The front bar is a popular karaoke spot. The outdoor courtyard draws crowds that gather to watch and comment on whatever is showing on the large-screen TV. Weekends, a back area known as the Stable Bar has DJs who turn the small room into a dance floor.

Brass Rail (✉ 3796 5th Ave., Hillcrest ☎ 619/298–2233), a fixture since the early 1960s, is the oldest gay bar in San Diego. There's dancing nightly, or you can just pass time playing pool on one of the three tables.

★ **Club Montage** (✉ 2028 Hancock St., Middletown ☎ 619/294–9590) is one of the largest and best clubs in town. The three-level nightspot was originally oriented to the gay crowd, but now all types come for the high-tech lighting system and world-class DJs. For a breath of fresh air, step out to view the skyline and enjoy a drink from the rooftop bar.

Flicks (✉ 1017 University Ave., Hillcrest ☎ 619/297–2056), a hip video bar that's popular with the see-and-be-seen crowd, plays music and comedy videos on four big screens. Drink specials vary each night.

Kickers (✉ 308 University Ave., Hillcrest ☎ 619/491–0400) rounds up country-music cowboys to do the latest line dance on its wooden dance floor Thursday through Saturday. It offers up disco, karaoke, and goth the rest of the time. Free lessons are given weeknights from 7 to 8:30. If you're hungry after all that dancing, Hamburger Mary's, on the premises, serves until 11 on weekends.

Numbers (✉ 3811 Park Blvd., North Park ☎ 619/294–9005) has a giant-screen TV, six pool tables, darts, and daily drink specials. A casually dressed crowd comes to hang out and watch showings of *Queer as Folk* and other gay-theme shows.

Rich's (✉ 1051 University Ave., Hillcrest ☎ 619/295–2195), a popular dance club, has frequent male revues. Thursday night's Club Hedonism spotlights groove house and tribal rhythms and is frequented by both gay and straight revelers.

Wolf's (✉ 3404 30th St., North Park ☎ 619/291–3730) is a Levi's-leather bar. There's no actual sign for the club, but look for the wolf painted on the exterior, beside the front door.

Women's Bars

6 Degrees (✉ 3175 India St., Middletown ☎ 619/296–6789), formerly Club Bom Bay, is still a popular hangout. It occasionally has live entertainment and always attracts a dancing crowd. It also hosts Sunday barbecues.

The Flame (✉ 3780 Park Blvd., Hillcrest ☎ 619/295–4163) has a red neon sign resembling a torch with a flame on top. A San Diego institution, this friendly dance club caters to lesbians most of the week. Sit at the bar amid vinyl upholstered walls or hang out and play darts or pool in the next room. On Tuesday the DJ spins for the popular and long-running Boys' Night.

Jazz

★ **Elario's Bistro & Sky Lounge** (✉ 7955 La Jolla Shores Dr., La Jolla ☎ 858/551–3620) is the reincarnation of one of San Diego's most famous jazz venues. Perched on the top floor of the Hotel La Jolla, Elario's delivers an ocean view and a lineup of locally acclaimed jazz musicians Tuesday through Saturday.

Croce's (✉ 802 5th Ave., Gaslamp Quarter ☎ 619/233–4355), the intimate jazz cave of restaurateur Ingrid Croce (singer-songwriter Jim Croce's widow), books superb acoustic-jazz musicians.

Next door to Croce's, **Croce's Top Hat** (✉ 818 5th Ave., Gaslamp Quarter ☎ 619/233–4355) puts on live R&B nightly from 9 to 2. Musician A. J. Croce, son of Jim and Ingrid, often headlines at both clubs.

Dizzy's (✉ 344 7th Ave., Gaslamp Quarter ☎ 858/270–7467) is one of the few venues in town that's totally devoted to music and the arts. The late-night jazz jam is your best bet on Friday after midnight. During the week you can count on the best in jazz, visual and performance art shows, and the occasional spoken-word event. Refreshments are sold, but no alcohol is served.

Humphrey's by the Bay (✉ 2241 Shelter Island Dr., Shelter Island ☎ 619/523–1010 for concert information), surrounded by water, is the summer stomping grounds for musicians such as Harry Belafonte and Chris Isaak. From June through September this dining and drinking oasis hosts the city's best outdoor jazz, folk, and light-rock concert series. The rest of the year the music moves indoors for some first-rate jazz most Sunday, Monday, and Tuesday nights, with piano-bar music on other nights.

Night Bay Cruises

Bahia Belle (✉ 998 W. Mission Bay Dr., Mission Bay ☎ 619/539–7779) is a paddlewheeler that offers relaxing evening cruises along Mission Bay that include cocktails, dancing, and live music. Board from the Bahia Hotel. Cruises run from Wednesday through Sunday in summer and Friday and Saturday in winter (but no cruises in December). The $6 fare is less than most nightclub covers.

Hornblower Cruises (✉ 1066 N. Harbor Dr., Downtown ☎ 619/686–8700) makes nightly dinner-dance cruises aboard the *Lord Hornblower*—passengers are treated to fabulous views of the San Diego skyline.

San Diego Harbor Excursion (✉ 1050 N. Harbor Dr., Downtown ☎ 619/234–4111 or 800/442–7847) welcomes guests aboard with a glass of champagne as a prelude to nightly dinner-dance cruises.

Piano Bars

Hotel Del Coronado (✉ 1500 Orange Ave., Coronado ☎ 619/435–6611), the famous fairy-tale hostelry, has piano music in its Crown Room and Palm Court. The Ocean Terrace Lounge has bands nightly 9–1.

Inn at the Park (✉ 525 Spruce St., Hillcrest ☎ 619/296–0057) offers large booths to tuck into as a piano player entertains nightly beginning at 7 PM. It makes for a nice stop after a day in Balboa Park.

Old Venice (✉ 2910 Canon St., Point Loma ☎ 619/222–1404), a small restaurant-bar, attracts a good crowd of locals on weekdays with its casual, artsy atmosphere. It's a good bar to go to if you prefer not to raise your voice just to have a conversation.

Palace Bar (✉ 311 Island Ave., Gaslamp Quarter ☎ 619/544–1886), in the historical Horton Grand Hotel, is one of the mellowest lounges in the Gaslamp Quarter. Rest up in an overstuffed chair and cradle your drink while deciding what sights to see next.

FodorsChoice **Top of the Hyatt** (✉ 1 Market Pl., Embarcadero ☎ 619/232–1234)
★ crowns the tallest waterfront building in California, affording great views of San Diego Bay, including Coronado to the west, the Coronado Bridge and Mexico to the south, and Point Loma and La Jolla to the North. The wood paneling and mood lighting affect one of the most romantic spots in town. Tables by the windows always seem to be occupied longer because of the view and the well-padded chairs. If this lounge were most anywhere else in the country, it would likely be filled with the self-satisfied puffing their cigars.

Top o' the Cove (✉ 1216 Prospect St., La Jolla ☎ 858/454–7779), also a magnificent Continental restaurant, has pianists playing show tunes and standards from the 1940s to the present. A well-heeled set hob nobs and peruses the extensive wine list, which includes over 1,400 selections. The candlelight, brick walls and overstuffed booths make a great setting from which to enjoy the panoramic views of La Jolla Cove.

Westgate Hotel (✉ 1055 2nd Ave., Downtown ☎ 619/238–1818) is one of the most elegant settings in San Diego. "Old Money" is evoked with leather upholstered seats, marble tabletops, and a grand piano.

Rock, Pop, Folk, Reggae & Blues

Belly Up Tavern (✉ 143 S. Cedros Ave., Solana Beach ☎ 858/481–9022), a fixture on local papers' "best of" lists, has been drawing crowds of all ages since it opened in the mid-'70s. The "BUT's" longevity attests to the quality of the eclectic entertainment on its stage. Within converted Quonset huts, critically acclaimed artists play everything from reggae and folk to—well, you name it.

Brick by Brick (✉ 1130 Buenos Ave., Bay Park ☎ 619/275–5483), an otherwise nondescript cinderblock box in an industrial neighborhood, is always cranking out punk, alternative, or hard rock. Occasionally blues acts or underground dance clubs will make an appearance, making this a very eclectic club.

Casbah (✉ 2501 Kettner Blvd., Middletown ☎ 619/232–4355), near the airport, is a small club with a national reputation for showcasing up-and-coming acts. Nirvana, Smashing Pumpkins, and Alanis Morissette all played the Casbah on their way to stardom. Within San Diego, it's widely recognized as the headquarters of the indie rock scene. You can hear every type of band here—except those that sound like Top 40.

Dream Street (✉ 2228 Bacon St., Ocean Beach ☎ 619/222–8131) is the place to see up-and-coming (or good enough to drink to) local rock bands. The music is on the heavy side and the biker and rocker crowd that hangs out here can have a scary look about them. This is not the place for a quiet evening out.

The Field (✉ 544 5th Ave., Gaslamp Quarter ☎ 619/232–9840) is San Diego's resident Irish pub. True to its Celtic pride, the pub promotes local Irish folksingers throughout the week and has Irish folkdancing on Sunday evenings.

4th & B (✉ 345 B St., Downtown ☎ 619/231–4343) is a live-music venue housed in a former bank that is only open when a concert is booked. All styles of music and occasional comedy acts take the stage.

Over the Border (✉ 3008 Main St., Chula Vista ☎ 619/427-5889) is the home of *rock en español* in San Diego. Cover bands usually play the weekends, but some of the top Latin Rock bands make this unassuming cinderblock club a destination for concertgoers from both sides of the border.

Patrick's II (✉ 428 F St., Gaslamp Quarter ☎ 619/233–3077) serves up live New Orleans–style jazz, blues, and rock in an Irish setting.

Soma (✉ 3350 Sports Arena Blvd., Sports Arena ☎ 619/226–7662) is a name that has been associated with the San Diego music scene since the '80s. Now near the Sports Arena, this all-ages club occupies a former cinema mulitplex converted into two concert halls. A smaller room features local acts while the huge main hall hosts some of the top touring indie rock and punk bands. Regardless of the room, Soma crowds love their mosh pits. There's no seating, so the uninitiated are advised to stand on the sidelines.

Winston's Beach Club (✉ 1921 Bacon St., Ocean Beach ☎ 619/222–6822) is a sure bet for quality music in Ocean Beach. In a bowling alley–turned–rock club, Winston's hosts local bands, reggae groups, and occasionally 1960s-style bands. The crowd, mostly locals, are typically mellow, but can get rowdy.

Singles Bars

Barefoot Bar and Grill (✉ San Diego Princess Resort, 1404 W. Vacation Rd., Mission Bay ☎ 858/274–4630), a beachfront watering hole and hotel bar with a tiki feel, attracts flocks of singles, especially on Sunday night in spring and summer. Live music and happy-hour specials fill the joint up early, making for long latecomer lines.

Dick's Last Resort (✉ 345 4th Ave., Gaslamp Quarter ☎ 619/231–9100) is not for Emily Post adherents. The surly waitstaff and abrasive service are part of the gimmick. The rudeness notwithstanding, fun-loving party people pile into this barnlike restaurant and bar. Dick's has live music nightly and one of the most extensive beer lists in San Diego.

Japengo (✉ 8960 University Center La., La Jolla ☎ 858/450–3355) is the post–work socializing spot for young La Jolla professionals. A sushi bar is one draw, but most come here for the singles scene that plays itself out nightly.

Jose's (✉ 1037 Prospect St., La Jolla ☎ 858/454–7655) is a hit with yuppies from La Jolla and other neighboring beach communities. This small but clean hole-in-the-wall's lack of space gives suave singles an excuse to get up close and personal.

Moose McGillycuddy's (✉ 535 5th Ave., Gaslamp Quarter ☎ 619/702–5595), a major pickup palace, is also a great place to go with friends or hang out with the locals. A DJ spins house and Top 40 dance music that powers the dance floor while the staff serves up drinks and Mexican food.

Old Bonita Store & Bonita Beach Club (✉ 4014 Bonita Rd., Bonita ☎ 619/479–3537), a South Bay hangout, has a DJ spinning retro house music every weekend. The decor is a cross between a family restaurant and a roadhouse, but since Bonita is so far removed from the city center, looks don't matter as it's the only place to go in this part of town.

RT's Longboard Grill (✉ 1466 Garnet Ave., Pacific Beach ☎ 858/270–4030) appeals to the young, tanned beach crowd that comes by to schmooze and booze under the indoor palapas that give this lively bar a south-of-the-border feel.

Typhoon Saloon (✉ 1165 Garnet Ave., Pacific Beach ☎ 858/373–3444) is an obligatory stop for college age singles club-hopping on weekend nights. There are several levels, four bars, and two small dance floors. DJs play a Top 40 mix.

U. S. Grant Hotel (✉ 326 Broadway, Gaslamp Quarter ☎ 619/232–3121), a favorite of the over-thirty business set, is the classiest spot in town for meeting fellow travelers while relaxing with a Manhattan or a martini at the mahogany bar. The best local Latin, jazz, and blues bands alternate appearances.

THE ARTS

National touring companies perform regularly at the 3,000-seat Civic Theatre and Golden Hall, and in Escondido at the California Center for the Arts. Programs at San Diego State University, the University of California at San Diego, private universities, and community colleges host a range of artists, from well-known professionals to students. The *San Diego Union-Tribune* lists attractions and complete movie schedules. The *Reader* weekly devotes an entire section to upcoming cultural events. *San Diego* magazine publishes monthly listings and reviews. Those in the know rely on San Diego's many community micromags found in most coffeehouses.

Book tickets well in advance, preferably at the same time you make hotel reservations. Outlets exist for last-minute tickets, although you risk either paying top rates or getting less-than-choice seats—or both.

You can buy half-price tickets to most theater, music, and dance events on the day of performance at **Times Arts Tix** (✉ Horton Plaza, Gaslamp Quarter ☎ 619/497–5000). Advance full-price tickets are also sold here. **Ticketmaster** (☎ 619/220–8497) sells tickets to many performances. Service charges vary according to the event, and most tickets are nonrefundable.

Dance

California Ballet Company (☎ 858/560–6741) performs high-quality contemporary and traditional works, from story ballets to Balanchine, September–May. The *Nutcracker* is staged annually at the **Civic Theatre** (✉ 202 C St., Downtown); other ballets are presented at the **Lyceum** (✉ 79 Horton Plaza, Gaslamp Quarter) and the **Poway Center for the Performing Arts** (✉ 15498 Espola Rd., Poway).

San Diego Ballet (✉ 5304 Metro St., Downtown ☎ 619/294–7378) performs a vast repertory of classic and contemporary ballet at several venues countywide.

Eveoke Dance Theater (✉ 644 7th Ave., Downtown ☎ 619/238–1153) is San Diego's major avant–garde dance company. It performs a regular season of dance theater works, produces several special events, and presents community-focused classes and exhibitions.

Film

Landmark Theatres (☎ 619/819–0236), known for first-run foreign, art, American independent, and documentary offerings, operates the following four theaters in the San Diego area. **La Jolla Village Cinemas** (✉ 8879 Villa La Jolla Dr., La Jolla ☎ 858/453–7831) is a modern multiplex set in a shopping center. **Hillcrest Cinemas** (✉ 3965 5th Ave., Hillcrest ☎ 619/299–2100) is a posh multiplex right in the middle of uptown's action. **Ken Cinema** (✉ 4061 Adams Ave., Kensington ☎ 619/283–5909) is considered by many to be the last bastion of true avant-garde film in San Diego. It plays a roster of art and revival films that changes almost every night (many programs are double bills), along with *The Rocky Horror Picture Show* every Saturday at midnight. It publishes its listings in the *Ken*, a small newspaper distributed in nearly every coffeehouse and music store in the county. In its 225-seat theater, the **Museum of Photographic Arts** (✉ 1649 El Prado, Balboa Park ☎ 619/238–7559) runs a regular film program that includes classic American and international cinema from prominent filmmakers, as well as the occasional cult film. Each screening is preceded by an informative introduction from the museum staff.

Part of the Museum of Contemporary Art, the **Sherwood Auditorium** (✉ 700 Prospect St., La Jolla ☎ 858/454–2594) hosts foreign and classic film series and special cinema events, including the wildly popular Festival of Animation, from January through March.

Science, space-documentary, observation-of-motion, and sometimes psychedelic films are shown on the IMAX screen at the **Reuben H. Fleet Science Center** (✉ 1875 El Prado, Balboa Park ☎ 619/238–1233).

Music

Coors Amphitheatre (✉ 2050 Otay Valley Rd., Chula Vista ☎ 619/671–3500), the largest concert venue in town, can accommodate 20,000 concertgoers with reserved seats and lawn seating. It presents top-selling national and international acts during its late spring to late summer season.

Copley Symphony Hall (✉ 750 B St., Downtown ☎ 619/235–0804) has great acoustics surpassed only by an incredible Spanish Baroque interior. Not just the home of the San Diego Symphony Orchestra, the renovated 2,200-seat 1920s-era theater has also presented such popular musicians such as Elvis Costello and Sting.

Cox Arena (✉ San Diego State University, 5500 Canyon Crest Dr., College Area ☎ 619/594–6947) attracts top-name acts like Eric Clapton and Depeche Mode to its 12,500-person confines.

East County Performing Arts Center (✉ 210 E. Main St., El Cajon ☎ 619/440–2277) hosts a variety of performing arts events, but mostly music. Internationally touring jazz, classical, blues, and world-beat musicians have ensured its popularity among locals.

La Jolla Chamber Music Society (☎ 858/459–3728) presents internationally acclaimed chamber ensembles, orchestras, and soloists at Sherwood Auditorium and the Civic Theatre.

Open-Air Theatre (✉ San Diego State University, 5500 Campanile Dr., College Area ☎ 619/594–6947) presents top-name rock, reggae, and popular artists in summer concerts under the stars.

San Diego Chamber Orchestra (☎ 760/753–6402), a 35-member ensemble, performs once a month, October–April, in a number of different venues, including St. Joseph's Cathedral downtown.

San Diego Opera (✉ Civic Theatre, 3rd Ave. and B St., Downtown ☎ 619/232–7636) draws international artists. Its season runs January–May. Past performances have included *The Magic Flute, Faust, Idomeneo,* and *Aida,* plus concerts by such talents as Luciano Pavarotti.

San Diego Sports Arena (✉ 3500 Sports Arena Blvd., Sports Arena ☎ 619/224–4176) holds 14,000-plus fans for big-name concerts.

San Diego State University School of Music and Dance (☎ 619/594–6884) presents concerts in many genres, including jazz, classical, and world music in different venues on campus.

The year-round special events of the **San Diego Symphony Orchestra** (✉ 750 B St., Downtown ☎ 619/235–0804) include classic concerts and summer and winter pops. Concerts are held at Copley Symphony Hall, except the Summer Pops series at the Navy Pier, on North Harbor Drive downtown.

Sherwood Auditorium (✉ 700 Prospect St., La Jolla ☎ 858/454–2594), a 550-seat venue in the Museum of Contemporary Art, hosts classical and jazz events.

Spreckels Organ Pavilion (✉ Balboa Park ☎ 619/702–8138) holds a giant outdoor pipe organ dedicated in 1915 by sugar magnates John and Adolph Spreckels. The beautiful Spanish Baroque pavilion hosts concerts by civic organist Carol Williams on most Sunday afternoons and on most Monday evenings in summer. Local military bands, gospel groups, and barbershop quartets also perform here. All shows are free.

Spreckels Theatre (✉ 121 Broadway, Downtown ☎ 619/235–0494), a designated-landmark theater erected in 1912, hosts musical events—everything from mostly Mozart to small rock concerts. Ballets and theatrical productions are also held here. Its good acoustics and historical status make this a special venue.

Theater

California Center for the Arts, Escondido (✉ 340 N. Escondido Blvd., Escondido ☎ 800/988–4253) presents mainstream theatrical productions such as *Grease* and *The Odd Couple.*

Coronado Playhouse (✉ 1775 Strand Way, Coronado ☎ 619/435–4856), a cabaret-type theater near the Hotel Del Coronado, stages regular dramatic and musical performances. Friday and Saturday dinner packages are available.

Diversionary Theatre (✉ 4545 Park Blvd., University Heights ☎ 619/220–0097) is San Diego's premier gay and lesbian company. It presents a range of original works that focus on gay and lesbian themes.

Horton Grand Theatre (✉ Hahn Cosmopolitan Theatre, 444 4th Ave., Gaslamp Quarter ☎ 619/234–9583) stages comedies, dramas, mysteries, and musicals at a 250-seat venue.

La Jolla Playhouse (✉ Mandell Weiss Center for the Performing Arts, University of California at San Diego, 2910 La Jolla Village Dr., La Jolla ☎ 858/550–1010) crafts exciting and innovative productions under the artistic direction of Michael Greif, May–November. Many Broadway shows, such as *Tommy* and *How to Succeed in Business Without Really Trying,* have previewed here before heading for the East Coast.

La Jolla Stage Company (✉ 5661 La Jolla Blvd., La Jolla ☎ 858/459–7773) presents lavish productions of Broadway favorites and popular comedies year-round on the La Jolla High School campus.

Lamb's Players Theatre (✉ 1142 Orange Ave., Coronado ☎ 619/437–0600) has a regular season of five productions from February through November and stages a musical, "Festival of Christmas," in December. "An American Christmas" is their dinner-theater event at the Hotel del Coronado.

Lyceum Theatre (✉ 79 Horton Plaza, Gaslamp Quarter ☎ 619/544–1000) is home to the San Diego Repertory Theatre and also presents productions from visiting theater companies.

Lyric Opera San Diego (✉ Casa del Prado Theatre, Balboa Park ☎ 619/239–8836) presents a variety of musical theater including several Gilbert and Sullivan works each season.

Marie Hitchcock Puppet Theatre (✉ 2130 Pan American Rd. W, Balboa Park ☎ 619/685–5990) entertains with amateur and professional puppeteers and ventriloquists five days a week. The cost is just a few dollars for adults and children alike. If you feel cramped in the small theater, don't worry; the shows rarely run longer than a half hour.

Old Globe Theatre (✉ Simon Edison Centre for the Performing Arts, 1363 Old Globe Way, Balboa Park ☎ 619/239–2255) is the oldest professional theater in California, performing classics, contemporary dramas, and experimental works. It produces the famous summer Shakespeare Festival at the Old Globe and its sister theaters, the Cassius Carter Centre Stage and the Lowell Davies Festival Theatre.

Poway Center for the Performing Arts (✉ 15498 Espola Rd., Poway ☎ 858/748–0505), an ambitious theater in suburban San Diego, presents musical comedy and other lighthearted fare.

San Diego Junior Theater (✉ Casa del Prado Theatre, Balboa Park ☎ 619/239–8355) is a highly regarded school where children ages 6–18 perform and stage productions. Call for performance dates.

San Diego Repertory Theatre (✉ Lyceum Theatre, 79 Horton Plaza, Gaslamp Quarter ☎ 619/235–8025), San Diego's first resident acting company, performs contemporary works year-round.

San Diego State University Drama Department (✉ Don Powell Theatre and elsewhere on campus, 5500 Campanile Dr., College Area ☎ 619/594–6947) presents contemporary and classic dramas.

Sledgehammer Theatre (✉ 1620 6th Ave., Uptown ☎ 619/544–1484), one of San Diego's cutting-edge theaters, stages avant-garde pieces in St. Cecilia's church.

Starlight Musical Theatre (✉ Starlight Bowl, 2005 Pan American Plaza, Balboa Park ☎ 619/544–7827 in season), a summertime favorite, is a series of musicals performed in an outdoor amphitheater mid-June–early September. Because of the theater's proximity to the airport, actors often have to freeze mid-scene while a plane flies over.

Sushi Performance & Visual Art (✉ 320 11th Ave., Downtown ☎ 619/235–8469), a nationally acclaimed group, provides an opportunity for well-known performance artists to do their thing in the old Carnation Milk building, now dubbed the "rein-Carnation building." The white-walled interior provides an intimate setting for many an avant-garde performance. The group will likely switch its venue periodically between late 2004 and late 2006 due to redevelopment in the area.

Theatre in Old Town (✉ 4040 Twiggs St., Old Town ☎ 619/688–2494) presents punchy revues and occasional classics. Shows like *Forbidden Broadway*, *Ruthless*, *Gilligan's Island*, and *Forbidden Hollywood* have made this a popular place.

UCSD Theatre (✉ Mandell Weiss Center for the Performing Arts, University of California at San Diego, 2910 La Jolla Village Dr. and Expedition Way, La Jolla ☎ 858/534–4574) presents productions by students of the university's theater department, September–May.

Welk Resort Theatre (✉ 8860 Lawrence Welk Dr., Escondido ☎ 760/749–3448 or 800/932–9355), a famed dinner theater about a 45-minute drive northeast of downtown on I–15, puts on polished Broadway-style productions.

SPORTS &
THE OUTDOORS

5

IDEAL FAMILY SAND
Silver Strand State Beach ⇨*p.141*

MOST POPULAR STRAND
Mission Beach ⇨*p.143*

WHERE TO SPOT SURFERS YEAR-ROUND
Tourmaline Surfing Park ⇨*p.145*

NOMINEE, PRETTIEST SPOT ANYWHERE
La Jolla Cove ⇨*p.145*

BEST PLACE NOT TO PLAY IN THE SAND
Torrey Pines Municipal Golf Course ⇨*p.153*

Updated by
Rob Aikins

SAN DIEGO HAS A REPUTATION as being an active, outdoors-oriented community. It's a reputation easy to earn given the near perfect weather and a wealth of places to play: ocean, bay, lakes, mountains, deserts, parks, and golf courses offer a chance to practice nearly any sport conceivable. The ocean especially is one of San Diego's most popular natural attractions. Surfers, swimmers, kayakers, divers, snorkelers, sailboarders, and even kiteboarders have 70 mi of shorefront from which to enter their arena. You can rent equipment and take lessons in any one of these sports or simply enjoy a fishing or whale-watching excursion on one of the many charter boats. Even if you're inclined to do no more than sightsee, you can take a low-impact sunset stroll on a wide, sandy beach or explore secluded coves at low tide and see the microcosm of a tidepool.

The north coastal section of the county has lured many resident professional triathletes, surfers, and bicyclists, who all take advantage of the climate, both meteorologic and social, which looks favorably upon them. There's excellent hiking, mountain biking, and horseback riding in the county's eastern foothills and mountains.

At the end of the day at any beach in the county, you'll see a daily ritual as locals cease all activity to silently observe the sunset over the water.

Ballooning

Enjoy the views of the Pacific Ocean, the mountains, and the coastline south to Mexico and north to San Clemente from a hot-air balloon at sunrise or sunset. The conditions are perfect: necessary winds and wide-open spaces. **A Balloon Adventure by California Dreamin'** (✉ 162 S. Rancho Santa Fe Rd., Suite F35, Encinitas ☎ 800/373–3359) offers sunset and sunrise flights from several North County spots, as well as a sunrise flight from Otay Mesa for visitors to the South Bay. Temecula wine country flights are also available. **Skysurfer Balloon Company** (✉ 1221 Camino del Mar, Del Mar ☎ 858/481–6800 or 800/660–6809) lifts off from several locations and will take you on one-hour flights in North County or Temecula. Hors d'oeuvres and beverages are included.

Baseball

Baseball is important in San Diego, where games are almost never rained out. After decades of playing at the multi-use Qualcomm Stadium, the **San Diego Padres** finally have a park designed specifically for baseball. Opening day 2004 also opened **Petco Park** (✉ 100 Park Blvd., Downtown ☎ 888/697–2373), which harkens back to the great ballparks of yesteryear. The park's design incorporates existing antique buildings to give it a classic ambience that preserves some of the area's heritage. Long-time fans are hoping the new digs will energize the team. Those not interested in baseball still look forward to the growth of the redevelopment district around the park, which will include shops, restaurants, a new library, and trendy residential developments. The team slugs it out for bragging rights in the National League West from April into October. Games with such rivals as the Los Angeles Dodgers and the San Francisco Giants are often the highlights of the home season. Tickets are usually available on game day.

Basketball

Although there have been a few attempts to bring pro and semi-pro basketball to San Diego, no team has endured. Diehard basketball fans instead rely on college teams to give them a basketball fix. Both San Diego State University and the private University of San Diego have teams that regularly reach the playoffs of their conferences.

The **San Diego State University Aztecs** (☎ 619/283–7378) compete in the Western Athletic Conference with such powers as the University of Utah and Brigham Young University. The Aztecs play December–March at **Cox Arena** (✉ College Ave. exit off I–8, San Diego State University ☎ 619/594–6947), home to the university's men's and women's basketball teams.

The **University of San Diego Toreros** (☎ 619/260–4803 or 619/260–4600) take on West Coast Conference opponents Pepperdine University, the University of San Francisco, the University of California at Santa Barbara, and other teams. Games are played in the state-of-the-art **Jenny Craig Pavilion** (✉ 5998 Alcalá Park, Linda Vista ☎ 619/260–4803 or 619/260–4600).

Beaches

Water temperatures are generally chilly, ranging from 55°F to 65°F from October through June, and 65°F to 75°F from July through September. For a surf and weather report, call 619/221–8824. For a general beach and weather report, call 619/289–1212. Pollution, which has long been a problem near the Mexican border, is inching north and is generally worse near rivermouths and storm drain outlets. The weather page of the *San Diego Union-Tribune* includes pollution reports along with listings of surfing and diving conditions.

Overnight camping is not allowed on any San Diego city beaches, but there are campgrounds at some state beaches throughout the county (☎ 800/444–7275 for reservations). Lifeguards are stationed at city beaches from Sunset Cliffs up to Black's Beach in the summertime, but coverage in winter is provided by roving patrols only. Leashed dogs are permitted on most San Diego beaches and adjacent parks from 6 PM to 9 AM; they can run unleashed anytime at Dog Beach at the north end of Ocean Beach and, from Memorial Day through Labor Day, at Rivermouth in Del Mar. It's rarely a problem, however, to take your pet to isolated beaches in winter.

Pay attention to signs listing illegal activities; undercover police often patrol the beaches, carrying their ticket books in coolers. Glass is prohibited on all beaches, and fires are allowed only in fire rings or elevated barbecue grills. Alcoholic beverages—including beer—are completely banned on some city beaches; others allow you to partake from 8 AM to 8 PM. Imbibing in beach parking lots, on boardwalks, and in landscaped areas is always illegal. Although it may be tempting to take a starfish or some other sea creature as a souvenir from a tide pool, it upsets the delicate ecological balance and is illegal to do, too.

Parking near the ocean can be hard to find in summer but is unmetered at all San Diego city beaches. Del Mar has a pay lot and metered street parking around the 15th Street Beach.

The beaches below are listed from south to north, starting near the Mexican border. County Highway S21 runs along the coast between Torrey Pines State Beach/Reserve and Oceanside, although its local name, Old Highway 101 or Coast Highway 101, for example, varies by community. Most of the beaches north of Del Mar are plagued by erosion and bluff failure. It's always a wise idea to stay clear of the bluffs, whether you're above or below them.

South Bay

Border Field State Beach. This southernmost San Diego beach is different from most California beaches; swimming is prohibited and the fence marking off the south end of the parking lot also marks the U.S.–Mexican border. On the other side of that fence is Tijuana's Bullring-by-the-Sea. Occasionally concerts are held with attendees and performers on both sides of the border. The beach is part of Border Field State Park, a marshy area with wide chaparral and wildflowers, a favorite among horseback riders and hikers. The park contains much of the Tijuana River Estuary, a haven for migrating birds. The beach is usually open 9–5. Beware that in winter the grounds are often posted with contamination signs because of sewer runoff from Tijuana. The beach has barbecue rings, parking is plentiful, and there are restrooms. ⊠ *Exit I–5 at Dairy Mart Rd. and head west along Monument Rd.; South San Diego.*

Imperial Beach. In August this classic southern California beach is the site of one of the nation's largest sand-castle competitions. The rest of the year, this laid-back town is a great place for long walks away from crowds. The surf here is often excellent, but sewage contamination can be a problem. There are lifeguards in summer, restrooms, parking, and nearby food vendors. A walk on the pier, the southernmost in California, allows views of Mexico to the south and Point Loma to the north. A walk on the wide, sandy beaches south toward Border Field State Beach is a great way to experience a quiet, uncrowded beach—not always an easy thing to do. ⊠ *Take Palm Ave. west from I–5 until it hits water; Imperial Beach.*

Coronado

Silver Strand State Beach. This quiet Coronado beach is ideal for families. The water is relatively calm, lifeguards and rangers are on duty year-round, and there are places to Rollerblade or ride bikes. Four parking lots provide room for more than 1,500 cars. Sites at a campground ($18) for self-contained RVs are available on a first-come, first-serve basis; stays are limited to seven nights. Foot tunnels under Route 75 lead to a bayside beach, which affords great views of the San Diego skyline. ⊠ *From San Diego–Coronado Bay Bridge, turn left onto Orange Ave., which becomes Rte. 75, and follow signs; Coronado* ☎ *619/435-5184.*

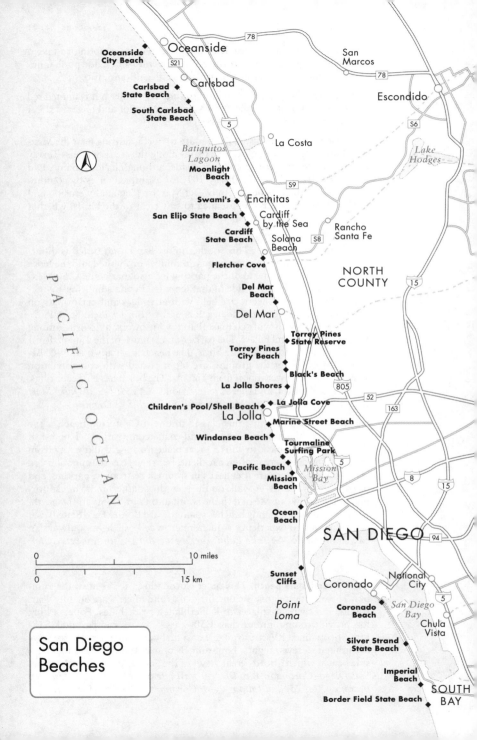

San Diego
Beaches

★ ☺ **Coronado Beach.** With the famous Hotel Del Coronado as a backdrop, this stretch of sandy beach is one of San Diego County's largest and most picturesque. It's perfect for sunbathing, people-watching, or Frisbee. Exercisers include Navy SEAL teams, as well as the occasional Marine Recon unit, who have training runs on the beaches in and around Coronado. Parking can be difficult on the busiest days. There are plenty of restrooms and service facilities, as well as fire rings. ⊠ *From the bridge, turn left on Orange Ave. and follow signs; Coronado.*

Point Loma

Sunset Cliffs. Beneath the jagged cliffs on the west side of the Point Loma peninsula is one of the more secluded beaches in the area. A few miles long, it's popular with surfers and locals. At the south end of the peninsula, near Cabrillo Point, tide pools teeming with small sea creatures are revealed at low tide. Farther north the waves lure surfers and the lonely coves attract sunbathers. Stairs at the foot of Bermuda and Santa Cruz avenues provide beach access, as do some (treacherous at points) cliff trails. There are no facilities. A visit here is more enjoyable at low tide; check the local newspaper for tide schedules. ⊠ *Take I–8 west to Sunset Cliffs Blvd. and head west; Point Loma.*

San Diego

Ocean Beach. Much of this mile-long beach is a haven for volleyball players, sunbathers, and swimmers. The area around the municipal pier at the south end is a hangout for surfers and transients; the pier itself is open to the public 24 hours a day for fishing and walking and there's a restaurant at the middle. The beach is south of the channel entrance to Mission Bay. You'll find food vendors and fire rings; limited parking is available. Swimmers should beware of unusually vicious rip currents here. ⊠ *Take I–8 west to Sunset Cliffs Blvd. and head west. Turn right on Santa Monica Ave.; Ocean Beach.*

Mission Beach. San Diego's most popular beach draws huge crowds on hot summer days. The 2-mi-long stretch extends from the north entrance of Mission Bay to Pacific Beach. A wide boardwalk paralleling the beach is popular with walkers, joggers, roller skaters, bladers, and bicyclists. Surfers, swimmers, and volleyball players congregate at the south end. Thinly clad volleyball players practice on Cohasset Court year-round. Toward its north end, near the Belmont Park roller coaster, the beach narrows and the water becomes rougher. The crowds grow thicker and somewhat rougher as well. For parking you can try for a spot on the street, but your best bet are the two big lots at Belmont Park. ⊠ *Exit I–5 at Garnet Ave. and head west to Mission Blvd. Turn south and look for parking; Mission Beach.*

Pacific Beach/North Pacific Beach. The boardwalk of Mission Beach turns into a sidewalk here, but there are still bike paths and picnic tables along the beachfront. Pacific Beach runs from the north end of Mission Beach to Crystal Pier. North Pacific Beach extends from the pier north. The scene here is particularly lively on weekends. There are designated surfing areas, and fire rings are available. Parking can be a challenge, but there are plenty of restrooms and restaurants in the area. ⊠ *Exit I–5*

SURFING SAN DIEGO

SURFING MAY HAVE originated in Hawai'i, but modern surfing culture is inextricably linked to the southern California lifestyle. From the Malibu settings of Beach Blanket Bingo and Gidget to the surf-city sounds of Jan and Dean and the Beach Boys, the entertainment industry brought a California version of surfing to the landlocked, and in the process created an enduring mystique.

Today the billion-dollar surfing industry centered around Orange and San Diego counties sells the California surfing "dude" image worldwide. However, surfing is not just for dudes anymore. Women are entering the sport at a rate twice that of men, a trend that represents a return to surfing's Hawaiian origins when surfing was enjoyed by people of both genders and all ages.

Surfing is a demanding sport that requires great reflexes, endurance, and balance. But besides being a strong athlete, a good surfer must be part oceanographer and part meteorologist in order to understand the subtle nuances of the ocean. Waves suitable for surfing are generated by the intense winds of offshore storms blowing across large expanses of water. When the waves reach the shallow water of the coast, they stand up and break. Because the quality and size of waves at any given spot is subject to many variables, including ocean bottom contour, tides, and local winds, even the best spots may not be consistent. But with a little knowledge and luck, a surfer can fulfill his or her quest for the perfect wave.

Watching surfing from the shore can be a test of patience. Surfers spend a lot of time paddling into position and waiting to "take off" on the next wave. When someone takes off, look for one of two types of surfing: longboarding and shortboarding. Longboarders tend to ride boards more than 8 feet in length with rounded noses. Shortboarders ride the lightweight, high-performance boards from 5 to 7 feet in length that have pointed noses. A great longboarder will have a smooth, fluid style and will shuffle up and down the board, maybe even riding on the nose with the toes of both feet on the very edge ("hanging ten"). Shortboarders tend to surf faster and more aggressively. The best shortboarders surf vertical to the wave face and may even break free of the wave—known as "aerials" or "catching air." Nonsurfers are often most impressed and amused by the mistakes. "Wipeouts," the sometimes spectacular falls, inevitably happen to all surfers.

In San Diego the biggest waves usually occur in winter, although good-size swells can come any time of the year. Generally, swells come from a northerly directionin winter, while in summer they tend to come from the south. Certain surf spots are better on different swells. In winter try beaches like Swami's in Encinitas or Black's Beach near La Jolla. Summer spots are Windansea in La Jolla and nearby Tourmaline Surfing Park.

Another good place for watching surfers is any municipal pier, which gives you a much closer vantage point on the action. To get a feel for the surfing culture at-large, spend some time in the laid-back shops and restaurants of towns like Ocean Beach, Pacific Beach, and Encinitas. The truly adventurous can seek instruction from a qualified surf school and soon understand the stoke that one feels after shredding clean epic peaks during a dawn patrol (or, in plain English, feeling the elation of surfing good waves during an early morning surf session).

— Rob Aikins

at Garnet Ave. and head west to Mission Blvd. Turn north and look for parking; Pacific Beach.

La Jolla

The beaches of La Jolla combine unusual beauty with good fishing, scuba diving, and surfing. On the down side, they are crowded and have limited parking. Don't think about bringing your pet; dogs aren't even allowed on the sidewalks above some beaches here.

Tourmaline Surfing Park. This is one of the area's most popular beaches for surfing and sailboarding year-round. No swimming is allowed and surfing etiquette is strongly enforced by the locals in and out of the water. There's a 175-space parking lot at the foot of Tourmaline Street that normally fills to capacity by midday. ⊠ *Take Mission Blvd. north (it turns into La Jolla Blvd.) and turn west on Tourmaline St.; La Jolla.*

Windansea Beach. If the scenery here seems familiar, it's because Windansea and its habitués were the inspiration for Tom Wolfe's satirical novel *The Pump House Gang,* about a group of surfers who protect their surf-turf from outsiders. The beach's sometimes towering waves (caused by an underwater reef) are truly world class. With its incredible views and secluded sunbathing spots set among sandstone rocks, Windansea is also one of the most romantic of West Coast beaches, especially at sunset. ⊠ *Take Mission Blvd. north (it turns into La Jolla Blvd.) and turn west on Nautilus St.; La Jolla.*

Marine Street Beach. Wide and sandy, this strand of beach often teems with sunbathers, swimmers, walkers, and joggers. The water is known as a great spot for bodysurfing, although the waves break in extremely shallow water and you'll need to watch out for riptides. ⊠ *Accessible from Marine St., off La Jolla Blvd.; La Jolla.*

Children's Pool. Because of the pool's location at the tip of the peninsula, you can actually look east back at the La Jolla Peninsula for unmatched panoramic views of the coastline and ocean. This shallow cove, protected by a seawall, has small waves and no riptide. The area just outside the pool is popular with scuba divers who explore the offshore reef when the surf is calm. The beach here is closed to humans ever since groups of harbor seals decided to call it home. Ironically, it seems more popular than ever as people come to the seawall just to watch these cute but unfriendly pinnipeds wallow in the sand. ⊠ *Follow La Jolla Blvd. north. When it forks, stay to the left, then turn right onto Coast Blvd.; La Jolla.*

Shell Beach. North of Children's Pool is a small cove, accessible by stairs, with a relatively secluded beach. The exposed rocks off the coast have been designated a protected habitat for sea lions; you can watch them sun themselves and frolic in the water. ⊠ *Continue along Coast Blvd. north from Children's Pool; La Jolla.*

Fodor's Choice **La Jolla Cove.** This is one of the prettiest spots in the world. A palm-lined
★ park sits on top of cliffs formed by the incessant pounding of the waves. At low tide the tide pools and cliff caves provide a destination for explorers. Divers, snorkelers, and kayakers can explore the underwater

delights of the San Diego–La Jolla Underwater Ecological Reserve. The cove is also a favorite of rough-water swimmers. ⊠ *Follow Coast Blvd. north to signs, or take the La Jolla Village Dr. exit from I–5, head west to Torrey Pines Rd., turn left, and drive downhill to Girard Ave. Turn right and follow signs; La Jolla.*

★ ☾ **La Jolla Shores.** On summer holidays all access routes are usually closed to one of San Diego's most popular beaches. Get here early to get a spot; you know you've missed out if the access road closes. The lures here are an incredible view of the La Jolla peninsula, a wide sandy beach, an adjoining grassy park, and the most gentle waves in San Diego. In fact, several surf schools teach here and kayak rentals are nearby. A concrete boardwalk parallels the beach. Arrive early to get a parking spot in the lot at the foot of Calle Frescota. ⊠ *From I–5 take La Jolla Village Dr. west and turn left onto La Jolla Shores Dr. Head west to Camino del Oro or Vallecitos St. Turn right; La Jolla.*

Black's Beach. The powerful waves at this beach, officially known as Torrey Pines City Park Beach, attract world-class surfers, and its relative isolation appeals to nudist nature lovers (although by law nudity is prohibited). Access to parts of the shore coincides with low tide. There are no lifeguards on duty, and strong rip currents are common—only experienced swimmers should take the plunge. Storms have weakened the cliffs in the past few years; they're dangerous to climb and should be avoided. ⊠ *Take Genesee Ave. west from I–5 and follow signs to Glider Port; easier access, via a paved path, available on La Jolla Farms Rd., but parking is limited to 2 hrs; La Jolla.*

Del Mar

★ **Torrey Pines State Beach/Reserve.** One of San Diego's best beaches encompasses 1,700 acres of bluffs and bird-filled marshes. A network of meandering trails lead to the sandy shoreline below. Along the way enjoy the rare Torrey Pine trees, found only here and on Santa Rosa Island offshore. The large parking lot is rarely full. Lifeguards are on duty weekends (weather permitting) from Easter until Memorial Day, then daily until Labor Day, and again on weekends through September. Torrey Pines tends to get crowded in summer, but more isolated spots under the cliffs are a short walk in either direction. ⊠ *Take the Carmel Valley Rd. exit west from I–5, turn left on Rte. S21; Del Mar* 🕿 *858/755–2063* 🅿 *Parking $6.*

Del Mar Beach. The numbered streets of Del Mar, from 15th north to 29th, end at a wide beach popular with volleyball players, surfers, and sunbathers. Parking can be a problem on nice summer days, but access is relatively easy. The portions of Del Mar south of 15th Street are lined with cliffs and are rarely crowded. Leashed dogs are permitted on most sections of the beach year-round; from October through May, dogs may run free at Rivermouth, Del Mar's northernmost beach. During the annual summer meeting of the Del Mar Thoroughbred Club, horse bettors sit on the beach in the morning, working on the *Daily Racing Form* before heading across the street to the track. ⊠ *Take the Via de la Valle exit from I–5 west to Rte. S21 (also known as Camino del Mar in Del Mar) and turn left; Del Mar.*

Solana Beach

Most of the beaches in this little city are nestled under cliffs, and access is limited to private stairways. However, at the west end of Lomas Santa Fe Drive (at an area known as Pill Box because of the bunkerlike structures on top of the cliffs), you'll find access to a small beach, known locally as **Fletcher Cove**. Also here are restrooms and a large parking lot. During low tide it's an easy walk under the cliffs to nearby beaches. High tide can make some of the beach impassable. Tides and surf conditions are posted at a kiosk on top of the bluffs. ☒ *From I–5 take Lomas Santa Fe Dr. west; Solana Beach.*

Cardiff-by-the-Sea

Cardiff State Beach. This beach begins at the parking lot immediately north of the cliffs at Solana Beach. A reef break draws surfers, although this cobbly beach otherwise is not particularly appealing. However, a walk south will give you great access to some of the secluded coves of Solana Beach. Pay attention to the incoming tide or you may have to wade or swim back to the parking lot. ☒ *From I–5 turn west on Lomas Santa Fe Dr. to Rte. S21 (Old Hwy. 101) and turn right; Cardiff-by-the-Sea* ☎ *760/753–5091* 🚗 *Parking $4.*

San Elijo State Beach. There are **campsites** (☎ 800/444–7275 for reservations) atop a scenic bluff at this park, which also has a store and shower facilities plus beach access for swimmers and surfers. Sites run $12–$18. ☒ *From I–5 turn west on Lomas Santa Fe Dr. to Rte. S21 (Old Hwy. 101) and turn right; Cardiff-by-the-Sea* ☎ *760/753–5091* 🚗 *Parking $4 per car, or park free nearby on U.S. 101.*

Encinitas

Swami's. Palms and the golden lotus-flower domes of the nearby Self-Realization Fellowship Retreat and Hermitage earned this picturesque beach its name. Extreme low tides expose tidepools that harbor anemones, starfish, and other sea life. Remember to look but don't touch; all sea life here is protected. The beach is also a top surfing spot; the only access is by a long stairway leading down from the cliff-top park. On big winter swells, the bluffs are lined with gawkers watching the area's best surfers take on, and be taken down by, one of the best big waves in the county. ☒ *Follow Rte. S21 north from Cardiff, or exit I–5 at Encinitas Blvd., go west to Rte. S21, and turn left; Encinitas.*

Moonlight Beach. Large parking areas and lots of facilities make this beach, tucked into a break in the cliffs, an easy getaway. To combat erosion sand is trucked in every year. The volleyball courts on the north end attract many competent players, including a few professionals who live in the area. ☒ *Take the Encinitas Blvd. exit from I–5 and head west to 3rd St. Turn left. Parking lot is on your right at the top of the hill; Encinitas.*

Carlsbad

Carlsbad State Beach, South Carlsbad State Beach. Erosion from winter storms has made the southern Carlsbad beaches rockier than most beaches in southern California. This is particularly true of South Carlsbad, a stretch of which is named in honor of Robert C. Frazee, a local politician and civic booster. Still, it's a good swimming spot, there are fine street- and beach-level promenades outside of downtown Carlsbad, and for self-contained RVs there's **overnight camping** (☎ 800/444–7275). No overnight camping is allowed at Carlsbad State Beach, farther to the north, but there's a fishing area and a parking lot. ✉ *Exit I–5 at La Costa Ave. and head west to Rte. S21. Turn north and follow coastline; Carlsbad* ☎ *760/438–3143* ✎ *Free at both beaches.*

Oceanside

Swimmers, surfers, and U.S. Marines (from nearby Camp Pendleton) often come to play on **Oceanside's beaches.** The surf is good around the Oceanside Pier near the foot of Mission Avenue and on either side of the two jetties. Self–serve RV day parking–overnight camping is at the northernmost end of Harbor beach for $8 per half-day or $16 overnight up to five days. Campers can pay at the machine. There are plenty of pay lots and meters around the pier and also in the Oceanside harbor area. ✉ *Take Vista Way west from I–5 to Rte. S21 (Coast Hwy.) and turn right. Best access points are from Cassidy St., the Oceanside Pier, and the Oceanside Harbor area. For direct access to Oceanside Harbor, take the Harbor Dr. exit from I–5 and follow the signs; Oceanside.*

Bicycling

On any given summer day **Route S21** from La Jolla to Oceanside looks like a freeway for cyclists. Never straying more than a quarter-mile from the beach, it's easily the most popular and scenic bike route around. Although the terrain is fairly easy, the long, steep Torrey Pines grade, heading south just past Del Mar, is world famous for weeding out the weak. Experienced cyclists follow **Lomas Santa Fe Drive** in Solana Beach east into Rancho Santa Fe, perhaps even continuing east on Del Dios Highway, past Lake Hodges, to Escondido. These roads can be narrow and winding in spots. For more leisurely rides, **Mission Bay, San Diego Harbor,** and the **Mission Beach boardwalk** are all flat and scenic. San Diego also has a **velodrome** in the Morley Field section of Balboa Park. Often thought of as only for racing, Balboa Park's ⅓ km, light banked, elliptical track is often more like a lap pool for bicyclists of all types who come for community, not competition. For those who want to take their biking experience to the extreme, the **Magdalena Ecke YMCA Skate/BMX park** (✉ 200 Saxony Rd., Encinitas ☎ 760/942–9622) has set times when BMXers can rip it up on the same wood vert ramp and street courses that skateboarders use.

Local bookstores and camping stores sell guides to some challenging mountain-bike trails in outer San Diego County. A free comprehensive map of all county bike paths is available from the local office of the **California Department of Transportation** (✉ 2829 Juan St., Old Town 92110 ☎ 619/688–6699).

Bicycle Barn (✉ 746 Emerald St., Pacific Beach ☎ 858/581–3665) rents a variety of bikes—from mountain bikes to beach cruisers and tandems—to get you cruising the boardwalk in no time. Once you're off the boat at Coronado Ferry Landing, explore the charming community with a bike from **Bikes and Beyond** (✉ 1201 1st Ave., Coronado ☎ 619/435–

7180). **Mission Beach Surf and Skate** (✉ 704 Ventura Pl., Mission Beach ☎ 858/488–5050) is right on the boardwalk and rents bikes, skates, and boards of all types.

Boccie

Italian fishermen immigrated to San Diego in the early 20th century, bringing with them their pastime sport. The Italian version of lawn bowling is played on Monday, Wednesday, and Friday from 1 to 5 on courts in the Morley Field section of **Balboa Park** (☎ 619/692–4919). The games are open to the public, and there are usually boccie balls at the courts.

Bullfighting

California Academy of Tauromaquia (✉ Point Loma ☎ 619/709–0664) is believed to be the only school of toreo in the United States. The academy promotes the art of bloodless bullfighting. They offer regular classes each week as well as four- to six-day intensive clinics that teach some fundamentals of bullfighting. Classes without animals are held in Ocean Beach or Point Loma. Instruction with live animals takes place on a bull ranch in northern Baja.

Diving

Enthusiasts the world over come to San Diego to snorkel and scuba-dive off La Jolla and Point Loma. At La Jolla Cove you'll find the **San Diego–La Jolla Underwater Ecological Park**. Because all sea life is protected here, it's the best place to see large lobster, sea bass, and sculpin, as well as numerous golden Garibaldi, the state marine fish. It's common to see hundreds of beautiful (and harmless) leopard sharks schooling on the north end of the cove, near La Jolla shores, especially in summer. Farther north, off the south end of Black's Beach, the rim of **Scripps Canyon** lies in about 60 feet of water. The canyon plummets to more than 900 feet in some sections.

The HMCS *Yukon,* a decommissioned Canadian warship, was intentionally sunk off of **Mission Beach** to create a diving destination. A mishap caused it to settle on its side, creating a surreal, M. C. Escher–esque diving environment. Beware and exercise caution: even experienced divers have become disoriented inside the wreck. Another popular diving spot is **Sunset Cliffs** in Point Loma, where the sea life and flora are relatively close to shore. Strong rip currents make it an area best enjoyed by experienced divers, who mostly prefer to make their dives from boats. It's illegal to take any wildlife from the ecological preserves in La Jolla or near Cabrillo Point. Spearfishing requires a license (available at most dive stores), and it's illegal to take out-of-season lobster and game fish. The *San Diego Union–Tribune* includes diving conditions on its weather page. For recorded diving information, contact the **San Diego City Lifeguard Service** (☎ 619/221–8824).

San Diego Divers Supply (✉ 4004 Sports Arena Blvd., Sports Arena ☎ 619/224–3439) provides equipment and instruction, as well as boat trips and maps of local wrecks and attractions. **Ocean Enterprises Scuba**

Diving (✉ 7710 Balboa Ave., Clairemont Mesa ☏ 858/565–6054), a sister location of San Diego Divers Supply, provides the same full range of services. **Diving Locker** (✉ 1020 Grand Ave., Pacific Beach ☏ 858/272–1120) has been a fixture in San Diego since 1959, making it the city's longest-running dive shop. Not for the faint of heart, **San Diego Shark Diving Expeditions** (✉ 6747 Friar's Rd., Suite 112, Mission Valley ☏ 619/299–8560) will chum the water with blood and lower you in a cage to the frenzy below the surface. They do not offer instruction and cater to experienced divers only.

Fishing

Live out your deep water fishing fantasies of wrestling with a bluefin tuna or hauling in a shark from a local pier. San Diego's waters are home to a plethora of game species and you never know what you'll hook into. Depending on the season, a half- or full-day ocean charter trip could bring in a yellowfin, dorado, sea bass, or halibut. Longer trips to Mexican waters can net you bigger game like a marlin or a bigeye tuna. Pier fishing doesn't offer as much potential excitement, but it's the cheapest ocean fishing option available. No license is required to fish from a public pier, such as the Ocean Beach, Imperial Beach and Oceanside piers. Public lakes are frequently stocked with a variety of trout and largemouth bass, but also have resident populations of bluegill and catfish. A fishing license from the state **Department of Fish and Game** (✉ 4949 Viewridge Ave., San Diego 92123 ☏ 858/467–4201), available at most bait-and-tackle and sporting-goods stores, is required for fishing from the shoreline. Nonresidents can purchase an annual license or a 10-day, 2-day, or 1-day short-term license. Children under 16 do not need a license.

County-operated **Lake Jennings** (✉ 10108 Bass Rd., Lakeside) and **Lake Morena** (✉ 2550 Lake Morena Dr., Campo) are popular for fishing and camping. For information or to make reservations call 619/565–3600 weekdays between 8 AM and 5 PM. City-operated reservoirs, like **Sutherland** (✉ Sutherland Dam Rd.) and **San Vicente** (✉ Moreno Ave.) are good spots for catching trout and bass, but have no campgrounds. Call 619/465–3474 for a 24-hour information line. Three freshwater lakes—**Dixon, Hodges, and Wohlford**—surround the North County city of Escondido. Camping is allowed at Wohlford at the **Oakvale RV Park** (☏ 760/749–2895) on the south shore; there's a supply store and a boat ramp. On the north shore of Lake Wohlford, there's camping at **Wohlford Resort** (☏ 760/749–2755), complete with stores selling food, drinks, bait, tackle, and camping supplies. Boats can be rented at the boat ramp. **Lyle's at Dixon Lake** (☏ 760/741–3328, 760/839–4680 ranger station) is a city-administered campground and offers similar amenities as the areas at Wohlford.

Fisherman's Landing (✉ 2838 Garrison St., Point Loma ☏ 619/221–8500) has a fleet of luxury vessels from 57 feet to 124 feet long, offering long-range multiday trips in search of yellowfin tuna, yellowtail, and other deep-water fish. Whale-watching and sometimes whale-petting trips are also available. **H&M Landing** (✉ 2803 Emerson St., Point Loma ☏ 619/222–1144) schedules fishing trips, plus whale-watching excursions from December through March. **Seaforth Boat Rentals** (✉ 1641 Quivira Rd., Mission Bay ☎ 619/223–1681) can take you out on Mission Bay in a rowboat or power skiff or can arrange a charter for an ocean adventure. **Helgren's Sportfishing** (✉ 315 Harbor Dr. S, Oceanside ☎ 760/722–2133) is your best bet in North County, offering the full assortment of trips from Oceanside Harbor.

Fitness

Most major hotels have full health clubs, with weight machines, stationary bicycles, and spas. Several hotels have elaborate spas that offer one-day spa-and-fitness programs for nonguests.

The spa at **Hotel Del Coronado** (✉ 1500 Orange Ave., Coronado ☎ 619/435–6611) offers body treatments and massages including the Del Aromatherapy Body Masque and the Del Massage. All services include full use of fitness facilities for the day. **L'Auberge Del Mar Resort and Spa** (✉ 1540 Camino Del Mar, Del Mar ☎ 858/259–1515) has a full-service European spa with services that range from single treatments to full-day affairs. Facials are custom-blended to each client's needs, with no two being alike. A package at the **Rancho Bernardo Inn** (✉ 17550 Bernardo Oaks Dr., Rancho Bernardo ☎ 858/675–8500) includes a massage, a facial, and use of the fitness center. Day-spa packages at the **Rancho Valencia Resort** (✉ 5921 Valencia Circle, Rancho Santa Fe ☎ 858/756–1123) include massage, aromatherapy, and use of fitness facilities. **The Spa at the Coronado Island Marriott Resort** (✉ 2000 2nd St., Coronado ☎ 619/435–3000) has pampering packages that include the use of fitness facilities and admission to exercise classes. **Chopra Center for Well Being** (✉ 7630 Fay Ave., La Jolla ☎ 888/424–6772) was founded by New Age guru Dr. Deepak Chopra to teach and treat guests according to his holistic view of life. Day spa treatments and longer visits are offered, as well as free courses to the general public.

Frog's Athletic & Racquet Club (✉ 901 Hotel Circle S, Hotel Circle ☎ 619/291–3500) has a weight room, saunas, and tennis and racquetball courts. Anyone can use the splendid facilities at the **Sporting Club at Aventine** (✉ 8930 University Center La., La Jolla ☎ 858/552–8000). The **24 Hour Fitness Centers** (✉ 5885 Rancho Mission Rd., Mission Valley ☎ 619/281–5543 ✉ 3675 Midway Dr., Sports Arena ☎ 619/224–2902 ✉ 4405 La Jolla Village Dr., La Jolla ☎ 858/457–3930) welcome nonmembers for a small fee. **Gold's Gym** (✉ 2949 Garnet Ave., Pacific Beach ☎ 858/272–3400) allows drop-ins. **Bodyworks Health & Fitness** (✉ 1130 7th Ave., Downtown ☎ 619/232–5500) allows nonmembers to use the facilities for a small fee. **Athletic Center** (✉ 1747 Hancock St., Middletown ☎ 619/299–2639) has a low daily rate for visitors.

Football

The **San Diego Chargers** (✉ 9449 Friars Rd., Mission Valley ☎ 619/280–2121) of the National Football League fill Qualcomm Stadium from August through December. Games with AFC West rivals the Oakland Raiders and Denver Broncos are particularly intense.

The **San Diego State University Aztecs** compete in the Western Athletic Conference and attract the most loyal fans in town, with attendance rivaling and sometimes surpassing that of the NFL Chargers. The biggest game of the year is always a showdown with Brigham Young University. The WAC champion plays in the **Holiday Bowl** (☎ 619/283–5808), around the end of December in Qualcomm Stadium. The Aztecs also play their home games at Qualcomm.

Frisbee Golf

This is like golf, except it's played with Frisbees. A course, laid out at Morley Field in Balboa Park, is open seven days a week from dawn to dusk. It costs $2 to play on weekdays and $2.50 on weekends. Equipment and playing times can be arranged with the Disc Golf Club on a first-come, first-serve basis. Rules are posted. Directions to the field are available from the **Balboa Park Disc Golf Club** (☎ 619/692–3607).

Golf

On any given day, it would be difficult to find a better place to play golf than San Diego. The climate—generally sunny, without a lot of wind—is perfect for the sport, and there are courses in the area to suit every level of expertise. Experienced golfers can play the same greens as PGA-tournament participants, and beginners or rusty players can book a week at a golf resort and benefit from expert instruction. You'd also be hard-pressed to find a locale that has more scenic courses—everything from sweeping views of the ocean to verdant hills inland.

During busy vacation seasons it can be difficult to get a good tee-off time. Call in advance to see if it's possible to make a reservation. You don't necessarily have to stay at a resort to play its course; check if the one you're interested in is open to nonguests. Most public courses in the area provide a list of fees for all San Diego courses. The **Southern California Golf Association** (☎ 818/980–3630) publishes an annual directory ($15) with detailed and valuable information on all clubs. Another good resource for golfers is the **Southern California Public Links Golf Association** (☎ 714/994–4747), which will answer questions over the phone or, for $5, will provide you with a roster of member courses.

The **Buick Invitational** (☎ 858/452–3226) brings the pros to the Torrey Pines Municipal Golf Course in mid-February. The **Accenture World Match Play Championship** (☎ 760/438–9111) is held at the La Costa resort in February.

Courses

The following is not intended to be a comprehensive list but provides suggestions for some of the best places to play in the area. The greens fee is included for each course; carts (in some cases mandatory), instruction, and other costs are additional.

The **Balboa Park Municipal Golf Course** (✉ 2600 Golf Course Dr., Balboa Park ☎ 858/570–1234) is in the heart of Balboa Park, making it convenient for downtown visitors. Greens fee: $34–$39.

Carmel Mountain Ranch Country Club (✉ 14050 Carmel Ridge Rd., Poway ☏ 858/487–9224) has 18 holes, a driving range, and equipment rentals. A challenging course with many difficult holes, Carmel Mountain Ranch is not particularly scenic: it's in a suburban area and runs through a housing development. Greens fee: $78–$98.

Coronado Municipal Golf Course (✉ 2000 Visalia Row, Coronado ☏ 619/435–3121) has 18 holes, a driving range, equipment rentals, and a snack bar. Views of San Diego Bay and the Coronado Bridge from the back nine holes on this course make it popular—but rather difficult to get on. Greens fee: $20–$35.

Cottonwood at Rancho San Diego Golf Club (✉ 3121 Willow Glen Rd., El Cajon ☏ 619/442–9891) has a driving range, rentals, a restaurant, and two 18-hole courses. The Monte Vista course is the easier of the two. Ivanhoe often hosts tournaments. Both are good walking courses, and have nice practice putting greens. Greens fee: $28–$45.

Eastlake Country Club (✉ 2375 Clubhouse Dr., Chula Vista ☏ 619/482–5757) has 18 holes, a driving range, equipment rentals, and a snack bar. A fun course for golfers of almost all levels of expertise, it's not overly difficult despite the water hazards. Greens fee: $52–$72.

Tucked away in the former flower fields of coastal north county, **Encinitas Ranch** (✉ 1275 Quail Gardens Dr., Encinitas ☏ 760/944–1936) is a hilly course that offers beautiful views of the Pacific as you play its championship 18 holes. Greens fee: $68–$88.

Mission Bay Golf Resort (✉ 2702 N. Mission Bay Dr., Mission Bay ☏ 858/490–3370) has 18 holes, a driving range, equipment rentals, and a snack bar. A not-very-challenging executive (par 3 and 4) course, Mission Bay is lighted for night play with final tee time at 7:53 PM. Greens fee: $19–$23.

Mount Woodson Country Club (✉ 16422 N. Woodson Dr., Ramona ☏ 760/788–3555) has 18 holes, equipment rentals, a golf shop, and a snack bar. This heavily wooded course in the mountains outside San Diego has scenic views and wooden bridges. Greens fee: $45–$70.

Singing Hills Country Club (✉ 3007 Dehesa Rd., El Cajon ☏ 619/442–3425) has 54 holes, a driving range, equipment rentals, and a restaurant. The lush course, set in a canyon, has many water hazards. One of *Golf Digest*'s favorites, Singing Hills comes highly recommended by everyone who's played it. Hackers will love the executive par-3 course; seasoned golfers can play the championship courses. Greens fee: $40–$67.

Fodor'sChoice ★ **Torrey Pines Municipal Golf Course** (✉ 11480 N. Torrey Pines Rd., La Jolla ☏ 800/985–4653) has 36 holes, a driving range, and equipment rentals. One of the best public golf courses in the United States, Torrey Pines has views of the Pacific from every hole and is sufficiently challenging to host the Buick Invitational in February. The par-72 South Course receives rave reviews from the touring pros. Designed by acclaimed course designer Rees Jones, it has more length and more challenges than the North Course and, fittingly, commands higher greens fees. It's not easy to get a good tee time here as professional brokers buy up the best ones. Check the yellow pages for broker's numbers. Out-of-towners are better off booking the instructional Golf Playing Package, which includes cart, greens fee, and a golf-pro escort for the first three holes. Greens fee: $65–$125.

Resorts

★ **Aviara Golf Club** (✉ 7447 Batiquitos Dr., Carlsbad ☎ 760/603–6900) is a top-quality course with 18 holes (designed by Arnold Palmer), a driving range, equipment rentals, and views of the protected adjacent Batiquitos Lagoon and the Pacific Ocean. Carts fitted with GPS systems that tell you distance to the pin, among other features, are included in the cost. Greens fee: $175–$195.

Barona Creek (✉ 1932 Wildcat Canyon Rd., Lakeside ☎ 619/387–7018) in East County is the newest resort in the area. Hilly terrain and regular winds add to the challenge. Fast greens will test your finesse. If your game is on, you can always see if your luck holds in the adjacent casino. Greens fee: $80–$100.

Carlton Oaks Lodge and Country Club (✉ 9200 Inwood Dr., Santee ☎ 619/448–4242) has 18 holes, a driving range, equipment rentals, a clubhouse, a restaurant, and a bar. Many local qualifying tournaments are held at this difficult Pete Dye–designed course with lots of trees and water hazards. Carts are included. Greens fee: $55–$80.

Carmel Highland Doubletree Golf and Tennis Resort (✉ 14455 Peñasquitos Dr., Rancho Peñasquitos ☎ 858/672–9100), a fairly hilly, well-maintained course in inland North County, has 18 holes, a driving range, equipment rentals, and a clubhouse with restaurant. Greens fee: $60–$80.

La Costa Resort and Spa (✉ 2100 Costa del Mar Rd., Carlsbad ☎ 760/438–9111 or 800/854–5000) has two 18-hole PGA-rated courses, a driving range, a clubhouse, equipment rentals, an excellent golf school, and a pro shop. One of the premier golf resorts in southern California, it hosts the Accenture World Match Play Championships each February. After a full day on the links you can wind down with a massage, steam bath, and dinner at the exclusive spa resort that shares this verdant property. All this doesn't come cheaply, but then again, how many courses will send a limo to pick you up at the airport? Greens fee: $185–$195.

Morgan Run Resort and Club (✉ 5690 Cancha de Golf, Rancho Santa Fe ☎ 858/756–2471), a very popular walking course near polo grounds and stables, has 27 holes (for members and resort guests only) that can be played in three combinations of 18; a driving range; equipment rentals; and a pro shop. Greens fee: $80–$100.

Pala Mesa Resort (✉ 2001 Old Hwy. 395, Fallbrook ☎ 760/728–5881) has 18 holes, a driving range, and equipment rentals. Narrow fairways help make this a challenging course, but it's well maintained and has views of the inland mountains. Greens fee: $69–$85.

Rancho Bernardo Inn and Country Club (✉ 17550 Bernardo Oaks Dr., Rancho Bernardo ☎ 858/675–8470 Ext. 1) has 45 holes, a driving range, equipment rentals, and a restaurant. Guests can play three other golf courses at company-operated resorts: Mount Woodson, Temecula Creek, and Twin Oaks. Ken Blanchard's Golf University of San Diego, based here, is world famous. And Rancho Bernardo Inn lays out one of the best Sunday brunches in the county. Greens fee: $85–$110.

Redhawk (✉ 45100 Redhawk Pkwy., Temecula ☎ 909/310–3850 or 800/ 451–4295) has 18 holes in an arboretumlike setting, a driving range, a putting green, and a restaurant. The par-72 course offers enough challenges to have earned a 4-star rating from *Golf Digest* and a top 10 ranking from *California Golf Magazine*. Greens fee: $48–$68.

Hang Gliding & Paragliding

The **Torrey Pines Glider Port** (✉ 2800 Torrey Pines Scenic Dr., La Jolla), perched on the cliffs overlooking the ocean north of La Jolla, is one of the most spectacular—and easiest—spots to hang glide in the world. However, it's definitely for experienced pilots only. Hang gliding and paragliding lessons and tandem rides for inexperienced gliders are available from the **Hang Gliding/Paragliding Center** (☎ 858/452–9858) based here.

Hiking & Nature Trails

San Diego has plenty of open space for hiking. From beachside bluffs and waterfront estuaries to the foothills and trails of the nearby Laguna mountains, or to the desert beyond, the county has several vegetation and climate zones. Those who lack the time to explore the outskirts will find a day hike through the canyons and gardens of Balboa Park a great way to escape to nature without leaving the city. A list of scheduled walks appears in the Night and Day section of the Thursday *San Diego Union-Tribune* and in the *Reader* weekly.

Guided hikes are conducted regularly through Los Peñasquitos Canyon Preserve and the Torrey Pines State Beach and Reserve.

The **San Dieguito River Park** (✉ 21 mi north of San Diego on I–5 to Lomas Santa Fe Dr., east 1 mi to Sun Valley Rd., north into park; Solana Beach ☎ 858/664–2270) is a 55-mi corridor that begins at the mouth of the San Dieguito River in Del Mar, heading from the riparian lagoon area through coastal sage scrub and mountain terrain to end in the desert just east of Volcan Mountain near Julian. The **Tijuana Estuary** (✉ 301 Caspian St. Exit I–5 at Coronado Ave., head west to 3rd St., turn left. Go to Caspian turn left into estuary parking lot; Imperial Beach ☎ 619/ 575–3613), mostly contained within Border Field State Park, is one of the last extant riparian environments in southern California. The freshwater and saltwater marshes give refuge to migrant and resident waterfowl. The visitor center has an amphitheater for interpretive talks. **Mission Trails Regional Parks** (✉ 1 Father Junípero Serra Trail, Mission Valley ☎ 619/668–3275 ⊕ www.mtrp.org), which encompasses nearly 6,000 acres of mountains, wooded hillsides, lakes, and riparian streams, is only 8 mi northeast of downtown. Trails range from easy to difficult; they include one with a superb city view from Cowles Mountain and another along a historic missionary path.

Horse Racing

For a few short weeks in summer, racing forms and racing fans can be seen all over Del Mar. Tradition says that women wear a hat on opening day of the annual summer meeting of the **Del Mar Thoroughbred Club** (✉ Take I–5 north to the Via de la Valle exit; Del Mar ☎ 858/755–1141) on the Del Mar Fairgrounds. The track attracts the best horses and jockeys in the country. Racing begins in July and continues through early September, every day except Tuesday. You can also bet on races at tracks throughout California, shown on TV via satellite at the **Del Mar Race Place** (☎ 858/755–1167) at the entrance to the track's parking lot.

Horseback Riding

Bright Valley Farms (✉ 12310 Campo Rd., Spring Valley ☎ 619/670–1871) offers lessons and rentals to ride on the winding trails of the Sweetwater River Valley. **Happy Trails Horse Rentals** (✉ 12115 Black Mountain Rd., Miramar ☎ 858/271–8777) offers guided trail rides through the Los Peñasquitos Reserve.

Sandi's Rental Stable (✉ 2060 Hollister St., Imperial Beach ☎ 619/424–3124) leads rides through Border Field State Park. They offer lessons for beginners and will accommodate more advanced riders. Be sure to tell them your needs before you saddle up.

Ice Hockey

The five-time Taylor Cup champion **San Diego Gulls** (☎ 619/224–4625) of the minor-league ECHL take to the ice from late October through March. The Gulls play at the **San Diego Sports Arena** (✉ 3500 Sports Arena Blvd., Sports Arena ☎ 619/224–4171). Take the Rosecrans exit off I–5 and turn right onto Sports Arena Boulevard.

Ice-Skating

Icetown (✉ University Towne Centre, 4545 La Jolla Village Dr., La Jolla ☎ 858/452–9110) offers open skating and hockey leagues. You can watch from the mall's food court above the rink. **Iceoplex Ice Center** (✉ 555 N. Tulip, Escondido ☎ 760/489–5550) has two Olympic-size rinks, a fitness center, a heated swimming pool, a sauna, and a restaurant. It offers lessons, hockey leagues, and public skate sessions. **San Diego Ice Arena** (✉ 11048 Ice Skate Pl., Mira Mesa ☎ 858/530–1825) is the place to learn hockey. There are lessons for youths, adults, and even adult pickup games, plus skate rentals and public sessions.

Jet Skiing

Jet Skis can be launched from most ocean beaches, although you must ride beyond surf lines, and some beaches have special regulations governing their use. The only freshwater lake that allows Jet Skis is **El Capitan Reservoir**, 30 mi northeast of the city near Lake Jennings. Waveless Mission Bay and the small **Snug Harbor Marina** (☎ 760/434–3089), east of the intersection of Tamarack Avenue and I–5 in Carlsbad, are favorite spots. **H2O Jet Ski Rentals** (✉ 1617 Quivira Rd., Mission Bay ☎ 619/226–2754) rents Jet Skis for use on Mission Bay. **Seaforth Boat Rentals** (☎ 619/223–1681) rents Jet Skis for use in the South Bay Marina in Coronado, and Mission Bay.

Jogging

Almost any beach in the county is great for running at low tide. Make sure to consult the tide charts in the local newspaper or your run may turn into a swim. The most popular run downtown is along the **Embarcadero,** which stretches for 2 mi around the bay. There are uncongested sidewalks all through the area. The alternative in the downtown area is to head east to **Balboa Park,** where trails snake through the canyons. Joggers can start out from any parking lot, but it's probably easiest to start anywhere along the 6th Avenue side. Entry to the numerous lots is best where Laurel Street connects with 6th Avenue. There's also a fitness circuit course in the park's **Morley Field** area. **Mission Bay** is renowned among joggers for its wide sidewalks and basically flat landscape. Trails head west around Fiesta Island, providing distance as well as a scenic route. **Del Mar** has the finest running trails along the bluff; park your car near 15th Street and run south along the cliffs for a gorgeous view of the ocean. The **Mission Beach boardwalk** is a great place to run while soaking up the scenery and beach culture. Organized runs occur almost every weekend. They're listed in *Competitor* magazine, which is available free at bike and running shops. **Roadrunner Sports** (✉ 5553 Copley Dr., San Diego ☎ 619/693–6377) has all the supplies and information you'll need for running in San Diego. Don't run in bike lanes!

Over-the-Line

As much a giant beach party as a sport, this game is a form of beach softball played with three-person teams. Every July the world championships are held on Fiesta Island, with two weekends of wild beer drinking and partying. Some good athletes take part in the games, too. Admission is free, but parking is impossible and traffic around Mission Bay can become unbearable. Call the **Old Mission Beach Athletic Club** (☎ 619/688–0817) for more information.

Rock Climbing

While there are few multipitch climbs opportunities, San Diego offers a variety of indoor and outdoor climbing options for beginners through experts. **Mission Trails Regional Parks** (✉ 1 Father Junípero Serra Trail, Mission Valley ☎ 619/668–3275) has a huge park of bouldering, top-roping, and single-pitch climbs. Call the park office for more information. With plenty of belay stations and holds that are regularly changed, the two locations of **Solid Rock Gym** (✉ 2074 Hancock St., Old Town ☎ 619/299–1124 ✉ 13025 Stowe Rd., Poway ☎ 858/748–9011) appeals to all skill levels. **Vertical Hold Sport Climbing Center** (✉ 9580 Distribution Ave., Mira Mesa ☎ 858/586–7572) is the largest full-service indoor rock-climbing gym in southern California. It offers lessons, rentals, and party packages.

Rollerblading & Roller-Skating

The sidewalks at **Mission Bay** are perfect for Rollerblading and skating; you can admire the sailboats and kites while you get some exercise. **Bicycle Barn** (✉746 Emerald St., Pacific Beach ☎858/581–3665) rents blades for leisurely skates along the Pacific Beach boardwalk. **Bikes and Beyond** (✉ 1201 1st Ave., Coronado ☎ 619/435–7180) is the place to go to rent skates, blades, and bikes to cruise the beachwalk of Coronado. **Mission Beach Surf & Skate** (✉ 704 Ventura Pl., Mission Beach ☎ 858/488–5050) is right next to the Mission Beach boardwalk. Their black, castlelike facade is easy to spot. You can also rent lockers, skateboards, and almost everything else a beachgoer could need. **Skateworld** (✉ 6907 Linda Vista Rd., Linda Vista ☎ 858/560–9349) has several public sessions daily, in addition to private group sessions for bladers and skaters.

Sailing & Boating

The city's history is full of seafarers, from the ships of the 1542 Cabrillo expedition to the America's Cup that once had a home here. Winds in San Diego are consistent, especially in winter. If you're bringing your boat, there are several marinas that rent slips. Vessels of various sizes and shapes—from small paddleboats to sleek 12-meters and kayaks to Hobie Cats—can be rented from specialized vendors. Plus, most bayside resorts rent equipment for on-the-water adventures. Most are not intended for the open ocean, which is wise for the inexperienced. The **Bahia Resort Hotel** (✉ 998 W. Mission Bay Dr., Mission Bay ☎ 858/539–7696) and its sister location, the **Catamaran Resort Hotel** (✉ 3999 Mission Blvd., Mission Beach ☎ 858/488–2582) will rent paddleboats, kayaks, Waverunners, and sailboats from 14 feet to 22 feet. The Bahia also rents out a ski boat. The Bahia dock is closed in winter, but Catamaran stays open year-round. **Harbor Sailboats** (✉ 2040 Harbor Island Dr., Suite 104, Harbor Island ☎ 619/291–9568) rents sailboats from 22 feet to 46 feet long for open-ocean adventures. **Coronado Boat Rentals** (✉ 1715 Strand Way, Coronado ☎ 619/437–1514) has kayaks, Jet Skis, fishing skiffs, and power boats from 15 feet to 19 feet in length as well as sailboats from 18 feet to 36 feet. They also can hook you up with a skipper. The **Mission Bay Sports Center** (✉ 1010 Santa Clara Pl., Mission Bay ☎ 858/488–1004) rents kayaks, catamarans, single-hull sailboats, and power boats. **Seaforth Boat Rentals** (✉ 1641 Quivira Rd., Mission Bay ☎ 619/223–1681) rents Jet Skis, paddleboats, sailboats, and skiffs. **Carlsbad Paddle Sports** (✉ 2002 S. Coast Hwy., Oceanside ☎ 760/434–8686) handles kayak sales, rentals, and instruction for coastal North County.

Sailboat and powerboat charters and cruises can be arranged through the **Charter Connection** (✉1715 Strand Way, Coronado ☎619/437–8877). Contact **Fraser Charters** (✉2353 Shelter Island Dr., Shelter Island ☎800/228–6779) for yachting excursions. **Hornblower Dining Yachts** (✉ 2825 5th Ave., Embarcadero ☎ 619/686–8700) operates sunset cocktail and dining cruises. **San Diego Harbor Excursion** (✉ 1050 N. Harbor Dr., Embarcadero ☎ 619/234–4111 or 800/442–7847) has one- and two-hour narrated harbor tours, as well as dinner cruises and a ferry to Coronado. **Classic Sailing Adventures** (✉ 2051 Shelter Island Dr., Shelter Island ☎ 619/224–0800) will take you on their 38-foot sailboat for champagne sunset cruises in summer, or daytime whale-watching in winter. For information, including tips on overnight anchoring, contact the **Port of San Diego Mooring Office** (☎ 619/686–6227). For additional information contact the **San Diego Harbor Police** (☎ 619/686–6272)

Skateboard Parks

Skateboarding culture has always thrived in San Diego, and recent changes in liability laws have encouraged a jump in the number of skateparks. A good number of top pro skateboarders live in San Diego and often practice and perfect new moves at local skate parks. Pads and helmets (always a good idea anywhere) are required at all parks.

★ The **Carlsbad Skate Park** (✉ 2560 Orion Way, Carlsbad ☎ 760/434–2824) offers 15,000 square feet of concrete bowls and ledges and a pyramid and rails. It's also the only skating venue that doesn't charge a fee. **Escondido Sports Center** (✉ 333 Bear Valley Pkwy., Escondido ☎ 760/738–5425) has a miniramp, street course, and vertical ramp. **Magdalena Ecke YMCA** (✉ 200 Saxony Rd., Encinitas ☎ 760/942–9622) is very popular among the many pros in this beach town. It has a bowl, competition street course, miniramp, and a classic vertical ramp from the 2003 X games. **Ocean Beach Skatepark at Robb Field** (✉ 2525 Bacon St., Ocean Beach ☎ 619/525–8486) is the largest park in the city. It has a huge street plaza, bowls, ledges, grind rails, and quarterpipes.

Surfing

If you're a beginner, consider paddling in the waves off Mission Beach, Pacific Beach, Tourmaline, La Jolla Shores, Del Mar, or Oceanside. More experienced surfers usually head for Sunset Cliffs, the La Jolla reef breaks, Black's Beach, or Swami's in Encinitas. All necessary equipment is included in the cost of all surfing schools. **Kahuna Bob's Surf School** (☎ 760/721–7700) conducts two-hour lessons in coastal North County seven days a week. **San Diego Surfing Academy** (☎ 858/565–6892) has surf camps and lessons in Cardiff-by-the-Sea. **Surf Diva Surf School** (✉ 2160-A Avenida de la Playa, La Jolla ☎ 858/454–8273) offers clinics, surf camps, surf trips, and private lessons especially formulated for women. Clinics and trips are for women only, but guys can book private lessons from the nationally recognized staff.

Many local surf shops rent both surf and bodyboards. **Mission Beach Surf & Skate** (✉ 704 Ventura Pl., Mission Beach ☎ 858/488–5050) is right on the boardwalk, just steps from the waves. **Star Surfing Company** (✉ 4652 Mission Beach, Pacific Beach ☎ 858/273–7827) can get you out surfing around the Crystal Pier. **La Jolla Surf Systems** (✉ 2132 Avenida de la Playa, La Jolla ☎ 858/456–2777) takes care of your needs if you want to surf the reefs or beachbreaks of La Jolla. **Hansen's** (✉ 1105 S. Coast Hwy. 101, Encinitas ☎ 760/753–6595) is just a short walk from Swami's beach.

Swimming

Built in 1925, Belmont Park's 58-yard-long **Plunge** (✉ 3115 Ocean Front Walk, Mission Beach ☎ 858/488–3110) is the largest heated indoor swimming pool in California. The **Copley Family YMCA** (✉ 3901 Landis St., North Park ☎ 619/283–2251) has a pool on the eastern edge of the city. The **Bud Kearns Memorial Pool** (✉ 2229 Morley Field Dr., Balboa Park ☎ 619/692–4920) is operated year-round by the City of San Diego.

The pools at the **Downtown YMCA** (✉ 500 W. Broadway Ave., Suite B ☎ 619/232–7451) are close to the Gaslamp Quarter and Balboa Park. The **Magdalena Ecke YMCA** (✉ 200 Saxony Rd., Encinitas ☎ 760/942–9622) is convenient for swimming in North County.

Tennis

Most of the more than 1,300 courts around the county are in private clubs, but a few are public. The **Balboa Tennis Club at Morley Field** (✉ 2221 Morley Field Dr., Balboa Park ☎ 619/295–9278) has 12 lighted courts. Courts are available on a first-come, first-serve basis for a $5-per-person fee. Heaviest usage is 9AM–11AM and after 5PM; at other times you can usually arrive and begin playing. The **La Jolla Tennis Club** (✉ 7632 Draper Ave., La Jolla ☎ 858/454–4434) has nine free public courts near downtown La Jolla; five are lighted. The 12 lighted courts at the privately owned **Peninsula Tennis Club** (✉ Robb Field, Ocean Beach ☎ 619/226–3407) are available to the public for a $4 per person day-use fee.

Several San Diego resorts have top-notch tennis programs staffed by big-name professional instructors. **Rancho Bernardo Inn** (✉ 17550 Bernardo Oaks Dr., Rancho Bernardo ☎ 858/675–8500) has 12 tennis courts and packages that include instruction, accommodations, and meals. **Rancho Valencia Resort** (✉ 5921 Valencia Circle, Rancho Santa Fe ☎ 858/756–1123), which is among the top tennis resorts in the nation, has 18 hard courts and several instruction programs. **La Costa Resort and Spa** (✉ Costa Del Mar Rd., Carlsbad ☎ 760/438–9111), where the annual Acura Tennis Classic is held, has 21 courts including two Wimbledon-quality grass courts and two clay courts, professional instruction, clinics, and workouts.

Volleyball

Ocean Beach, South Mission Beach, Del Mar Beach, Moonlight Beach, and the western edge of Balboa Park are major congregating points for volleyball enthusiasts. These are also the best places to find a pickup game. Contact the **San Diego Volleyball Club** (☎ 858/486–6885) to find out about organized games and tournaments.

Waterskiing

Mission Bay is one of the most popular waterskiing areas in southern California. It's best to get out early, when the water is smooth and the crowds are thin. Boats and equipment can be rented from **Seaforth Boat**

Rentals (✉ 1641 Quivira Rd., Mission Bay ☎ 619/223–1681). The private **San Diego and Mission Bay Boat and Ski Club** (✉ 2606 N. Mission Bay Dr. ☎ 858/270–0840) operates a slalom course and ski jump in Mission Bay's Hidden Anchorage. Permission from the **Mission Bay Harbor Patrol** (☎ 619/221–8985) is required.

Windsurfing

Also known as sailboarding, windsurfing is a sport best practiced on smooth waters, such as Mission Bay or the Snug Harbor Marina at the intersection of I–5 and Tamarack Avenue in Carlsbad. More experienced windsurfers will enjoy taking a board out on the ocean. Wave jumping is especially popular at the Tourmaline Surfing Park in La Jolla and in the Del Mar area, where you can also occasionally see kiteboarders practice their variation on the theme. Sailboarding rentals and instruction are available at the **Bahia Resort Hotel** (✉ 998 W. Mission Bay Dr., Mission Bay ☎ 858/488–0551). The **Catamaran Resort Hotel** (✉ 3999 Mission Blvd., Mission Beach ☎ 858/488–1081) is a sister location of the Bahia Resort Hotel and offers the same services. **Mission Bay Sports Center** (✉ 1010 Santa Clara Pl., Mission Bay ☎ 858/488–1004) is well equipped to handle your windsurfing equipment needs. Head to **Windsport** (✉ 844 W. Mission Bay Dr., Mission Bay ☎ 858/488–4642) to see Mission Bay from a sailboard. The **Snug Harbor Marina** (✉ 4215 Harrison St., Carlsbad ☎ 760/434–3089) has rentals and instruction and can advise those looking to windsurf on Agua Hedionda lagoon.

SHOPPING

6

Updated by
Lenore Greiner

A MÉLANGE OF HISTORIC DISTRICTS, homey villages, funky neighborhoods, megamalls, and chic suburbs make up the shopping areas of San Diego. Malls and shopping areas are outdoors; the architecture, such as that of Horton Plaza or Seaport Village, is often creative and you can enjoy the legendary sunny weather at the same time. In the beach towns, cruising the shops provides a break from the surf and sun. Hillcrest and the Gaslamp Quarter are known for their hip stores, La Jolla's Prospect Street and Girard Avenue for its world-class boutiques, and the quaint village of Coronado for its gift shops. If you poke around some of the smaller neighborhoods—Del Mar, Solana Beach's Cedros Design District, Carlsbad's upscale outlet mall, and Julian—you may turn up some real finds.

Most major malls, many in the Westfield Shoppingtown chain, offer merchandise you can find nearly anywhere. For San Diego–related memorabilia, browse the gift shops at major attractions like the zoo, Wild Animal Park, and Bazaar del Mundo in Old Town. You can also pick up a real-live San Diego keepsake at the flower nurseries around Carlsbad and Encinitas, and along inland farm trails.

Establishments are usually open daily 10–6; department stores and shops within the larger malls stay open until 9 on weekdays. Just about all will ship your purchase for you domestically or internationally. Sales are advertised in the *San Diego Union-Tribune* and in the *Reader*, a free weekly that comes out on Thursday. Also, check out the Web sites ⊕ www.signonsandiego.com and ⊕ www.sandiegoinsider.com for more details on local shops and sales. Click on the San Diego Convention & Visitors Bureau's Web site (www.sandiego.org) for shopping coupons.

Coronado

Shopping Center

Fodor'sChoice
★
Ferry Landing Marketplace. A staggering view of San Diego's downtown skyline across the bay, 30 boutiques, and a Tuesday afternoon Farmers' Market provide a delightful place to shop while waiting for a ferry. **Lavender Gift Shop** (☏ 619/522–9868) stocks a sweet-smelling selection of herbs and soaps as well as vintage-inspired gifts and antiques. **Men's Island Sportswear** (☏ 619/437–4696) has hats, tropical sportswear, and accessories. ⊠ *1201 1st St., at B Ave., Coronado.*

Specialty Stores

Friendly shopkeepers make the boutiques lining **Orange Avenue,** Coronado's main drag, a good place to browse.

BOOKS
★
Bay Books. This old-fashioned bookstore is the spot to sit, read, and sip coffee on an overcast day by the sea. International travelers will love the large selection of foreign-language magazines and newspapers and a section in the back is devoted to children's books and games. There are plenty of secluded reading nooks and a sidewalk reading area with coffee bar. ⊠ *1029 Orange Ave., Coronado* ☏ *619/435–0070.*

GOURMET FOODS
In Good Taste. Come here for smooth-as-silk chocolates and fudge, specialty cheeses, wine, truffles, and fresh bread. ⊠ *1146 Orange Ave., Coronado* ☏ *619/435–8356.*

HOME
ACCESSORIES
& GIFTS

Forget-Me-Not. This relatively tacky gift shop has a few surprises, including lots of reasonably priced glass baubles and miniature figures by Eickholt, Glass Eye Studio, and Goebel. ⊠ *1009-A Orange Ave., Coronado* ☎ *619/435–4331.*

Hotel Del Coronado. At the 20 gift shops within the peninsula's main historic attraction, you can purchase everything from sweatshirts to Christmas ornaments and designer handbags. ⊠ *1500 Orange Ave., Coronado* ☎ *619/435–6611.*

Island Provenance. Sophisticated bedding, crystal, porcelains, and home accessories are sold here. ⊠ *1053 B Ave., Coronado* ☎ *619/435–8232.*

La Provencale. The shop carries lots of imported linens, tableware, fashion accessories, and paintings, all in sunny colors. A line of remarkable French-made acrylic trays and salad bowls are filled with dried herbs and flowers by Amalgam. ⊠ *1122 Orange Ave., Coronado* ☎ *619/437–8881.*

WOMEN'S &
MEN'S CLOTHING

Dale's Swim Shop. Something is bound to catch your eye in this crammed shop of swim suits, hats, sunglasses, and sunscreen. ⊠ *1150 Orange Ave., Coronado* ☎ *619/435–7301.*

Kippys. The horse and rodeo sets comes here for fine leather shirts, chaps, skirts, belts, and bags, most trimmed with gold and silver spangles and beads. ⊠ *1114 Orange Ave., Coronado* ☎ *619/435–6218.*

Pollack's Men's Shop. The fine men's sportswear here includes many sweaters and a line of colorful Hawaiian shirts by Ryne Spooner. ⊠ *1162 Orange Ave., Coronado* ☎ *619/435–3203.*

Downtown

Shopping Centers

Seaport Village. Horse and carriage rides, an 1890 Looff carousel, and frequent public entertainment are the side attractions to this waterfront complex of 74 shops and restaurants. There's a parking lot and the Seaport is within walking distance of hotels and the San Diego Convention Center. **Discover Nature** (☎ 619/231–1299) is where you can find gifts for the office, table-top fountains, wind chimes, and jewelry. **Magic Shop** (☎ 619/236–1556) specializes in magic, games, and gifts. **Seaport Village Shell Company** (☎ 619/234–1004) carries shells, coral, jewelry, and craft items. **Latitudes** (☎ 619/235–0220) sells casual beachwear. **Wyland Galleries** (☎ 619/544–9995) offers the marine life art of Wyland; there's another branch in La Jolla. ⊠ *W. Harbor Dr. at Kettner Blvd., Embarcadero* ☎ *619/235–4014.*

Westfield Shoppingtown Horton Plaza. Within walking distance of most downtown hotels, the Horton Plaza is bordered by Broadway, 1st Avenue, G Street, and 4th Avenue. The multilevel shopping, dining, and entertainment complex is an open-air visual delight, with a terra-cotta color scheme and flag-draped facades. There are department stores, including Macy's, Nordstrom, and Mervyn's; fast-food counters; upscale restaurants; the Lyceum Theater; cinemas; and 140 other stores. Park

★ in the plaza garage and any store where you make a purchase will validate your parking ticket, good for three free hours. The **San Diego City Store** (☎ 619/238–2489) sells city artifacts and memorabilia, such as street signs and parking meters. Yellow signs such as SURFING OK sign is a typical San Diego–inspired souvenir. ✉ *Gaslamp Quarter* ☎ *619/ 238–1596.*

Gaslamp Quarter

Within Victorian buildings and renovated warehouses along 4th and 5th avenues, the historic heart of San Diego beats with fine restaurants catering to conventioneers and partying locals, plus fantastic shops that have opened in the last few years. The art galleries, antiques, and specialty stores in this area tend to close early, starting as early as 5PM.

Specialty Stores

ANTIQUES **Olde Cracker Factory.** The historic home of the Bishop Cracker Factory now houses a collection of antique shops. **Bobbie's Paper Dolls** (☎ 619/ 233–0055) displays Victorian paper goods. **Bert's Antiques** (☎ 619/239– 5531) specializes in military memorabilia. ✉ *448 W. Market, Gaslamp Quarter* ☎ *619/233–1669.*

San Diego Hardware. If you've been hunting for a piece of reproduction Victorian hardware, this store dating to 1892 may have that piece you've been seeking. ✉ *840 5th Ave., Gaslamp Quarter* ☎ *619/232–7123.*

CLOTHING & **Jacques Lelong.** Within the 1882 Yuma Building, you'll find unique
ACCESSORIES women's fashions with reasonable prices for the high-end look. From formal dresses to T-shirts and jeans, there's also the shoes, jewelry, scarves and accessories to go with them. ✉ *635 5th Ave., Gaslamp Quarter* ☎ *619/234–2583.*

Le Travel Store. Among the travel accessories sold here are luggage, totes, guidebooks, and maps. ✉ *745 4th Ave., Gaslamp Quarter* ☎ *619/ 544–0005.*

Splash Wearable Art. The reasonably priced clothing here includes one-of-a-kind things not found at the malls, such as dresses crafted from Balinese fabrics and a fine collection of hand-beaded evening wear. ✉ *376 5th Ave., Gaslamp Quarter* ☎ *619/233–5251.*

Western Hat Works. Western Hat Works has been selling every kind of hat from fedora to Stetson on this corner since 1922. ✉ *868 5th Ave., Gaslamp Quarter* ☎ *619/234–0457.*

GALLERIES **Golden Pacific Arts.** This gallery carries striking handmade silver, pearl and agate jewelry and vivid paintings reminiscent of Picasso. ✉ *520 5th Ave., Gaslamp Quarter* ☎ *619/234–0700.*

Many Hands Crafts Gallery. This cooperative crafts gallery showcases local pottery, glass, woodwork, photography, fibers, and basketry. ✉ *302 Island Ave., Gaslamp Quarter* ☎ *619/557–8303.*

Opium Gallery. Furniture and accessories from the world over are sold here. ✉ *425 Market St., Gaslamp Quarter* ☎ *619/234–2070.*

CloseUp

SHOPPING BLITZ TOUR

A shopping safari in San Diego means casting a wide net, so give yourself plenty of time to navigate the freeways to the malls and to spot parking in the neighborhoods. Stores are arranged by special interest; exact addresses can be found in the store listings below.

Gifts

Before releasing a single card from your wallet, charge yourself with a fortifying espresso at **Caffe Italia** in Little Italy and then set off on India Street, where **Bella Stanza, Simply Italian** and **The Art Store** sell handmade wares. Charming boutiques make up the **Fir Street Cottage Shops,** between India and Columbia streets.

The nearby Gaslamp Quarter holds more art galleries, antique shops, and specialty stores. The **Le Travel Store** supplies the accessories that travelers love (and sometimes forget to pack). One of the most indulgent places for your four-footed best friend is the **Lucky Dog Pet Boutique.**

Bargains

For the best bargains in town, join the locals on Friday, Saturday, and Sunday at **Kobey's Swap Meet** in Point Loma. Then head to Mission Valley to the **Park Valley Center** for designer discounts at Saks Fifth Avenue's outlet, OFF 5th. Across the street in the **Westfield Shoppingtown Mission Valley,** comb the men's and women's clothing racks at Loehmann's and Nordstrom's Rack for inexpensive basics to designer items.

Galleries

It may be a village setting, but the intersection of Prospect and Girand streets in La Jolla is one of the most glamourous places to shop. Overlooking the ocean is **Lamano Gifts,** a small shop jam-packed with artful, hand-made Venetian-style Carnival masks in leather, ceramic, and papier-mâché. **Gallery Eight** has lovely hand-blown glass vases and bowls. A true California artist, Wyland showcases his talent in depicting whales and other sealife at **Wyland Galleries. Fingerhut Gallery** hangs local works—such as the whimsical lithographs of La Jolla's own Dr. Seuss—along with those by Chagall and Lautrec. Liquid art in a bottle is the mainstay of **Alexander Perfumes and Cosmetics,** a European-style perfumery that stocks French fragrances not usually found in the United States.

GIFTS **Cuban Cigar Factory.** Master Cuban cigarmakers hand-roll the goods for
★ this factory, the largest hand-rolled cigar maker on the West Coast. Its
walk-in humidor also carries cigars from Nicaragua, Dominican Republic,
and many other countries for the man (or woman) who loves to puff.
They'll ship domestically and internationally. Retail outlets are at the
Horton Plaza and Fashion Valley malls. ⊠ *551 5th Ave., Gaslamp
Quarter* ☎ *619/238–2496.*

La Paperie. Fine stationery, cards, and gift wrap from around the world
are offered here. ⊠ *363 5th Ave., Gaslamp Quarter* ☎ *619/234–5457.*

Lucky Dog Pet Boutique. If nothing is too good for Fifi or Fido, show your
loyalty to them with a sweater, raincoat, or shoes. The dog gifts here
even include hats, bags, and perfume. ⊠ *557 4th Ave., Gaslamp Quarter* ☎ *619/696–0364.*

Little Italy

Italians arrived here in the 1920s to work in the city's once-massive tuna
fleet. Their working-class neighborhood has turned into a lively urban
village, hip and cozy, artsy and bohemian, and is noted for its bold architecture. Bound by the waterfront, Interstate–5 to the east, and Laurel and Ash streets, the heart of Little Italy is India Street, between Cedar
and Grape streets. This main thoroughfare has a collection of creative
restaurants, boutiques, and art galleries. Take a break from shopping
at **Caffe Italia** (⊠ 1804 India St., Little Italy ☎ 619/234–6767), where
you can catch up on fashion trends and news at its extensive magazine
and newspaper rack.

Specialty Stores

GALLERIES **The Gargoyle.** This modern arts-and-crafts gallery and café offers hard-
to-find Moroccan handicrafts, such as hand-painted octagonal tables.
⊠ *1845 India St., Little Italy* ☎ *619/234–1344.*

2400 Kettner Street. Several fine art galleries are in this building, including
Candy Kuhl (☎ 619/696–7230) and **David Zapf Gallery** (☎ 619/232–
5004). ⊠ *2400 Kettner Blvd., Little Italy.*

GIFTS **The Art Store.** Beside supplying artists with their tools, the Art Store also
carries fine stationery, beautiful leather-bound journals, and a fine selection of art books. ⊠ *1844 India St., Little Italy* ☎ *619/687–0050.*

Bella Stanza. The elegant Italian handmade gifts for the home include a
large collection of colorful ceramics, glass, and art pieces. ⊠ *1501 India
St., No. 120, Little Italy* ☎ *619/239–2929.*

The Fir Street Cottage Shops. These colorful cottages hold upscale boutiques. **Cathedral Home** (☎ 619/255–5861), just like its Hillcrest outpost, has fragrant candles, tall Japanese floral vases, and astrologically
themed body lotions. For small designers not found at the malls, visit
Sorella Boutique (☎ 619/232–9322), whose racks include red silk
dresses, cotton Bermuda shorts, and calico cowboy shirts. ⊠ *600 block
of Fir St., between India and Columbia Sts., Little Italy.*

Simply Italian. The fine selection of *artigianato*, or Italian handicrafts, includes hand-blown Murano glass goblets. ⊠ *1646 India St., Little Italy* ☎ *619/702–7777.*

Hillcrest, North Park, Uptown & Mission Hills

Although their boundaries blur, each of these four established neighborhoods north and northeast of downtown contains a distinct urban village with shops, many ethnic restaurants and cafés, and entertainment venues. Most of the activity is on University Avenue and Washington Street, and along the side streets connecting the two.

Gay-popular and funky Hillcrest, north of Balboa Park, has many gift, book, and music stores. Retro rules in North Park. Nostalgia shops along Park Boulevard and University Avenue at 30th Street carry clothing, accessories, furnishings, wigs, and bric-a-brac of the 1920s–1960s. The Uptown District, an open-air shopping center on University Avenue, includes several furniture, gift, and specialty stores. Sophisticated, old monied elegance is the tone in the well-heeled Mission Hills neighborhood.

Specialty Stores

BOOKSTORE **Obelisk.** The shelves here hold a bounty of gay and lesbian literature, cards, and gifts. ⊠ *1029 University Ave., Hillcrest* ☎ *619/297–4171.*

GOURMET FOOD **Henry's Marketplace.** This market is a San Diego original for fresh produce, bulk grains, nuts, snacks, dried fruits, and health foods. ⊠ *4175 Park Blvd., North Park* ☎ *619/291–8287.*

Original Paw Pleasers. At this bakery for dogs and cats you'll find oatmeal "dogolate" chip cookies, carob brownies, and "itty bitty kitty treats." ⊠ *1220 Cleveland Ave., Hillcrest* ☎ *619/670–7297.*

Trader Joe's. This shop stocks an affordable and eclectic selection of gourmet foods and wines from around the world. ⊠ *1090 University Ave., Hillcrest* ☎ *619/296–3122.*

HOME **Auntie Helen's.** The nonprofit thrift emporium sells heirlooms, collectibles, seasonal items, furniture, and brand-name clothing. Proceeds provide medical equipment, clothing, and laundry service to people with AIDS. ⊠ *4028 30th St., North Park* ☎ *619/584–8438.*

Babette Schwartz. This zany pop-culture store sells toys, books, T-shirts, and magnets. ⊠ *421 University Ave., Hillcrest* ☎ *619/220–7048.*

California Fleurish. This perfumery has lots of extras: silk scarves, delicate Japanese pottery, and fine vinegars and soaps. ⊠ *4011 Goldfinch St., Mission Hills* ☎ *619/291–4755.*

Cathedral. This store, voted the "Best Place to Smell" in a local poll, is worth a sniff around. As with its Little Italy sister, Cathedral specializes in candles and home and bath goods. You can find creative combinations, such as in the cocoa-hazelnut spice candles, coriander-lavender bath foams, and Asian pear–and–ginger body scrubs. ⊠ *435 University Ave., Hillcrest* ☎ *619/296–4046.*

Circa a.d. The eclectic collection of gifts and home decor includes items from Asia and Europe such as kimono, Thai spirit houses, Russian icons, and Indonesian puppets. ⊠ *3867 4th Ave., Hillcrest* ☎ *619/293–3328.*

Hillcrest Hardware. Don't let the name fool you. Hardware carries hard-to-find, expensive holiday decorative accessories. ⊠ *1007 University Ave., Hillcrest* ☎ *619/291–5988.*

Maison en Provence. There really is a house in Provence and you can rent it from the French proprietors, Pascal and Marielle Giai, who bring sunny fabrics and pottery from the region. There's also fine soaps, antique postcards, and bottles of flower syrups, lavender honey or violet, to mix with champagne. ⊠ *820 Fort Stockton Dr., Mission Hills* ☎ *619/298–5318.*

Metropolis. This store specializes in reproduction Arts and Crafts items, antiques, and decorative accessories. ⊠ *1003 University Ave., Hillcrest* ☎ *619/220–0632.*

P. B. Home & Garden. If you don't make it south of the border, this is a good resource for Mexican pottery and folk art. ⊠ *3795 4th Ave., Hillcrest* ☎ *619/295–4851.*

Pomegranate Home Collection. Housed in one of Hillcrest's oldest buildings, the Pomegranate has gifts, cards, and home accessories along with contemporary furnishings. ⊠ *1037 University Ave., Hillcrest* ☎ *619/ 220–0225.*

Royal Monkey. This eclectic gift shop has something for babies, pets, and grown-ups, including finger puppets, books, home accessories, and bath potions. ⊠ *142-D University Ave., Hillcrest* ☎ *619/299–4663.*

WOMEN'S & MEN'S CLOTHING
Le Bel Age Boutique. Owners Valerie Lee and Michala Lawrence design the women's silk hostess pants and jewelry themselves. ⊠ *1607 W. Lewis St., Mission Hills* ☎ *619/297–7080.*

Wear It Again Sam. Among the trendy men's and women's vintage clothes are 1960s ballgowns, panama hats, and collectible cowboy shirts. ⊠ *3823 5th Ave., Hillcrest* ☎ *619/299–0185.*

La Jolla

This seaside village has chic boutiques, art galleries, and gift shops lining narrow twisty streets, often celebrity soaked. Parking is tight in the village and store hours vary widely, so it's wise to call in advance. Most shops on Prospect Street in the village stay open until 10 PM on weeknights to accommodate evening strollers. On the east side of I–5 office buildings surround Westfield Shoppingtown UTC, where you'll find department stores and chain stores.

Shopping Center
Westfield Shoppingtown UTC. This handy outdoor mall east of La Jolla village has 155 shops, a cinema, and 25 eateries, plus an ice-skating rink. Department stores include Nordstrom, Robinsons-May, Macy's, and Sears Roebuck. **Charles David** (☎ 858/625–0275) sells high-fashion women's shoes. **The Walking Company** (☎ 858/453–9033) offers comfortable

walking shoes, backpacks, hats, jackets, and accessories. **Royal Nursery** (☎ 858/450–1317) sells sophisticated clothing and accessories for babies. **Papyrus** (☎ 858/458–1399) carries a collection of San Diego postcards, whimsical notecards, gifts and fine stationery. ⊠ *La Jolla Village Dr., between I–5 and I–805, La Jolla* ☎ *858/546–8858.*

Specialty Stores

Shops in the **Coast Walk Plaza** on Prospect Street, feature designer clothing and handmade crafts amid stunning Pacific Ocean views.

Green Dragon Colony. A loose collection of buildings housing galleries and boutiques, the colony is La Jolla's historic shopping area. It dates back to 1895, when the first structure was built by Anna Held, who was governess for Ulysses S. Grant Jr. ⊠ *Prospect St. near Ivanhoe St., La Jolla.*

ANTIQUES   **Glorious Antiques.** Profits from the sale of the truly glorious selection of antiques, fine china, silver, crystal, and fine art benefit the San Diego Humane Society. ⊠ *7616 Girard Ave., La Jolla* ☎ *858/459–2222.*

BOOKSTORE   **Warwick's.** An upscale bookstore and La Jolla fixture since 1896, Warwick's often hosts big-name author signings. ⊠ *7812 Girard Ave., La Jolla* ☎ *858/454–0347.*

CHILDREN'S   **Gap Kids.** The best bet for children's togs is this international chain.
CLOTHING   ⊠ *7835 Girard Ave., La Jolla* ☎ *858/454–2052.*

FINE ART &   **Africa and Beyond.** This gallery carries Shona stone sculpture, textiles, crafts,
CRAFTS   masks, and jewelry. ⊠ *1250 Prospect St., La Jolla* ☎ *858/454–9983.*

The Artful Soul. The contemporary craft gallery carries jewelry, handbags, and gifts, many by local artists. ⊠ *1237-C Prospect St., La Jolla* ☎ *858/ 459–2009.*

Fingerhut Gallery. Fingerhut carries the art of Dr. Seuss and Grace Slick alongside works by Peter Max and etchings and lithographs by Picasso, Chagall, and Lautrec. ⊠ *1205 Prospect St., La Jolla* ☎ *858/456–9900.*

Gallery Eight. Hand-blown glass, quilted silk jackets from India, and ceramics with a botanical motif are on display. ⊠ *7464 Girard Ave., La Jolla* ☎ *858/454–9781.*

Prospect Place Fine Art. Etchings and lithographs by 19th- and 20th-century masters include works by Miró, Matisse, Rufino Tamayo, and Chagall. ⊠ *1268 Prospect St., La Jolla* ☎ *858/459–1978.*

Wyland Galleries. California artist Wyland is famous for his murals depicting whales and other marine life. The gallery showcases his bronzes, original paintings, and limited-edition work. The mural on the ceiling is by the maestro himself. There's also a gallery in Seaport Village. ⊠ *1025 Prospect St., Suite 100, La Jolla* ☎ *858/459–8229.*

HOME   **Alexander Perfumes and Cosmetics.** Products rarely seen in the United States
ACCESSORIES   are available in this European-style perfumery, which claims to have the
& GIFTS   largest selection of fragrances in California. Its unusual French cosmetic lines include Lancaster, Darphin, and Orlane. ⊠ *7914 Girard Ave., La Jolla* ☎ *858/454–2292.*

Bo Danica. The tantalizing selection includes contemporary tabletops, Lynn Chase jungle-motif china, Orrefors crystal, and handmade decorator items. ⊠ *7722 Girard Ave., La Jolla* ☎ *858/454–6107.*

Everett Stunz. This store offers the finest in luxury home linens, robes, and sleepwear in cashmere, silk, or Swiss cotton. ⊠ *7624 Girard Ave., La Jolla* ☎ *800/883–3305.*

★ **Lamano Gifts.** Save yourself a trip to La Serenissima and explore the wide selection of delightful papier-mâché and ceramic Venetian Carnival masks, many hand-made. You'll also find the traditional costumes worn during Venice's Carnival, including black hooded capes. ⊠ *1298 Prospect St., La Jolla* ☎ *858/454–7732.*

JEWELRY **Fogel's Antique Beads.** Among the European precious beads from the 1920s are dazzling Austrian and Czech crystal beads. Restringing is done here. ⊠ *1128 Wall St., La Jolla* ☎ *858/456–2696.*

Philippe Charroil Boutique. This is the U.S. flagship store for the Charroil boutiques. It's reserved exclusively for the brand's fine Swiss timepieces and jewelry designs in their patented Celtic steel cable fashioned into necklaces and bracelets. The boutique also carries fine leather goods and writing instruments. It's open 12–6 daily. ⊠ *1227 Prospect St., La Jolla* ☎ *858/551–4933.*

Pomegranate. Antique and estate jewelry are paired here with fashions by Eileen Fisher and Harari. ⊠ *1152 Prospect St., La Jolla* ☎ *858/459–0629.*

WOMEN'S & **Ascot Shop.** The classic Ivy League look is king here—this traditional MEN'S CLOTHING menswear shop offers fashions by Kenneth Gordon and Talbott, but you have the option of loosening up with one of the Hawaiian shirts. Local stockbrokers are the biggest customers of a La Jolla village fixture, Gene Williams, who in the afternoon offers professional shoeshines afternoons in the back of the shop. ⊠ *7750 Girard Ave., La Jolla* ☎ *858/454–4222.*

Gentleman's Quarter. This high-end specialist in European-designed suits and sportswear is known for its excellent customer service. The shop also specializes in bespoke Armani, Canali, and Zegna suits made with European specifications and fabrics. ⊠ *1200 Prospect St., La Jolla* ☎ *858/459–3351.*

La Jolla Surf Systems. One block from La Jolla Shores Beach, this La Jolla institution for vivid California beach and resort wear has been anchored here for 25 years. Tame the waves with surfboards by Olas or Tuberville and boogie boards by BZ and Morey. This shop also rents surfboards and boogie boards, as well as beach chairs, umbrellas, snorkel gear. ⊠ *2132 Avenida de la Playa, La Jolla* ☎ *858/456–2777.*

Rangoni of Florence. This boutique carries its own house brand, Rangoni of Florence, as well as seasonal selections of medium-price European footwear for men and women. Brands include Amalfi, Donald Pliner, and Cole Haan, all fashioned in Italy. ⊠ *7870 Girard Ave., La Jolla* ☎ *858/459–4469.*

Sigi Boutique. Fashionistas seeking very high-end European designer fashions and accessories will discover Italian lines such as Loro Piana for cashmere pieces and Max Mara for sportswear. ✉ *7888 Girard Ave., La Jolla* ☎ *858/454–7244.*

Mission Valley–Hotel Circle Area

The Mission Valley–Hotel Circle area, northeast of downtown near I–8 and Route 163, has two major shopping centers, plus a number of smaller shopping centers that cater to residents.

Shopping Centers

FodorsChoice
★

Fashion Valley Center. San Diego's upscale mall has a contemporary Mission theme, lush landscaping, and more than 200 shops and restaurants. To get here, you can use the San Diego Trolley or a shuttles that goes to and from major hotels. Every store has Spanish-speaking sales associates. The major department stores are Macy's, Nordstrom, Saks Fifth Avenue, Neiman Marcus, and Robinsons-May. **April Cornell** (☎ 619/298–8482) carries designer home decor items. **Gallery One** (☎ 619/688–6588) has a selection of reproduction Fabergé eggs. **Smith & Hawkin** (☎ 619/298–0441) stocks fancy gardening supplies and gifts. ✉ *7007 Friars Rd., Mission Valley.*

Park Valley Center. This U-shape strip mall is across the street from Westfield Shoppingtown Mission Valley. It's anchored by **OFF 5th** (☎ 619/296–4896), where fashions by Ralph Lauren, Armani, and Burberry seen last season in Saks Fifth Avenue are now sold at Costco prices. ✉ *1750 Camino de la Reina, Mission Valley.*

Westfield Shoppingtown Mission Valley. The discount stores at San Diego's largest outdoor mall sometimes reward shoppers with the same merchandise as in the mall up the road, but at lower prices. Shops include Macy's Home Store; Loehmann's; Bed, Bath and Beyond; Nordstrom Rack; Charlotte Russe; and Fredericks of Hollywood. ✉ *1640 Camino del Rio N, Mission Valley.*

Specialty Stores

BOOKSTORE

Prince & the Pauper Collectible Children's Books. You'll find some old friends here, ones you can introduce to your kids. Snaking bookcases in the 4,000-square-foot store reveal 75,000 books and little corners perfect for tucking into a book. Most titles are gently used hardbacks, some are rare, many are collectible, and there are out-of-print, first edition, and signed volumes, too. This is why prices will range from one buck to a thousand. The rarer and more valuable volumes are kept under glass. Contemporary titles, like the popular (and hilarious) Captain Underpants books are also available. ✉ *3201 Adams Ave., Normal Heights* ☎ *619/283–4380.*

Ocean Beach, Mission Beach & Pacific Beach

Among the T-shirt shops, yogurt stands, and eateries that line the coast within San Diego proper are a few stores worthy of a browse.

Great News Discount Cookware. Cooks drool over the discount kitchen tools and gadgets, especially over the mandolines and chinois. There's a cooking school in the back, an extensive selection of cookbooks, and excellent customer service. ⊠ *1789 Garnet Ave., Pacific Beach* ☎ *858/ 270–1582.*

Mallory's OB Attic. Mallory's handles collectibles and antique and used furniture. ⊠ *4921 Newport Ave., Ocean Beach* ☎ *619/223–5048.*

★ **Pilar's Beach Wear.** Come to Pilar's for one of California's largest selections of major-label swimsuits. ⊠ *3745 Mission Blvd., Mission Beach* ☎ *858/488–3056.*

Trader Joe's. Snacks on the beach are as necessary as sunscreen, so stop here for gourmet food and dried fruits and nuts, and for the evening, wine and cheese. ⊠ *1211 Garnet Ave., Pacific Beach* ☎ *858/272–7235.*

Old Town

North of downtown, off I–5, the colorful Old Town historic district recalls a Mexican marketplace. Adobe architecture, flower-filled plazas, fountains, and courtyards decorate the shopping areas of Bazaar del Mundo and Old Town Esplanade, where you'll find international goods, toys, souvenirs, and arts and crafts.

Shopping Centers

FodorsChoice
★

Bazaar del Mundo. A San Diego institution, the bazaar is a colorful shopping complex with boutiques selling designer items, crafts, fine arts, and fashions from around the world. The best time to visit is during the annual Santa Fe Market in March, when you can browse collections of jewelry, replica artifacts, wearable-art clothing and accessories, pottery, and blankets—all crafted by Southwestern artists. **Ariana** (☎ 619/ 296–4989) carries ethnic and artsy fashions. **The Guatemala Shop** (☎ 619/296–3161) specializes in clothing, fabrics, and decorator items from Central America. **Earth, Wind and Sea** (☎ 619/294–2028) sells decorative fountains, ceramics, wind chimes, and cacti. ⊠ *2754 Calhoun St., Old Town* ☎ *619/296–3161.*

Kobey's Swap Meet. Not far from Old Town is San Diego's premier flea market. The open-air weekend event seems to expand every week, with sellers displaying everything from futons to fresh strawberries. The back section, with secondhand goods, is a bargain-hunter's delight. The swap meet is open Friday–Sunday 7–3; admission is 50¢ on Friday and $1 on weekends; parking is free. ⊠ *San Diego Sports Arena parking lot, 3500 Sports Arena Blvd., Sports Arena* ☎ *619/226–0650.*

Specialty Shops

FINE ART &
CRAFTS
★

Gallery Old Town. The rare collection of photojournalism by Alfred Eisenstaedt, Margaret Bourke-White, and Gordon Parks lies within an historic building on one of San Diego's oldest streets. ⊠ *2513 San Diego Ave., Old Town* ☎ *619/296–7877.*

Studio Gallery of Old Town. This gallery, often crowded at night with after-dinner strollers, is devoted to the extensive animation art of Chuck Jones, the famous Warner Bros. cartoon director. ⊠ *2501 San Diego Ave., Old Town* ☎ *619/294–9880.*

GIFT SHOPS **Apache Indian Arts Center.** Southwestern Indian jewelry, paintings, sculpture, and Pueblo baskets are sold here. ⊠ *2425 San Diego Ave., Old Town* ☎ *619/296–9226.*

Maidhof Bros. This is one of California's oldest and largest dealers in nautical and brass items. ⊠ *1891 San Diego Ave., Old Town* ☎ *619/ 574–1891.*

Ye Olde Soap Shoppe. This shop carries a full line of soap-making supplies including kits, herbs, and vegetable bases, as well as hand-fashioned soaps. ⊠ *2497 San Diego Ave., Old Town* ☎ *619/543–1300.*

NORTH COUNTY
& ENVIRONS

7

THE SAN DIEGO NORTH COAST
FROM DEL MAR TO OCEANSIDE

Updated by
Bobbi Zane

TO SAY THE NORTH COAST OF SAN DIEGO COUNTY IS DIFFERENT from the city of San Diego is an understatement. From the northern tip of La Jolla to Oceanside, a half dozen small communities developed separately from urban San Diego—and from one another. Connecting them is U.S. Highway 101, marked by replicas of old black-and-white signs. The historic highway nearly disappeared into a series of city streets when Interstate 5 was completed. Due to the efforts of dedicated preservationists, the roadway once more displays its historic designation most of the way. It's a delightful scenic drive with beach views most of the way and it passes through communities embracing their historic southern California beach culture. As you drive, recall the Beach Boys, surfing movies, and Woodies (wood-bodied cars).

The rich and famous were drawn to Del Mar because of its wide beaches and Thoroughbred horse-racing complex. Up the road, agriculture played a major role in the development of Solana Beach and Encinitas. The former farming area of Carlsbad is reinventing itself as tourist destination with Legoland California, several museums, an upscale outlet shopping complex, and the Four Seasons Resort Aviara. Its roots are in the old Mexican rancheros and the entrepreneurial instinct of John Frazier, who promoted the area's water as a cure for common ailments. In the late 19th century, a few miles from the site of the luxurious La Costa Resort and Spa, Frazier attempted to turn the area into a massive replica of a German mineral-springs resort.

Oceanside, home of one of the longest wooden piers on the West Coast, promotes its beach culture with a yacht harbor and the projected construction of beachside resort hotels. But the city is also the southern portal to the massive Camp Pendleton Marine Base, home of the bulk of marines on active duty in Iraq.

An explosion of development begun in the 1980s continues to intensify the north coast's suburbanization. Once-lovely hillsides have been bulldozed and leveled to make room for bedroom communities in Oceanside, Carlsbad, and even in such high-price areas as Rancho Santa Fe and La Jolla.

Highway S21 (also known as Historic U.S. 101) connects the beach towns Del Mar, Solana Beach, Cardiff-by-the-Sea, Encinitas, Leucadia, Carlsbad, and Oceanside, though the road is known by a different name in each different town. (Signs say Highway 101 in Solana Beach and Oceanside. In Del Mar it's called Camino del Mar, and in Carlsbad, Carlsbad Boulevard.) Whatever the alias, it's an awesome drive up the coast past fragile bluffs, rare Torrey pines, and ever-present surfers bobbing in the blue waters.

Numbers in the margin correspond to points of interest on the San Diego North County map.

7

Beaches Locals stake out their favorite sunning, surfing, bodyboarding, and walking territories at the easily accessible beaches of Del Mar, Solana Beach, Encinitas, Carlsbad, or Oceanside.

Desert Adventures Anza-Borrego Desert State Park encompasses more than 600,000 acres, most of it wilderness. Springtime, when the wildflowers are in full bloom, is a good season to visit. In the sandstone canyons you can walk in the footsteps of prehistoric camels, zebras, and giant ground sloths.

Dining People in downtown San Diego don't think twice about driving north for dinner, as prominent chefs oversee chic restaurants in wealthy communities such as Del Mar, Carlsbad, Encinitas, Rancho Santa Fe, and Rancho Bernardo. By contrast, casual dining is the rule in the beach towns, inland mountain towns, and desert communities.

WHAT IT COSTS				
	$$$$	$$$	$$	$	¢
AT DINNER	over $30	$23–$30	$16–$22	$10–$15	under $10

Prices are for a main course at dinner, excluding 7.75% tax.

Flowers The North County is a prolific flower-growing region. Nurseries, some open to the public, line the hillsides on both sides of I-5 in Encinitas, Leucadia, and Carlsbad. In winter most of the poinsettias sold in the United States get their start here. Quail Botanical Gardens in Encinitas displays native and exotic plants year-round. The gardens at the San Diego Wild Animal Park attract nearly as many people as the animals do.

Lodging If you stay overnight in the North County, your choices are diverse, from stylish hotels providing courtly, traditional service to basic motels catering to the beach crowd. Tennis and golf resorts and health-oriented spas abound, and some fine bed-and-breakfast inns are tucked into wooded hillsides around Julian.

WHAT IT COSTS				
	$$$$	$$$	$$	$	¢
FOR 2 PEOPLE	over $250	$176–$250	$121–$175	$90–$120	under $90

Prices are for a standard double room in high (summer) season, excluding 10.5% tax.

Del Mar

23 mi north of downtown San Diego on I–5, 9 mi north of La Jolla on Rte. S21.

Del Mar is best known for its glamorous racetrack, chic shopping strip, celebrity visitors, and wide beaches in its quaint old beach town west of Interstate 5. Its new face is the Del Mar Gateway business complex with high-rise hotels and fast-food outlets east of the interstate at the entrance to Carmel Valley. Access to Del Mar's beaches is from the streets that run east–west off Coast Boulevard; access to the business complex is via Highway 56. Along with its collection of shops, **Del Mar Plaza** also contains outstanding restaurants and landscaped plazas and gardens with Pacific views.

Summer evening concerts take place at the west end of **Seagrove Park** (⊠ 15th St., Del Mar), a small stretch of grass overlooking the ocean.

❶ The Spanish mission–style **Del Mar Fairgrounds** is home of the **Del Mar Thoroughbred Club** (⊠ 2260 Jimmy Durante Blvd., Del Mar ☎ 858/ 755–1141 ⊕ www.delmarracing.com). Crooner Bing Crosby and his Hollywood buddies—Pat O'Brien, Gary Cooper, and Oliver Hardy, among others—organized the club in the 1930s, primarily because Crosby wanted to have a track near his Rancho Santa Fe home. Del Mar soon developed into a regular train stop for the stars of stage and screen. Even now the racing season here (usually July–September, Wednesday–Monday, post time 2 PM) is one of the most fashionable in California. One of the best places to see and be seen is in the Paddock, where you can watch horses being saddled and the jockies mount and get ready to trot out to the track. If you're new to horse racing, stop by the Plaza de Mexico where you'll find a table staffed by an employee who can explain how to place a bet on a horse. The track also hosts free Four O'Clock Friday concerts following the races during the season. During off-season, horse players can bet on races at other California tracks televised via satellite at the Surfside Race Place. Times vary, depending on which tracks in the state are operating. Del Mar Fairgrounds hosts more than 100 different events each year, including the Del Mar Fair (San Diego County) and a number of horse shows. ⊠ *Head west at I–5 Via de la Valle Rd. exit* ☎ *858/793–5555* ⊕ *www.sdfair.com.*

☾ **Freeflight,** a small exotic-bird training aviary adjacent to the Del Mar Fairgrounds, is open to the public. You are allowed to handle the birds— a guaranteed child pleaser. ⊠ *2132 Jimmy Durante Blvd., Del Mar* ☎ *858/ 481–3148* 🎫 *$1* ☾ *Daily 10–4.*

Where to Stay & Eat

$$–$$$$ ✕ **J. Taylor's.** Jacob Taylor built the first hotel in Del Mar early in the 20th century, and nearly a century later the posh L'Auberge Del Mar Resort and Spa tipped their hat to him in their thoroughly revitalized dining room. Elegant but relaxed, it offers some of the best cooking in town. Breakfast and lunch are excellent, but the dinner menu truly takes off with such appetizers as a "steak" of fresh foie gras with blackberry sauce, followed by entrées like roasted guinea hen with citrus wild

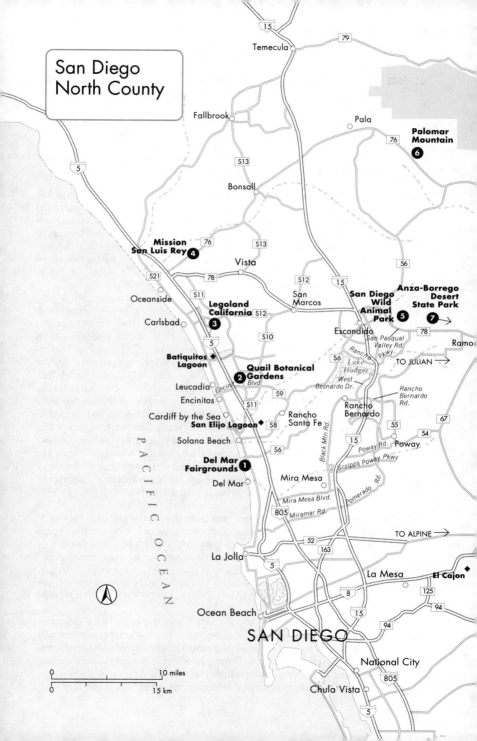

San Diego North County

PACIFIC OCEAN

Temecula

Fallbrook

Pala

Palomar Mountain 6

Bonsall

Mission San Luis Rey 4

Vista

Oceanside

San Marcos

Legoland California 3

Escondido

San Diego Wild Animal Park 5

Anza-Borrego Desert State Park 7

Carlsbad

Ramo

Batiquitos Lagoon

Quail Botanical Gardens 2

San Pasqual Valley Rd.

TO JULIAN

Lake Hodges

Leucadia

West Bernardo Dr.

Rancho Bernardo Rd.

Encinitas

Cardiff by the Sea

San Elijo Lagoon

Rancho Santa Fe

Rancho Bernardo

Solana Beach

Poway Rd.

Poway

Del Mar Fairgrounds 1

Scripps Poway Pkwy

Del Mar

Mira Mesa

Mira Mesa Blvd.

Miramar Rd.

Pomerado Rd.

TO ALPINE

La Jolla

La Mesa

El Cajon

Ocean Beach

SAN DIEGO

National City

Chula Vista

0   10 miles
0   15 km

rice. ⊠ *1540 Camino del Mar, Del Mar* ☎ *858/259–1515* ▭ *AE, D, DC, MC, V.*

$$–$$$$ ╳ **Ruth's Chris Steak House.** In a spacious, handsomely decorated setting with a vast outdoor sculpture installation and a narrow view of the Pacific, this outpost of the upscale chain serves over-size portions on red-hot metal plates. You might open with lobster bisque, a shrimp cocktail, or a fancy salad. Steaks range in size from a petite filet to a huge "cowboy" rib eye. Maine lobsters start at 2½ pounds. Although devouring dessert may seem improbable after consuming such mass quantities, keep in mind the chocolate-chunk bread pudding. ⊠ *11582 El Camino Real, Del Mar* ☎ *858/755–1454* ▭ *AE, D, DC, MC, V* ☺ *No lunch.*

$–$$$$ ╳ **Jake's Del Mar.** This enormously popular oceanfront restaurant has a close-up view of the water and a menu of simple but well-prepared fare that ranges from an appetizer of mussels steamed in aromatic saffron broth, to a dressy halibut sandwich and mustard-crusted lamb rack with port-flavored garlic sauce. A menu note reminds that the legendary, ice-cream stuffed hula pie is "what the sailors swam ashore for in Lahaina." ⊠ *1660 Coast Blvd., Del Mar* ☎ *858/755–2002* ⚫ *Reservations essential* ▭ *AE, D, MC, V* ☺ *No lunch Mon.*

$$–$$$ ╳ **Nugent's Seafood Grille.** The view of the lagoon is a plus, but it's the menu that distinguishes this comfortable eatery from the competition. The kitchen respects the integrity of old-style seafood favorites, especially from the owner–chef's native East Coast. Choose from clam chowder and lightly breaded, deep-fried shellfish (served in baskets with spiced french fries), steamed Maine lobster and Chesapeake Bay–style crab cakes, and seafood pastas. ⊠ *2282 Carmel Valley Rd., Del Mar* ☎ *858/792–6100* ▭ *AE, D, MC, V* ☺ *No lunch weekends.*

$$–$$$ ╳ **Pacifica Del Mar.** This lovely restaurant overlooks the sea from the plush precincts of Del Mar Plaza. Highly innovative, the restaurant frequently rewrites the menu to show off such show-stoppers as a barbecued sugar-spiced salmon with mustard sauce and filet mignon with potato–white cheddar gratin; the menu also lists low-carb items. The crowd ranges from young hipsters at the bar to well-dressed businesspeople on the terrace, where glass screens block any hint of a chilly breeze. ⊠ *Del Mar Plaza, 1515 Camino del Mar, Del Mar* ☎ *858/792–0476* ▭ *AE, D, MC, V.*

$$–$$$ ╳ **Scalini.** A favorite of horse fans from the nearby Del Mar racetrack, Scalini overlooks the playing fields of the region's most exclusive polo club from the second floor of a shopping center. The elegant eatery offers pizza for those who must; otherwise, the menu concentrates on fine pastas, such as the linguine frutti di mare, and on entrées like Italian-style bouillabaisse, and pistachio-crusted lamb chops in port sauce. ⊠ *3790 Via de la Valle, Del Mar* ☎ *858/259–9944* ▭ *AE, D, DC, MC, V* ☺ *No lunch.*

$–$$$ ╳ **Epazote.** The menu changes seasonally at this casual-chic eatery. Innovative Southwestern-style dishes range from vegetable tamales with goat cheese to turkey- and wild-mushroom enchiladas or sesame-honey–seared ahi. Desserts, like the creamy, traditional caramel custard, help to cut the spice effects of the main dishes. The hand-shaken margaritas are on the expensive side but superb. There's an ocean view from the patio, which gets busy on weekend nights and during Sunday brunch. ⊠ *Del Mar Plaza, 1555 Camino del Mar, Suite 322, Del Mar* ☎ *858/ 259–9966* ▤ *AE, D, DC, MC, V.*

★ **$–$$$** ✕**Fish Market.** There's no ocean view at the North County branch of downtown's waterfront restaurant, but this eatery remains popular with residents and tourists for its simple preparations of very fresh fish and shellfish. The scene is lively, crowded, and noisy. Singles flock here, but it's also a great place to bring the kids. ⊠ *640 Via De La Valle, Del Mar* ☎ *858/755–2277* ▤ *AE, D, DC, MC, V.*

$–$$ ✕**Villa Capri.** This suave, reasonably priced Italian bistro serves out-of-the-ordinary fare, with appetizers like sautéed prawns in a cognac-enriched grain-mustard sauce and thinly sliced smoked duck breast dressed with truffle oil and shavings of Parmesan. The pasta list shines with such offerings as rigatoni with sausage ragu, artichoke hearts, and mozzarella. Among the entrées, consider the grilled chicken with rosemary-garlic sauce or the sea bass in a pungent tomato sauce flavored with capers and olives. ⊠ *3870 Valley Center Dr., Del Mar* ☎ *858/720–8777* ▤ *AE, DC, MC, V* ⊗ *No lunch weekends.*

¢–$$ ✕**Barone's Trattoria del Mare.** True to its name, this is a lively, small, Italian seafood restaurant with an outdoor terrace. On the southern rim of town, Barone's specializes in good service and a sizable menu of ample dishes; you are expected to be hungry, and you will be after reading the listings for crab-stuffed mushrooms, linguine with assorted shellfish, grilled swordfish, and grilled beef filet. ⊠ *2234 Carmel Valley Rd., Unit A, Del Mar* ☎ *858/259–9063* ▤ *AE, MC, V* ⊗ *No lunch Wed., Sat., and Sun.*

$ ✕**Le Bambou.** Small, carefully decorated, and more elegant than any Vietnamese restaurant in San Diego proper, Le Bambou snuggles into the corner of a neighborhood shopping center and is easy to overlook. Those in the know, however, seek it out for authoritative versions of such classics as ground shrimp grilled on sugar cane; Imperial rolls generously stuffed with shrimp, noodles, and bamboo shoots; and cooked-at-the-table beef dishes. ⊠ *2634 Del Mar Heights Rd., Del Mar* ☎ *858/259–8138* ▤ *MC, V* ⊗ *Closed Mon.*

$ ✕**Milton's Delicatessen, Grill, Bakery.** There's a bunkerlike quality to this cavernous, semi-underground, Flower Hill Mall restaurant. It was built so that sunlight cascades down the walls, which are decorated with vintage magazine covers. Milton's offers belly-busting portions of traditional deli fare. The vast menu lists some 50 sandwiches, from a simple egg salad on rye to a pork chop sandwich with grilled onions. Traditionally the "poor man's meal" in Germany, *hoppel poppel,* an egg scramble of salami, peppers, onions, and potatoes, makes a filling breakfast. ⊠ *2660 Via De La Valle, Del Mar* ☎ *858/792–2225* ⊕ *www. miltonsbaking.com* ▤ *AE, MC, V.*

¢–$ ✕**Elijah's Delicatessen.** San Diegans are known to complain about the scarcity of decent, East Coast–type delicatessens. Well, this comfortable, no-frills establishment fits the bill. The vast menu extends to all the Jewish deli classics, including blintzes, chopped liver, smoked fish platters, skyscraping sandwiches, and baked beef brisket with potato pancakes. As a plus—this is Del Mar, after all—you can be served on a pleasant outdoor terrace. ⊠ *2638 Del Mar Heights Rd., Del Mar* ☎ *858/259–4880* ⊟ *AE, D, MC, V.*

¢–$ ✕ **Taste of Thai.** Tucked into a corner at the east end of the Flower Hill Mall, this café is a crowd-pleaser. Flashing lights in the ceiling and other artistic tricks delight young and old as they await plates of crispy mee krob noodles, minced beef salad flavored with mint and chilies, and batter-fried calamari with sweet chili sauce. After these substantial snacks diners get down to business with carefully prepared Thai curries, noodle dishes, and such house specialties as crisp-skinned duck in garlic sauce and grilled freshwater prawns in mild curry sauce. The mood is quite informal and the service low-key and pleasant. ⊠ *15770 San Andreas Rd., Del Mar* ☎ *858/793–9695* ⊟ *AE, MC, V.*

$$$$ ▦ **L'Auberge Del Mar Resort and Spa.** Although it looks rather like an upscale condominium complex, L'Auberge is modeled on the Tudor-style hotel that once stood here, a playground for the early Hollywood elite. Today's inn has a relaxed elegance, fitting for the repeat celebrity guests. The beach is a three-minute walk downhill, and the outdoor Pacific Terrace provides a glimpse of the ocean horizon between pine trees. Rooms are done in pink-and-green pastels and have marble bathrooms. Most rooms have balconies and gas fireplaces. Across the street are boutiques and restaurants at Del Mar Plaza. ⊠ *1540 Camino del Mar, Del Mar 92014* ☎ *858/259–1515 or 800/901–9514* 🖶 *858/755–4940* ⊕ *www.laubergedelmar.com* ⟿ *112 rooms, 8 suites* ⌂ *Restaurant, room service, in-room data ports, minibars, cable TV with movies, 2 tennis courts, 2 pools, gym, outdoor hot tub, massage, sauna, spa, steam room, bar, meeting room, parking (fee); no smoking* ⊟ *AE, D, DC, MC, V.*

$$$ ▦ **San Diego Marriott Del Mar.** Convenient for business travelers in the Carmel Valley Corporate Center, this hotel is within walking distance of AMN Healthcare, Peregrine, and Fair Isaacs. It's adjacent to two freeways and apt to be noisy outside. However, guest rooms are quiet and services include two-line phones, voice mail, high-speed Internet access, and weekday newspaper delivery. The locally popular Arterra Restaurant has indoor and outdoor seating and holds a sushi bar. Parking in an adjacent structure is $11 per night. ⊠ *11966 El Camino Real, San Diego 92130* ☎ *858/523–2700* 🖶 *858/523–1355* ⊕ *www.marriott.com* ⟿ *281 rooms, 3 suites* ⌂ *Restaurant, room service, in-room data ports, cable TV with movies, pool, outdoor hot tub, gym, bar, shop, babysitting, dry cleaning, laundry service, concierge, concierge floor, business services, meeting rooms, car rental, parking (fee), no-smoking rooms* ⊟ *AE, D, DC, MC, V.*

$$–$$$ ▦ **Clarion Del Mar Inn.** Del Mar's Tudor theme prevails at this hotel with steep gabled roofs and colorful English gardens. The inn is within walking distance to the beach, shopping, restaurants, and a local fitness center, which you can use at no charge. A continental breakfast and afternoon tea are included in the room rate. ⊠ *720 Camino del Mar, Del Mar 92014* ☎ *858/755–9765 or 800/451–4515* 🖶 *858/792–8196* ⊕ *www.delmarinn.com* ⟿ *81 rooms* ⌂ *Some kitchenettes, some microwaves, some refrigerators, cable TV, pool, outdoor hot tub, library, dry cleaning, laundry facilities, business services, meeting rooms, free parking; no smoking* ⊟ *AE, D, DC, MC, V* ⏃️ *CP.*

$–$$$ ☒ **Best Western Stratford Inn of Del Mar.** During racing season this equestrian-theme inn hosts horse owners and jockeys. Ample rooms, many with ocean views or kitchenettes, are surrounded by six lushly landscaped acres. There's a European day spa on the property, Spa Cucina. The staff is multilingual. Continental breakfast is included in the price. ☒ *710 Camino del Mar, Del Mar 92014* ☎ *858/755–1501 or 888/478–7829* ☒ *858/755–4704* ⊕ *www.bestwestern.com* ⌨ *64 rooms, 30 suites* ⚎ *In-room data ports, some kitchenettes, refrigerators, cable TV with movies, 2 pools, outdoor hot tub, spa, laundry service, business services, meeting room, free parking, no-smoking rooms* ☰ *AE, D, DC, MC, V* ⦿ *CP.*

Shopping

The tiered, Mediterranean-style **Del Mar Plaza** (☒ 15th St. and Camino Del Mar, Del Mar ☎ 858/792–1555) has flower-filled courtyards, fountains, a spectacular view of the Pacific, and some fine restaurants. Some businesses validate parking, which is underground. For women's fashions, **White House/Black Market** (☎ 858/794–0355) stocks fashionable apparel mainly in basic black and white. **Silver Goose West Gifts** (☎ 858/ 755–4810) specializes in jewelry, gifts, and collectibles.

Thinker Things (☒ 2670 Via de la Valle, Del Mar ☎ 858/755–4488) carries children's dolls, puppets, crafts, and games.

Solana Beach

1 mi north of Del Mar on Rte. S21, 25 mi north of downtown San Diego on I–5 to Lomas Santa Fe Dr. west.

Once-quiet Solana Beach is *the* place to look for antiques, collectibles, and contemporary fashions and artwork. The Cedros Design District, occupying four blocks south of the Amtrak station, contains shops, galleries, designers' studios, restaurants, and a popular performance venue, the Belly Up Tavern. The tavern and businesses surrounding it occupy a group of World War II–style Quonset huts standing side by side. Solana Beach is known for its excellent restaurants, but most area lodging is in the adjacent towns of Del Mar and Encinitas.

Where to Stay & Eat

★ **$$–$$$$** ✕ **Pamplemousse Grille.** Justly celebrated as one of North County's best restaurants, the "Grapefruit Grill," across the street from the racetrack, offers French-country dining California style. Chef–proprietor Jeffrey Strauss brings a caterer's sensibilities to the details, like a mix-or-match selection of sauces—wild mushroom, grey mustard, or peppercorn—to complement the simple but absolutely top-quality grilled meats and seafood. Appetizers can be very clever, like the huge wild mushroom ravioli. The comfortable rooms are painted with murals of bucolic country scenes, and the service is quiet and professional. ☒ *514 Via de la Valle, Solana Beach* ☎ *858/792–9090* ☰ *AE, D, DC, MC, V* ⦿ *No lunch Sat.–Thurs.*

$$–$$$$ ✕ **Red Tracton's.** Across the street from the Del Mar racetrack, this deluxe steak and seafood house is a high-roller's heaven. Everyone from the bar pianist to the exceptional waitresses is well aware that smiles and prompt service can result in tips as generously sized as the gigantic Australian lobster tails that the menu demurely lists at "market price." Tracton's serves simple but good food, and the menu highlights roasted prime rib in addition to prime New York sirloin and filet mignon, top-grade pork back ribs, panfried scallops, and such starters as lobster bisque and "jumbo" shrimp on ice. ⊠ *550 Via de la Valle, Solana Beach* ☎ *858/755–6600* ⊟ *AE, D, DC, MC, V* ⊘ *No lunch Sun.*

¢–$ ✕ **Don Chuy.** Small, family-run, unassuming, and utterly charming, Don Chuy serves authentic Mexican cuisine to southern Californians that, before dining here, may have tasted only a pale version of the real thing. The flavors are savory and convincing, and the portions sufficient to banish hunger until the following day. For something straight from the soul of Mexican home cooking, try the *nopales con chorizo y huevos,* a scramble of tender cactus leaves, crumbled spicy sausage, and eggs; this is served with piles of rice and beans as well as a warm tortilla and the palate-warming house salsa. ⊠ *650 Valley Ave., Solana Beach* ☎ *858/794–0535* ⊟ *AE, D, DC, MC, V.*

$–$$ ⊡ **Holiday Inn Express.** Straddling the border between Del Mar and Solana Beach, this modern hotel offers good value in a pricey area. Simply furnished rooms have balconies with pool views and coffeemakers. A continental breakfast is included in the room rate. ⊠ *621 S. Coast Hwy. 101, Solana Beach 92075* ☎ *858/350–0111* ⊟ *858/481–9177* ⊕ *www.hinnexpress.com* ⤺ *64 rooms, 16 suites* �⅄ *In-room data ports, some microwaves, refrigerators, cable TV with movies, pool, outdoor hot tub, gym, meeting rooms, free parking, no-smoking rooms* ⊟ *MC, V* ¶⦶ *CP.*

Nightlife

Belly Up Tavern (⊠ 143 S. Cedros Ave., Solana Beach ☎ 858/481–9022), a fixture on local papers' "best of" lists, has been drawing crowds of all ages since it opened in the mid-'70s. The "BUT's" longevity attests to the quality of the eclectic entertainment on its stage. Within converted Quonset huts, critically acclaimed artists play everything from reggae and folk to—well, you name it.

Shopping

★   The **Cedros Design District** (⊕ www.cedrosdesigndistrict.com) is a collection of nearly 100 shops that specialize in interior design and gifts.

Antique Warehouse (⊠212 S. Cedros Ave. ☎858/755–5156) carries American and European antiquities, art, books, glass, dolls, and jewelry. **Birdcage** (⊠ 143 S. Cedros Ave., Suite J ☎ 858/793–6263) specializes in unusual home accessories. David Turner, owner of **Elements Furniture and Gifts** (⊠ 118 S. Cedros Ave. ☎ 858/792–7773), designed furnishings for TV's *Ellen* and *Seinfeld,* and sells copies of the chairs, sofas, and accessories seen on those and other shows. You'll find sarongs and aloha shirts at **Frangipani, Resort Wear** (⊠ 130 S. Cedros Ave., No. 130 ☎ 858/259–0288), which also has south seas fragrances, hats, and shoes. You'll find cool accessories such as designer beds and totes for *haute* dogs and cats at **Muttropolis** (⊠ 227 S. Cedros Ave. ☎ 858/755–3647). **Trios Gallery** (⊠ 130 S. Cedros Ave. ☎ 858/793–6040) showcases the work of local artists, glass art from the Pacific Northwest, and designer jewelry.

Rancho Santa Fe

4 mi east of Solana Beach on Rte. S8 (Lomas Santa Fe Dr.), 29 mi north of downtown San Diego on I–5 to Rte. S8 east.

Groves of huge, drooping eucalyptus trees cover the hills and valleys of exclusive Rancho Santa Fe. East of I–5 on Via de la Valle Road, Rancho Santa Fe is horse country. It's common to see entire families riding the many trails that crisscross the hillsides.

Lillian Rice, one of the first women to graduate with a degree in architecture from the University of California, designed the town, modeling it after villages in Spain. Her first structure, a 12-room house built in 1922, evolved into the Inn at Rancho Santa Fe, which became a gathering spot for celebrities such as Bette Davis, Errol Flynn, and Bing Crosby. The challenging Rancho Santa Fe Golf Course, the original site of the Bing Crosby Pro-Am and considered one of the best courses in southern California, is open only to members of the Rancho Santa Fe community and guests of the inn.

Where to Stay & Eat

★ **$$$–$$$$** ✕**Mille Fleurs.** Mille Fleurs has a winning combination, from its location in the heart of wealthy, horsey Rancho Santa Fe to the warm Gallic welcome extended by proprietor Bertrand Hug, and the talents of chef Martin Woesle. The quiet dining rooms are decorated like a French villa. Menus are written daily to reflect the market and Woesle's mood, but sometimes feature a soup of *musque de Provence* (pumpkin with cinnamon croutons), sautéed *lotte* (monkfish) with okra and curry sauce, stuffed quail with peaches, and oven-roasted baby lamb with summer vegetable ratatouille. ⊠ *Country Squire Courtyard, 6009 Paseo Delicias, Rancho Santa Fe* ☎ *858/756–3085* ⚑ *Reservations essential* ⊟ *AE, DC, MC, V* ☾ *No lunch weekends.*

$$$$ ✕⬚**Rancho Valencia Resort.** One of southern California's hidden trea-
Fodor'sChoice sures has luxurious accommodations in Spanish-style casitas scattered
★ on 40 acres of landscaped grounds. Suites have corner fireplaces, luxurious Berber carpeting, and shuttered French doors leading to private patios. Six suites also have private outdoor hot tubs and wall-mounted plasma flat screen TVs. Rancho Valencia is one of the top tennis resorts in the nation and is adjacent to three well-designed golf courses. The inn's first-rate restaurant ($$$$) has a seasonal menu that might include a foie gras Napoleon; pasilla-chili crab cakes; farm-raised abalone steaks with a miso shiro butter sauce; and prime rib-eye steak in a Calvados-scented brown sauce. ⊠ *5921 Valencia Circle, Rancho Santa Fe 92067* ☎ *858/756–1123 or 800/548–3664* ⊟ *858/756–0165* ⊕ *www. ranchovalencia.com* ⬒ *49 suites* ⚭ *Restaurant, room service, in-room safes, some in-room hot tubs, minibars, refrigerators, cable TV with movies, 18 tennis courts, 2 pools, health club, 3 outdoor hot tubs, spa, bicycles, croquet, hiking, bar, shops, meeting rooms, business services, free parking, no-smoking rooms* ⊟ *AE, DC, MC, V.*

★ **$$$** ⬚**Inn at Rancho Santa Fe.** Understated elegance is the theme of this genteel old resort in the heart of the Spanish Colonial village of Rancho Santa Fe. Guest rooms are in red-tiled cottages spread around the property's

20 lushly landscaped acres. Many have private patios and woodburning fireplaces. The inn also has membership at the exclusive Rancho Santa Fe Golf Club and privileges at five other nearby, exclusive courses. ✉ *5951 Linea del Cielo, Rancho Santa Fe 92067* ☎ *858/756–1131 or 800/843–4661* 🖷 *858/759–1604* ⊕ *www.theinnatrsf.com* ⇗ *73 rooms, 5 suites, 8 private 1-, 2- and 3-bedroom cottages* ♿ *Dining room, room service, in-room data ports, in-room safes, some in-room hot tubs, some kitchens, minibars, microwaves, cable TV with movies, 3 tennis courts, pool, exercise equipment, croquet, bar, library, meeting room, free parking, some pets allowed; no smoking* ☰ *AE, DC, MC, V.*

Shopping

Tony boutiques here cater to the ultrawealthy. However, a couple of shops are worthy of note, even if you don't have a fat wallet. **Country Friends** (✉ 6030 El Tordo ☎ 858/756–1192) is a great place for unusual gifts. Operated by a nonprofit foundation, it carries collectibles, silver, and antiques donated or consigned by the community's residents. **Chino's Vegetable Shop** (✉ 6123 Calzada del Bosque ☎ 858/756–3184) at Chino's farm grows premium (and very expensive) fruits and rare baby vegetables for many of San Diego's upscale restaurants, as well as for famed California eateries such as Chez Panisse in Berkeley and Spago in Los Angeles.

Encinitas

6 mi north of Solana Beach on Rte. S21, 7 mi west of Rancho Santa Fe on Rte. S9, 28 mi north of downtown San Diego on I–5.

Flower breeding and growing has been the major industry in Encinitas since 1922; the town now calls itself the Flower Capital of the World due to the large number of nurseries operating here. The city, which encompasses the coastal towns of Cardiff-by-the-Sea and Leucadia as well as inland Olivenhain, is home to Paul Ecke Poinsettias (open only to the trade), the largest producer and breeder of the Christmas blossom. During the spring blooming season some commercial nurseries east of I–5 are open to the public. The palms and the golden domes of the Self-Realization Fellowship Retreat and Hermitage mark the southern entrance to downtown Encinitas.

U.S. 101 (now Route S21) was the main route connecting all the beach towns between southern Orange County and San Diego before the I–5 freeway, to the east of Encinitas, was constructed. Local civic efforts are bringing back the historic California–U.S. 101 signs on Route S21 and restoring the boulevard's historic character.

ʘ ❷ **Quail Botanical Gardens** displays more than 4,000 rare and exotic plants on 30 landscaped acres. There are 15 collections. Individual displays include Central American, Himalayan, Australian, and African tropical gardens; the largest collection of bamboo in North America; California native plants; an old-fashioned demonstration garden; and subtropical fruit. Kids can roll around in the Seeds of Wonder garden, explore a baby dinosaur forest, discover a secret garden, or play in a playhouse. ✉ *230 Quail Gardens Dr., Encinitas* ☎ *760/436–3036* ⊕ *www.qbgardens.com* 🎫 *$8* ☉ *Daily 9–5.*

BOUNTIFUL BEAUTY

SOUTHERN CALIFORNIA'S FAMOUS WARM, SUNNY CLIMATE *has blessed this corner of the continent with an ever-changing, year-round palette of natural color. It's hard to find a spot anywhere around the globe that produces as spectacular a scene as spring in San Diego—from the native plant gardens found tucked away in mountain canyons and streambeds to the carpets of wildflowers on the desert floor. You'll have to see it yourself to believe just how alive the deceptively barren desert really is.*

Spring debuts in late February or early March. Heavy winter rains always precede the best bloom seasons. And good blooms also bring even more beauty—a bounty of butterflies. But here in this generally temperate climate, the bloom season lasts nearly all year.

Although wildfires in the Cuyamaca and Laguna mountains in 2002 and 2003 destroyed much of the ancient forest, the wildflowers should put on brilliant and unusual displays as a result. The years following wildfires produce a profusion of plantlife not normally seen. Some drought-tolerant plants rely on fire to germinate. Look for rare western redbud trees erupting into a profusion of crimson flowers, sometimes starting as early as February. Native California lilacs (ceanothus) blanket the hillsides throughout the backcountry with fragrant blue-and-white blossoms starting in May and showing until August.

Native varieties of familiar names show up in the mountain canyons and streambeds. A beautiful white western azalea would be the star in anyone's garden. A pink California rose blooms along streambeds in spring and summer. Throughout the year three varieties of native dogwood show off white blooms and beautiful crimson fall foliage. The Cuyamaca

Mountains usually put on a display of fall color as the native oaks turn gold and red. By winter the rare toyon, known as the California Christmas tree, shows off its red berries alongside the roads.

You can get a good introduction to mountain wildflowers by visiting Julian in early May, when the Women's Club puts on its annual Wildflower Show. For more than seven decades members have collected and displayed native plants and flowers from hillsides, meadows, and streambeds surrounding the mountain town. For information on exact dates call the Julian Chamber of Commerce (☎ 760/765–1857).

Farther east in the Anza-Borrego Desert State Park, the spring wildflower display can be spectacular: carpets of pink, purple, white, and yellow verbena and desert primrose as far as the eye can see. Rocky slopes yield clumps of beavertail cactus topped with showy pink blossoms, clumps of yellow brittlebush tucked among the rocks, and crimson-tip ocotillo trees. For a good introduction to desert vegetation, explore the visitor center garden, adjacent to the park's underground headquarters.

San Diego County is a leading flower supplier to the nation, with dozens of nurseries turning out poinsettias, ranunculuses, bromeliads, orchids, begonias, and other subtropical plants. Many can be seen and visited in the western part of the county. In the spring, tour the brilliant acres of ranunculus blooms at the Flower Fields at Carlsbad Ranch (Palomar Airport Rd., east of I–5, ☎ 760/431–0352, www.theflowerfields.com).

For a vivid view of both the mountain and desert spring flora, take Interstate 8 east to Route 79, go north to Julian, and then east on Route 78 into Anza-Borrego park.

The **San Elijo Lagoon Reserve,** between Solana Beach and Encinitas, is the most complex of the estuary systems in San Diego North County. A network of trails surrounds the area, where more than 189 species of birds, 300 species of plants, and many fish and migrating birds live. Docents offer free public walks here; call for dates and times. ⊠ *2710 Manchester Ave., Encinitas* ☎ *760/436-3944* ⊕ *www.sanelijo.org* ▧ *Free* ☉ *Daily dawn–dusk.*

The **Self-Realization Fellowship Retreat and Hermitage** was founded in 1936 as a retreat and place of worship by Paramahansa Yogananda. There are two beautiful meditation gardens open to the public that have sweeping views of the Pacific. The gardens are planted with flowering shrubs and trees, and contain a series of ponds connected by miniature waterfalls populated by tropical fish. Wandering through this peaceful place, you may encounter acouple exchanging wedding vows against the backdrop of the Pacific Ocean. ⊠ *215 K St., Encinitas* ☎ *760/753-2888* ⊕ *www.encinitastemple.org* ▧ *Free* ☉ *Tues.–Sun. 9–5.*

At the **Magdalena Ecke YMCA Skate/BMX Park,** the world's top pro skaters Tony Hawk and Bob Burnquist practice among those destined to take their thrones. This 37,000-square-foot skate park includes a 33,000-square-foot street course with quarter pipes, bank ramps, roll-in ramps, pyramids, hips, handrail stations, slider boxes, a 12-foot vert wall, and a little kids' course. Ask your nearest 13-year-old what these things mean. There's also a classic cement pool. But the gnarliest feature is the 13-foot-tall vert ramp that Tony Hawk designed. At 80-feet wide it offers plenty of room to play. The day is broken up into sessions exclusively for the acrobatics and street tricks of BMX bikers. Even if you don't skate or ride it's exciting just to sit and watch. ⊠ *200 Saxony Rd., Encinitas* ☎ *760/942-9622* ⊕ *www.ecke.ymca.org* ▧ *$10* ☉ *Weekdays 2:30–5, weekends 9–5.*

Where to Stay & Eat

$$–$$$ ✕ **La Bonne Bouffe.** A longtime North County favorite, this restaurant offers expertly prepared classic French fare, including a delicious beef bourguignonne, roast duckling in green peppercorn sauce, Dover sole, and frogs' legs. With lace curtains, white tablecloths, and bistro chairs, you can pretend you're dining in France. ⊠ *471 Encinitas Blvd., Encinitas* ☎ *760/436-3081* ⌕ *Reservations essential* ▭ *AE, D, DC, MC, V* ☉ *Closed Sun. and Mon. No lunch.*

$–$$ ✕ **Hershel's.** Morning, noon, and night, this cheerful deli and restaurant is packed with diners who flock here for the enormous omelets, lox and bagel noshes, and overstuffed sandwiches that range from four variations on the Reuben to kippered salmon salad. Breakfast is served all day, and Hershel's serves a small selection of dinner specials, too. Beware—the desserts are more than enough for two. Give yourself some time to peruse the menu; it's enormous. ⊠ *1486 Encinitas Blvd., Encinitas* ☎ *760/942-9655 or 800/656-3354* ▭ *AE, D, DC, MC, V.*

¢–$$ ✕ **Italian Market.** A gregarious Franco-Italian couple, Jean and Rosanna, run this small restaurant in old Encinitas. At lunch there are great deli sandwiches on homemade bread (try the prosciutto and provolone on focaccia) and excellent pizzas. There are a few tables inside and several more on the front and back patios. ⊠ *806 1st St. (U.S. 101), Encinitas* ☎ *760/942–0738* ▭ *AE, D, DC, MC, V.*

¢–$$ ✕ **La Especial Norte.** Casual to the point of funkiness, this Mexican café is a great hit with locals who flock here to slurp up large bowls of delicious homemade soups. Try the chicken, beans, and rice, or the Seven Seas fish soup accompanied by tortillas and a dish of cabbage salad. You can also order renditions of the standard burrito, enchilada, and taco, and premium margaritas. ⊠ *644 N. U.S. 101, Encinitas* ☎ *760/942–1040* ▭ *AE, MC, V.*

$$–$$$ ⊞ **Best Western Encinitas Inn and Suites at Moonlight Beach.** This hotel, tucked into a hillside west of I–5 with ocean or city views from all rooms, offers a great deal. Unusually spacious rooms are well equipped for business travelers. Most rooms have private balconies. There's an attractive swimming pool area and a popular Japanese restaurant, Tomiko, on-site. Continental breakfast is complimentary. ⊠ *85 Encinitas Blvd., Encinitas 92024* ☎ *760/942–7455* 🖷 *760/632–9481* ⊕ *www.bestwestern.com* ⬐ *60 rooms, 34 suites* ⬩ *Restaurant, in-room data ports, in-room safes, refrigerators, cable TV with movies, pool, outdoor hot tub, sauna, bar, laundry service, concierge, business services, meeting room, airport shuttle, free parking, no-smoking rooms* ▭ *AE, D, DC, MC, V* ¶◎ *CP.*

★ $ ⊞ **Country Inn by Ayers.** Just off I–5, this inn has a European ambience. Rooms are decorated with reproduction French antiques including pencil point beds and mahogany armoires. The large lobby resembles a living room with a huge fireplace. Breakfast and afternoon refreshments (mid-week) are included in the room rate. ⊠ *1661 Villa Cardiff Dr., Cardiff by the Sea 92007* ☎ *760/944–0427 or 800/450–2272* 🖷 *760/944–7708* ⊕ *www.ayershotels.com* ⬐ *100 rooms* ⬩ *In-room data ports, refrigerators, cable TV with movies, pool, outdoor hot tub, meeting room, business services, free parking, no-smoking rooms* ▭ *AE, D, DC, MC, V* ¶◎ *CP.*

$ ⊞ **Moonlight Beach Motel.** This folksy, laid-back motel is a short walk from the beach. Rooms are basic but spacious and clean, and most have balconies and ocean views. ⊠ *233 2nd St., Encinitas 92024* ☎ *760/753–0623* 🖷 *760/944–9827* ⬐ *24 rooms* ⬩ *Kitchenettes, cable TV, free parking, no-smoking rooms; no a/c* ▭ *AE, D, DC, MC, V.*

¢–$ ⊞ **Ocean Inn.** Across from the train tracks on the main drag through town, this lodging is apt to be somewhat noisy. The simple guest rooms are done in pleasant shades of nautical blue and white. Continental breakfast is included in the price. ⊠ *1444 N. Coast Hwy. 101, Encinitas 92024* ☎ *760/436–1988 or 800/546–1598* 🖷 *760/436–3921* ⊕ *www.oceaninnhotel.com* ⬐ *50 rooms* ⬩ *Some in-room hot tubs, kitchenettes, microwaves, refrigerators, cable TV, laundry facilities, free parking; no-smoking rooms* ▭ *AE, MC, V* ¶◎ *CP.*

Shopping

Souvenir items are sold at shops along U.S. 101 and in the Lumberyard shopping center. Encinitas also abounds in commercial plant nurseries where you can pick up a bit of San Diego to take home. Look for bulbs, cut flowers, seeds, starter cuttings, unusual small plants, and cactus in nursery gift shops.

Anderson's La Costa Nursery (✉ 400 La Costa Ave., Encinitas ☎ 760/753–3153) offers rare and hard-to-find orchids, bromeliads, cactus, and succulents. **Bailey's–That Cat Place** (✉ 162 S. Rancho Santa Fe Rd., Encinitas ☎ 760/944–5783), caters to cat-lovers with feline toys and supplies, and cat-theme human apparel, jewelry, and gifts. **Hansen's** (✉ 1105 S. Coast Hwy. 101, Encinitas ☎ 760/753–6595 ⊕ www.hansensurf.com), one of San Diego's oldest surfboard manufacturers, is owned by Don Hansen, surfboard shaper extraordinaire, who came here from Hawai'i in 1962. The store, about a block south of the Lumberyard strip mall, also stocks a full line of recreational clothing and casual wear.

The **Lumberyard Shopping Center** (✉ S. Coast Hwy. 101, Encinitas) contains several specialty shops. **Heaven on Earth** (✉ 765 S. Coast Hwy. 101, Encinitas ☎ 760/753–2345) offers a selection of New Age books, tapes, gifts, and candles.

Weideners' Gardens (✉ 695 Normandy Rd., Encinitas ☎ 760/436–2194) carries begonias, fuchsias, and other flowers. It's closed sporadically in fall and winter; call for hours.

Carlsbad

6 mi from Encinitas on Rte. S21, 36 mi north of downtown San Diego on I–5.

The millennium marked a turning point for once laid-back Carlsbad, a Bavarian-inspired coastal community that is popular with beachgoers and sun seekers. On a clear day you can get sweeping ocean views that stretch from La Jolla to Oceanside by walking along a 2-mi-long seawalk that runs between the Encina power plant and Pine Street. Along the walk, you'll find several stairways leading to the beach and quite a few benches. The Legoland California theme park has moved much of the visitor appeal inland east of I–5. The park is at the center of a tourist complex that includes resort hotels, a discount shopping mall with a winery, colorful spring-blooming flower fields, and golf courses. During the mid-20th century, farming was the main industry in Carlsbad, with truckloads of avocados, potatoes, and other vegetables shipped out year-round. Carlsbad strawberries are some of the sweetest you'll find in southern California; in spring you can pick them yourself in fields on both sides of I–5. Area farmers develop and grow new varieties of flowers including the ranunculus that transform a hillside into a rainbow each spring.

Carlsbad owes its name and Bavarian look to John Frazier, who lured people to the area a century ago with talk of the healing powers of mineral water bubbling from a coastal well. The water was found to have the same properties as water from the German mineral wells of Karlsbad—hence the name of the new community. Remnants from this era, including the original well and a monument to Frazier, are found at the **Alt Karlsbad Haus** (✉ 2802 Carlsbad Blvd., Carlsbad ☎ 760/434–1887), a stone building that houses a small day spa and the Carlsbad Famous Water Company, a 21st-century version of Frazier's waterworks.

Development has destroyed many of the lagoons and saltwater marsh wildlife habitats that punctuated the North County coastline, but **Batiq-**

uitos Lagoon has been restored to support fish and bird populations. A local group is developing trails to the best viewing spots around the lagoon. This is a quiet spot for contemplation or a picnic. ☒ *Batiquitos Dr. S, east of I–5's Poinsettia La. exit, Carlsbad* ☎ *760/845–3501* ⊕ *www. batiquitosfoundation.org* ☉ *Tours on weekends and Friday; call ahead.*

③ **Legoland California,** the centerpiece of a development that includes resort hotels and a designer discount shopping mall, offers a full day of entertainment for pint-size fun-seekers and their parents. The mostly outdoor experience is best appreciated by kids ages 2 to 10, who often beg to ride the mechanical horses around the Royal Joust again and again, or take just one more turn through the popular Driving School. Miniland, an animated collection of cities constructed entirely of Lego blocks, captures the imaginations of all ages. In 2004 the park added several attractions. The Block of Fame is a collection of busts of famous people such as George Washington and Marilyn Monroe, created from Lego bricks. Kids get a chance to dig for buried fossils on Dino Island, which holds the Coastearaurus junior roller coaster and Dig Those Dinos archaeological dig. At the Fun Town Fire Academy, families compete at fire fighting by racing in a model fire truck and hosing down a simulated burning building. Dads beg to be taken to Miniland Florida, a diminutive race course where they can race remote Lego brick cars. Other attractions include a castle; pint-size Dragon and Spellbound roller coasters; and Aquazone Wave Racers, the first power-ski water ride in North America. Kids can climb on and over, operate, manipulate, and explore displays and attractions constructed out of plastic blocks. Included are a nature maze and power tower with an ocean view; a driving school with miniature cars and boats; a waterworks operated by joysticks; and a junior roller coaster. Stage shows and restaurants with kid-friendly buffets are also part of the mix. ☒ *1 Lego Dr., exit I–5 at Cannon Rd. and follow signs east ¼ mi, Carlsbad* ☎ *760/918–5346* ⊕ *www.legolandca.com* ☒ *$41.95* ☉ *Days, hrs vary. Mid-Sept.–mid-June, daily 10–5; mid-June–Labor Day, daily 9–9.*

Fodor'sChoice ★

In spring the hillsides are abloom at **Flower Fields at Carlsbad Ranch,** the largest bulb production farm in southern California, where you can walk through fields planted with thousands of ranunculus displayed against a backdrop of the blue Pacific Ocean. The rose walk of fame is lined with examples of award-winning roses selected during the last half century. Artists who normally work with paint and easels created the pair of demonstration gardens. The unusually large and well-stocked Armstrong Garden Center at the exit carries plants, garden accessories, and ranunculas bulbs. ☒ *5704 Paseo del Norte, east of I–5, Carlsbad* ☎ *760/431–0352* ⊕ *www.theflowerfields.com* ☒ *$7* ☉ *Mar.–May, daily 9–6.*

Take an interactive journey through 100 years of popular music at the **Museum of Making Music,** which displays more than 450 vintage instruments and samples of memorable tunes from the past century. Hands-on activities include playing a digital piano, drums, guitar, and electric violin. ☒ *5790 Armada Dr., east of I–5, Carlsbad* ☎ *760/438–5996* ⊕ *www.museumofmakingmusic.org* ☒ *$5* ☉ *Tues.–Sun. 10–5.*

CloseUp

SPAS

KNOWN FOR ITS HEALTHY AND FIT POPULATION, San Diego is also home to one of the largest concentrations of European-style spa resorts in the United States.

Hollywood hides out and freshens up at **Cal-a-Vie Spa** (✉ 29402 Spa Havens Way, Vista ☎ 760/945-2055 or 866/772-4283 ⊕ www.cal-a-vie.com), an intimate destination spa in the hills near Escondido. Sharon Stone, Russell Crowe, and Oprah Winfrey have come to this French country–style estate to hike, work out, attend health and nutrition lectures, be massaged and wrapped, and devour delicious healthy meals. When new owners acquired what was already one of the best spas in California, they added European antiques and elegant touches to the 24 individual cottages. They also built a light-filled, frescoed Turkish–style bathhouse with travertine marble tile, where hydrotherapy and seaweed wrap treatments are given. A fitness facility with weight room, Olympic pool, exercise classrooms, and tennis courts were scheduled for completion in late 2004. A new chef prepares delicious nutritionally balanced meals and teaches you how to cook that way at home.

The spa and fitness center at **Four Seasons Resort Aviara** (✉ 7100 Four Seasons Point, Carlsbad ☎ 760/603-6800 ⊕ www.fourseasons.com/aviara) holds 25 treatment rooms including a Couple's Suite with side-by-side massage tables, a lounge with marble fireplace and double shower, and a private patio with whirlpool. There's also a Zen garden holding five outdoor massage cabanas. Facilities include a fitness center with machines and free weights, plus an indoor solarium with fireplace whirlpools. The spa offers a full menu of massages, scrubs, body wraps, facials and bath rituals. Indigenous Southern California treatments include a hydrating avocado body wrap.

The venerable spa at **La Costa Resort and Spa** (✉ 2100 Costa Del Mar Rd., Carlsbad ☎ 760/931-7570 or 800/729-4772 ⊕ www.lacosta.com) got a major makeover in 2003 and joined forces with the Chopra Center to add therapies for the body and mind, including medical consultation, philosophy, psychology, and ayurvedic oils, herb, and aroma treatments. La Costa's new spa facilities are available à la carte and individuals and couples can select from a menu of one-day themed Spa Journeys. Facilities now include 42 treatment rooms, a Roman waterfall shoulder-pounding massage, sunbathing areas, outdoor pool and Jacuzzi, and an outdoor aromatic–herbal steam gazebo. There's also a full-service Athletic Club; a Yamaguchi Salon; a spa café, and boutique.

The Spa at Torrey Pines (✉ 11480 N. Torrey Pines Rd., La Jolla ☎ 858/453-4420 ⊕ www.spatorreypines.com) focuses on ancient rituals and techniques from four distinct cultures. The tranquil setting is the Craftsman-style Lodge at Torrey Pines. Choose from the Ancient Oceans Ritual, Indian Aruyveda Ayoma Ritual, a Scen Tao Ritual with Shiatsu and accupressure, and the Aboriginal Australian Li'Tya Sacred Earth Ritual. Each features massage, wraps, facials, herbs, and essential oils; they each last 140 minutes. An intimate full-service facility, it holds 14 treatment rooms, saunas, herbal-infused steam rooms, and aromatherapy inhalation rooms. Also offered are a full menu of massage, group fitness classes, yoga, meditation, and tai chi. Skin care treatments include mud or champagne facials, body masks, and wraps.

— Bobbi Zane

○ The **Children's Discovery Museum of North County** provides playful, hands-on activities that teach kids about science and the environment. Kids can assemble art projects to take home, play color games, and discover the world of sound. ⊠ *2787 State St., Carlsbad* ☎ *760/720–0737* ⊕ *www.museumforchildren.org* ✇ *$6* ◷ *Tues.–Sat. 10–4, Sun. noon–4.*

Where to Stay & Eat

○ **$$$$**
Fodor'sChoice
★

🏨 **Four Seasons Resort Aviara.** This hilltop resort sitting on 30 acres overlooking Batiquitos Lagoon is one of the most luxurious in the San Diego area, with gleaming marble corridors, original artwork, crystal chandeliers, and enormous flower arrangements. Rooms have every possible amenity: oversize closets, private balconies or garden patios, and marble bathrooms with double vanities and deep soaking tubs. The resort is exceptionally family friendly, providing a wide selection of in-room amenities designed for the younger set. The kids also have their own pool, nature walks with wildlife demonstrations, video and board games. ⊠ *7100 Four Seasons Point, Carlsbad 92009* ☎ *760/603–6800 or 800/332–3442* 🖷 *760/603–6878* ⊕ *www.fourseasons.com/aviara* ⇆ *285 rooms, 44 suites* ⌕ *4 restaurants, room service, in-room data ports, in-room safes, minibars, cable TV with movies and games, 18-hole golf course, 6 tennis courts, 3 pools, 2 whirlpools, health club, massage, sauna, spa, steam room, bicycles, hiking, volleyball, shops, babysitting, children's programs (ages 5–12), laundry service, concierge, business services, meeting room, airport shuttle, car rental, some pets allowed (fee), parking (fee); no smoking* ▤ *AE, D, DC, MC, V.*

$$$$
🏨 **La Costa Resort and Spa.** This famous resort is surprisingly low-key, a collection low-slung buildings on more than 100 tree-shaded acres. Unusually large rooms, totally redecorated in a major renovation in 2003–2004, have a traditional look with lots of dark wood and opulent marble bathrooms. Also revamped is the legendary spa, now home of the Deepak Chopra Center, which provides integrated medical consultations to complement spa services. The resort also has one of the most comprehensive sports programs in the area. There are two PGA championship golf courses and the Jim McLean golf school, plus a large tennis center. ⊠ *2100 Costa del Mar Rd., Carlsbad 92009* ☎ *760/438–9111 or 800/854–5000* 🖷 *760/931–7569* ⊕ *www.lacosta.com* ⇆ *474 rooms, 77 suites* ⌕ *Restaurant, room service, in-room data ports, in-room safes, minibars, some refrigerators, cable TV with movies, driving range, 2 18-hole golf courses, putting green, 21 tennis courts, pro shop, 4 pools, health club, hair salon, 3 outdoor hot tubs, sauna, spa, steam room, bicycles, croquet, hiking, lounge, shops, babysitting, children's programs (ages 5–12), dry cleaning, laundry service, concierge, business services, meeting rooms, car rental, pets allowed (fee), no-smoking rooms* ▤ *AE, D, DC, MC, V.*

○ **$$$–$$$$**
🏨 **Carlsbad Inn Beach Resort.** Gabled roofs, half-timber walls, and stone supports are among the architectural elements of note at this sprawling inn and time-share condominium complex, steps from the beach. Rooms, which range from cramped to large, are furnished European fashion, with pencil-post beds and wall sconces. Many have ocean views and kitchenettes; some also have fireplaces and hot tubs. With sprawling, landscaped grounds the inn is well-equipped to accommodate families. Kids

are included in a number of the resort's scheduled activities. ✉ *3075 Carlsbad Blvd., Carlsbad 92008* ☎ *760/434–7020 or 800/235–3939* 🖷 *760/729–4853* ⊕ *www.carlsbadinn.com* 🛏 *61 rooms, 1 suite* 🕭 *In-room data ports, some in-room hot tubs, some kitchenettes, cable TV, pool, gym, hair salon, outdoor hot tub, sauna, bicycles, shops, playground, laundry facilities, laundry service, business services, meeting rooms, free parking, no-smoking rooms* 🖃 *AE, D, DC, MC, V.*

$–$$$ 🏨 **Pelican Cove Inn.** Two blocks from the beach and surrounded by palm trees and mature colorful gardens with secluded nooks, this two-story bed-and-breakfast has spacious rooms with gas fireplaces, feather beds, and private entrances. The innkeepers provide beach chairs and towels and can make arrangements for biplane rides or balloon excursions. Breakfast is included in the price. ✉ *320 Walnut Ave., Carlsbad 92008* ☎ *888/735–2683* ⊕ *www.pelican-cove.com* 🛏 *10 rooms* 🕭 *Cable TV, some room phones, some in-room hot tubs, free parking; no a/c, no smoking* 🖃 *AE, MC, V* ❑ *BP.*

$–$$ 🏨 **Inns of America Suites.** An excellent choice to stay with your family on a trip to Legoland, this hotel is less than a mile from the park. You can buy tickets at the hotel and catch a free shuttle to the entrance. Despite proximity to I-5, the suites are very quiet; and all are equipped with kitchenettes or full kitchens. A Mexican fountain in the marble lobby and details like granite counters and hand-painted ceramic sinks complete the picture. Included in the price, breakfast is served in a pleasant, south-of-the-border-style room. ✉ *5010 Avenida Encinas, Carlsbad 92008* ☎ *760/929–8200* 🖷 *760/929–8219* ⊕ *www.innsofamerica.com* 🛏 *73 rooms, 23 suites* 🕭 *Dining room, in-room data ports, some kitchens, some kitchenettes, microwaves, refrigerators, cable TV with movies and video games, pool, gym, outdoor hot tub, dry cleaning, laundry facilities, business services, meeting rooms, free parking, no-smoking rooms* 🖃 *AE, D, DC, MC, V* ❑ *CP.*

Shopping

★ **Carlsbad Company Stores** (✉ 5620 Paseo Del Norte, Carlsbad ☎ 760/804–9000 or 888/790–7467 ⊕ www.carlsbadcompanystores.com) is the only upscale designer factory outlet in the San Diego area. Within this attractively landscaped complex you'll find Wedgewood, Lennox, Donna Karan Company Store, and Polo Ralph Lauren. **Thousand Mile Outdoor Wear** (☎ 760/804–1764) makes the bathing suits used by most lifeguards in southern California and also has a line of outerwear manufactured from recycled soft-drink bottles. **Barney's New York** (☎ 760/929–9600) carries a large selection of designer women's and men's fashions. You'll find home accessories at the **Crate & Barrel Outlet** (☎ 760/692–2100). **Dooney & Bourke** sells their popular handbags and accessories at discounted prices (☎ 760/476–1049).

Oceanside

8 mi north of Carlsbad on Rte. S21, 37 mi north of downtown San Diego on I-5.

California Welcome Center Oceanside offers complete state travel information, foreign language assistance, and a concierge service inside a mission-style, white-arched building. You can buy discount tickets to many Southern California attractions. ✉ *928 Coast Hwy., Oceanside 92054* ☎ *800/350–7873* ⊕ *www.oceansidechamber.com* ⊗ *Daily 9–5.*

With 900 slips, **Oceanside Harbor** (☎ 760/435–4000) is North County's center for fishing, sailing, and watersports. **Helgren's Sportfishing** (✉ 315 Harbor Dr. S, Oceanside ☎ 760/722–2133) schedules daily ocean fishing trips and whale-watching coastal excursions. South of the Harbor, **Oceanside Pier**, at 1,942 feet, is one of the longest on the West Coast. A restaurant, Ruby's Diner, stands at the end of the wooden pier's long promenade.

California Surf Museum displays a large collection of surfing memorabilia, photos, vintage boards, apparel, and accessories. ✉ *223 N. Coast Hwy., Oceanside* ☎ *760/721–6876* ⊕ *www.surfmuseum.org* ⊠ *Free* ⊗ *Thurs.–Mon. 10–4.*

Camp Pendleton encompasses 17 mi of Pacific shoreline as the nation's largest amphibious military training complex. It's not unusual to see herds of tanks and flocks of helicopters maneuvering through the dunes and brush alongside I–5. You may also see herds of sheep keeping the bushland down and fertile fields growing next to the Pacific coastline.

🐾 ❹ **Mission San Luis Rey** was built by Franciscan friars in 1798 under the di-
Fodor'sChoice rection of Father Fermin Lasuen to help educate and convert local Na-
★ tive Americans. Once a location for filming Disney's *Zorro* TV series, the well-preserved mission is still owned by Franciscan friars. The San Luis Rey was the 18th and largest and most prosperous of California's missions. The *sala* (parlor), a friar's bedroom, a weaving room, the kitchen, and a collection of religious art convey much about early mission life. Retreats are still held here, but a picnic area, a gift shop, and a museum (which has the most extensive collection of old Spanish vestments in the United States) are also on the grounds. Visitors are welcome to explore the mission's grounds, sunken gardens, the *lavanderia* (open-air laundry), and museum. Self-guided and docent tours are available. The mission's retreat center has limited, inexpensive dormitory-style overnight accommodations. ✉ *4050 Mission Ave., Oceanside* ☎ *760/757–3651* ⊕ *www.sanluisrey.org* ⊠ *$5* ⊗ *Daily 10–4:30.*

Oceanside Museum of Art, housed in the old City Hall designed by architect Irving Gill, presents changing exhibits of local artwork and exhibitions loaned from major art museums. Recent exhibits include photography, art books, and works of regional artists. ✉ *704 Pier View Way, Oceanside* ☎ *760/721–2787* ⊕ *www.oma-online.org* ⊠ *$5* ⊗ *Tues.–Sat. 10–4, Sun. 1–4.*

The **Wave Waterpark** is a 3-acre waterpark run by the City of Vista. It's also one of the few places in the country with a flow-rider, a type of standing wave that allows riders on bodyboards to turn, carve, and slash almost like surfing on a real wave. If you haven't learned how to do that, you can tube down their own river or slip down the 35-foot water slide. ✉ *161 Recreation Dr., Vista* ☎ *760/940–9283* ⊠ *$11.50* ⊗ *Memorial Day–Labor Day, daily 10:30 to 5:30; weekends only until last weekend of Sept. 11–5.*

Where to Stay & Eat

$–$$$ ✕ **A Taste of Europe.** French with a German accent is the theme at this comfortable little restaurant where candlelight, white table linens, and attentive service prevail. You can dine on such well-prepared entrées as rack of lamb Provençale, steak *au poivre vert* (with green pepper), or Wiener schnitzel. There's a good wine list featuring Californian and imported vintages. ⊠ *1733 S. Coast Hwy., Oceanside* ☎ *760/722–7006* 🝙 *AE, D, DC, MC, V* ☉ *Closed Mon. No lunch.*

$–$$$ ✕ **Jolly Roger.** This casual restaurant is a good choice for waterside dining. You can watch traffic move through the harbor while savoring nicely prepared salmon, halibut, ahi or even teriyaki steak or prime rib. The dining room is a bit old-fashioned, with leather-lined booths and laminate-topped tables. Entertainment is presented on weekends. ⊠ *1900 Harbor Dr. N* ☎ *760/722–1831* 🝙 *AE, D, MC, V.*

$–$$ ✕ **Monterey Bay Cannery.** A pleasant place to dine while watching small fishing and pleasure boats moving through the Oceanside Harbor, this restaurant has tables outside and inside. The menu lists chowders, halibut, steamed clams, grilled ahi, and steak. The Sunday brunch here is a popular event. There's entertainment most nights. ⊠ *1325 Harbor Dr.* ☎ *760/722–3474* 🝙 *AE, DC, MC, V.*

¢ ✕ **Johnny Manana's.** This locally popular store-front eatery serves up Costa Rican–themed Mexican platters including tacos, burritos, enchiladas, and four types of fajitas. ⊠ *308 Mission Ave., Oceanside* ☎ *760/721–9999* 🝙 *No credit cards.*

¢ ✕ **101 Cafe.** A diner dating back to 1928, this is both a local hangout and the headquarters for the historic Highway 101 movement. You'll find all kinds of Highway 101 memorabilia here along with breakfast, lunch, and dinner. The menu lists the usual suspects: biscuits and gravy, chicken-fried steak, spaghetti, and meat loaf. ⊠ *631 S. Coast Hwy.* ☎ *760/722–5220* 🝙 *No credit cards.*

★ **$$–$$$$** 🏨 **Oceanside Marina Suites.** Of all the oceanfront lodgings in North County towns, this motel occupies the best location—a spit of land surrounded by water and cool ocean breezes on all sides. All rooms have either ocean or harbor views. The rooms are unusually large and have fireplaces and expansive balconies. There are barbecues for guest use. A free boat shuttles you to the beach in summer. Continental breakfast is included in the price. ⊠ *2008 Harbor Dr. N, Oceanside 92054* ☎ *760/722–1561 or 800/252–2033* 🖶 *760/439–9758* ⊕ *www.omihotel. com* 🛏 *64 suites* ♿ *In room data ports, kitchens, cable TV with movies, pool, hot tub, sauna, Ping-Pong, volleyball, laundry facilities, free parking; no a/c, no smoking* 🝙 *AE, MC, V* ⏍ *CP.*

¢–$$ 🏨 **Marina Comfort Suites.** Convenient to I–5 and Route 76 but also noisy at times, this Mediterranean-style, all-suite hotel is close to the marina, the beach, and downtown Oceanside. A morning newspaper, continental breakfast, and afternoon refreshments are included. ⊠ *888 N. Coast Hwy., Oceanside 92054* ☎ *760/722–8880 or 800/228–5150* ⊕ *www.choicehotels.com* 🖶 *760/722–7280* 🛏 *47 rooms, 25 suites* ♿ *Fans, in-room data ports, some in-room hot tubs, microwaves, refrigerators, cable TV with movies, pool, gym, laundry service, meeting room, free parking; no smoking* 🝙 *AE, D, DC, MC, V* ⏍ *CP.*

$ ⊞ **Best Western Marty's Valley Inn.** This attractive family-owned motel, east of I–5, is a good choice for families. Rooms are ample with contemporary furniture. The hotel's La Mision Mexican restaurant is one of Oceanside's most popular eateries. Continental breakfast is included. ⊠ *3240 Mission Ave., Oceanside 92054* ☎ *760/757–7700 or 800/ 747–3529* 🖷 *760/439–3311* ⊕ *www.bwmartys.com* ☞ *108 rooms, 2 suites* ♿ *Restaurant, in-room data ports, some microwaves, some refrigerators, cable TV with movies, pool, gym, outdoor hot tub, business services, meeting rooms, free parking, no-smoking rooms* ⊟ *AE, D, DC, MC, V* ¶◎¶ *CP.*

¢ ⊞ **Guesthouse Inn & Suites.** This is a convenient, but noisy location, just steps from I–5 and the railroad tracks. The hotel is close to the marina and convenient to Camp Pendleton. There's an on-site restaurant, the Flying Bridge, and a breakfast room, where a complimentary continental breakfast is served. RV and truck parking is available. ⊠ *1103 N. Coast Hwy., Oceanside 92054* ☎ *760/722–1904 or 800/914–2230* 🖷 *760/722–1168* ⊕ *www.guesthouseintl.com* ☞ *80 rooms* ♿ *Restaurant, dining room, microwaves, refrigerators, cable TV with movies, pool, business services, meeting room, free parking, no-smoking rooms* ⊟ *AE, D, DC, MC, V* ¶◎¶ *CP.*

Shopping

Oceanside Photo & Telescope (⊠ 1024 Mission Ave., Oceanside ☎ 760/ 722–3348 ⊕ www.optcorp.com) is the place to pick up a telescope or binoculars to view San Diego County's dazzling night sky; call for information about stargazing parties the store holds regularly.

San Diego North Coast A to Z

To research prices, get advice from other travelers, and book travel arrangements, visit www.fodors.com

AIR TRAVEL

McClellan Palomar Airport is run by the county of San Diego. America West Express and United Express operate flights between here and Los Angeles International Airport and Phoenix Sky Harbor Airport.

🛂 Airport Information **McClellan Palomar Airport** ⊠ 2198 Palomar Airport Rd., Carlsbad ☎ 760/431–4646 ⊕ www.sdcdpw.org/airports/.

BUS TRAVEL

The San Diego Transit District covers the city of San Diego up to Del Mar. The North County Transit District serves San Diego County from Del Mar north.

🛂 Bus Information **The North County Transit District** ☎ 800/266–6883. **San Diego Transit District** ☎ 619/233–3004.

CAR TRAVEL

Interstate 5 is the main freeway artery connecting San Diego to Los Angeles. Running parallel west of I–5 is Route S21, also known and sometimes indicated as Highway 101, Old Highway 101, or Coast Highway 101, which never strays too far from the ocean.

TRAIN TRAVEL

Amtrak stops in Solana Beach and Oceanside. The last train leaves San Diego at about 7 each night (9 on Friday; the last arrival is about midnight). Coaster operates commuter rail service between San Diego and Oceanside.

🚆 Train Information **Amtrak** ☎ 760/722-4622 in Oceanside, 800/872-7245 ⊕ www. amtrakcalifornia.com. **Coaster** ☎ 800/262-7837 ⊕ www.sdcommute.com.

TOURS

Civic Helicopters gives whirlybird tours of the area along the beaches for about $100 per person per half hour. Barnstorming Adventures conducts open-cockpit vintage biplane excursions and military-style Top Dog air combat flights from McClellan Palomar Airport. Tours start at $98 per couple.

🚆 Tour Companies **Barnstorming Adventures** ☎ 760/438-7680 or 800/759-5667 ⊕ www.barnstorming.com. **Civic Helicopters** ⊠ 2192 Palomar Airport Rd., Carlsbad ☎ 760/438-8424 ⊕ www.civichelicopters.com.

VISITOR INFORMATION

🚆 **Carlsbad Convention and Visitors Bureau** ⟳ 400 Carlsbad Village Dr., Carlsbad 92008 ☎ 760/434-6093 or 800/227-5722 ⊕ www.visitcarlsbad.com. **Greater Del Mar Chamber of Commerce** ⊠ 1104 Camino del Mar, Del Mar 92014 ☎ 858/755-4844 ⊕ www.delmarchamber.org. **Oceanside Welcome Center** ⊠ 928 N. Coast Hwy., Ocean-side 92054 ☎ 800/350-7873 ⊕ www.oceansidechamber.com. **San Diego North Con-vention and Visitors Bureau** ⊠ 360 N. Escondido Blvd., Escondido 92025 ☎ 760/745-4741 or 800/848-3366 ⊕ www.sandiegonort.com.

INLAND NORTH COUNTY
RANCHO BERNARDO, ESCONDIDO, FALLBROOK & TEMECULA

Long regarded as San Diego's beautiful backyard, replete with green hills, quiet lakes, and citrus and avocado groves, inland San Diego County is now one of the fastest-growing areas in southern California. Subdivi-sions, many containing palatial homes, now fill the hills and canyons around Escondido, and Rancho Bernardo, and even extend north into Temecula, the wine-making area of southern Riverside County. Growth notwithstanding, the area still has such natural settings as the San Diego Wild Animal Park, Rancho Bernardo, and the Welk Resort Center.

Numbers in the margin correspond to points of interest on the San Diego North County map.

Rancho Bernardo

23 mi northeast of downtown San Diego on I–15.

Rancho Bernardo straddles a stretch of I–15 between San Diego and Es-condido and technically is a neighborhood of San Diego. Originally a suburban community where many wealthy retirees settled down, Ran-cho Bernardo is now home to a number of high-tech companies, the most notable of which is Sony. It's the location of the Rancho Bernardo Inn, one of San Diego's most delightful resorts.

Where to Stay & Eat

$$$–$$$$ ✕ **El Bizcocho.** Wealthy locals rate this restaurant at the Rancho Bernardo
Fodor'sChoice Inn tops for style and cuisine. The tranquil setting features candlelit ta-
★ bles, plush banquettes, and quiet, live music. The menu offers updated versions of classic entrées such as roasted rack of lamb, grilled chateaubriand carved tableside, medallions of veal with morel mushroom cream sauce, and grilled rib-eye steak with pinot noir sauce. Try Maine lobster salad with Spanish red bell pepper mousse, or halibut poached in a lime and sea bean broth. The wine list has more than 1,000 selections, including rare vintages. ✉ *Rancho Bernardo Inn, 17550 Bernardo Oaks Pkwy., Rancho Bernardo* ☎ *800/267–5662 or 858/675–8500* ⚏ *Jacket and tie* ▤ *AE, D, DC, MC, V* ☾ *No lunch, no dinner Sun.*

$$–$$$$ ✕ **Bernard'O.** The California-European menu consists of classic and innovative seasonal interpretations of French favorites such as rack of lamb roasted with pungent *herbes de Provence* and such fresh fish selections as sea bass with a ragout of white beans and balsamic vinegar. There's an enclosed patio, indoor and outdoor fireplaces, and an expanded, elegant dining room. ✉ *12457 Rancho Bernardo Rd., Rancho Bernardo* ☎ *858/487–7171* ▤ *AE, D, DC, MC, V* ☾ *No lunch weekends.*

$$–$$$ ✕ **Carver's Steak House.** Dried-leaf and bark arrangements adorn the entrance to this upscale restaurant whose walls and tables are made of finished wood. House specialties here include prime rib and filet mignon. Seafood and chicken are also available. ✉ *11940 Bernardo Plaza Dr., Rancho Bernardo* ☎ *858/485–1262* ⚏ *Reservations essential* ▤ *AE, D, DC, MC, V* ☾ *No lunch Mon. and Tues.*

$$–$$$ ✕ **French Market Grille.** The Grille's stylish dark-wood dining room and the twinkling lights will help you forget that you're eating in a shopping center. The French fare changes with the seasons; typical entrées include grilled beef tenderloin, roasted scallops Dijonnaise, or roasted chicken with fresh herbs. On Tuesday night, opera is presented by local and guest artists. ✉ *Ralph's Shopping Center, 15717 Bernardo Heights Pkwy., Rancho Bernardo* ☎ *858/485–8055* ▤ *AE, D, DC, MC, V.*

$–$$$ ✕ **Cafe Luna.** The setting is low-key and intimate in this candlelit café with exposed brick. The house specialty is tournedos gorgonzola—two petit filets mignon, pan-seared with a cabernet demi-glace and topped with mushroom caps and gorgonzola. Pastas and desserts are homemade daily. ✉ *11040 Rancho Carmel Dr., Carmel Mountain Ranch* ☎ *858/ 673–0077* ⚏ *Reservations essential* ▤ *AE, D, DC, MC, V* ☾ *Closed Sun. No lunch Mon. and Tues.*

¢–$$ ✕ **Chiêu-Anh.** Local Asian families frequent this Vietnamese café that's set in a remote corner of the Bernardo Center shopping center. It's small, but has elegant touches such as fresh flowers and waitresses clad in traditional flowing gowns. Try the spring rolls, the herb salad with steamed shrimp and pork, the rice noodles with charbroiled shrimp, one of the clay-pot dishes, or the shrimp on sugarcane. ✉ *16769 Bernardo Center Dr., Rancho Bernardo* ☎ *858/485–1231* ▤ *AE, DC, MC, V* ☾ *Closed Mon. No lunch weekends.*

¢–$ ✕ **Spices Thai Cafe.** One of the North County's most stylish ethnic restaurants serves beautiful Thai dishes. The traditional *pad thai* is a feast of shrimp, bean sprouts, bean curd, and noodles, and the seafood selections and salads are highly recommended. ✉ *16441 Bernardo Center Dr., Rancho Bernardo* ☎ *858/674–4665* 🖃 *AE, D, DC, MC, V.*

★ 🖼 **Rancho Bernardo Inn.** This gem of a resort is on 265 oak-shaded acres surrounded by a well-established residential community. The two-story, red-roof adobe buildings are complemented by bougainvillea-decked courtyards. Public areas are a collection of small sitting rooms where Spanish mission–style sofas and chairs invite you to linger with a good book. There are fireplaces everywhere, overstuffed furniture, and Oriental rugs on tile floors. Rooms inside are ample, but simply furnished and appointed with early California and Mexican art. All have private patios or balconies with views. Suites have fireplaces. Seasonal children's activities included science and sports instruction. ✉ *17550 Bernardo Oaks Dr., Rancho Bernardo 92128* ☎ *858/675–8500 or 877/517–9342* 🖷 *858/675–8501* ⊕ *www.ranchobernardoinn.com* ⤳ *287 rooms, 15 suites* ⚅ *2 restaurants, room service, in-room data ports, in-room safes, minibars, refrigerators, cable TV with movies and games, driving range, 18-hole golf course, 27-hole golf course, putting green, 12 tennis courts, 2 pools, gym, 7 outdoor hot tubs, sauna, spa, steam room, bicycles, volleyball, 2 bars, shops, children's programs (ages 5–13), concierge, business services, meeting rooms, no-smoking rooms* 🖃 *AE, D, DC, MC, V.*

$$–$$$$

Shopping

A trip to **Bernardo Winery** (✉ 13330 Paseo Del Verano, Norte, Rancho Bernardo ☎ 858/487–1866 ⊕ www.bernardowinery.com) feels like traveling back to early California days; some of the vines on the former Spanish land grant property are more than 100 years old. The winery was founded in 1889 and has been operated by the Rizzo family since 1928. Besides the wine-tasting room selling cold-pressed olive oil and other gourmet goodies, Cafe Merlot serves lunch daily except Monday. About a dozen shops offer apparel, home decor items, and arts and crafts. If you're lucky, the glassblowing artist will be working at the outdoor furnace. The winery is open daily 9–5; the shops are open Tuesday–Sunday 10–5.

Escondido

8 mi north of Rancho Bernardo on I–15, 31 mi northeast of downtown San Diego on I–15.

Escondido and the lovely rolling hills around it originally comprised a land grant bestowed on Juan Bautista Alvarado in 1843 by Mexican Governor Manuel Micheltorena. The Battle of San Pasqual, a bloody milestone in California's march to statehood, took place just east of the city. For a century and a half, the hills supported citrus and avocado trees, plus large grape vineyards. The rural character began to change when the San Diego Zoo established its Wild Animal Park in the San Pasqual Valley east of town in the 1970s. By the late 1990s, suburban development had begun to transform the hills into housing tracts. The California Center for the Arts, opened in 1993, now stands as a downtown centerpiece of a burgeoning arts community that includes a branch of the Mingei Folk Art Museum and a collection of art galleries along Grand Avenue. Despite its urbanization, Escondido still supports several pristine open-space preserves that attract nature-lovers, hikers, and mountain bikers.

San Diego Wild Animal Park is an extension of the San Diego Zoo, a 35-minute drive south. The 1,800-acre preserve in the San Pasqual Valley is designed to protect endangered species of animals from around the world. Exhibit areas have been carved out of the dry, dusty canyons and mesas to represent the animals' natural habitats—North Africa, South Africa, East Africa, Heart of Africa, Australian Rain Forest, Asian Swamps, and Asian Plains.

The best way to see these preserves is on the 60-minute, 5-mi Wgasa Bushline Railway (included in the price of admission). As you pass in front of the large, naturally landscaped enclosures, you can see animals bounding through prairies and mesas as they would in the wild. More than 3,000 animals of 450 species roam or fly above the expansive grounds. Predators are separated from prey by deep moats, but only the elephants, tigers, lions, and cheetahs are kept in isolation. Photographers with zoom lenses can get spectacular shots of zebras, gazelles, and rhinos (a seat on the right-hand side of the monorail is best for viewing). The trip is especially enjoyable in the early evening, when the heat has subsided and the animals are active and feeding. In summer the monorail travels through the park after dark, and sodium-vapor lamps highlight the active animals.

The park is as much a botanical garden as a zoo, and botanists collect rare and endangered plants for preservation. Unique gardens include cacti and succulents from Baja California, a bonsai collection, fuchsia display, native plants, protea, and water-wise plantings. The park sponsors a number of garden events throughout the year, including a spring orchid show.

Pride of the Park, the lion exhibit opened in 2004, gives you a close-up view of the king of beasts in a slice of African wilderness complete with sweeping plains and rolling hills. You walk through this encounter to an observation station where you can watch the giant cats lounging around through a 40-foot-long window. The next stop offers an overview of the cats at work, and the last stop is a research station where you can see the cats all around you through glass panels.

The 1¼-mi-long **Kilimanjaro Safari Walk** winds through some of the park's hilliest terrain in the East Africa section, with observation decks overlooking the elephants and lions. A 70-foot suspension bridge spans a steep ravine, leading to the final observation point and a panorama of the entire park and the San Pasqual Valley.

The ticket booths at **Nairobi Village,** the park's center, are designed to resemble the tomb of an ancient king of Uganda. Animals in the **Petting Kraal** affectionately tolerate tugs and pats and are quite adept at posing for pictures with toddlers. At the **Congo River Fishing Village** 10,000 gallons of water pour each minute over a huge waterfall into a large lagoon. **Hidden Jungle,** an 8,800-square-foot glass house, houses creatures that creep, flutter, or just hang out in a tropical habitat. Gigantic cockroaches and bird-eating spiders share the turf with colorful butterflies and hummingbirds and oh-so-slow-moving two-toed sloths. **Lorikeet Landing** holds 75 of the loud and colorful small parrots—you can buy a cup of nectar at the aviary entrance to induce them to land on your hand. Along the trails of 32-acre **Heart of Africa** you can travel in the footsteps of an early explorer through forests and lowlands, across a floating bridge to a research station where an expert is on hand to answer questions; finally you arrive at Panorama Point where you capture an up-close-and-personal view of cheetahs, a chance to feed the giraffes, and a distant glimpse of the expansive savanna where rhinos, impalas, wildebeest, oryx, and beautiful migrating birds reside. The Wild Animal Park, which conducts captive breeding programs to save rare and endangered species, shows off one of its most successful efforts, the California Condor, at **Condor Ridge.** The exhibit, perched like one of the ugly black vultures it features, occupies nearly the highest point in the park, and affords a sweeping view of the surrounding San Pasqual Valley. Also on exhibit here is a herd of rare desert bighorn sheep.

Ravens, vultures, hawks, and a great horned owl perform throughout the day at the **Bird Show Amphitheater.** All the park's animal shows are entertainingly educational. The gift shops here offer wonderful merchandise, much of it limited-edition items. Rental camcorders, strollers, and wheelchairs are available. Serious shutterbugs might consider joining one of the park's special photo caravans ($119.50–$159.50, including admission). You can also overnight in the park in summer on a Roar and Snore Campover ($139.50, kids 8–11 $112.50, including admission), take a Sunrise Safari in August, and celebrate the holidays during the annual Festival of Lights. ⊠ *15500 San Pasqual Valley Rd., Escondido, take I–15 north to Via Rancho Pkwy. and follow signs (6 mi)* ☎ *760/747–8702* ⊕ *www.wildanimalpark.org* ⊠ *$29.50 includes all shows and monorail tour; a $52.65 combination pass grants entry, within 5 days of purchase, to San Diego Zoo and San Diego Wild Animal Park; parking $6* ☉ *Mid-June–Labor Day, daily 9–8; Mid-Sept.–mid-June, daily 9–4* ⊟ *D, MC, V.*

☜ The **California Center for the Arts,** an entertainment complex with two theaters, an art museum, and a conference center, presents operas, musicals, plays, dance performances, and symphony and chamber-music concerts. Performers conduct free workshops for children; check the Web site for dates. The museum, which focuses on 20th-century art, occasionally presents blockbuster exhibits such as the glass art of Dale Chilhuly and photos by Ansel Adams, making a side trip here worthwhile. ⊠ *340 N. Escondido Blvd., Escondido* ☎ *760/839–4138, 800/988–4253 box office, 760/839–4100* ⊕ *www.artcenter.org* ⊠ *Museum price varies* ☉ *Museum hrs vary.*

The outdoor **Heritage Walk Museum** in Grape Day Park is adjacent to the Center for the Arts. Several historic buildings illustrate local history from the late 1800s, when grape growing and gold mining supported the economy. Exhibits include the 1888 Santa Fe Depot and railroad car, Escondido's first library, the Bandy Blacksmith shop, a furnished 1890 Victorian house, and other 19th-century buildings. ⊠ *321 N. Broadway, Escondido* ☎ *760/743–8207* ⊕ *www.escondidohistoricalsociety.com* ⊠ *$3* ⊙ *Thurs.–Sat. 1–4.*

The **Escondido Municipal Gallery** showcases works by local artists. The Arts Bazaar gift shop carries locally crafted jewelry, blown glass, and textiles. ⊠ *142 W. Grand Ave., Escondido* ☎ *760/480–4101* ⊙ *Tues.–Sat. 11–4.*

Occupying a former JCPenney store at the foot of Escondido's emerging arts district, **Mingei International Museum North County** is a satellite of the larger facility in San Diego's Balboa Park. All the Mingei art is classified as folk art; collections include pre-Columbian items, ceramics, textiles, glass, and a variety of Japanese arts of daily life. Initial exhibits include a retrospective on local sculptor Niki de Saint Phalle and Horses Circling the Globe. ⊠ *155 W. Grand Ave.* ☎ *760/735–3355* ⊕ *www.mingei.org* ⊠ *$6* ⊙ *Tues.–Sun. 1–4.*

Ⓒ A 3,058-acre conservation area and historic ranch site, **Daley Ranch** holds 20 mi of multipurpose trails for hikers, mountain bikers, and equestrians. The 2.4-mi Boulder Loop affords sweeping views of Escondido and the 2.5-mi Ranch House Loop passes two small ponds, the Daley family ranch house built in 1928, and the site of the original log cabin. Private motorized vehicles are prohibited on the ranch. Sunday shuttle service is provided from the parking area to the entrance. ⊠ *3024 La Honda Dr., Escondido 92027* ☎ *760/893–4680* ⊕ *www.ci.escondido. ca.us* ⊠ *Free* ⊙ *Dawn–dusk.*

off the beaten path

LAVENDER FIELDS – A spring visit to the Lavender Fields is worth a detour. A self-guided walking tour takes you through 6 acres planted with 28 varieties of lavender and to an area where plants are distilled into essential oils. A gift shop sells lavender products and plants. ⊠ *12460 Keys Creek Rd., Valley Center* ☎ *760/742–1489* ⊕ *www. thelavenderfields.com* ⊠ *Free* ⊙ *Weekends May and June 10–5.*

Orfila Vineyards offers tours and tastings of award-winning Syrah, Sangiovese, and Viongier produced from grapes harvested from the 10,000-acre vineyard. The Rose Arbor has a picnic area and there's a gift shop with wine-related merchandise. ⊠ *13455 San Pasqual Valley Rd., Escondido* ☎ *760/738–6500 or 800/858–9463* ⊕ *www.orfila.com* ⊙ *Daily 10–6, guided tours at 2.*

Ⓒ The last work by sculptor Niki de Saint Phalle (1930–2002), the garden **Queen Califia's Magical Circle** consists of eight totemic figures up to 21 feet tall. Adorned with stylized monsters, protective deities, geometric symbols, crests, human skulls and animals, they evoke ancient tales and legends. Saint Phalle designed the garden for the entertainment of children, who can scramble around and on the giant fanciful figures. ⊠ *Kit Carson Park, Bear Valley Pkwy. and Mary La., Escondido* ☎ *760/745–9396* ⊕ *www.queencalifia.org* ⊠ *Free* ⊙ *9–dusk.*

☺ **San Dieguito River Park** maintains several hiking and walking trails in the Escondido area. These are part of the 55-mi-long Coast to Crest Trail that will link the San Dieguito Lagoon near Del Mar with the river's source on Volcan Mountain, north of Julian. Three trails circle Lake Hodges. The **Piedras Pintadas Trail** informs about native American Kumeyaay lifestyles and uses for native plants; the first half mile of the **Highland Valley Trail** comprises the Ruth Merrill Children's Walk. Three trails in **Clevenger Canyon** lead to sweeping views of the San Pasqual Valley. Visit the Web site for a list of upcoming guided hikes. ⊠ *18327 Sycamore Creek Rd., Escondido* ☎ *760/674–2270* ⊕ *www.sdrp.org* ⌷ *Free* ⊙ *Daily.*

San Pasqual Battlefield State Historic Park and Museum commemorates an important moment in the Mexican-American War. On December 6, 1846, a contingent of Americans, including famous frontier scout Kit Carson, suffered defeat by a group of Californios (Spanish-Mexican residents of California). This was the Californios' most notable success during the war, but the Americans, with support from Commodore Stockton in San Diego, regained control of the region. A historic battle reenactment is held every December. ⊠ *15808 San Pasqual Valley Rd., Escondido* ☎ *760/737–2201* ⊕ *www.sanqpasqual.org* ⌷ *Free* ⊙ *Weekends 10–5.*

Where to Stay & Eat

★ **$$–$$$$** ✕ **150 Grand Cafe.** This pretty storefront restaurant lies a block from the California Center for the Arts. It consists of a collection of individually decorated dining rooms, all with a garden ambience, and an outdoor dining area. The seasonal menu might feature miso-braised salmon on barley risotto, hoisin-crusted pork tenderloin with couscous, or open-faced seafood ravioli with broccoli rabe. ⊠ *150 W. Grand Ave., Escondido* ☎ *760/738–6868* ⊟ *AE, DC, MC, V* ⊙ *Closed Sun.*

$$–$$$ ✕ **Vincent's Sirino's.** Here's an excellent choice for dining before attending an event at the nearby California Center for the Arts. Original paintings decorate the walls and crisp white tablecloths cover the tables, adorned with fresh flowers. The menu changes frequently; offerings include rack of lamb with fresh herb-garlic sauce or veal prosciutto ravioli. The wine list is serious, as are the desserts. The service is friendly and attentive. ⊠ *113 W. Grand Ave., Escondido* ☎ *760/745–3835* ⊟ *AE, D, MC, V* ⊙ *Closed Mon. No lunch weekends.*

$–$$ ⊞ **Castle Creek Inn Resort and Spa.** European ambience and unusually lush gardens mark this small resort tucked into a canyon just north of Escondido. Public areas feature antique armoires, gilded mirrors, and crystal chandeliers. Rooms, all with patios or balconies affording garden or golf course views, are simply appointed with antique chairs and desks, hand-painted wall stenciling, and down comforters. ⊠ *29850 Circle R Way, 92026* ☎ *760/751–8800 or 800/253–5341* ⊟ *760/751–8787* ⊕ *www.castlecreekinn.com* ⇄ *30 rooms, 1 suite* �ဒ *In-room data ports, microwaves, refrigerators, cable TV, pool, gym, 4 outdoor hot tubs, sauna, spa, meeting room, free parking; no smoking* ⊟ *AE, D, DC, MC, V.*

$–$$ ⊞ **Welk Resort Center.** This resort sprawls over 600 acres of rugged, oak-studded hillside. Built by band leader Lawrence Welk in the 1960s, the resort includes a hotel, time-share condominiums, and a recreation and entertainment complex. A museum displays Welk memorabilia, a theater presents Broadway-style musicals year-round, and there are many shops on the premises. Hotel rooms, decorated with a Southwestern flair, have golf-course views. ⌧ *8860 Lawrence Welk Dr., Escondido 92026* ☎*760/749–3000 or 800/932–9355* 🖷*760/749–6182* ⊕*www.welkresort. com* ↪ *137 rooms, 10 suites* ♿ *3 restaurants, grocery, in-room data ports, cable TV, 2 18-hole golf courses, 5 tennis courts, 6 pools, health club, 7 hot tubs, bar, theater, shops, meeting room, travel services, free parking, no-smoking rooms* 🖃 *AE, D, DC, MC, V.*

¢–$ 🖻 **Holiday Inn Express.** This basic motel is one of the closest to the Wild Animal Park, about 6 mi away. It's on a busy thoroughfare, but close to the California Center for the Arts and civic center. Simply decorated rooms sport a vague African theme. Continental breakfast is included in the price. ⌧ *1250 W. Valley Pkwy., 92029* ☎ *760/741–7117* 🖷 *760/ 839–1601* ⊕ *www.hiexescondido.com* ↪ *84 rooms, 25 suites* ♿ *Snack bar, in-room data ports, some kitchenettes, cable TV with movies, pool, outdoor hot tub, exercise equipment, dry cleaning, laundry facilities, concierge, business service, meeting rooms, car rental, free parking, no-smoking rooms* 🖃 *AE, D, DC, MC, V* ◎ *CP.*

Shopping

In the 1990s farmland began giving way to suburbs, and the fruit, nut, and vegetable bounty has diminished. You can still find overflowing farmstands in the San Pasqual Valley and in Valley Center, just east of the city. In 2000 the city began to look to the arts to sustain its economy. As a result the downtown streets surrounding the California Center for the Arts are getting make-overs, attracting mid-to-high-end art galleries and restaurants to replace the thrift stores and diners.

☼ **Bates Nut Farm** (⌧ 15954 Woods Valley Rd., Valley Center ☎ 760/ 749–3333 ⊕ www.batesfarm.com) is home of San Diego's largest pumpkin patch in fall, where you might find 200-pound squash. The 100-acre historic farm sells locally grown pecans, macadamia nuts, and almonds. There's a petting zoo holding farm animals, a picnic area, and gift shop. **Canterbury Gardens** (⌧ 2402 S. Escondido Blvd., Escondido ☎ 760/746–1400 ⊕ www.canterburygardens.com) specializes in seasonal designer decorator items and giftware, plus a year-round selection of Christmas ornaments and collectibles. Interior decorations and silk plants are all designed and crafted on-site.

The **Lillian Berkley Collection** (⌧ 128 E. Grand Ave., Escondido ☎ 760/ 480–9434 ⊕ www.lillianberkley.com) presents colorful paintings by several contemporary Russian artists including Vachagan Narazyan and Vigen Sogomonyan. **Rave Reviews** (⌧ 120 W. Grand Ave., Escondido ☎ 760/743–0056) carries high-end vintage clothing and accessories from the 1940s, '50s, and '60s. The **Woodcrafter Design Gallery** (⌧ 135 E. Grand Ave., Escondido ☎ 760/741–0124) offers handmade one-of-a-kind wood products ranging from small bowls and cutting boards to exquisite desks and chairs.

Palomar Mountain

❻ *35 mi northeast of Escondido on I–15 to Rte. 76 to Rte. S6, 66 mi northeast of downtown San Diego on Rte. 163 to I–15 to Rte. 76 to Rte. S6.8*

Palomar Observatory, atop Palomar Mountain and home to the 200-inch Hale telescope, is the site of some of the most important astronomical discoveries of the 20th century. And in 2004, Sedna, the tiny platentoid and most distant object in the solar system, was photographed through observatory's 48-inch telescope. The small museum at the observatory contains photos of some of these discoveries and presents informative videos. A park with picnic areas surrounds the observatory. ⊠ *Rte. S6, north of Rte. 76, east of I–15, Palomar Mountain* ☎ *760/742–2119* ⊕ *www.astro.caltech.edu/palomarpublic* ⌨ *Free* ☉ *Observatory for self-guided tours daily 9–4, except Dec. 24 and 25.*

Mission San Antonio de Pala, built in 1816, is a living remnant of the mission era and serves the local Native American community. In fact, it's the only original Spanish mission to continue with its purpose in serving Native American Indians. Displays in a small museum include a mineral collection. The old jail and cemetery are part of the original mission. ⊠ *Pala Mission Rd. off Rte. 76, 6 mi east of I–15, Pala* ☎ *760/742–1600* ⌨ *$2* ☉ *Museum and gift shop Wed.–Sun. 10–4.*

One of the few areas in Southern California with a Sierra-like atmosphere, **Palomar Mountain State Park** holds a forest of pines, cedars, western dogwood, native azalea, and other plants. Wildflower viewing is good in spring. **Boucher Lookout,** on one of several nature–hiking trails, affords a sweeping view to the west. There's trout fishing in Doane Pond. The campground holds 31 sites with tables, firepits, and flush toilets. ⊠ *Off Hwy. S6 at Hwy. S7, Palomar Mountain* ☎ *760/742–3462 ranger station, 800/444–7275 campsite reservations* ⊕ *www.palomar.statepark.org* ⌨ *$4, camping $14–$19.*

Fallbrook

19 mi northwest of Escondido on I–15 to Mission Rd. (Rte. S13) to Mission Dr.

With 6,000 hillside acres planted, Fallbrook bills itself as the avocado capital of the world. Citrus and macadamia nuts are grown in the region, too. Historic Old Main Street, a few antiques malls, and agriculture are the attractions in this small walkable town. There's an Avocado Festival every April where you can sample great guacamole or even avocado ice cream.

Under the 20-foot ceilings with exposed beams, spacious **Fallbrook Art and Cultural Center** hosts local and regional art shows of watercolors, oils, glass sculpture, bronzework, ceramics, and even gourd art. You can also watch bronze casting and glass-blowing (call ahead for firing times). ⊠ *103 S. Main St.* ☎ *760/728–1414 or 800/919–1159* ⌨ *$5* ☉ *Open days vary with exhibit; call ahead.*

Where to Stay & Eat

$–$$$ ✕ **Bistro Restaurant.** In summer you can eat on the patio, or upstairs in the casual indoor dining room. Rack of lamb, black pepper filet mignon, Stroganoff, duck, and shrimp are part of the continental menu. ⊠ *119 N. Main St.* ☎ *760/723–3559* ⊟ *AE, D, DC, MC, V* ☉ *Closed Mon. No lunch Sun.*

★ **$–$$** ⌂ **Pala Mesa Resort.** In the secluded rolling foothills of a former ranch, this two-story resort offers excellent value and is popular with convention groups. It was built in the 1970s, but fully renovated in 2003, and boasts a championship golf course. All guest rooms have golf course or foothills views, and many have balconies or private patios. ⊠ *2001 Old Hwy. 395, 92028* ☎ *760/728–5881 or 800/722–4700* ⊟ *760/723–8292* ⊕ *www.palamesa.com* ↝ *133 rooms* ⌂ *Restaurant, room service, in-room data ports, minibars, cable TV with movies, driving range, 18-hole golf course, putting green, 4 tennis courts, pool, gym, outdoor hot tub, massage, spa, bar, business services, meeting rooms, free parking, no-smoking rooms* ⊟ *AE, D, DC, MC, V.*

$ ⌂ **Fallbrook Country Inn.** This motel-like building wraps around a swimming pool. Decor is country style with fluffy floral bedspreads and overstuffed chairs. Each room has a private balcony. Breakfast is included in the price. ⊠ *1425 S. Mission Rd., 92028* ☎ *760/728–1114* ⊟ *760/728–1114* ⊕ *www.pinnaclehotelusa.com* ↝ *28 rooms* ⌂ *In-room data ports, fans, some kitchenettes, some microwaves, some refrigerators, cable TV, pool, outdoor hot tub, free parking, no-smoking rooms* ⊟ *AE, D, DC, MC, V* �◉| *CP.*

¢–$ ⌂ **La Estancia.** This Italian-style lodge offers a convenient, but not glamorous, stop right alongside the freeway. Rooms are small and somewhat dark. Grounds support mature landscaping with plenty of flowers year-round to decorate the many weddings held here. The restaurant is open daily. ⊠ *3135 Hwy. 395 S, 92028* ☎ *760/723–2888* ⊟ *760/451–3528* ⊕ *www.laestanciainn.com* ↝ *40 rooms, 4 suites* ⌂ *Restaurant, in-room data ports, some in-room safes, some in-room hot tubs, some kitchenettes, some microwaves, some refrigerators, cable TV, pool, outdoor hot tub, free parking, no-smoking rooms* ⊟ *AE, D, MC, V.*

¢ ⌂ **Fallbrook Lodge.** This two-story no-frills motel was built in 1991 and is in a commercial area 1 mi from downtown. Continental breakfast is included in the price. ⊠ *1608 S. Mission Rd., 92028* ☎ *760/723–1127* ⊟ *760/723–2917* ↝ *36 rooms* ⌂ *Some kitchenettes, cable TV, no-smoking rooms* ⊟ *AE, D, DC, MC, V* �◉| *CP.*

Temecula

29 mi from Escondido, 60 mi from San Diego on I–15 north to Rancho California Rd. east.

Once an important stop on the Butterfield Overland Stagecoach route and a market town for the huge cattle ranches in the surrounding hillsides, Temecula (pronounced teh-*mec*-yoo-la) is southern California's only developed wine region. Premium wineries, most of which allow tasting for a small fee, can be found along Rancho California Road as it snakes through oak-studded hills. Temecula draws thousands of people to its Balloon and Wine Festival held in the spring. Hot-air-balloon excursions are a good choice year-round. **Grape Escape Balloon Adventure** (☎ 800/965–2122 ⊕ www.hotairtours.com) has morning lift-offs.

Temecula is home to 18 wineries. The **Temecula Valley Winegrowers Association** (✉ 34567 Rancho California Rd., Temecula ☎ 951/699–6586 or 800/801–9463 ⊕ www.temeculawines.org ⊙ Weekdays 8:30–4:30) distributes brochures and sells tickets to special wine events. **Thornton Winery** (✉ 32575 Rancho California Rd., Temecula ☎ 951/699–0099 ⊕ www. thorntonwine.com) produces several varieties of wine, including sparkling white wine; it offers weekend tours and daily tastings. **Callaway Vineyard & Winery** (✉ 32720 Rancho California Rd., Temecula ☎ 951/676–4001 ⊕ www.callawaycoastal.com) produces several lines of wines made from grapes grown along the coast including Cabernet Sauvignon, Chadonnay, and Merlot. It offers tastings, tours, and there's a gift shop. **Maurice Car'rie Vineyard & Winery** (✉ 34225 Rancho California Rd., Temecula ☎ 951/ 676–1711 ⊕ www.mauricecarriewinery.com) produces 16 varieties of wine. It has a tasting room, a gift shop, and a picnic area.

Once a hangout for cowboys, **Old Town Temecula** still looks the part. Park on Front Street and walk along the six-block stretch past the large 19th-century wooden buildings; several antiques shops here specialize in local and Wild West memorabilia.

☾ **Temecula Valley Museum,** adjacent to Sam Hicks Monument Park, focuses on the history of life in the Temecula Valley including early–Native American life, Butterfield stage routes, and the ranchero period. A hands-on interactive area for children holds a general store, photographer's studio, and ride-a-pony station. Outside there's a playground and picnic area. ✉ *28314 Mercedes St., Temecula* ☎ *951/694–6450* ⌂ *$2 donation requested* ⊙ *Tues.–Sat. 10–5, Sun. 1–5.*

The **Santa Rosa Plateau Ecological Reserve** provides a glimpse of what this countryside was like before the developers took over. Trails wind through oak forests and past vernal pools and rolling grassland. A visitor and operations center has interpretive displays and maps; some of the reserve's hiking trails begin here. ✉ *Take I–15 south to Clinton Keith Rd. exit and head west 5 mi, Murrieta* ☎ *951/677–6951* ⊕ *www. santarosaplateau.org* ⌂ *$2* ⊙ *Daily dawn–dusk.*

Where to Stay & Eat

$$–$$$$ ✕ **Cafe Champagne.** The Thornton Winery's airy country restaurant, whose big windows overlook the vineyards, serves contemporary cuisine. Menu highlights include grilled eggplant with Portobello mushroom Napoleon and grilled peppered filet mignon with Maytag blue cheese. If you're in the mood for something small, pick one of the appetizers as your main course. ✉ *32575 Rancho California Rd., Temecula* ☎ *951/699–0088* ▤ *AE, D, MC, V.*

$$–$$$ ✕ **Temet Grill.** The lovely brass-and-glass room at the Temecula Creek Inn has wall-to-wall views of the resort's golf courses. Dinner entrées change from time to time; typical options include porterhouse of pork with green peppercorn sauce and roasted vegetable ravioli on a bed of spinach. The inn's signature dessert is a bread pudding created by late actor Vincent Price. The Temet is also open daily for breakfast. ⊠ *44501 Rainbow Canyon Rd.* ☎ *951/587–1465* ☰ *AE, D, DC, MC, V.*

¢–$ ✕ **Bank of Mexican Food.** *Flautas*—shredded beef or chicken rolled in a flour tortilla and deep fried—crab enchiladas, and other south-of-the-border dishes are served in this place that was a bank in 1913. There's a ceramic-tile patio if you want to eat outside. Meals come with beans and rice and there's a kids' menu, too. ⊠ *28645 Front St.* ☎ *951/676–6160* ☰ *MC, V.*

$$–$$$ ▥ **Temecula Creek Inn.** This upscale golf resort occupies a hillside adjacent to I–15 and is a short distance from the wine-touring area. Rooms are in a collection of low-slung, red-roof buildings; those facing the freeway are apt to be noisy. Unusually large and bright rooms are nicely appointed with double vanity areas and expansive windows revealing a tranquil golf-course view (which you also get from a private balcony or patio). Rooms, decorated in soft desert colors, contain interesting displays of Native American pottery, basket remnants, and antique tribal weavings. ⊠ *44501 Rainbow Canyon Rd., Temecula 92592* ☎ *951/694–1000 or 877/517–1823* 🖷 *951/676–2466* ⊕ *www.temeculacreekinn.com* ⤳ *120 rooms, 10 suites* ⟐ *Restaurant, café, in-room data ports, in-room safes, cable TV, driving range, 27-hole golf course, putting green, 2 tennis courts, pool, gym, outdoor hot tub, massage, croquet, hiking, horseshoes, volleyball, bar, meeting room, free parking, no-smoking rooms* ☰ *AE, D, DC, MC, V.*

$–$$ ▥ **Loma Vista Bed and Breakfast.** This mission-style inn has tranquil views of vineyards, citrus groves, and gardens. Most rooms have private balconies or outdoor sitting areas, some have private entrances or fireplaces. A full breakfast, with champagne, is included in the price. ⊠ *33350 La Serena Way, Temecula 92592* ☎ *951/676–7047* ⤳ *10 rooms* ⟐ *Some in-room hot tubs, outdoor hot tub; no room phones, no room TVs, no smoking* ⦿ *BP* ☰ *MC, V.*

Inland North County A to Z

To research prices, get advice from other travelers, and book travel arrangements, visit www.fodors.com

BUS TRAVEL

🛈 Bus Information **North County Transit District** ☎ 800/266–6883.

CAR TRAVEL

Escondido sits at the intersection of Route 78, which heads east from Oceanside, and I–15, the inland freeway connecting San Diego to Riverside, which is 30 minutes north of Escondido. Del Dios Highway winds from Rancho Santa Fe through the hills past Lake Hodges to Escondido. Route 76, which connects with Interstate 15 north of Escondido, veers east to Palomar Mountain. Interstate 15 continues north to Fallbrook and Temecula.

TOURS

Several companies offer individual and group tours of the Temecula wine country with departures from San Diego and Temecula. Some include lunch or refreshments as part of the package.

🚘 Limousine Tours **Destination Temecula** ☎ 951/695–1232 or 800/584–8162 ⊕ www. destem.com. **Grapeline Wine County Shuttle** ☎ 951/693–5463 ⊕ www.gogrape.com.

VISITOR INFORMATION

🛈 **Escondido Chamber of Commerce** ✉ 720 N. Broadway, Escondido 92025 ☎ 760/ 745–2125 ⊕ www.escondidochamber.org. **Fallbrook Chamber of Commerce** ✉ 233 E. Mission Rd., Suite A, Fallbrook 92028 ☎ 760/728–5845 ⊕ www.fallbrookca.org. **Rancho Bernardo Chamber of Commerce** ✉ 11650 Iberia Pl., Suite 220, San Diego 92128 ☎ 858/487–1767 ⊕ www.ranchobernardochamber.com. **San Diego North Convention and Visitors Bureau** ✉ 360 N. Escondido Blvd., Escondido 92025 ☎ 760/745–4741 ⊕ www.sandiegonorth.com. **Temecula Valley Chamber of Commerce** ✉ 26790 Ynez Court, Temecula 92591 ☎ 951/676–5090 or 866/676–5090 ⊕ www.temecula.org.

EAST COUNTY

San Diego's East County, the area that extends directly east of the city to the Anza Borrego Desert, is one vast outdoor playground. It holds the alpinelike Cuyamaca, Laguna, and Volcan mountains, where camping, hiking, birding, andstargazing are popular pursuits. Lakes and reservoirs lure boaters and fishermen. The East County is the least developed area of San Diego County, but development pressures are visible not only in the area's major cities, but also along major highways such as Interstate 8, which bisects the region in an east–west direction.

La Mesa

15 mi east of San Diego via I–8.

La Mesa is the first of several small cities you'll encounter as you head east from San Diego on I–8. Most, including La Mesa, fall into the category of suburban bedroom communities. But villagelike La Mesa holds secrets. During the first two decades of the 20th century, it was a center of a burgeoning film industry. Alan Dwan, a president of the Motion Picture Directors Association and director of Shirley Temple films, shot more than 150 silent flicks in and around lemon groves that covered the hillsides. His Flying A Studio, now gone, was on La Mesa Boulevard and 3rd Street. The village holds antiques shops and there's a farmers' market on Friday afternoon (3 PM–6 PM).

Lake Murray is not far from the San Diego city center and offers boating and fishing for bass, bluegill, channel catfish, and rainbow trout, which are stocked regularly. Fishing is allowed normally Wednesday and weekends (dawn to dusk) from early November through Labor Day. There are trails for walking, jogging, and picnicking. ✉ *Kiowa Dr. off Lake Murray Blvd., La Mesa* ☎ *619/390–0222* 🆓 *Free* ☉ *Daily dawn–dusk.*

Mission Trails Regional Park has nearly 5,800 acres of open land. Some of it represents what the area looked like before settlers and developers discovered San Diego. There are 40 mi of well-marked trails for hikers of all abilities, a visitor center with interpretive displays, boating and fishing on Lake Murray, and camping at the Kumeyaay campground. In the Mission Gorge section of the park are great areas for mountain biking and light rock climbing. Plants damaged in the fires of 2003 are coming back well. ⊠ *1 Father Junipero Serra Trail, La Mesa* ☎ *619/668–3275* ⊕ *www.mtrp.org* ☞ *Free* ⊙ *Visitor center daily 9–5.*

SIMPSON'S GARDEN TOWN NURSERY AND CAR BARN – More than just a place to buy potted plants, these 25 acres also have barnyard animals, a small historic museum, and 50 antique automobiles. All this ambience makes the long drive from San Diego worthwhile. ⊠ *13925 Hwy. 94, Jamul* ☎ *No phone* ⊕ *www.simpsonsnursery.com* ☞ *Free* ⊙ *Daily 8:30–5.*

Shopping

Literary adventures await kids who venture into **The Yellow Book Road** (⊠ 8315 La Mesa Blvd. ☎ 619/463–4900 ⊕ www.yellowbookroad.com), a huge surprise-filled bookstore. If you're lucky, you may meet an author of a popular children's book at this venue, which hosts signings and readings on a regular basis.

El Cajon

18 mi from San Diego, on I–8.

El Cajon is nestled in a valley surrounded on four sides by hills or mountains, hence its name, which means the big Box Valley. Now home to 95,000 people, El Cajon was part of a Mexican land grant where agriculture was the main activity. Following the discovery of gold to the east in Julian in 1869, El Cajon became a waystation for commerce and travelers. The city holds a satellite government for the east county, a major regional shopping center, an arts complex, and a downtown that is rediscovering its heritage.

The theater of the **East County Performing Arts Center** has 1,142 seats and good sight lines. The schedule has included George Winston, Olivia Newton John, Marvin Hamlish, and the San Diego Symphony Orchestra. ⊠ *210 E. Main St.* ☎ *619/440–2277* ⊕ *www.ecpac.com.*

Aircraft intended for display at the San Diego Aerospace Museum in Balboa Park are restored at **Gillespie Field,** a small general aviation airport in the East County. Recent projects have included restoration of a Convair F102A Delta Dagger, which was first built at the Convair facility in San Diego. ⊠ *Off Hwy. 67 at Prospect Ave.* ☎ *619/234–8291* ⊕ *www.aerospacemuseum.org/gillespie* ⊙ *Mon., Wed., and Fri. 8–3.*

The **Santee Drive-In** (⊠ 10990 N. Woodside Ave., Santee ☎ 619/448–7447 ⊙ Mon.–Thurs. 7:30 PM, Fri. and Sat. 8 PM) is one of the last drive-in theaters in the county and the only one that operates year-round. Many viewers bring lawn chairs or blankets and set up just in front or to the sides of their cars.

The **Heritage of the Americas Museum** is dedicated to the natural and human history of the Americas, which it displays in a variety of forms, including meteorites, tribal tools, and jewelry. The museum overlooks the Cuyamaca Community College campus. ⊠ *12110 Cuyamaca College Dr. W* ☎ *619/670–5194* ☞ *$3* ⊙ *Tues.–Fri. noon–4, Sat. noon–5.*

The storefront **Olaf Wieghorst Museum** celebrates the work of western artist Olaf Wieghorst, who produced lifelike bronzes, paintings, and watercolors that focus on the beauty and strength of horses. The artist lived in El Cajon during the mid-20th century. Many western film celebrities including Gene Autry, John Wayne, and Clint Eastwood have acquired Wieghorst works for their private collections. ⊠ *131 Rea Ave.* ☎ *619/590–3431* ⊕ *www. wieghorstmuseum.org* ⊡ *Donation* ⊙ *Tues.–Fri. 10–3.*

At **Summers Past Farms** you can stroll among the many herb and flower gardens, learn about fairies, flowers, and gardening or just play with the resident birds, dogs, cats, and rabbits that make this a great place for kids and adults to spend an idyllic afternoon. ⊠ *16502 Olde Hwy. 80, Flinn Springs* ☎ *619/390–1523* ⊕ *www.summerspastfarms.com* ⊡ *Free* ⊙ *Wed.–Sat. 9–5, Sun. 10–5.*

Cajon Speedway is a ⅜-mi professional track of the NASCAR Southwest Region featuring a variety of NASCAR-rated stock cars. Races are generally scheduled on Saturday evenings with qualifying laps starting at 5:15 and the first race at 6:45. There are occasional Friday and Sunday races. ⊠ *1888 Wing Ave., at Denny Ave., El Cajon 92020* ☎ *619/448–8900* ⊕ *www.cajonspeedway.com* ⊡ *$10.*

Where to Stay & Eat

$–$$$$ ✕ **Jasmine Bistro.** Flavors from China, Singapore, and Thailand mingle in every lovely dish that comes from the open kitchen at this restaurant tucked into Westfield Shoppingtown. Specialties include Crouching Tiger Hidden Dragon (sautéed lobster tail and tiger prawns), Malay prawns and scallops, and Thai hot basil shrimp. You can dine inside or out, but the patio has a view of the parking lot. ⊠ *315 Parkway Plaza* ☎ *619/588–8228* ⊟ *AE, D, DC, MC, V.*

¢–$ ✕ **Por Favor.** A popular dining spot in El Cajon's up-and-coming downtown, Por Favor presents a variety of interesting entrées including a chile relleno filled with shrimp, carne asada made with dried beef, and several versions of fajitas. Soup-bowl–size margaritas are a specialty. You can dine indoors or out in the large patio area. ⊠ *148 E. Main St.* ☎ *619/440–8228* ⊟ *AE, D, MC, V.*

$$–$$$ ▦ **Singing Hills Resort.** Established in 1955, Singing Hills Resort on 425 acres is all about golf, boasting one of the best championship facilities in San Diego County. Guest rooms are fairly basic, but have views of the mountains, the Dehesa Valley, and golf courses. This resort is owned by the Sycuan Indians, who also operate a nearby casino. ⊠ *3007 Dehesa Rd., 92019* ☎ *619/442–3425 or 800/457–5568* 🖷 *619/442–9574* ⊕ *www.singinghills.com* ➥ *102 rooms* ⚘ *Restaurant, dining room, some microwaves, refrigerators, 2 pools, outdoor hot tub, massage, 3 golf courses, 3 putting greens, 11 tennis courts, gym, bar, laundry facilities, business services, no-smoking rooms* ⊟ *AE, D, MC, V.*

¢–$$ ▦ **Best Western Continental Inn.** This modern motel is easily accessed off I-8 in downtown El Cajon. Bright rooms are simply furnished. Continental breakfast is included in the price. ⊠ *650 N. Mollison Ave., 92021* ☎ *619/442–0601* 🖷 *619/442–0152* ⊕ *www.bestwestern.com* ➥ *85 rooms, 12 suites* ⚘ *In-room data ports, some in-room hot tubs, some kitchenettes, microwaves, refrigerators, cable TV, pool, outdoor* *hot tub, gym, business services, meeting room, free parking, no-smoking rooms* ⊟ *AE, D, DC, MC, V* ⸍◎⸌ *CP.*

Shopping

Not your typical outlet mall, **Viejas Outlet Center** occupies a beautiful Indian-themed landscaped setting complete with an interactive fountain kids can play with. There are 57 stores including Big Dog, Gap, Nike, and Tommy Hilfinger. Eight food outlets include Rubios and McDonalds. There's free entertainment here throughout the year. ⊠ *5005 Willows Rd., Alpine* ☎ *619/659–2070* ⊕ *www.shopviejas.com* ⊘ *Mon.–Sat. 10–9, Sun. 10–7.*

East County A to Z

To research prices, get advice from other travelers, and book travel arrangements, visit www.fodors.com

PUBLIC TRANSPORTATION

San Diego Transit provides bus and trolley service to East County cities including La Mesa, El Cajon, and Santee. The Northeast Rural Bus System has service from the El Cajon Transit Center to Alpine, Harbison Canyon, and points east.

🔃 Bus Information **Northeast Rural Bus System (NERBS)** ☎ 800/858-0291. **San Diego Transit** ☎ 619/233-3004, 619/234-5005 TTY/TDD ⊕ www.sdcommute.com.

VISITOR INFORMATION

The Web site of La Mesa Village's merchants association has information about annual events and festivals, like Oktoberfest.

🔃 **La Mesa Village Merchants Association** ⊕ www.lmvma.com. **San Diego East County Visitors Bureau** ⊠ 5005 Willows Rd., #208, Alpine 91901 ☎ 619/445-0180 or 800/463-0669 ⊕ www.visitsandiegoeast.com

THE BACKCOUNTRY & JULIAN

The Cuyamaca and Laguna mountains to the east of Escondido—sometimes referred to as the backcountry by county residents—are favorite weekend destinations for hikers, nature lovers, stargazers, and apple-pie fanatics. Most of the latter group head to Julian, a historic mining town now better known for apple pie than for the gold once extracted from its hills. Nearby Cuyamaca Rancho State Park, once a luscious ancient oak and pine forest, burned completely in a 2003 fire.

The **Sunrise National Scenic Byway,** in the Cleveland National Forest, is the most dramatic approach to Julian—its turns and curves reveal amazing views of the desert from the Salton Sea all the way to Mexico. You can spend an entire day roaming these mountains; an early-morning hike to the top of Garnet Peak (mile marker 27.8) is the best way to catch the view. Springtime wildflower displays are spectacular, particularly along Big Laguna Trail from Laguna Campground. There are picnic areas along the highway at Desert View and Pioneer Mail.

On summer weekends you can view the heavens through a 21-inch telescope in the **Mount Laguna Observatory** (⊠ Morris Ranch Rd., off Sunrise Scenic Byway, Mt. Laguna ☎ 619/594–6182), which sits at an altitude of 6,100 feet. It's operated by San Diego State University at Mount Laguna.

Cuyamaca Mountains

An alternative route into the mountains is through **Cuyamaca Rancho State Park** (⊠ 12551 Rte. 79, Descanso 92016 ☎ 760/765–0755 ⊕ www. cuyamaca.statepark.org). The park spreads over 24,677 acres of open meadows, mountains, and oak woodlands. Cuyamaca Peak rises to 6,512 feet. Much of the park, including all of its infrastructure, burned during a wildfire in 2003 and the park was closed; no stopping along Highway 79 was permitted. Local volunteers commenced rebuilding early in 2004, hoping to get some areas of the park open by the year's end. Reconstruction of the 120 mi of hiking and nature trails, picnic areas, campgrounds, and museum is underway. However, even a drive through the park will reveal nature's healing processes as abundant seasonal wildflowers and other native plants emerge from the blackened earth in a breathtaking display. For an inspirational desert view, stop at the lookout about 2 mi south of Julian on Route 79; on a clear day you can see several mountain ranges in hues ranging from pink to amber stepped back behind the Salton Sea.

Behind a dam constructed in 1888, the 110-acre **Lake Cuyamaca** offers fishing, boating, picnicking, nature hikes, and wildlife watching. Anglers regularly catch trout, smallmouth bass, and sturgeon. A shaded picnic area occupies the lakeshore. Families can rent small motorboats, rowboats, canoes, and paddleboats by the hour. Free guided nature walks take place the first Sunday of the month along the 3.5-mi perimeter trail. Free fishing classes for kids are held Saturday at 10 AM. Fishing licenses and advice are available at the tackle shop. Two rental condominiums, 40 RV campsites with hookups, and 10 tent sites are available at Chambers Park on a first-come basis. ⊠ *15027 State Hwy. 79, Julian* ☎ *760/ 765–0515* ⊕ *www.lakecuyamaca.org* 🖾 *$6* ☉ *Daily dawn–dusk.*

Where to Eat

$ ✕ **Lake Cuyamaca Restaurant.** This tidy, lace-curtain lakefront café specializes in Austrian fare, highlights of which include a selection of schnitzels and wursts, plus several chicken and steak entrées. Austrian beers are are on tap. The restaurant, as well as the adjacent food market, are popular with anglers and locals. ⊠ *15027 Rte. 79, Julian* ☎ *760/765–0070* ▤ *AE, D, DC, MC, V.*

Julian, Santa Ysabel & Wynola

62 mi from San Diego to Julian, east on I–8 and north on Rte. 79.

Gold was discovered in the Julian area in 1869 and gold-bearing quartz a year later. More than $15 million worth of gold was taken from local mines in the 1870s. Today this mountain town retains some historic false-front buildings from its mining days. Many of the buildings along Julian's Main Street and the side streets date back to the gold-rush period; others are reproductions. When gold and quartz became scarce the locals turned

SAN DIEGO COUNTY'S CASINO COUNTRY

INCE THE STATE GRANTED 12 Native American tribes permission to operate casinos in greater San Diego, the county has become the undisputed casino capital of California. The casinos range from sprawling Las Vegas–style resorts, with big-name entertainment and golf courses, to small card rooms tucked away on rural crossroads. Although the gaming options may resemble what you might find in Las Vegas, the action is definitely different. The casinos stand alone on back roads, so it's not practical to travel from one to another. The big casinos—Viejas, Barona and Sycuan—are popular with local seniors, some Asian visitors to San Diego, and the tour bus crowd from the Los Angeles area. The three most central of these are described below followed by another found on North County backroads. More are on their way. Many casinos offer bus transport, so call before visiting and save on gas. Also, note that the gambling age is 21 years and over.

Viejas Casino and Turf Club (⊠ 5000 Willows Rd., Alpine ☎ 619/445–5400 ⊕ www.viejas.com) is a massive Native American–themed entertainment–shopping complex with the largest casino in San Diego County, but it has no hotel. It's just east of El Cajon and Lakeside off I–8. Viejas has 2,000 slot machines, plus blackjack, poker, bingo, pai gow, and off-track wagering. There are five restaurants and a cocktail lounge, and the Dream Catcher Showroom presents top-of-the-line entertainment. Weekends have Top 40 bands, Sunday is Big Band night, and big names include George Thorogood and Big Bad Voodoo Daddy. A Native American–theme factory outlet mall across from the casino has 57 shops, restaurants, and a landscaped amphitheater where evening shows are presented.

Barona Valley Ranch Resort and Casino (⊠ 1000 Wildcat Canyon Rd., Lakeside ☎ 619/443–2300 ⊕ www.barona.com) is an all-in-one western-style destination with gaming, hotel, restaurants, and golf course. In 2004 the resort was alcohol-free, pending approval of a liquor license. In the casino you'll find 2,000 video slot machines including progressives like Wheel of Fortune, 59 gaming tables including blackjack, a bingo hall, a poker room, and off-track betting. There are three restaurants including Barona Oaks Steakhouse, Branding Iron Cafe, and the Ranch House buffet. The 400-room Barona Valley Ranch hotel holds a fitness center, day spa, pool and outdoor whirlpool tub, business center, and meeting rooms. Adjacent is the well-regarded 18-hole Barona Creek Golf Club.

More compact than other area casinos, **Sycuan Casino** (⊠ 5469 Dehesa Rd., El Cajon ☎ 619/445–6002 ⊕ www. sycuan.com) has 2,000 slot machines, table games such as blackjack, poker, and pai gow, a bingo parlor, and off-track betting. The Showcase Theatre hosts top name acts such as Little Richard and Wayne Newton. On-site restaurants include Wachena Falls Cafe, Pearl of the Sea, and Paipa's Oasis buffet. The tribe also owns the nearby Singing Hills Resort and Country Club.

Tropically themed **Casino Pauma** (⊠ 777 Pauma Reservation Rd., Pauma Valley ☎ 760/742–2177), a huge tent surrounded by orange orchards in the Pauma Valley, has 850 slot machines, 24 gaming tables, a café, and two bar-lounges. In 2003 the casino announced plans to enlarge the facility, adding restaurants and lounges.

— Bobbi Zane

to growing apples and pears. During the fall harvest season you can buy fruit, sip cider, eat apple pie, and shop for antiques and collectibles. But spring is equally enchanting (and less congested), as the hillsides explode with wildflowers, lilacs, and peonies. More than 50 artists have studios tucked away in the hills surrounding Julian; they often show their work in local shops and galleries. The Julian area comprises three small crossroads communities: Santa Ysabel, Wynola, and historic Julian. You'll find bits of history, shops, and dining options in each community. Most visitors come to spend a day in town, but the hillsides support many small bed-and-breakfast establishments for those who want to linger longer.

The rundown-looking **Banner Queen Ranch Trading Post Gallery** is a remnant of an old gold mine dug into a hillside on Banner Grade, 5 mi east of Julian. A step inside reveals a wealth of contemporary art in what was the superintendent's home. Five rooms are filled with paintings, photos, sculpture, ceramics, stained glass (even some fire glass), and woven pieces by Julian artists. Prices range from $30 or less for photos and pottery to hundreds for paintings and sculptures by widely recognized artists such as James Hubbell and Bob Verdugo. ⊠ *36766 Hwy. 78, Julian* ☎ *760/765–2168* ☉ *Fri.–Sun. 1–5.*

One of the few places in North America where you can get an up-close view of the gray wolves that once roamed much of North America lies just outside Julian. Now an endangered species, the wolves are being ★ ☪ bred for release into the wild once again. The **California Wolf Center** holds 28 gray wolves, including nine rare Mexican grays and two people-friendly ambassador wolves. The animals are kept secluded from public view in 3-acre pens, but some may be seen by visitors during weekly educational tours. Private tours are available by appointment. ⊠ *Hwy. 79 at KQ Ranch Rd., Julian* ☎ *760/765–0030* ⊕ *www.californiawolfcenter.org* ▣ *$8, reservations required* ☉ *Tour Sat. 2 PM.*

☪ Five blocks east of the center of Julian, the **Eagle Mining Company** leads an hour-long tour of an authentic Julian gold mine. A small rock shop and gold-mining museum are also on the premises. ⊠ *C St., Julian* ☎ *760/765–0036* ▣ *$10* ☉ *Daily 10–3, weather permitting.*

☪ In Julian's heyday, mobs of gold miners invaded the tiny hamlet. When the mines played out, the gold miners left, leaving behind discarded mining tools and empty houses. Today the **Julian Pioneer Museum**, a 19th-century brewery, displays remnants of that time, including pioneer clothing, a collection of old lace, and old photographs of the town's historic buildings and mining structures. ⊠ *4th and Washington Sts.* ☎ *760/765–0227* ▣ *$2* ☉ *Apr.–Nov., daily 10–4; Dec.–Mar., weekends 10–4.*

> **off the beaten path**
>
> **JULIAN OPEN STUDIOS –** A group of professional artists can arrange private visits to the studios of member artists. Most studios are along Julian's scenic backroads. Advance reservations are required. ⊠ *Julian* ☎ *760/765–1774* ⊕ *www.julianstudios.org.*

The 1¼-mi trail through **Volcan Mountain Wilderness Preserve** passes through Engleman oak forest, native manzanita, and rolling mountain meadows to a panoramic viewpoint extending north all the way to Palomar Mountain. On a clear day you can see Point Loma in San Diego. At the entrance you pass through gates designed by local artist James Hubbell, who is known for his ironwork, wood carving, and stained glass. ✥ *From Julian take Farmer Rd. to Wynola Rd., go east a few yards, and then north on Farmer Rd.* ☎ *760/765–2300* ⊕ *www.volcanmt.org* ⛌ *Free* ☉ *Open daily.*

The Santa Ysabel Valley, where three Native American tribes live, looks pretty much the way the backcountry appeared a century ago, with sweeping meadows surrounded by oak-studded hillsides. The Indians run cattle here and operate small farms. In recent years, the valley's beautiful pasturelands have been threatened by development. However, in 2000 the Nature Conservancy acquired large portions of the valley to set aside as a nature preserve. The village of **Santa Ysabel**, 7 mi west of Julian, has several interesting shops. West of Santa Ysabel, tiny **Mission Santa Ysabel** (⊠ Rte. 79 ☎ 760/765–0810) is a late-19th-century adobe mission that continues to serve several local Native American communities.

Where to Stay & Eat

$$–$$$ ✕ **Julian Grille.** The menu at this casual restaurant inside a historic home appeals to a variety of tastes, including vegetarian. Chicken dishes are popular, as are steaks and the smoked pork chops served with applesauce. Lunch options include good burgers, whopping sandwiches, and soups. There's a tree-shaded dining area that is heated on cool evenings. ⊠ *2224 Main St., Julian* ☎ *760/765–0173* ⊟ *AE, D, MC, V* ☉ *No dinner Mon.*

$–$$ ✕ **Romano's Dodge House.** You can gorge on huge portions of antipasto, pizza, pasta primavera, sausage sandwiches, and seafood in a cozy, historic house. This is a casual, red-checker tablecloth kind of place. ⊠ *2718 B St., Julian* ☎ *760/765–1003* ⊟ *No credit cards* ☉ *Closed Tues.*

$$ ✕ **Pine Hills Lodge Dinner Theater.** Weekend musical and comedy shows staged by the Pine Hills Players include a barbecue dinner with an all-you-can-eat salad bar. The historic theater was built as a gymnasium for world heavyweight champion Jack Dempsey. The lodge has a pub, which is popular with locals. ⊠ *2960 La Posada Way, Julian* ☎ *760/765–1100* ⊟ *AE, MC, V.*

¢ ✕ **Julian Tea and Cottage Arts.** Sample finger sandwiches, scones topped with whipped cream, and lavish sweets during afternoon tea inside the Clarence King House, built by Will Bosnell in 1898. Sandwiches, soups, and other lunch items are also available. ⊠ *2124 3rd St., Julian* ☎ *760/765–0832* ☉ *No dinner* ⊟ *AE, D, MC, V.*

¢–$ ✕ **Wynola Pizza Express.** Locals come to this casual indoor–outdoor restaurant for delicious, single portion pizzas such as pesto pizza, Thai chicken pizza, and tostada pizza. Other items include chili, lasagna, and sandwiches. Entertainers usually perform on weekends in the adjacent Red Barn, or in fine weather, outdoors. ⊠ *4355 Hwy. 78, Wynola* ☎ *760/765–1004* ⊟ *AE, MC, V.*

★ $ ✕ **Julian Pie Company.** The apple pies that made Julian famous come from the Smothers family bakery, which occupies a one-story house on

Main Street. In pleasant weather you can sit on the front patio and watch the world go by while savoring a slice of hot pie topped with homemade cinnamon ice cream or, at lunch time, a sandwich. Many of the apples used in the pies, from Dutch Apple to Apple Mountain Berry Crumb, are grown in Julian. Soup and sandwiches are served at lunchtime at the Julian location. The larger Santa Ysabel bakery just makes the pies. ⌧ *2225 Main St., Julian* ☎ *760/765–2449* ⌧ *21976 Hwy. 79, Santa Ysabel* ☎ *760/765–2400* ⊕ *www.julianpie.com* ▭ *MC, V.*

★ **$$$–$$$$** 🔲 **Orchard Hill Country Inn.** On a hill above town, this lodge and five Craftsman-style cottages have a sweeping view of the countryside. The luxurious backcountry accommodations are decorated with antiques, original art, and handcrafted quilts. The cottage suites have see-through fireplaces, double whirlpool tubs, and wet bars—even private patios or balconies. Guests gather in the evening for wine and hors d'oeuvres in the Great Room, where a fire blazes in the stone fireplace. Breakfast is included. Dinner is served nightly except Monday and Wednesday to guests only at an extra charge. ⌧ *Washington St., Julian 92036* ☎ *760/765–1700 or 800/716–7242* 🖷 *760/765–0290* ⊕ *www.orchardhill. com* 🗗 *10 rooms, 12 suites* 🜪 *Dining room, in-room data ports, some in-room hot tubs, some minibars, cable TV, in-room VCRs with movies, hiking, wine bar, meeting room; no smoking* ▭ *AE, MC, V* ❙◯❙ *BP.*

$$–$$$ 🔲 **Butterfield Bed and Breakfast.** Built in the 1930s, this inn on a 4-acre hilltop is cordial and romantic with knotty pine ceilings, Laura Ashley accents, and a gazebo in the backyard. Rooms, ranging from small to ample, have fireplaces or woodstoves, CD players, and private entrances. The property is beautifully landscaped with terraced rose gardens. The innkeepers can arrange for a horse and carriage to take you to Julian for dinner or sightseeing. Full breakfast and afternoon refreshments are included. ⌧ *2284 Sunset Dr., Julian 92036* ☎ *760/765–2179* 🖷 *760/765–1229* ⊕ *www.butterfieldbandb.com* 🗗 *5 rooms* 🜪 *Dining room, cable TV with movies; no a/c* ▭ *AE, D, MC, V* ❙◯❙ *BP.*

$$–$$$ 🔲 **Wikiup Bed and Breakfast.** Best known for its herd of 18 llamas, Wikiup appeals to animal lovers. There are angora goats, a donkey, a parrot, plus assorted dogs and cats to keep you company. The inn consists of a main contemporary cedar-and-brick structure, with cedar paneling, modern Danish furnishings, and high, open-beam ceilings holding sky lights. Guest rooms in the main house and a pair of cottages have private entrances, fireplaces, and outdoor hot tubs for stargazing. The innkeepers offer full and half-day llama treks to guests. A full breakfast is included in the price. ⌧ *1645 Whispering Pines Dr., 92036* ☎ *760/765–1890 or 800/526–2725* 🖷 *760/765–1512* ⊕ *www.wikiupbnb.com* 🗗 *4 rooms* 🜪 *Microwaves, refrigerators, some in-room hot tubs, library, lounge, no-smoking rooms; no room phones, no room TVs* ▭ *AE, MC, V.*

$–$$$ 🔲 **Julian Gold Rush Hotel.** Built in 1897 by freed slave Albert Robinson and his wife Margaret, the over 100-year-old hotel is Julian's only designated national landmark. Current owners Steve and Gig Ballanger have brought the old place into the 21st century, but the ambience is thoroughly Victorian. Smallish rooms hold antique furnishings and colorful quilts. Cottage accommodations have private entrances and fireplaces. The innkeepers serve afternoon tea and invite guests to sit on the porch.

Full breakfast is included in the price. ⊠ *2032 Main St., Julian 92036* ☎ *760/765–0201 or 800/734–5854* ⊕ *www.julianhotel.com* ⌁ *14 rooms, 2 suites △ Breakfast room, fans, lobby lounge; no a/c, no room phones, no room TVs* ▤ *AE, MC, V.*

$–$$$ ⊡ **All Seasons Lodge.** A convenient stop along the highway through the Cuyamaca Mountains, this bed-and-breakfast occupies a wooded setting that qualifies it for natural backyard wildlife habitat designation. Large rooms and suites are designed for two couples or families. Most have kitchens, private entrances, fireplaces, and hot tubs. The lodge is well suited for children; toys and videos are available. ⊠ *569 K.Q. Ranch Rd., Julian 92036* ☎ *760/765–4880 or 877/495–4880* ⊕ *www. allseasonslodge.com* ⌁ *2 rooms, 3 suites △ Fans, some in-room hot tubs, kitchenettes, cable TV, in-room VCRs, hiking, library; no a/c* ▤ *AE, MC, V* ◉| *CP.*

$ ⊡ **Apple Tree Inn.** This basic motel is set alongside busy Highway 78 in the Wynola area, about 3 mi west of Julian. Simply furnished ground-floor rooms with private entrances surround a parking lot and swimming pool with gazebo. ⊠ *4360 Rte. 78, Wynola 92070* ☎ *760/765– 0222* ⊕ *www.julianappletreeinn.com* ⌁ *16 rooms △ Cable TV, pool, some pets allowed* ▤ *AE, MC, V.*

¢–$ ⊡ **Julian Lodge.** A replica of a late-19th-century Julian hotel, this two-story lodge calls itself a bed-and-breakfast, but instead of having a common area in which guests can gather, there's a small lobby, large enough for four or five guests. The rooms and public spaces are furnished with antiques; on chilly days you can warm yourself at the large stove in the lobby. Buffet-style continental breakfast is included in the price. ⊠ *4th and C Sts., Julian 92036* ☎ *760/765–1420 or 800/542–1420* ⊕ *www. julianlodge.com* ⌁ *23 rooms △ Dining room, cable TV, library, piano, no-smoking rooms* ▤ *AE, MC, V* ◉| *CP.*

Shopping

Julian, Wynola, and Santa Ysabel have a number of unique shops that are open weekends, but midweek hours vary considerably. In autumn locally grown apples, pears, nuts, and cider are available in town and at a few roadside stands. The best apple variety produced here is a Jonagold, a hybrid of Jonathan and Golden Delicious.

The **Birdwatcher** (⊠ 2775 B St., Julian ☎ 760/765–1817) offers wild-bird items, including birdhouses, birdseed, hummingbird feeders, plus bird-themed accessories such as jewelry, apparel, novelties, and guidebooks for serious birders. The **Julian Bell, Book and Candle** (⊠ 2007 Main St., Julian ☎ 760/765–2377 or 800/664–5851) displays an unusual collection of handcrafted candles and accessories.

Once Upon a Time (⊠ Rte. 78 and Rte. 79, Santa Ysabel ☎ 760/765– 1695) comprises three tiny cottages, each devoted to antiques, florals, gifts, and Christmas decorations. **Santa Ysabel Art Gallery** (⊠ Rte. 78 and Rte. 79, Santa Ysabel ☎ 760/765–1676) shows watercolors, stained glass, sculptures, and other creations by local artists.

★ **King Leo Chocolate Factory and Store** (⊠ 4510 Rte. 78, Wynola ☎ 760/ 765–0188) makes and sells creamy chocolates and fudges, including seasonal flavored items such as apple pie and butterscotch fudge. **Meyer Orchards** (⊠ 3962 Rte. 78, Wynola ☎ 760/765–0233) carries different kinds of local apples, including a few heirloom varieties such as Northern Spy and Arkansas Black.

The Backcountry & Julian A to Z

To research prices, get advice from other travelers, and book travel arrangements, visit www.fodors.com

CAR TRAVEL

A loop drive beginning and ending in San Diego is a good way to explore this area. You can take the Sunrise National Scenic Byway (sometimes icy in winter) from I–8 to Route 79 and return through Cuyamaca Rancho State Park (also icy in winter). If you're only going to Julian (a 75-minute trip from San Diego in light traffic), take either the Sunrise Byway or Route 79, and return to San Diego via Route 78 past Santa Ysabel to Ramona and Route 67; from here I–8 heads west to downtown.

VISITOR INFORMATION

🛈 Julian Chamber of Commerce ⊠ 2129 Main St., Julian 92036 ☎ 760/765–1857 ⊕ www. julianca.com.

THE DESERT

In most spring seasons the stark desert landscape east of the Cuyamaca Mountains explodes with colorful wildflowers. The beauty of this spectacle, as well as the natural quiet and blazing climate, lures many tourists and natives each year to Anza-Borrego Desert State Park, less than a two-hour drive from central San Diego.

For hundreds of years the only humans to linger in the area were Native Americans from the Cahuilla and Kumeyaay tribes, who made their winter homes in the desert. It was not until 1774, when Mexican explorer Captain Juan Bautista de Anza first blazed a trail through the area seeking a shortcut from Sonora, Mexico, to San Francisco, that Europeans had their first glimpse of the oddly enchanting terrain.

The desert is best visited from October through May to avoid the extreme summer temperatures. Winter temperatures are comfortable, but nights (and sometimes days) are cold, so bring a warm jacket.

Numbers in the margin correspond to points of interest on the San Diego North County map.

Anza-Borrego Desert State Park

❼ *88 mi from downtown San Diego (to park border due west of Borrego Springs), east on I–8, north on Rte. 67, east on Rte. S4 and Rte. 78, north on Rte. 79, and east on Rtes. S2 and S22. Alternately take I–8 east to Hwy. 79, follow Hwy. 79 to Julian, where it intersects with Hwy. 78, take Hwy. 78 east to Yaqui Pass Rd., which will take you to Borrego Springs.*

Today more than 600,000 acres are included in the Anza-Borrego Desert State Park, making it the largest state park in the contiguous United States. It is also one of the few parks in the country where people can camp anywhere. No campsite is necessary; follow the trails and pitch a tent wherever you like. Rangers and displays at an excellent underground **Visitors Information Center** (✉ 200 Palm Canyon Dr., Borrego Springs ☎ 760/767–5311, 760/767–4684 wildflower hotline ⊕ www. anzaborrego.statepark.org ⊗ Oct.–May, daily 9–5; June–Sept., weekends and holidays 9–5) can point you in the right direction.

Five hundred mi of paved and dirt roads traverse the park, and you are required to stay on them so as not to disturb the ecological balance. There are also 110 mi of hiking and riding trails that allow you to explore canyons, capture scenic vistas, and tip-toe through fields of wildflowers in spring. In addition, 28,000 acres have been set aside in the eastern part of the desert near Ocotillo Wells for off-road enthusiasts. General George S. Patton conducted field training in the Ocotillo area to prepare for the World War II invasion of North Africa.

Many of the park's sites can be seen from paved roads, but some require driving on dirt roads. Rangers recommend using four-wheel-drive vehicles when traversing dirt roads. Carry the appropriate supplies: shovel and other tools, flares, blankets, and plenty of water. Canyons are susceptible to flash flooding; inquire about weather conditions before entering.

Wildflowers that typically bloom from January through mid-March attract thousands of visitors. A variety of factors including rainfall and winds determine how extensive the bloom will be in a particular year. However, good displays of low-growing sand verbena can be found along Airport Road and DiGeorgio Road. Most of the desert plants can also be seen in the demonstration desert garden at the visitor center.

Narrows Earth Trail is a short walk off Route 78, east of Tamarisk Grove, that reveals the many geologic processes involved in forming the desert canyons. Water, wind, and faulting created the commanding vistas along **Erosion Road**, a self-guided, 18-mi auto tour along Route S22. The **Southern Emigrant Trail** follows the route of the Butterfield Stage Overland Mail through the desert.

At **Borrego Palm Canyon,** a few minutes west of the Anza-Borrego Visitors Information Center, a 1½-mi trail leads to a small oasis with a waterfall and palms. The Borrego Palm Canyon campground is one of only two developed campgrounds with flush toilets and showers in the park. (The other is Tamarisk Grove Campground, at the intersection of Route 78 and Yaqui Pass Road; sites at both are $17, $26 with hookup at Borrego Palm Canyon.)

Geology students from all over the world visit the Fish Creek area of Anza-Borrego to explore a famous canyon known as **Split Mountain** (✉ Split Mountain Rd., south from Rte. 78 at Ocotillo Wells), a narrow gorge with 600-foot perpendicular walls that was formed by an ancestral stream. Fossils in this area indicate that a sea covered the desert floor at one time. A 2-mi nature trail west of Split Mountain rewards hikers with a good view of shallow caves created by erosion.

Borrego Springs

31 mi from Julian, east on Rte. 78 and Yaqui Pass Rd., and north on Rte. S3.

A quiet town with a handful of year-round residents, Borrego Springs is emerging as a laid-back destination for desert-lovers, where you can enjoy activities such as hiking, nature study, golf, tennis, horseback riding, and mountain-bike riding from September through June when temperatures hover in the 80s and 90s. Even during the busier winter season, Borrego Springs feels quiet. There are three golf resorts, two bed-and-breakfast inns, and a growing community of winter residents, but the laid-back ambience prevails. If winter rains cooperate, Borrego Springs puts on some of the best wildflower displays in the low desert.

Where to Stay & Eat

$–$$ ✕ **Carlee's Bar & Grill.** The local watering hole, Carlee's is the place to go any night of the week. A large dimly-lit room holds both bar and dining tables. The menu lists pasta and pizza in addition to old-fashioned entrées such as liver and onions, lamb chops, and mixed grill. Dinners come with soup or salad. ⊠ *660 Palm Canyon Dr.* ☎ *760/767–3262* ⊟ *AE, D, MC, V.*

$–$$ ✕ **The Pavilion at Rams Hill.** Colorful original paintings add to the Southwestern style of this spot, where specialties include grilled items such as salmon with red pesto sauce and Cornish game hens. Open-air dining on the deck looks out to mountain views and the adjacent golf course. Brunch is served Sunday. ⊠ *1881 Rams Hill Rd.* ☎ *760/767–5000* ⊟ *AE, MC, V.*

¢–$ ✕ **Bernard's.** In a single large room with a wall of windows overlooking the Mall, chef-owner Bernard offers casual dining with a unique Alsatian flavor (Alsatia is a French region that has some influence from Germany, which is just across the border). Try sauerkraut Alsatian style, plus daily regional Alsatian preparations of duck, pork, and roast leg of lamb. ⊠ *501 Palm Canyon Dr.* ☎ *760/767–5666* ⊟ *AE, D, MC, V* ☉ *Closed Sun.*

$$$$ 🏨 **La Casa del Zorro.** This serene resort owned by San Diego's prominent Copley family pampers guests with spectacular desert scenery, luxurious accommodations, and gracious and superb service. You need walk only a few hundred yards from your room to find yourself in a quiet desert garden surrounded by ocotillo and cholla or at night alone under the stars. Accommodations range from ample standard rooms to private casitas with their own pools or private garden outdoor hot tubs. The elegant restaurant puts on a good Sunday brunch. La Casa schedules a number of wine, music, and astronomy weekends throughout the year. In summer, prices are deeply discounted. ⊠ *3845 Yaqui Pass Rd., Borrego Springs 92004* ☎ *760/767–5323 or 800/824–1884* 🖷 *760/767–5963* ⊕ *www.lacasadelzorro.com* ⏏ *48 rooms, 12 suites, 19 1- to 4-bedroom casitas* � *Restaurant, room service, BBQs, fans, in-room data*

Fodor's Choice ★

ports, some in-room hot tubs, minibars, microwaves, cable TV with movies, putting green, 6 tennis courts, 5 pools, exercise equipment, fitness classes, hair salon, 3 outdoor hot tubs, massage, bicycles, archery, boccie, croquet, hiking, horseback riding, horseshoes, Ping-Pong, shuffleboard, volleyball, lounge, children's programs (ages 7–12), concierge, business services, meeting rooms, airport shuttle, free parking, no-smoking rooms ⊟ AE, D, MC, V.

★ **$$–$$$** 🏨 **Borrego Valley Inn.** Desert gardens of mesquite, ocotillo, and creosote surround adobe southwestern-style buildings of this inn. Spacious rooms with plenty of light are decorated in Indian-design fabrics and hold original art. Furnishings include lodgepole beds with down comforters and sarape-stripe bedspreads, walk-in showers with garden views, and double futons facing corner fireplaces. Every room opens out to its own enclosed garden with chaises, chairs, and table. Friendly innkeepers serve a tasty continental breakfast and invite guests to enjoy the courtyard desert garden while dining. The inn is very pet friendly; the innkeepers even have bowls of water in the lobby. ⊠ *405 Palm Canyon Dr., Borrego Springs 92004* 🕾 *760/767–0311 or 800/333–5810* 🖨 *760/767–0900* ⊕ *www.borregovalleyinn.com* 🛏 *14 rooms, 1 suite* ⟁ *In-room data ports, cable TV, some kitchenettes, microwaves, refrigerators, 2 pools, 2 hot tubs, pets allowed (fee); no smoking* ⊟ *D, MC, V* 🍽 *CP.*

$$–$$$ 🏨 **Palms at Indian Head.** Spectacular desert views of the Anza-Borrego Desert State Park can be had from this small romantic hotel. Large guest rooms are decorated in hand-crafted, Southwest lodgepole furniture and original art by local artists. Two rooms have fireplaces. When it was called the Old Hoberg Resort, celebrities Marilyn Monroe, Bing Crosby, and Lon Chaney Jr., among others, vacationed here. ⊠ *2220 Hoberg Rd., 92004* 🕾 *760/767–7788 or 800/519–2624* 🖨 *760/767–9717* ⊕ *www. thepalmsatindianhead.com* 🛏 *12 rooms* ⟁ *Restaurant, microwaves, refrigerators, pool, outdoor hot tub, bar; no room phones, no smoking* ⊟ *AE, D, DC, MC, V.*

$–$$ 🏨 **Borrego Springs Resort and Country Club.** This low-key resort is surrounded by expansive desert views, visible from every room. Rooms are simply furnished with contemporary oak and upholstered pieces. Amenities include hair dryers and in-room coffeemakers. The restaurant on premises serves lunch and dinner daily except Monday. ⊠ *1112 Tilting T Dr., Borrego Springs 92004* 🕾 *760/767–5700 or 888/826–7734* 🖨 *760/767–5710* ⊕ *www.borregospringsresort.com* 🛏 *66 rooms, 34 suites* ⟁ *Restaurant, in-room data ports, some kitchenettes, microwaves, refrigerators, 27-hole golf course, putting green, 6 tennis courts, 2 pools, exercise equipment, outdoor hot tub, bar, meeting rooms, free parking, no-smoking rooms* ⊟ *AE, D, MC, V.*

$–$$ 🏨 **Palm Canyon Resort.** One of the largest properties around Anza-Borrego Desert State Park includes a hotel, an RV park, a restaurant, and recreational facilities. Decor is western style and some rooms have balconies. ⊠ *221 Palm Canyon Dr., Borrego Springs 92004* 🕾 *760/ 767–5341 or 800/222–0044* 🖨 *760/767–4073* ⊕ *www.pcresort.com* 🛏 *60 rooms, 1 suite* ⟁ *Restaurant, in-room data ports, refrigerators, cable TV with movies, pool, gym, outdoor hot tub, lounge,* *shop, laundry facilities, meeting room, no-smoking rooms* ▤ *AE, D, DC, MC, V.*

Sports & the Outdoors

The 18-hole **Rams Hill Country Club** (☎ 760/767–5000) course is open to the public. The greens fee is $85–$95, which includes a mandatory cart. **Roadrunner Club** (☎ 760/767–5374) has an 18-hole par-3 golf course. The greens fee is $25.

off the beaten path

OCOTILLO WELLS STATE VEHICULAR RECREATION AREA – The sand dunes and rock formations at this 78,000-acre haven for off-road enthusiasts are fun and challenging. Camping is permitted throughout the area, but water is not available. The only facilities are in the small town (really no more than a corner) of Ocotillo Wells. ⊠ *Rte. 78, 18 mi east from Borrego Springs Rd., Ocotillo Wells* ☎ *760/767–5391.*

The Desert A to Z

To research prices, get advice from other travelers, and book travel arrangements, visit www.fodors.com

BUS TRAVEL

The Northeast Rural Bus System connects Julian, Borrego Springs, Agua Caliente, and many other small communities with La Mesa, 15 mi east of downtown San Diego. There's no service Sunday or Monday.

🚍 Bus Information The **Northeast Rural Bus System** (NERBS) ☎ 800/858-0291.

CAR TRAVEL

From downtown San Diego, take I–8 east to Route 67 north, to Route 78 east, to Route 79 north, to Routes S2 and S22 east.

VISITOR INFORMATION

🏙 **Anza-Borrego Desert State Park** ⊠ 200 Palm Canyon Dr., Borrego Springs 92004 ☎ 760/767-5311 ⊕ www.anzaborrego.statepark.org. **Borrego Springs Chamber of Commerce** ⊠ 622 Palm Canyon Dr., Borrego Springs 92004 ☎ 760/767-5555 ⊕ www.borregosprings.org. **State Park Reservations** ☎ 800/444-7275 ⊕ www.reserveamerica.com. **Wildflower Hotline** ☎ 760/767-4684.

NORTH OF THE BORDER

CHULA VISTA & SAN YSIDRO

Chula Vista and San Ysidro mark the southernmost communities in San Diego County. Chula Vista is transforming from a small town with limited attractions to a much larger community that is well worth visiting due to the U.S. Olympic Training Center and Coors Amphitheatre. The border town of San Ysidro, where thousands cross back and forth daily, is working to lose its shady image with construction of the Las Americas shopping/hotel/dining complex.

Numbers in the margin correspond to points of interest on the San Diego North County map.

Chula Vista

10 mi south of San Diego via I–5.

This suburban San Diego community of more than 200,000 residents is the second largest city in San Diego County and the seventh fastest growing city in the nation. Comprised of 52 square mi, the city stretches from the southern shore of San Diego Bay east to the San Miguel Mountains. It has bayside parks, a harbor with two marinas, and coastal wetlands, master planned communities, and the crowning U.S. Olympic Training Center and Coors Amphitheater. The town's name means "beautiful view" in Spanish. It's one of several towns along I–5 that link downtown San Diego with Tijuana, just across the Mexican border.

The **U. S. Olympic Training Center** is a year-round, warm-weather facility with sport venues and support facilities for nine Olympic sports: archery, canoe–kayak, cycling, field hockey, rowing, soccer, softball, tennis, and track and field. The visitor center at this 150-acre facility tells the history of the Olympics using displays and videos. Free tours are offered every day during business hours. The tour follows an elevated visitor promenade called the Conrad N. Hilton Olympic Path from which you can see athletes in training for the Olympic Gold. A gift shop is also on-site. ⊠ *2800 Olympic Pkwy., Chula Vista 91915* ☎ *619/482–6222* ⊕ *www.usolympicteam.com* ☐ *Free* ☉ *Mon.–Sat. 10–3, Sun. 11–3.*

☺ **Chula Vista Nature Interpretive Center.** Plants and animals native to the San Diego bay are on exhibit at this zoo and aquarium in the 316-acre Sweetwater Marsh National Wildlife Refuge. Major displays include the Shark and Ray Experience, comprised of a 4,000-gallon touch-tank containing five species of sharks and rays; a free swimming tank with underwater viewing areas; and a number of hands-on displays. Eagle Mesa, which holds both a golden eagle and bald eagle, was installed in 2004. Hands-on exhibits focus on marine life as well as other animal life typical of salt marshes; there's a walk-through shore bird aviary, as well as six aviaries of other native birds, including hawks, owls, and falcons. One and a half miles of trails lead to San Diego Bay. Free interpretive tours are given on Wednesday, Saturday, and Sunday at 2 PM. Park in the small lot off I–5 at E St. and get the free shuttle to the center. ⊠ *1000 Gunpowder Point Dr., Chula Vista* ☎ *619/409–5900* ⊕ *www.chulavistanaturecenter.org* ☐ *$3.50; includes round-trip shuttle* ☉ *Tues.–Sun. 10–5. Shuttle runs 10–4.*

Knott's Soak City U.S.A. is a 32-acre waterpark with 22 water rides including four high-speed slides, six tube slides, and six body slides for action-packed and waterlogged fun. There are also plenty of wading pools, a family raft ride, and tamer slides for the littlest visitors. You can even choose to just lounge around in a deck chair or an innertube. Food is readily available. Be certain to bring sunscreen. ⊠ *2252 Entertainment Circle, Chula Vista* ☎ *619/661–7373* ⊕ *www.knotts.com/soakcity* ☐ *$23.95* ☉ *Daily 10 AM–6 PM.*

Rohr Park and Miniature Train cuts a green swath in between Chula Vista and Bonita. It boasts open space for picnicking, a playground, an equestrian ring, a 3.3-mi hiking trail, and a working, scale model steam engine that you can ride the second weekend of each month. The Chula Vista Live Steamers club operates it 1 PM–3 PM. ⊠ *4548 Sweetwater Rd., Chula Vista* ☎ *619/267–5675* ☜ *Free* ⊙ *Daily dawn–dusk.*

Where to Stay & Eat

🕒 **$$–$$$$** ✕ **Bob's on the Bay.** You can watch boats come in and out of the San Diego Bay marina while you eat on an indoor–outdoor patio. House specials are steak and seasonal lobster, catfish, mahi mahi, halibut, and king crab legs. The Sunday brunch is popular and the restaurant has a kids menu. ⊠ *570 Marina Pkwy.* ☎ *619/476–0400* ▭ *AE, D, MC, V.*

¢–$$ ✕ **Galley at the Marina.** The view is the attraction at this popular seafood eatery, but there are also bargains on the eclectic menu. The restaurant offers all-you-can-eat fish-and-chips on Thursday night and spaghetti on Tuesday night. Other options include Jamaican chicken with mango sauce and chicken fried steak. ⊠ *550 Marina Pkwy.* ☎ *619/422–5714* ▭ *AE, D, MC, V.*

$ 🏨 **Holiday Inn Express.** This southwest-style motel just west of I–805 at the southern end of Chula Vista is 4 mi from the Mexican border at San Ysidro. Continental breakfast is included in the price. ⊠ *4450 Main St., 91911* ☎ *619/422–2600* 🖷 *619/425–4605* ⊕ *www.holiday-inn.com* 📮 *118 rooms* ♿ *In-room data ports, refrigerators, microwaves, cable TV with movies, pool, outdoor hot tub, laundry facilities, business services, no-smoking rooms; no a/c* ▭ *AE, D, DC, MC, V.*

San Ysidro

19 mi south of San Diego via I–5.

San Ysidro, perhaps the world's busiest border crossing in the world with more than 30 million vehicles crossing in 2002, is 14 mi south of San Diego via I–5. The town is busy, somewhat dirty, and just a bit scary with unsavory looking characters and a heavy Border Patrol and law enforcement presence. In recent years, Tijuana has moved north to meet the border and you can soon walk across a footbridge to Mexico and to the better restaurants south of the border. In the early 20th century, San Ysidro was called the Little Landers Colony after a "back to the land" settlement begun by William Smythe, which eventually included 150 inhabitants. The town was renamed San Ysidro in honor of the patron saint of farmers. According to legend, the saint was a virtuous farmer whose fields were plowed by angels.

The easiest, most convenient way to get to San Ysidro is via the San Diego Trolley; the trip takes about 30 minutes from downtown San Diego. If you're driving, you can park at **Border Station Parking** (⊠ 4570 Camino de la Plaza ☎ 619/451–6200 ⊕ www.gototijuana.com/bs), a secure facility that's open 24 hours and runs a shuttle bus to Mexico.

★ Set right against the international border, **Las Americas** is a open-air multicultural retail and entertainment complex with 75 shops, including two duty-free outlets. A second phase of the project, which will eventually include the International Gateway, a footbridge over the Tijuana River directly into Mexico, was scheduled to open in 2004 or 2005. Still to come are more outlet stores, a library and cultural center, and a hotel. One of the largest outlets in the world, the **Nike Factory Store** (☎ 619/428–8859) sells shoes, clothing, and accessories. You'll find trendy fashions at **Guess Factory Store** (☎ 619/934–7216). Clothing and fragrances are among the finds at **Tommy Hilfiger Company Store** (☎ 619/934–7182). ⊠ *4211 Camino de la Plaza* ☎ *619/934–8400* ⊕ *www.lasamericas.com* 🖅 *Free* ☉ *Weekdays 10–9, Sat. 10–8, Sun. 10–6.*

Where to Stay

¢ 🖭 **Best Value Inn.** This three-story standard hotel has a shopping center adjacent, and Mexican and fast-food restaurants ½ mi away. ⊠ *930 W. San Ysidro Blvd., 92173* ☎ *619/690–2633* 🖳 *619/690–1360* ⊕ *www. bestvalueinn.com* 🖅 *75 rooms* ⚷ *In-room data ports, refrigerators, cable TV, pool* ⊟ *AE, D, MC, V.*

¢ 🖭 **Travelodge.** This four-story chain hotel is just a block from the international border. A shuttle to Mexico is available. A continental breakfast is included in the rates. ⊠ *643 E. San Ysidro Blvd., 92173* ☎ *619/428–2800* 🖳 *619/428–8136* ⊕ *www.travelodge.com* 🖅 *68* ⚷ *In-room data ports, cable TV with movies, laundry facilities* ⊟ *AE, D, DC, MC, V.*

North of the Border A to Z

To research prices, get advice from other travelers, and book travel arrangements, visit www.fodors.com

BUS TRAVEL

🚌 Bus Information **Chula Vista Transit** ☎ 619/233-3004 ⊕ www.sdcommute.com.

CAR TRAVEL

Both Chula Vista and San Ysidro can be reached by car. For Chula Vista take I–5 south from San Diego 8 mi to Highway 54. Go east to reach downtown and the Otay Lakes area. To reach the Chula Vista Nature Center, continue south on I–5 to E Street and turn west to the gate. To reach San Ysidro, continue south on I–5 8 mi; follow signs to the international border.

TROLLEY TRAVEL

The San Diego Trolley Blue Line offers a convenient means of reaching the international border. You can catch the trolley at any downtown San Diego location for the 30-minute ride to the border. The last north-bound trolley leaves San Ysidro at 1 AM nightly.

🚋 San Diego Trolley **San Diego Transit** ☎ 619/233-3004 ⊕ www.sdcommute.com.

VISITOR INFORMATION

🚩 **Chula Vista Chamber of Commerce** ⊠ 233 4th Ave., 91910 ☎ 619/425-4444 ⊕ www. chulavistaconvis.org. **San Ysidro Chamber of Commerce** ⊠ 663 E. San Ysidro Blvd., 92173 ☎ 619/428-1281 ⊕ www.sanysidrochamber.org.

TIJUANA, PLAYAS DE ROSARITO & ENSENADA

8

BEST SECOND COMING OF A SIN CITY
History, art exhibits, and films at
Tijuana's civilized Centro Cultural ⇨*p.233*

BEST SUNSET STROLL
The pier at Rosarito Beach Hotel ⇨*p.240*

BEST SOMBRERO ALTERNATIVE
Piñatas from Mercado Hidalgo ⇨*p.238*

BEST NEIGHBORHOOD WATCH
Spotting whales on Ensenada's coast ⇨*p.249*

BEST BOUNTY OF THE SEA
Fish taco stands at Ensenada's
Mercado de Mariscos ⇨*p.243*

GREATEST SOUND AND FURY
Rowdy revelry at Hussong's Cantina ⇨*p.247*

By Maribeth
Mellin

SEPARATED FROM MAINLAND MEXICO BY THE SEA OF CORTEZ, the Baja California peninsula stretches 1,625 km (1,000 mi) from Tijuana to Los Cabos. The desert landscape harbors isolated fishing retreats, Prohibition-era gambling palaces, world-class golf courses, and one of the busiest international borders in the world. Adventurers delight in kayaking alongside migrating gray whales, diving with hammerhead sharks, and hiking to hidden cave paintings.

Tijuana, just 29 km (18 mi) south of San Diego at the international border, is home to more than 2 million people, making it more populous than the entire remainder of the peninsula. It's also the most popular destination for day-trippers from San Diego, who come for the souvenir shopping, sports events, and sophisticated Mexican dining.

On the Pacific Coast of *Baja Norte* (meaning north Baja), travelers stream down the Transpeninsular Highway (Highway 1) to the beach community of Rosarito (and Ensenada, 75 km [47 mi] south of Rosarito), in search of a more laid-back Mexico. Here, English is spoken as freely as Spanish, and the dollar is as readily accepted as the peso. Between Baja's towns, the landscape is unlike any other, with cacti growing beside the sea, and stark mountains and plateaus rising against clear blue skies.

It's possible to visit all three cities in a long, busy day. Begin by bypassing Tijuana and heading straight for the toll road to Playas de Rosarito, about a 40-mi drive south. Stop at the Rosarito Beach Hotel for breakfast, take a walk on the beach in front of the hotel, and check out a few of the shops on Boulevard Benito Juárez. Return to the toll road south of the hotel and continue south for 45 mi to Ensenada. Take your time along this stretch of road, and exit at Salsipuedes and El Mirador to admire the view.

In Ensenada, park at the Plaza de Marina on the waterfront and do your exploring on foot. Spend an hour or two wandering along Avenida López Mateos and its side streets, where you may find bargains on leather goods and jewelry in high-quality shops. Culture-seekers should tour the Riviera del Pacifico, a former gambling palace built in the 1920s. Return to the waterfront for a quick run through the fish market, and try to be back on the road by early afternoon. On the way, stop for a lobster lunch in Puerto Nuevo, about 10 mi south of Rosarito.

If you finish lunch by mid-afternoon, you'll be able to reach Tijuana by evening. Once in the city, park in a lot by Calle 2A, the road that ties the highway to the border; walk up Calle 2A to Avenida Revolución, finish your souvenir shopping, and have dinner at a restaurant on the way back to your car. It's smart to wait until after 7 to cross the border, when rush-hour traffic has diminished.

A more leisurely tour would include an overnight stay in Playas de Rosarito. By doing so, you can spend the morning in Tijuana seeing the sights and pricing possible purchases. Check into your hotel in the early afternoon, and then visit the beach or the shops. Dine in town or in Puerto Nuevo, get to bed early, and start off to Ensenada in the morning. Spend a half day there, and then head back to Tijuana, where you can pick up that last tacky souvenir from a vendor along the border traffic lines.

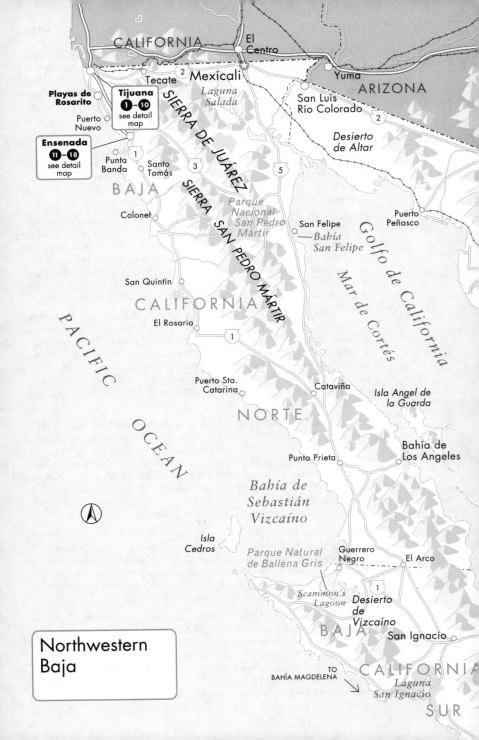

CALIFORNIA

El Centro

Tecate

2 Mexicali

Yuma

ARIZONA

Playas de Rosarito

Tijuana **1**–**10** see detail map

Laguna Salada

San Luis Río Colorado

2

Puerto Nuevo

Ensenada **11**–**18** see detail map

Punta Banda

1

Santo Tomás

3

Desierto de Altar

5

SIERRA DE JUÁREZ

Parque Nacional San Pedro Mártir

San Felipe

Bahía San Felipe

Puerto Peñasco

Colonet

SIERRA SAN PEDRO MÁRTIR

B A J A

Golfo de California

San Quintín

C A L I F O R N I A

Mar de Cortés

El Rosario

1

PACIFIC

OCEAN

Puerto Sta. Catarina

Cataviña

Isla Angel de la Guarda

N O R T E

Punta Prieta

Bahía de Los Angeles

Bahía de Sebastián Vizcaíno

Isla Cedros

Parque Natural de Ballena Gris

Guerrero Negro

El Arco

1

Scammon's Lagoon

Desierto de Vizcaíno

San Ignacio

B A J A

Northwestern Baja

C A L I F O R N I A

TO BAHÍA MAGDELENA

BAHÍA MAGDELENA

Laguna San Ignacio

S U R

Exploring Tijuana, Playas de Rosarito & Ensenada

Border city Tijuana has close ties to the southwestern United States, while Playas de Rosarito and Ensenada, on Baja's northern Pacific coast, are practically extensions of southern California. South of Ensenada the natural side of Baja appears in desolate mountain ranges and fields of cacti and boulders.

If you plan to drive the peninsula, you must have Mexican auto insurance. Always carry water, and make sure your vehicle is in good condition. Keep your gas tank at least half full at all times—remote stations may be out of gas just when you need it. For the most part, the Carretera Transpeninsular is well maintained, although some areas are marred by potholes or gravel and rocks. In addition, the route often has only two lanes, and sharing them with semis and speeding buses can be unnerving.

About the Restaurants

Restaurants as a rule are low-key and casual, though in Tijuana and Ensenada you're as apt to find upscale continental dining rooms as you are *taquerías* (taco stands). Dress is accordingly informal, and reservations aren't generally required. Moderate prices prevail, though some places add a 15% service charge to the bill.

About the Hotels

You can find great deals at small, one-of-a-kind hostelries. A few out-of-the-way and budget-price hotels don't accept credit cards; some of the more lavish places add a 10%–20% service charge to your bill. Most properties also raise their rates for the December–April high season (and raise them even higher for the days around Christmas). Expect to pay 25% less during the off-season. Many hotels offer midweek discounts of 30%–50% off the weekend rates.

Reservations are a must on holiday weekends for most coastal towns. Some hotels require a minimum two-night stay; resorts might also have minimum-night requirements in high season. Several hotels in Baja have direct toll-free numbers; although the operator may answer in Spanish, there's usually someone who speaks English in the office. Hotels don't always keep their fax machines on, so you may have to call to ask a staffer to connect it. If making a reservation on the Web, ask for a confirmation and print it out before you leave. Note also that several U.S. agencies book reservations at Baja hotels, condos, and time-share resorts, which may cost less than hotels if you're traveling with a group of four or more.

WHAT IT COSTS				
	$$$$	**$$$**	**$$**	**$**	**¢**
RESTAURANTS	over $25	$15–$25	$10–$15	$5–$10	under $5
HOTELS	over $250	$150–$250	$75–$150	$50–$75	under $50

Restaurant prices are for a main course at dinner excluding tax and tip. Hotel prices are for two people in a standard double room in high season, based on the European Plan (EP, with no meals) and excluding service and 17% tax.

Timing

Baja's climate is extreme, thanks to its desert locale. Temperatures in Tijuana, Ensenada, and Rosarito are similar to those in southern California.

TIJUANA

29 km (18 mi) south of San Diego.

Tijuana is the only part of Mexico many people see—a distorted view of the country's many cultures. Before the city became a gigantic recreation center for southern Californians, it was a ranch populated by a few hundred Mexicans. In 1911 a group of Americans invaded the area and attempted to set up an independent republic; they were quickly driven out by Mexican soldiers. When Prohibition hit the United States in the 1920s and the Agua Caliente Racetrack and Casino opened (1929), Tijuana boomed. Americans seeking alcohol and gambling flocked across the border, spending freely and fueling the region's growth. Tijuana became the entry port for what some termed a "sinful, steamy playground" frequented by Hollywood stars.

Then Prohibition was repealed, Mexico outlawed gambling, and Tijuana's fortunes declined. Although the flow of travelers from the north slowed to a trickle, Tijuana still captivated those in search of the sort of fun not allowed back home. Drivers heading into Baja's wilderness passed through downtown Tijuana, stopping along Avenida Revolución and its side streets for supplies and souvenirs.

When the toll highway to Ensenada was finished in 1967, travelers bypassed the city. But Tijuana began attracting residents from throughout Latin America at the same time, and the population mushroomed from a mere 300,000 in 1970 to more than 2 million today. As the government struggles to keep up with the growth and demand for services, thousands live without electricity, running water, or adequate housing in squatters' villages along the border. Petty crime is a significant problem; moreover, the area has become headquarters for serious drug cartels, and violent crime—reaching the highest levels of law enforcement and business—is booming. You're unlikely to witness a shooting or some other frightening situation, but be mindful of your surroundings, stay in the tourist areas, and guard your belongings.

City leaders, realizing that tourism creates jobs and bolsters Tijuana's fragile economy, are working hard to attract visitors. Avenida Revolución, the main street in the commercial Centro district, is lined with shopping arcades, restaurants, and bars. The Zona Río district—with its impressive Centro Cultural, several shopping complexes, fine restaurants, and fashionable discos—competes with Avenida Revolución for your attention. A massive 10-story-high cathedral dedicated to the Virgin of Guadalupe is under construction in this neighborhood. The Avenida Paseo de los Héroes, one of the city's main thoroughfares, cuts through the Zona Río, running parallel to the dry Río Tia Juana (Tia Juana River).

The avenue is notable for its large statues of historic figures, including Abraham Lincoln.

The city has an international airport; a fine cultural center that presents international music, dance, and theater groups; and deluxe high-rise hotels. The demand for business-class services has increased with the growth of *maquiladoras* (foreign manufacturing plants). There's even a nascent opera company. Although it's no longer considered just a bawdy border town, the city remains best known as a place for an intense, somewhat exotic daylong adventure.

And then there's shopping. From the moment you cross the border, people will approach you or call out and insist that you look at their wares. If you drive, workers will run out from auto-body shops to place bids on new paint or upholstery for your car. All along Avenida Revolución and its side streets, shops sell everything from tequila to Tiffany-style lamps. If you intend to buy food in Mexico, get the U.S. customs list of articles that are illegal to bring back so that your purchases won't be confiscated.

What to See

② Avenida Revolución. This infamous strip, lined with shops and restaurants that cater to uninhibited travelers, has long been Tijuana's main tourism zone. Shopkeepers call out from doorways, offering low prices for garish souvenirs and genuine folk art treasures. Many shopping arcades open onto Avenida Revolución; inside the front doors are mazes of stands with low-price pottery and other crafts.

★ ☾ ❼ Centro Cultural (CECUT). The cultural center was designed by architects Manuel Rosen and Pedro Ramírez Vásquez, who also created Mexico City's Museo Nacional de Antropología. The stark, low-slung, tan buildings fronted by the globelike Omnimax Theater are beloved landmarks. The center's Museo de las Californias provides an excellent overview of Baja's history, geography, and flora and fauna. The Omnimax shows films on a rotating schedule; some are in English. The film *Marine Oasis: The Riches of the Sea of Cortez* has fabulous underwater scenes. Exhibitions on art and culture change frequently, and the center's stage hosts performances by international groups. ✉ *Paseo de los Héroes and Av. Mina, Zona Río* ☎ 664/687–9600 ⊕ *www.cecut.gob.mx* ✉ *Museum $2, museum and Omnimax Theater $4* ☉ *Tues.–Sun. 10–6.*

❹ L.A. Cetto Winery. Most of Baja's legendary wineries are in the Ensenada region, but Tijuana does have this branch of one of Mexico's finest wineries. You can tour the bottling plant and sample the wines while watching a video on operations in the Guadalupe Valley. The shop's prices are far lower than those in regular liquor stores. ✉ *Cañon Johnson 2108, at Av. Constitución Sur, Centro* ☎ 664/685–3031 or 664/685–1644 ✉ *$2 for tour and wine tasting* ☉ *Mon.–Sat. 10–5.*

☾ ❺ Mundo Divertido. This popular amusement park includes a miniature golf course, batting cages, bumper boats, go-carts, a roller coaster, and a video-game parlor. Admission is free, and the rides cost just a few pesos.

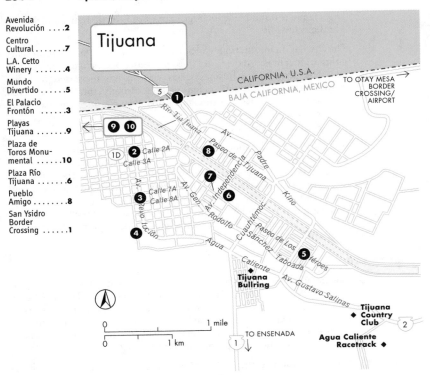

⊠ *Calle Velasco 2578, at Paseo de los Heroes, Zona Río* ☎ 664/634–3213 *or* 664/634–3214 ☾ *Weekdays noon–8:30, weekends 11–9:30.*

❸ El Palacio Frontón. For many years, the magnificent Moorish-style Jai Alai Palace hosted fast-paced jai alai games. The sport has declined in popularity, however, and the palacio is now occasionally used for boxing contests and concerts. ⊠ *Av. Revolución at Calle 7, Centro* ☎ 664/634–3213 ☾ *Open only for special events.*

❾ Playas Tijuana. Along the oceanfront is this mix of modest and expensive residential neighborhoods, with a few restaurants and hotels. The isolated beaches are visited mostly by residents.

❿ Plaza de Toros Monumental. The "Bullring by the Sea" is at the northwest corner of the beach area near the U.S. border. It's occasionally used for summer concerts. ☎ 664/688–0125.

❻ Plaza Río Tijuana. The area's largest shopping complex has good restaurants, department stores, hundreds of shops, and the Cineopolis multiplex theater that usually shows English-language films. Shade trees and flowers line the sidewalks that lead from the complex to the Centro Cultural. ⊠ *Paseo de los Héroes across from Centro Cultural, Zona Río* ☎ 664/684–0402.

❽ Pueblo Amigo. This entertainment center resembles a colonial village, with stucco facades and tree-lined paths leading to a domed gazebo. The complex includes a hotel, several restaurants and clubs, a huge grocery store, and a large branch of the Caliente Race Book, where gambling on televised sporting events is legal. Things get lively at night. ⊠ *Paseo de Tijuana between Puente Mexico and Av. Independencia, Zona Río.*

❶ San Ysidro Border Crossing. Locals and tourists jostle each other along the pedestrian walkway through the Viva Tijuana dining and shopping center and into the center of town. Artisans' stands line the walkway and adjoining streets, offering a quick overview of the wares to be found all over town.

Where to Stay & Eat

$$–$$$$ ✕ **Palmazul.** A mural of Baja's cave paintings and a tiled map of the peninsula reflect this restaurant's devotion to all things Baja. Seafood highlights include chocolate clams, red snapper, and shrimp prepared with fruit or chile salsas. Amid the quail, venison, and duck entrées are a few classics such as marinated *arrachera* beef. The wine list has several excellent Baja varieties by the glass; you can sip in the dining room or in the cantina, which is often filled with young professionals. ⊠ *Blvd. Salinas 11154, Colonia Aviación* ☎ *664/622–9773* ⊟ *MC, V.*

$$–$$$ ✕ **El Faro de Mazatlán.** Fresh fish prepared simply is the hallmark of one of Tijuana's best seafood restaurants. This is the place to try ceviche, abalone, squid, and lobster without spending a fortune. Frequented by professionals, the dining room is a peaceful spot for a long, leisurely lunch. Appetizers and soup are included in the price of the meal. ⊠ *Blvd. Sánchez Taboada 9542, Zona Río* ☎ *664/684–8883* ⊟ *MC, V.*

$–$$$ ✕ **Cien Años.** In this Spanish colonial–style restaurant, dishes include crêpes
Fodor'sChoice   filled with *huitlacoche* (fungus that grows on corn), shrimp with nopal
★   cactus, and tender beef with avocado and cheese. An unusual blend of flavors—tamarind, Mexican oregano, mango, poblano chilies—distinguishes the taste of each dish, including the *queso fundido* (melted cheese wrapped in tortillas). ⊠ *Blvd. Sánchez Taboada 10451, Zona Río* ☎ *664/634–7262* ⊟ *AE, MC, V.*

$–$$$ ✕ **La Diferencia.** It's a cozy restaurant that stands out for its bold use of unusual ingredients. If you're feeling adventuresome, go for the rabbit *mixiote,* with the shredded meat marinated in achiote sauce (ground annatto seeds and bitter orange juice) and wrapped in maguey cactus leaves. Also good are the squash-blossom or creamy poblano soups, the chile relleno stuffed with *huitlacoche* (corn fungus), and the beef fillet with guajillo chili strips. ⊠ *Blvd. Sánchez Taboada 10611, Zona Río* ☎ *664/634–7078* ⊟ *AE, MC, V.*

$–$$$ ✕ **Señor Frog's.** Kitschy license plates, posters, and Mexican crafts cover the walls of this wildly popular restaurant, where waiters encourage patrons to eat, drink, and sing along with the blaring music. Known for its barbecued ribs and chicken, the kitchen also prepares good standards such as tacos and *carne asada* (grilled strips of marinated meat). ⊠ *Pueblo Amigo, Paseo Tijuana 60, Zona Río* ☎ *664/682–4962* ⊟ *AE, MC, V.*

$–$$ ✕ **Chiki Jai.** The Monje family moved to Tijuana from Madrid in 1947, bringing Basque and Spanish cuisine to a tiny restaurant by El Palacio Frontón. They specialize in paella but also have a way with calamari. Meals start with hot homemade bread and Roquefort cheese—the perfect accompaniment to a jug of sangria. ⊠ *Av. Revolución 1388, Centro* ☎ *664/685–4955* ▭ *No credit cards.*

¢–$$ ✕ **Carnitas Uruapan.** You'll need to take a cab to this festive restaurant, where patrons mingle at picnic tables and toast one another to live mariachi music. The main attraction here is *carnitas* (marinated pork roasted over an open pit), sold by weight and served with homemade tortillas, salsa, cilantro, guacamole, and onions. ⊠ *Blvd. Diaz Ordaz 12650, at Fracc. El Prado, Otay Mesa* ☎ *664/681–6181* ▭ *No credit cards.*

★ ¢–$ ✕ **La Especial.** At the foot of the stairs that run down to an underground shopping arcade you'll find the best place in the tourist zone for homestyle Mexican cooking. The gruff, efficient waiters shuttle platters of carne asada, enchiladas, and burritos, all with a distinctive flavor found only at this busy, cavernous basement dining room. ⊠ *Av. Revolución 718, Centro* ☎ *664/685–6654* ▭ *MC, V.*

$$–$$$ ✕☷ **Real Del Mar Residence Inn by Marriott.** Golfers and escapists relish this all-suites hotel a short drive south of Tijuana. The suites' living rooms have vaulted brick ceilings, fireplaces, and kitchens. The on-site Rincón San Román restaurant ($–$$$) is excellent and attracts diners from Tijuana and Rosarito. It nods to both France and Mexico; for instance, you could have beef with either an escargot garlic sauce or a chipotle chili sauce. The spa provides ample diversion for nongolfers. ⊠ *Ensenada toll road, Km 19.5, 22710* ☎ *661/631–3670, 800/803–6038 in U.S.* 🖷 *661/631–3677* ⊕ *www.realdelmar.com.mx* ↴ *75 suites* ♨ *2 restaurants, snack bar, room service, in-room safes, some refrigerators, cable TV, 18-hole golf course, pool, gym, massage, spa, bar, laundry service, meeting rooms, no-smoking rooms* ▭ *AE, MC, V* ⊠ *CP.*

$$–$$$ ☷ **Grand Hotel.** The twin, mirrored towers of the hotel and a high-rise office building are Tijuana's most ostentatious landmarks. The rooms could use modernization, but are large; ask for one with good city views. It's an ideal spot for business travelers and anyone looking for a touch of luxury. The hotel mall has an Internet café. A stay here gets you access to the nearby Tijuana Country Club 18-hole golf course. ⊠ *Blvd. Agua Caliente 4558, Zona Río 22420* ☎ *664/681–7000 or 800/ 343–7825 in U.S.* 🖷 *664/681–7016* ⊕ *www.grandhoteltij.com.mx* ↴ *412 rooms, 10 suites* ♨ *3 restaurants, room service, in-room safes, minibars, cable TV, golf privileges, 2 tennis courts, pool, gym, bar, nightclub, shops, laundry service, business services, meeting rooms, travel services* ▭ *AE, MC, V.*

$$–$$$ ☷ **Lucerna.** Once one of the most charming hotels in Tijuana, the Lucerna is now showing its age. Still, the lovely gardens, large pool surrounded by palms, touches of tile work, and folk art lend the hotel a distinct Mexican character. ⊠ *Paseo de los Héroes 10902, at Av. Rodríguez, Zona Río 22320* ☎ *664/633–3900, 800/582–3762 in U.S.* 🖷 *664/634–2400* ⊕ *www.hotel-lucerna.com.mx* ↴ *156 rooms, 9 suites* ♨ *Restaurant, coffee shop, room service, cable TV, pool, gym,* *nightclub, laundry service, Internet, business services, meeting rooms, travel services* ☰ *AE, MC, V.*

$$ ▦ **Fiesta Inn.** It's a quirky hotel between two boulevards, on a landscaped island and next to the thermal spring for the 1920s-era Agua Caliente Spa. Rooms are modern and comfortable. The Vita Spa has individual and couples' hot tubs fed from the healing spring; it also has spa treatments at reasonable prices. ✉ *Paseo de los Héroes 18818, Zona Río 22320* ☏ *664/634–6360, 800/343–7821 in U.S.* ☏ *664/634–6912* ⊕ *www.fiestainn.com* ↪ *122 rooms, 5 suites* ⚘ *Restaurant, coffee shop, room service, in-room data ports, in-room fax, cable TV, pool, gym, hot tubs, massage, spa, laundry service, Internet, meeting rooms, no-smoking rooms* ☰ *AE, MC, V.*

¢–$ ▦ **La Villa de Zaragoza.** This brown stucco motel's strong suit is location; it's near El Palacio Frontón and around the corner from Avenida Revolución. The neighborhood can be noisy, though, so request a room at the back. Some rooms have kitchenettes; the guarded parking lot is a major plus. The motel is used by tour groups, so book ahead for holidays and weekends. ✉ *Av. Madero 1120, Centro 22000* ☏ *664/685–1832* ☏ *664/685–1837* ⊕ *www.hotellavilla.biz* ↪ *66 rooms* ⚘ *Restaurant, room service, cable TV, some kitchenettes, bar, no-smoking rooms* ☰ *MC, V.*

Nightlife & the Arts

Nightlife

Tijuana has toned down its Sin City image, but there are still plenty of boisterous bars on Avenida Revolución. Locals prefer the classier nightclubs in the Zona Río. Tijuana's discos usually have strict dress codes—no T-shirts, jeans, or sandals allowed.

Baby Rock (✉ Calle Diego Rivera 1482, Zona Río ☏ 664/634–1313), an offshoot of a popular Acapulco disco, attracts a young, hip crowd. The **Hard Rock Cafe** (✉ Av. Revolución 520, between Calles 1 and 2, Centro ☏ 664/685–0206) has the same menu and decor as other branches of the ubiquitous club.

Businessmen (there's a definite shortage of women here) favor **María Bonita** (✉ Camino Real hotel, Paseo de los Héroes 10305, Zona Río ☏ 664/633–4000). Designed after the L'Opera bar in Mexico City, this small clublike tavern serves several brands of fine tequila along with beer and mixed drinks. You're encouraged to play dominoes, chess, and card games at the tables.

Tijuana has its own brand of beer, thanks to the Czech brew master at
★ **Tijuana Brewery Company/La Cervecería** (✉ Blvd. Fundadores 2951, Centro ☏ 664/638–8662). The European-style pub serves Tijuana Claro and Tijuana Oscura, the light and dark beers brewed in the glassed-in brewery beside the bar. *Botanes*, or appetizers, include chiles rellenos and smoked tuna. Bands play some nights.

The Arts

Tijuana's cultural scene is thriving, with visiting music and theater groups from around the world performing at the Centro Cultural. **El Lugar del**

Nopal (✉ Callejón Cinco de Mayo, at Calle 6, Centro ☎ 664/685–1264) hosts evening performances by jazz groups, classical guitarists, and other performers. You can usually reach an English speaking person on the phone.

Sports & the Outdoors

Bullfighting

Skilled matadors from throughout Mexico and Spain face down bulls in Tijuana. Admission to bullfights varies, depending on the fame of the matador and the location of your seat—try for one in the shade. Fights are held at **El Toreo de Tijuana** (✉ Blvd. Agua Caliente, Zona Río ☎ 664/686–1510 ⊕ www.bullfights.org) most Sundays at 4:30, May through September. Ticket prices range from $15–$50. In July and August you can see bullfights at the **Plaza de Toros Monumental** (✉ Ensenada Hwy., Playas Tijuana ☎ 664/686–1219 ⊕ www.bullfights.org) Sunday at 4:30. Expect to pay $15–$50.

Shopping

The Avenida Revolución shopping area spreads across Calle 2 to a pedestrian walkway leading from the border. Begin by checking out the stands along this walkway. You may find that the best bargains are closer to the border; you can pick up your piñatas and serapes on your way out of town. Between Calles 1 and 8, Avenida Revolución is lined with establishments that are stuffed with crafts and curios. Bargaining is expected on the streets and arcades, but not in the finer shops.

More than 40 stands display crafts from around Mexico at **Bazaar de Mexico** (✉ Av. Revolución, at Calle 7, Centro). **Importaciones Sara** (✉ Av. Revolución 635, Centro ☎ 664/688–0488) sells imported perfumes and fine clothing at attractive prices. High-quality furnishings and art are tastefully displayed at **Mallorca** (✉ Calle 4, at Av. Revolución, Centro ☎ 664/688–3502). **El Vaquero** (✉ Av. Revolución 1006, Centro ☎ 664/685–5236) is a dependable place to buy leather jackets, boots, and saddles. The shops in **Plaza Revolución** (✉ Calle 1, at Av. Revolución, Centro) sell well made crafts.

You can find great buys on fashionable clothing and shoes at the **Plaza Río Tijuana** (✉ Paseo de los Héroes 96 and 98, Zona Río ☎ 664/684–0402) center. **Sanborns** (✉ Av. Revolución at Calle 8, Centro ☎ 664/688–1462) has beautiful crafts from throughout Mexico, an excellent bakery, and chocolates from Mexico City. The **Tijuana Tourist Terminal** (✉ Av. Revolución, between Calles 6 and 7, Centro ☎ 664/683–5681) is a one-stop center with clean restrooms. The nicest folk-art store, **Tolán** (✉ Av. Revolución 1471, between Calles 7 and 8, Centro ☎ 664/688–3637), carries everything from antique wooden doors to ceramic miniature village scenes.

Market

★ The **Mercado Hidalgo** (✉ Av. Independencia, at Av. Sánchez Taboada, 5 blocks east of Av. Revolución, Zona Río) is Tijuana's municipal market, with rows of fresh produce, some souvenirs, and Baja's best selection of piñatas.

PLAYAS DE ROSARITO

29 km (18 mi) south of Tijuana.

What was once a suburb of Tijuana has become a separate self-governed municipality. The region attracted considerable attention when 20th Century Fox built a permanent movie-production studio on the coastline south of town to film the mega-success *Titanic*. Today, the complex doubles as a theme park and a working studio.

Meanwhile, Rosarito's population, now about 100,000, has been growing steadily. The main drag, alternately known as the Old Ensenada Highway and Boulevard Benito Juárez, reflects the unrestrained growth and speculation that have both helped and harmed Rosarito. The street is packed with restaurants, bars, and shops in a jarring juxtaposition of building styles. The building boom has slowed, however, and the town's boosters are attempting to beautify the boulevard.

Southern Californians use Rosarito as a weekend getaway, and the crowd is far from subdued—the town's on the spring break circuit. The police do their best to control the revelers, but spring and summer weekend nights can be outrageously noisy. But hedonism shares the bill with healthier pursuits. Surfers, swimmers, and sunbathers enjoy the beach, which stretches from the power plant at the north end of town to about 8 km (5 mi) south. Horseback riding, jogging, and strolling are popular along this uninterrupted strand, where whales swim within viewing distance on their winter migration. Americans and Canadians continue to swell the ranks in vacation developments and gated retirement communities.

Sightseeing consists of strolling along the beach or down Boulevard Benito Juárez's collection of shopping arcades, restaurants, and motels. Nearly everyone stops at the landmark Rosarito Beach Hotel. It was built during Prohibition and has huge ballrooms, tiled fountains and stairways, murals, and a glassed-in pool deck overlooking the sea. A wooden pier stretches over the ocean; on calm days, there's no better place to watch the sun set than from the café tables along its glassed-in edges.

Museo Wa-Kuatay. Rosarito's history is illustrated in exhibits on the Kumiai Indians, the early missions, and ranching in the region at this small museum. ⊠ *Blvd. Juárez, next to the Rosarito Beach Hotel* ☎ *No phone* 🖼 *Free* ⊘ *Tues.–Sun. 9–5.*

☺ **Foxploration.** Fox Studios has expanded its operation to include a film-oriented theme park. You learn how films are made by visiting one set that resembles a New York street scene and another filled with props from *Titanic*. Exhibits on filming, sound-and-light effects, and animation are both educational and entertaining, and Fox's most famous films are shown in the large state-of-the-art theater. The park includes a children's playroom where kids can shoot thousands of foam balls out of air cannons, a food court with U.S. franchises, and a large retail area.

✉ *Old Ensenada Hwy., Km 32.8* ☎ *661/614–9444, 866/369–2252 in U.S.* ⊕ *www.foxploration.com* ▣ *$9–$12* ⊗ *Wed.–Fri. 9–5:30, weekends 10–6:30.*

Galería Giorgio Santini. Baja's finest painters and sculptors display their work in this architecturally stunning gallery. Stop by for a glass of wine or an espresso in the coffee shop, and learn something about Baja's vibrant art scene. ✉ *Old Ensenada Hwy., Km 40* ☎ *661/614–1459* ⊕ *www.giorgiosantini.com* ▣ *Free* ⊗ *Thurs.–Tues. 11–8.*

Where to Stay & Eat

★ **$$–$$$** ✕ **La Leña.** The cornerstone restaurant of the Quinta Plaza shopping center, La Leña is spacious and impeccably clean, with tables spread far enough apart for privacy. Try any of the beef dishes, especially the tender carne asada with tortillas and guacamole or the steak and lobster combo. ✉ *Quinta Plaza, Blvd. Juárez 2500* ☎ *661/612–0826* ▭ *MC, V.*

$–$$$ ✕ **El Nido.** A dark, wood-paneled restaurant with leather booths and a large central fireplace, this is one of Rosarito's oldest eateries. Diners unimpressed with newer, fancier places come here for mesquite-grilled steaks and grilled quail from the owner's farm in the Baja wine country. ✉ *Blvd. Juárez 67* ☎ *661/612–1430* ▭ *No credit cards.*

$–$$$ ✕ **El Patio.** Although it's amid the bustle of the Festival Plaza complex, this tasteful, colonial-style restaurant is the best spot for a relaxed, authentic Mexican meal. The aromas of chilies, mole, and grilled meats spark the appetite. Try the grilled quail, shrimp crêpes, or chicken with poblano sauce. The bar is a good place to enjoy a cocktail away from the street-side crowds. ✉ *Festival Plaza, Blvd. Juárez 1207* ☎ *661/612–2950* ▭ *MC, V.*

¢–$ ✕ **La Flor de Michoacán.** Michoacán-style (deep fried) carnitas, served with homemade tortillas, guacamole, and salsa, are the hallmark of this rustic Rosarito landmark, established in 1950. The tacos, *tortas* (sandwiches), and tostadas are great. Takeout is available. ✉ *Blvd. Juárez 291* ☎ *661/612–1858* ▭ *No credit cards* ⊗ *Closed Wed.*

¢–$ ✕ **Tacos El Yaqui.** For true down-home Mexican cooking, nothing beats this taco stand. Carne asada tacos with fresh corn tortillas are superb— the perfect fix for late-night munchies. The stand is clean, and the cooks use purified water. ✉ *Calle de la Palma, off Blvd. Juárez, across from Rosarito Beach Hotel* ☎ *No phone* ▭ *No credit cards.*

$$–$$$ 🏨 **Rosarito Beach Hotel and Spa.** Charm rather than comfort is the main reason for staying here. The rooms in the oldest section have hand-painted wooden beams and heavy dark furnishings. The more modern rooms in the tower have air-conditioning and pastel color schemes. ✉ *Blvd. Juárez s/n, south end of town* 🕭 *Box 430145, San Diego, CA 22710* ☎ *661/612–0144, 800/343–8582 in U.S.* ⊕ *www.rosaritobeachhotel.com* ⇝ *180 rooms, 100 suites* ♨ *2 restaurants, in-room safes, tennis court, 2 pools, gym, spa, beach, racquetball, bar, shops, playground, laundry service; no a/c in some rooms* ▭ *MC, V.*

$$ 🏨 **Festival Plaza.** The Festival is the perfect place if you have unrestrained fun in mind. The motel-like rooms are in an eight-story building beside the road and bars. A central courtyard serves as a concert stage, playground, and party headquarters. The casitas close to the beach are the quietest accommodations and have small hot tubs as well as living rooms with sofa beds. The villas just south of Rosarito have full kitchens. ⊠ *Blvd. Juárez 1207, 22710* ☎ *661/612–2950, 800/453–8606 in U.S.* 🖷 *661/612–0124* ⊕ *www.festivalplaza.com* ⤸ *203 rooms, 5 suites, 7 casitas, 13 villas* ♧ *6 restaurants, cable TV, pool, 2 hot tubs, 7 bars, dance club, shops* ⊟ *MC, V.*

$$ 🖵 **Las Rocas.** This white hotel with blue-tile domes would be the most romantic lodging in town if only it were renovated. The least expensive rooms are small; larger quarters have fireplaces and microwaves. All rooms have ocean views, and the pool and whirlpool seem to spill into the Pacific. An excellent spa offers reasonably priced state-of-the-art treatments. ⊠ *Old Ensenada Hwy., Km 38.5, 22710* ☎ *661/614–0357, 888/527–7622 in U.S.* 🖷 *661/614–0360* ⊕ *www.lasrocas.com* ⤸ *40 rooms, 34 suites* ♧ *2 restaurants, some kitchenettes, cable TV, 2 pools, exercise equipment, hot tub, massage, spa, beach, 2 bars* ⊟ *MC, V.*

$ 🖵 **Los Pelicanos Hotel.** Guests return annually to their favorite rooms in this small hotel by the beach. Rooms without ocean views are inexpensive; rates are higher for quarters on the top floors. Some rooms have little outside light. The restaurant is a local favorite for sunset cocktails. ⊠ *Calle Ebano 113, 22710* ☎ *661/612–0445 or 661/612–1757* ⤸ *39 rooms* ♧ *Restaurant, cable TV, bar* ⊟ *AE, MC, V.*

Nightlife

Rosarito's many restaurants keep customers entertained with live music, piano bars, or *folklórico* (folk music and dance) shows, and the bar scene is hopping as well. Drinking-and-driving laws are stiff. If you drink, take a cab or assign a designated driver. The police also enforce laws that prohibit drinking in the streets; confine your revelry to the bars.

The **Festival Plaza** (⊠ Blvd. Juárez 1207 ☎ 661/612–2950, 661/612–2950 cantina) presents live concerts on the hotel's courtyard stage most weekends. In the hotel complex are El Museo Cantina Tequila, dedicated to the art of imbibing tequila and stocked with more than 130 brands of the fiery drink. Rock & Roll Taco is an on-site taco stand that's also the town's largest (and most rambunctious) dancing and drinking hangout.

Papas and Beer (⊠ On beach off Blvd. Juárez near Rosarito Beach Hotel ☎ 661/612–0444) draws a young, energetic crowd for drinking and dancing on the beach and small stages. **Rene's Sports Bar** (⊠ Carretera Transpeninsular, Km 28 ☎ 661/612–1061) attracts a somewhat quiet, older crowd; the restaurant isn't great, but a few pool tables, TVs broadcasting sporting events, and a convivial gaggle of gringos make the bar a great hangout.

There's a lot going on at night at the **Rosarito Beach Hotel** (⊠ Blvd. Juárez s/n ☎ 661/612–0144): live music at the ocean-view Beach Comber Bar; a Mexican Fiesta on Friday and Saturday nights; and occasional live bands and dances in the cavernous ballroom.

Sports & the Outdoors

Golf

The **Real del Mar Golf Club** (✉ 18 km [11 mi] south of border on Ensenada toll road ☎ 661/631–3670) has 18 holes overlooking the ocean. Greens fees are $59 Monday through Thursday and $69 Friday through Sunday. Golf packages are available at some Rosarito Beach hotels.

Horseback Riding

You can hire horses at the north and south ends of Boulevard Juárez and on the beach south of the Rosarito Beach Hotel for $10 per hour. If you're a dedicated equestrian, ask about tours into the countryside, which can be arranged with the individual owners.

Surfing

Surfers head south of Rosarito to long beaches where there are good beach breaks. The most popular are just known by the kilometer marking on the Old Ensenada Highway, and include Popotla (Km 33), Calafía (Km 35.5), and Costa Baja (Km 36). The water is chilly most of the year, but it reaches the mid-70s in August and September. The **Inner Reef Surf Shop** (✉ Old Ensenada Hwy., Km 34.5 ☎ 661/613–2065 or 661/615–0841) rents surfboards, boogie boards, and wet suits. Surfboards cost about $20 a day.

Shopping

Shopping is far better in Rosarito than in most Baja cities, especially for pottery, wooden furniture, and high-end household items favored by condo owners in nearby expat clusters. Curio stands and open-air artisans' markets line Boulevard Juárez both north and south of town. Major hotels have shopping arcades with decent crafts stores.

★ **Apisa** (✉ Blvd. Juárez 2400 ☎ 661/612–0125) sells contemporary furnishings and iron sculptures from Guadalajara. At **Casa la Carreta** (✉ Old Ensenada Hwy., Km 29 ☎ 661/612–0502) you can see woodcarvers shaping elaborate desks, dining tables, and armoires. **Casa Torres** (✉ Rosarito Beach Hotel Shopping Center, Blvd. Juárez s/n ☎ 661/612–1008) sells imported perfumes.

The **Mercado de Artesanías** (✉ Blvd. Juárez 306 ☎ no phone) is a great place to find manufactured souvenirs—everything from sombreros to serapes. Resembling a colonial church with its facade of hand-painted tiles, **La Misión del Viejo** (✉ Blvd. Juárez 139 ☎ 661/612–1576) purveys hand-carved chairs, tin lamps shaped like stars, and glazed pottery.

ENSENADA

75 km (47 mi) south of Rosarito.

In 1542 Juan Rodríguez Cabrillo first discovered the seaport that Sebastián Vizcaíno named Ensenada-Bahía de Todos Santos (All Saints' Bay) in 1602. Since then the town has drawn a steady stream of explorers and developers. First ranchers made their homes on large plots along the coast and into the mountains. Gold miners followed in the late 1800s. After mine stocks were depleted, the area settled back into a bucolic state. The harbor gradually grew into a major port for shipping agricultural goods, and today Baja's third-largest city (population 369,000) is one of Mexico's largest seaports. It also has a thriving fishing fleet and fish-processing industry.

There are no beaches in Ensenada proper, but sandy stretches north and south of town are satisfactory for swimming, sunning, surfing, and camping. On summer and holiday weekends the population swells, but the town rarely feels overcrowded. Ensenada tends to draw those who want to explore a more traditional Mexican city.

Many cruise ships stop for at least a few hours in Ensenada to clear Mexican customs; thus, Ensenada is called Baja's largest cruise-ship port. Both the waterfront and downtown's main street are pleasant places to stroll. If you're driving, be sure to take the Centro exit from the highway, since it bypasses the commercial port area.

What to See

⑫ Las Bodegas de Santo Tomás. One of Baja's oldest wineries gives tours and tastings at its downtown winery and bottling plant. The restaurant, La Embotelladora Vieja, is one of Baja's finest. The winery also operates La Esquina de Bodegas, a café, shop, and gallery in a bright-blue building across Avenida Miramar. ⊠ *Av. Miramar 666, Centro* ☎ *646/174–0836 or 646/174–0829* ⊡ *$2* ☉ *Tours, tastings daily at 11, 1, and 3.*

⑱ Catedral Nuestra Señora de Guadalupe. The city's largest cathedral is named for the country's patron saint, and is the center of celebrations on December 12, the feast of the Virgin of Guadalupe. Though modest in comparison to mainland cathedrals, the church does have impressive stained-glass windows. ⊠ *Av. Floresta, at Av. Juárez, Centro.*

★ **⑬ Mercado de Mariscos.** At the northernmost point of Boulevard Costero, the main street along the waterfront, is an indoor-outdoor fish market where row after row of counters display piles of shrimp, tuna, dorado, and other fish caught off Baja's coasts. Outside, stands sell grilled or smoked fish, seafood cocktails, and fish tacos. You can pick up a few souvenirs, eat well for very little money, and take some great photographs. The original fish taco stands line the dirt path to the fish market. If your stomach is delicate, try the fish tacos at the cleaner, quieter Plaza de Mariscos in the shadow of the giant beige Plaza de Marina that blocks the view of the traditional fish market from the street.

⑭ Muelle de Pescador. Fishing and whale-watching boats depart from this pier. The area around it has been remodeled, and a broad *malecón* (seaside walkway) with park benches and palms runs along the waterfront. ⊠ *Blvd. Costero, at Av. Alvarado, Centro.*

⑪ Parque Revolución. Revolution Park is Ensenada's most traditional plaza, with a bandstand, playground, and plenty of benches in the shade. The plaza is festive on weekend evenings, when neighbors congregate here

to chat and children chase seagulls. ✉ *Av. Obregón, between Calles 6 and 7, Centro.*

⓰ Paseo Calle Primera. The renamed Avenida López Mateos is the center of Ensenada's traditional tourist zone. High-rise hotels, souvenir shops, restaurants, and bars line the avenue for eight blocks, from its beginning at the foot of the Chapultepec Hills to the dry channel of the Arroyo de Ensenada. The avenue also has cafés and most of the town's souvenir shops. Businesses use one or both street names for their addresses, though most stick with López Mateos. Locals shop for furniture, clothing, and other necessities a few blocks inland on Avenida Juárez, in Ensenada's downtown area.

⓯ Plaza Cívica. This block-long concrete park—with sculptures of Mexican heroes Benito Juárez, Miguel Hidalgo, and Venustiano Carranza—feels more like a monument than a gathering spot. Still, there are benches and horse-drawn carriages at the ready. ✉ *Blvd. Costero, at Av. Riveroll, Centro.*

⓱ Riviera del Pacífico. Officially called the Centro Social, Cívico y Cultural de Ensenada, the Riviera is a rambling, white, hacienda-style mansion built in the 1920s. An enormous gambling palace, hotel, restaurant, and bar, the glamorous Riviera was frequented by wealthy U.S. citizens and Mexicans, particularly during Prohibition. When gambling was outlawed in Mexico and Prohibition ended in the United States, the palace lost its raison d'être. You can tour some of the elegant ballrooms and halls, which occasionally host art shows and civic events. Many of the rooms are locked; check at the main office to see if someone is available to show you around. The gardens alone are worth visiting, and the building houses the Museo de Historia de Ensenada, a museum on Baja's history. ☒ *Blvd. Costero, at Av. Riviera, Centro* ☎ *646/177–0594* ☒ *Bldg. and gardens free; museum donations requested* ☉ *Daily 9:30–2 and 3–5.*

---

off the beaten path

LA BUFADORA – Seawater splashes up to 75 feet in the air, spraying sightseers standing near this impressive tidal blowhole (*la bufadora* means the buffalo snort) in the coastal cliffs at Punta Banda. Legend has it that the blowhole was created by a whale or sea serpent trapped in an undersea cave; both these stories, and the less romantic scientific facts, are posted on a roadside plaque here. The road to La Bufadora along Punta Banda—an isolated, mountainous point that juts into the sea—is lined with stands selling olives, tamales, strands of chilies and garlic, and terra-cotta planters. The drive gives you a sampling of Baja's wilderness. There are public restrooms as well as a few restaurants, including the extremely popular Gordo's, which is open Friday through Sunday. There's a small fee to park near the blowhole. A public bus runs from the downtown Ensenada station to Maneadero, the nearest town on the highway to La Bufadora. Here you can catch a minibus labeled Punta Banda that goes to La Bufadora. ☒ *Carretera 23, 31 km (19 mi) south of Ensenada, Punta Banda.*

Where to Stay & Eat

★ **$$–$$$$** ✕ **El Rey Sol.** From its chateaubriand *bouquetière* (garnished with a bouquet of vegetables) to the savory chicken chipotle, this family-owned French restaurant sets a high standard. Louis XIV–style furnishings and an attentive staff make it both comfortable and elegant. The sidewalk tables are a perfect place to dine and people-watch. The small café in the front sells pastries, all made on the premises. ☒ *Av. López Mateos 1000, Centro* ☎ *646/178–1733* ☐ *AE, MC, V.*

$–$$$ ✕ **La Embotelladora Vieja.** This elegant restaurant was once the wine-aging room of the Santo Tomás winery. The Baja French menu could include smoked tuna, grilled lobster in cabernet sauvignon sauce, or quail with sauvignon blanc sauce. Some dishes are available without alcohol-enhanced sauces. ☒ *Av. Miramar 666, Centro* ☎ *646/178–1660* ☐ *AE, MC, V* ☉ *Closed Mon.*

$–$$$ ✕ **Mariscos de Bahía de Ensenada.** Red lights flicker around the front door, making this seafood house just off the main drag easy to spot. The place is packed on weekends. Clams, shrimp, lobster, red snapper, squid, and other fresh seafood are fried, baked, broiled, or grilled, and served with a basic iceberg-lettuce salad, white rice, and tortillas made fresh at the window-front tortillería. There are a few canopied sidewalk tables. ✉ *Av. Riveroll 109, Centro* ☎ *646/178-1015* ▭ *AE, MC, V.*

$-$$ ✕ **Hacienda Del Charro.** Hungry patrons hover over platters of chiles rel-
Fodor's Choice lenos, enchiladas, and fresh chips and guacamole at heavy wooden pic-
★   nic tables. Plump chickens slowly turn over a wood-fueled fire by the
front window, and the aroma of simmering beans fills the air. ✉ *Av. López
Mateos 454, Centro* ☎ *646/178-2114* ▭ *No credit cards.*

$-$$ ✕ **Oxidos Café.** Baja meets L.A. at this new-wave café, where the metal
sculptures and other original art are as interesting as the food. The menu
aims to satisfy hunger pangs with hearty burgers, ribs, and pasta. The
bar is a gathering spot for local artists—you're sure to get into some interesting conversations if you hang out here. ✉ *Av. Ruíz 108, Centro*
☎ *646/178-8827* ▭ *No credit cards.*

¢-$ ✕ **Bronco's Steak House.** A great find near the Riviera del Pacífico,
Bronco's serves exceptional steaks and Mexican specialties. Try the *pun-
tas de filete al chipotle,* tender beef tips with smoke-flavored chipotle
chilies. Tripe appears frequently on the menu, satisfying the cravings
of the locals that fill many of the wood tables. Brick walls, wood-plank
floors, and hanging spurs and chaps evoke the Wild West, but the
mood truly is subdued and relaxed. Locals rave about the weekend breakfast buffet. ✉ *Av. López Mateos 1525, Centro* ☎ *646/172-4892*
▭ *AE, MC, V.*

☺ $$ ▦ **Estero Beach Resort.** Families love this long-standing resort on Ense-
nada's top beach. The best rooms (some with kitchenettes) are by the
sand; the worst are by the parking lot. Be sure to check out the outstanding
collection of folk art and artifacts in the resort's small museum. Mid-
week winter rates are a real bargain. There's also an on-site RV park;
its 38 sites have hookups for water, sewer, and electricity. ✉ *Mexico Car-
retera 1, 10 km (6 mi) south of Ensenada, Estero Beach* ☎ *482 W. San
Ysidro Blvd., San Ysidro, CA 92173* ☎ *646/176-6230 or 646/176-6235*
☎ *646/176-6925* ⊕ *www.hotelesterobeach.com* ⤴ *94 rooms, 2 suites*
& *Restaurant, some kitchenettes, cable TV, 4 tennis courts, pool, horse-
back riding, volleyball, bar, shops, playground* ▭ *MC, V.*

$$ ▦ **Hotel Coral & Marina.** This all-suites resort is enormous. It has a spa,
tennis courts, a water-sports center, and marina with slips for 350 boats
and customs-clearing facilities. All guest quarters have refrigerators and
coffeemakers. Suites in the two eight-story towers are done in burgundy
and dark green; most have waterfront balconies, seating areas, and international phone service. ✉ *Mexico Carretera 1, Km 103, Zona Play-
itas 22860* ☎ *646/175-0000, 800/862-9020 in U.S.* ☎ *646/175-0005*
⊕ *www.hotelcoral.com* ⤴ *147 suites* & *Restaurant, room service, refrigerators, cable TV, 2 tennis courts, 3 pools (1 indoor), gym, hot tub,
massage, spa, boating, marina, fishing, bar, laundry service, meeting rooms*
▭ *MC, V.*

$$ ▦ **Posada El Rey Sol.** A glass elevator rises three floors to rooms that
have comfy armchairs, sculpted headboards, and carpeting. The rooms
are the loveliest in downtown, and the proximity to restaurants and shops
is a big plus. Room service is provided by the El Rey Sol restaurant across
the street. ✉ *Av. Blancarte 130, 22860 Centro* ☎ *646/178-1641, 888/
315-2378 in U.S.* ☎ *646/174-0005* ⊕ *www.posadaelreysol.com* ⤴ *52*

rooms ⌂ Restaurant, room service, in-room data ports, in-room safes, minibars, pool, hot tub, bar, laundry service, meeting room, no-smoking rooms ▭ MC, V.

$$ 📺 **Las Rosas.** All rooms in this intimate hotel north of Ensenada face
FodorsChoice the ocean and pool; some have fireplaces and hot tubs, and even the least
★   expensive are lovely. The atrium lobby has marble floors, mint-green-and-pink couches that look out at the sea, and a glass ceiling that glows at night. Make reservations far in advance. ✉ Mexico Carretera 1, north of Ensenada, Zona Playitas ⬧ 374 E. H St. Chula Vista, CA 91910 ☎ 646/174–4320 or 646/174–4360 🖷 646/174–4595 ⊕ www.lasrosas.com ⚲ 48 rooms ⌂ Restaurant, 2 tennis courts, pool, hot tub, gym, massage, spa, bar, laundry service ▭ AE, MC, V.

★ **$$**   📺 **Punta Morro.** Five minutes from Ensenada, this secluded all-suites hotel is a great place to relax. The restaurant overlooks crashing waves and has an excellent combination of continental cuisine and fresh seafood. All rooms have seaside terraces, fireplaces, coffeemakers, and refrigerators. One-room studios are the least expensive units; the one-bedroom suite costs about $20 more. Two- and three-bedroom suites are also available. ✉ Mexico Carretera 1, Km 106, Zona Playitas ⬧ Box 434263 San Diego, CA 92143 ☎ 646/178–3507, 800/526–6676 in U.S. 🖷 646/174–4490 ⊕ www.punta-morro.com ⚲ 24 suites ⌂ Restaurant, in-room data ports, refrigerators, cable TV, pool, hot tub, beach, bar; no a/c ▭ AE, MC, V.

¢   📺 **Hotel del Valle.** Fishermen and budget travelers frequent this small hotel on a quiet side street. Rooms are basic and well maintained. You can use a coffeemaker in the lobby and parking spaces out front. Ask about rate discounts—those posted behind the front desk are about 40% higher than guests in the know normally pay. ✉ Av. Riveroll 367, Centro 22800 ☎ 646/178–2224 🖷 646/174–0466 ⚲ 43 rooms ⌂ Cable TV; no a/c ▭ MC, V.

¢   📺 **Joker Hotel.** A bizarre, colorful mishmash of styles makes it hard to miss the Joker. Rooms, which vary in size and level of maintenance, have balconies. The hotel is popular with Mexican families and there may not be an English-speaking staff member on duty. Traffic noise from the highway and from guests leaving at the crack of dawn can be a problem; try to stay away from the road and the busiest parts of the parking lot. ✉ Mexico Carretera 1, Km 12.5, Ejido Chapultepec 22800 ☎ 646/176–7201 🖷 646/177–4460 ⚲ 40 rooms ⌂ Restaurant, some refrigerators, TV, pool, hot tub, bar, nightclub ▭ MC, V.

Nightlife

Ensenada is a party town for college students, surfers, and other young tourists, though it's also possible to enjoy a mellow evening out. **La Capilla** (✉ Hotel El Cid, Paseo Calle Primera 997, Centro ☎ 646/178–2401 Ext. 104) attracts an older crowd that enjoys live Cuban music and romantic ballads in a relaxed setting. **Hussong's Cantina** (✉ Av. Ruíz 113, Centro ☎ 646/178–3210) has been an Ensenada landmark since 1892 and has changed little since then. A security guard stands by the front door to handle the often rowdy crowd—a mix of locals and visitors of all ages over 18. The noise is usually deafening, pierced by mariachi and ranchera musicians and the whoops and hollers of the pie-eyed. **Papas and Beer** (✉ Av. Ruíz 102, Centro ☎ 646/174–0145) attracts a collegiate crowd.

Sports & the Outdoors

Beaches
The waterfront in Ensenada proper is taken up by fishing boats, repair yards, and commercial shipping. The best swimming beaches are south of town. Estero Beach is long and clean, with mild waves; the Estero Beach Hotel takes up much of the oceanfront, but the beach is public. Surfers populate the strands off Carretera 1 north and south of Ensenada, particularly San Miguel, Tres Marías, and Salsipuedes; scuba divers prefer Punta Banda, by La Bufadora. Lifeguards are rare, so be cautious. The tourist office in Ensenada has a map that shows safe diving and surfing beaches.

Fishing
Boats leave the Ensenada sportfishing pier regularly. The best angling is from April through November, with bottom fishing good in winter. Charter vessels and party boats are available from several outfitters along Avenida López Mateos and Boulevard Costero and off the sportfishing pier. Mexican fishing licenses for the day or year are available at the tourist office or from charter companies.

Ensenada Clipper Fleet (✉ Sportfishing Pier, Blvd. Costero at Av. Alvarado, Centro ☎ 646/178–2185) has charter and group boats. The fee for a day's fishing is $50 including a fishing license. **Sergio's Sportfishing** (✉ Sportfishing Pier, Blvd. Costero at Av. Alvarado, Centro ☎ 646/178–2185 ⊕ www.sergios-sportfishing.com), one of the best sportfishing companies in Ensenada, has charter and group boats as well as boat slips for rent. The fee for a day's fishing is $50 per person on a group boat, including the cost of a license.

Hiking
★ **Expediciones de Turismo Ecológico y Aventura** (✉ Blvd. Costero 1094–14, Centro ☎ 646/178–3704 or 619/279–7503 ⊕ www.mexonline.com/ecotur.htm) runs hiking and camping trips in the San Pedro de Martir National Park. Prices start at $150.

Water Sports
Estero Beach and Punta Banda (en route to La Bufadora south of Ensenada) are both good kayaking areas, although facilities are limited. **Dale's La Bufadora Shop** (✉ Rancho La Bufadora, Punta Banda ☎ 646/154–2092) offers scuba diving trips (with all gear available for rent) to seamounts and walls off Punta Banda. They also have whale-watching trips in winter.

Some of the best surf on the coast is found off Islas de Todos Santos, two islands about 19 km (12 mi) west of Ensenada. Only the best and boldest challenge the waves here, which can reach 30 feet in winter. Surfers must hire a boat to take them to the waves. Calmer, but still exciting, waves crash on the beaches at San Miguel, Tres Marías, and Salsipuedes.

San Miguel Surf Shop (✉ Av. López Mateos, at Calle Ruíz, Centro ☎ 646/
178–1007) is the unofficial local surfing headquarters. They can guide
you toward the best areas and to gear rental.

Whale-Watching

Boats leave the Ensenada sportfishing pier for whale-watching trips
from December through February. The gray whales migrating from the
north to bays and lagoons in southern Baja pass through Todos Santos
Bay, often close to shore. Binoculars and cameras with telephoto capa-
bilities come in handy. The trips last about three hours. Vessels and tour
boats are available from several outfitters at the sportfishing pier. A three-
hour tour costs about $30.

Shopping

Most of the tourist shops are along Avenida López Mateos beside the
hotels and restaurants. There are several two-story shopping arcades,
many with empty shops. Dozens of curio shops line the street, all selling similar selections of pottery, serapes, and more.

Artes Don Quijote (✉ Av. López Mateos 503, Centro ☎ 646/174–4082)
has carved wood doors, huge terra-cotta pots, and crafts from Oaxaca.
It's closed Tuesday. **Bazar Casa Ramirez** (✉ Av. López Mateos 510, Centro ☎ 646/178–8209) sells high-quality Talavera pottery and other ceramics, wrought-iron items, and papier-mâché figurines. Be sure to
check out the displays upstairs. At **Los Castillo** (✉ Av. López Mateos 1076,
Centro ☎ 646/178–2335), the display of silver jewelry from Taxco is
★ limited but of excellent quality. The **Centro Artesenal de Ensenada** has a
smattering of galleries and shops. By far, the best shop there is **Galería
de Pérez Meillón** (✉ Blvd. Costero 1094–39, Centro ☎ 646/174–0394),
with its museum-quality Casas Grandes pottery and varied folk art by
indigenous northern Mexican peoples.

La Esquina de Bodegas (✉ Av. Miramar at Calle 6, Centro ☎ 646/178–
3557) is an innovative gallery, shop, and café in a century-old winery
building. **Los Globos** (✉ Calle 9, 3 blocks east of Reforma, Centro ☎ No
phone) is a daily open-air swap meet. Vendors and shoppers are most
abundant on weekends. **Mario's Silver** (✉ Calle Primera 1090–6, Centro
☎ 646/178–2451) has several branches along the main street tempting
shoppers with silver and gold jewelry. **La Mina de Salomón** (✉ Av. López
Mateos 1000, Centro ☎ 646/178–1733) carries elaborate jewelry in a
tiny gallery next to El Rey Sol restaurant. It also has a pastry shop.

TIJUANA, PLAYAS DE ROSARITO &
ENSENADA A TO Z

*To research prices, get advice from other travelers, and travel arrange-
ments, visit www.fodors.com.*

ADDRESSES

The Mexican method of naming streets can be exasperatingly arbitrary,
so **be patient when searching for street addresses.** Streets in the centers of

many colonial cities (those built by the Spanish) are laid out in a grid surrounding the *zócalo* (main square) and often change names on different sides of the square. Other streets simply acquire a new name after a certain number of blocks. Numbered streets are usually designated *norte–sur* (north–south) or *oriente–poniente* (east–west) on either side of a central avenue. (Three of these are abbreviated: Nte., Ote., and Pte. Sur is spelled out.) In many cities, streets that have proper names, such as Avenida Benito Juárez, change names when they cross some other street—and only a map will show where one begins and the other ends. Blocks are often labeled numerically, according to distance from a chosen starting point, as in "la Calle de Pachuca," "2a Calle de Pachuca," etc. Many Mexican addresses have "s/n" for *sin número* (no number) after the street name. Similarly, many hotels give their address as "Old Ensenada Highway Km 30," which indicates that the property is at the 30th kilometer on the highway heading to Ensenada.

BUS TRAVEL

Greyhound buses head to Tijuana from downtown San Diego several times daily. Buses to San Diego and Los Angeles depart from the Greyhound terminal in Tijuana 14 times a day. Fares are $5 to San Diego and $18 to Los Angeles. Mexicoach runs buses from the trolley depot in San Ysidro and the large parking lot on the U.S. side of the border to the Tijuana Tourist Terminal at Avenida Revolución between Calles 6 and 7. These shuttles make the circuit every 15 minutes between 8 AM and 9 PM; the fare is $1.50.

Buses connect all the towns in Baja Norte and are easy to use; stations are in Ensenada, Mexicali, San Felipe, Tecate, and Tijuana. There are usually three buses a day. Those traveling to Rosarito stop at a small terminal on Boulevard Juárez across from the Rosarito Beach Hotel. There's no official bus station here; check at the hotels for schedule information.

Buses to destinations in Baja and mainland Mexico depart from Tijuana's Central de Autobuses. Autotransportes de Baja California covers the entire Baja route and connects in Mexicali with buses to Guadalajara and Mexico City. Elite has first-class service to mainland Mexico.

Tijuana's Camionera de la Línea station is just inside the border and has service to Rosarito and Ensenada along with city buses to downtown. The downtown station is at Calle 1a and Avenida Madero. To catch the bus back to the border from downtown, go to Calle Benito Juárez (also called Calle 2a) between Avenidas Revolución and Constitución.

Colectivos (small, often striped vans) cover neighborhood routes in most Baja cities and towns. The destination is usually painted on the windshield; look for them on main streets. You can flag the vans down anywhere along their routes; fares are 3 pesos and up, depending on the distance you travel.

🚍 Bus Lines **Autotransportes de Baja California** ☎ 664/686–9010. **Elite** ☎ 664/688–1979 ⊕ www.abc.com.mx. **Greyhound** ☎ 664/686–0697, 664/688–0165 in Tijuana, 800/231–2222 in U.S. ⊕ www.greyhound.com. **Mexicoach** ☎ 664/685–1440, 619/428–9517 in U.S. ⊕ www.mexicoach.com.

▣ Bus Stations **Ensenada bus station** ✉ Av. Riveroll 1075, between Calles 10 and 11, Centro, Ensenada ☎ 646/178-6680. **San Diego** ✉ 120 W. Broadway ☎ 619/239-2366. **Tijuana city bus station** ✉ Calle 1a, at Av. Madero, Centro, Tijuana ☎ 664/688-0752. **Tijuana Camionera de la Línea** ✉ Centro Comercial Viva Tijuana, Vía de la Juventud Oriente 8800, Zona Río, Tijuana ☎ No phone. **Tijuana Central de Autobuses** ✉ Calz. Lázaro Cárdenas, at Blvd. Arroyo Alamar, La Mesa, Tijuana ☎ 664/621-2982 or 664/621-7640.

CAR RENTAL

Many U.S. car-rental companies don't allow you to drive their cars into Mexico. Avis permits its cars to go from San Diego into Baja as far as 724 km (450 mi) south of the border. You must declare your intention to take the car into Mexico and buy Mexican auto insurance; the person who rents the car must be the one to return it back in San Diego. Southwest Car Rentals allows its cars as far as Ensenada. California Baja Rent-A-Car rents four-wheel-drive vehicles, convertibles, and sedans for use throughout Mexico (the only company to do this). If you plan to rent your car in Tijuana or San Diego and drop it in Los Cabos, be prepared to pay a hefty sum (up to $900) on top of the rental price.

Fiesta Rent-a-Car and Hertz have offices in Ensenada. The larger U.S. rental agencies have offices at Tijuana's Aeropuerto Alberado Rodriguez, and Avis and Budget have offices in downtown Tijuana.

▣ **Avis** ✉ Blvd. Cuauhtémoc 1705, Zona Río, Tijuana ☎ 664/683-0605 ⊕ www.avis.com. **Budget** ✉ Paseo de los Héroes 77, Zona Río, Tijuana ☎ 664/634-3303 ⊕ www.budget.com. **California Baja Rent-A-Car** ✉ 9245 Jamacha Blvd., Spring Valley, CA 91977 ☎ 619/470-7368, 888/470-7368 in U.S. ⊕ www.cabaja.com. **Fiesta Rent-a-Car** ✉ Hotel Corona at Blvd. Costero, Centro, Ensenada ☎ 646/176-3344. **Hertz** ✉ Av. Blancarte, between Calles 1 and 2, Centro, Ensenada ☎ 646/178-2982 ⊕ www.hertz.com. **Southwest Car Rentals** ✉ 2975 Pacific Hwy. ☎ 619/497-4811, 800/476-8849 in U.S. ⊕ www.southwestcarrental.net.

CAR TRAVEL

The best way to thoroughly tour Baja Norte is by car, although the driving can be complicated. If you're just visiting Tijuana, Tecate, or Mexicali, it's easiest to park on the U.S. side of the border and walk across.

From San Diego, U.S. 5 and I–805 end at the San Ysidro border crossing; Highway 905 leads from I–5 and I–805 to the Tijuana border crossing at Otay Mesa. U.S. 94 from San Diego connects with U.S. 188 to the border at Tecate, 57 km (35 mi) east of San Diego. I–8 from San Diego connects with U.S. 111 at Calexico—203 km (126 mi) east—and the border crossing to Mexicali. San Felipe is on the coast, 200 km (124 mi) south of Mexicali via Carretera 5.

To head south into Baja from Tijuana, follow the signs for Ensenada Cuota, the toll road (also called Carretera 1 and, on newer signs, the Scenic Highway) that runs south along the coast. There are two clearly marked exits for Rosarito, and one each for Puerto Nuevo, Bajamar, and Ensenada. The road is excellent, although it has some hair-raising curves atop the cliffs and is best driven in daylight (the stretch from Rosarito to Ensenada is one of the most scenic drives in Baja). Tollbooths accept U.S. and Mexican currency; tolls are about $3. Restrooms are available near toll stations. The alternative free road—Carretera 1D or Ensenada Libre—may be difficult for first-timers to navigate. (The entry to the 1D is on a side street in a congested area of downtown Tijuana, and the highway is quite curvy.) Carretera 1 continues south of Ensenada through San Quintín to Guerrero Negro, at the border between Baja California and Baja Sur, and on to Baja's southernmost point; there are no tolls past Ensenada.

Mexico Carretera 2 runs east from Tijuana to Tecate and Mexicali. There are toll roads between Tijuana and Tecate and between Tecate and Mexicali. The 134-km (83-mi) journey from Tecate east to Mexicali on La Rumorosa, as the road is known, is as exciting as a roller-coaster ride, with the highway twisting and turning down steep mountain grades and over flat, barren desert.

If you're traveling only as far as Ensenada or San Felipe, you don't need a tourist card, unless you stay longer than 72 hours. If you're heading south of Ensenada, you can get the card at the Mexican Customs Office. You must have Mexican auto insurance, available at agencies near the border.

The combination of overpopulation, lack of infrastructure, and heavy winter rains makes many of Tijuana's streets difficult to navigate by automobile. It's always best to stick to the main thoroughfares. Most of Rosarito proper can be explored on foot, which is a good idea on weekends, when Boulevard Juárez has bumper-to-bumper traffic. To reach Puerto Nuevo and other points south, continue on Boulevard Juárez (also called Old Ensenada Highway and Ensenada Libre) through town. Most of Ensenada's attractions are within five blocks of the waterfront; it's easy to take a long walking tour of the city. A car is necessary to reach La Bufadora and most of the beaches.

PARKING Large lots stretch on both sides of I–5 at San Ysidro, close to the border. They charge $8 to $12 per day; though most have an attendant, they aren't actually guarded, so don't leave any valuables in your car. In Tijuana, there are lots along Avenida Revolución and at most major attractions. There's plenty of waterfront parking along Avenida Costera in Ensenada. Parking spaces are harder to find in Rosarito; try the large lot on Avenida Juárez by the Commercial Mexicana grocery store.

🄵 **Mexican Customs Office** ✉ Inside San Ysidro border crossing ☎ 664/682-3439 or 664/684-7790.

CHILDREN IN MEXICO
Mexico has one of the strictest policies about children entering the country. All children, including infants, must have proof of citizenship (a birth certificate) for travel to Mexico. All children up to age 18 traveling with a single parent must also have a notarized letter from the other parent stating that the child has his or her permission to leave their home country. If the other parent is deceased or the child has only one legal parent, a notarized statement saying so must be obtained as proof. In addition, parents must now fill out a tourist card for each child over the age of 10 traveling with them.

CONSULATES

🇨 **Canadian Consulate** ✉ Calle Germán Gedovius 10411, Zona Río, Tijuana ☎ 664/684-0461. **U.K. Consulate** ✉ Av. Salinas 1500, Fracc. Aviación, Tijuana ☎ 664/686-5320. **U.S. Consulate** ✉ Tapachula 96, Tijuana ☎ 664/622-7400 ⊕ www.usembassy-mexico.gov/tijuana/Tenglish.htm.

EMERGENCIES

In an emergency anywhere in Baja Norte, dial 066. The operators speak at least a bit of English. For tourist assistance with legal problems, accidents, or other incidents dial the Tourist Information and Assistance hotline at 078.

The Tijuana government publishes a small guide to crime for tourists, available at information desks. It lists the agencies to contact if you've been involved in a crime, and lists the crimes that tourists most often commit (carrying weapons, purchasing illegal drugs, public drunkenness). Crime victims should contact the State District Attorney's Office or the U.S. Consulate General.

🇸 **State District Attorney** ☎ 664/638-5206.

ENTRY REQUIREMENTS

Standard tourist visa forms are available through travel agents, Mexican consulates, and at the Mexico border if you're entering by land. A tourist visa costs about $18. You're exempt from the fee if you enter by land and do not stray past the 26–30-km (16–18-mi) checkpoint into the country's interior.

In addition to presenting the visa form, U.S. citizens must prove citizenship by presenting a valid passport, certified copy of a birth certificate, or voter-registration card (the last two must be accompanied by a government-issue photo ID). However, a passport is your best option, because that's what officials are used to dealing with. Minors traveling with one parent need notarized permission from the absent parent. *See* Children in Mexico. You're allowed to stay 180 days as a tourist; frequently, though, immigration officials will give you less. Be sure to ask for as much time as you think you'll need up to 180 days; going to a Mexican immigration office to extend a visa can easily take a whole day, plus you'll have to pay an extension fee of approximately $18.

Canadians, New Zealanders, and citizens of the United Kingdom may also request up to 180 days; Australians are allowed up to 90 days. A passport is required for all.

LODGING

Several companies specialize in arranging hotel reservations in northern Baja. Baja Information is one of the oldest and best agencies working with Baja hotels and tourism departments. Baja California Tours books hotel rooms in the cities and outlying areas. Mexico Condo Reservations books hotel and condo accommodations and represents La Pinta Hotels, a chain with several hotels on the peninsula.

🇧 **Baja California Tours** ✉ 7734 Herschel Ave., Suite O, La Jolla, CA 92037 ☎ 858/454-7166 or 800/336-5454 ⊕ www.bajaspecials.com. **Baja Information** ✉ 6855 Friars Rd., Suite 26, San Diego, CA 92108 ☎ 619/298-4105, 800/522-1516 in CA, NV, AZ,

800/225-2786 elsewhere in U.S. **Mexico Condo Reservations** ✉ 4420 Hotel Circle Ct., Suite 230, San Diego, CA 92108 ☎ 619/275-4500 or 800/262-9632 ⊕ www. mexicocondores.com.

TELEPHONES

The country code for Mexico is 52. When calling a Mexico number from abroad, dial any necessary international access code, then the country code and then all of the numbers listed for the entry.

To make an international call, dial 00 before the country code, area code, and number. The country code for the United States and Canada is 1, the United Kingdom 44, Australia 61, New Zealand 64, and South Africa 27.

Directory assistance is 040 nationwide. For assistance in English, dial 090 first for an international operator; tell the operator in what city, state, and country you require directory assistance, and he or she will connect you.

TOURS & PACKAGES

Baja California Tours has comfortable, informative bus trips throughout northern Baja. Seasonal day and overnight trips focus on whale-watching, fishing, shopping, wineries, sports, dude ranches, and art and cultural events in Tijuana, Rosarito, Ensenada, and San Felipe. Rainbows Over Baja has bus tours to the major towns in Baja, starting and ending in Phoenix, Arizona. Cali-Baja Tours runs bus trips to La Bufadora from Ensenada, and offers transportation between Baja. Five Star Tours runs a daily Tijuana shuttle and tours to Rosarito Beach, Puerto Nuevo, and Ensenada. San Diego Scenic Tours offers half- and full-day bus tours of Tijuana, with time allowed for shopping.

🚩 **Baja California Tours** ✉ 7734 Herschel Ave., Suite 0, La Jolla, CA 92037 ☎ 858/454-7166 or 800/336-5454 ⊕ www.bajaspecials.com. **Rainbows Over Baja** ✉ 416 W. San Ysidro Blvd., San Ysidro, CA 92173 ☎ 888/311-8034 ⊕ www.rainbowsoverbajatours.com. **Five Star Tours** ✉ 1050 Kettner Blvd., San Diego, CA 92101 ☎ 619/232-5049 ⊕ www.efivestartours.com. **Cali-Baja Tours** ✉ Av. Macheros, at Blvd. Costero, Centro, Ensenada, BC 92037 ☎ 646/178-1641. **San Diego Scenic Tours** ✉ 2255 Garnet Ave., San Diego, CA 92109 ☎ 858/273-8687 ⊕ www.sandiegoscenictours.com.

VISITOR INFORMATION

Baja tours, Mexican auto insurance, a monthly newsletter, and workshops are available through Discover Baja, which is a membership club for Baja travelers.

Baja's largest cities have tourism offices operated by different agencies. These offices are usually open weekdays 9–7 (although some may close in early afternoon for lunch) and weekends 9–1. Some of the smaller areas don't have offices. The excellent Baja California State Secretary of Tourism distributes information on the entire state.

Of Ensenada's two tourist bureaus, the one on Boulevard Costero has the most information. Mexicali has both a Convention and Tourism Bureau and a State Secretary of Tourism office, as does Tijuana. Tijuana Convention and Tourism Bureau has two offices, one within the San Ysidro border crossing, and one on Avenida Revolución. The Tijuana Tourist Trust operates an office in the Zona Río. Rosarito, San Felipe, and Tecate also each have a tourist office. The best Web sites for different cities are often private ones that are casually linked to the tourism bureau.

🔳 **Baja California State Secretary of Tourism** ✉ Paseo de los Héroes 10289, Zona Río, Tijuana ☎ 664/634-6330 ⊕ www.discoverbajacalifornia.com. **Discover Baja** ✉ 3089 Clairemont Dr., San Diego, CA 92117 ☎ 619/275-4225 or 800/727-2252 ⊕ www. discoverbaja.com. **Ensenada Tourism** ✉ Blvd. Costero 1477, Centro, Ensenada ☎ 646/ 172-3022 ⊕ www.ensenada-tourism.com. **Ensenada Tourist Board** ✉ Blvd. Cárdenas 609, Centro, Ensenada ☎☎ 646/178-8578 ⊕ www.enjoyensenada.com. **Rosarito Tourist Board** ✉ Blvd. Juárez 907, Oceana Plaza Shopping Center, Rosarito ☎ 624/ 612-0396 ⊕ www.rosarito.org. **Tijuana Convention and Tourism Bureau** ✉ Inside the San Ysidro border crossing, Border, Tijuana ☎ 664/683-1405 ✉ Av. Revolución, between Calles 3 and 4, Centro, Tijuana ☎ 664/684-0481 or 664/688-0555 ⊕ www. tijuanaonline.org. **Tijuana Tourist Trust** ✉ Paseo de los Héroes 9365-201, Zona Río, Tijuana ☎ 664/684-0537, 888/775-2417 in U.S. ⊕ www.seetijuana.com.

UNDERSTANDING
SAN DIEGO

SAN DIEGO AT A GLANCE

Fast Facts

Type of government: Mayor elected every four years, but must share power with City Manager appointed by City Council, composed of eight members elected from within their council districts.
Population: 1.3 million (city), 3 million (metro area)

Population Density: 705 people per square mi
Median age: 33.7
Ethnic groups: White 53%; Latino 29%; Asian 9%; black 5%; other 4%

Geography & Environment

Latitude: 33° N (same as Charleston, South Carolina; Casablanca, Morocco; Dallas, Texas; Jerusalem, Israel; Shanghai, China)
Longitude: 117° W (same as Beijing, China; Perth, Australia)
Elevation: 85 feet
Land area: 324 square mi (city) 4,200 square mi (metro)
Terrain: Seventy miles of beaches along the west coast, with elevations rising through gentle foothills to forested mountains in east and desert beyond. The 600,000-acre Anza Borrego Desert State Park straddles San Diego County and Imperial County to the east

Natural hazards: Earthquakes, heavy surf and riptides at some beaches, landslides, wildfires in dry eastern desert
Environmental issues: Urban runoff and sewage spills close most beaches during wet weather; summer droughts are a persistent problem; wildlife and plant preservation as the city continues robust growth, particularly with new home building; concerns over the effects of San Onofre, a nuclear power plant, on Pacific Ocean and local residents' long-term safety

Economy

Per capita income: $32,515
Unemployment: 3.9%
Work force: 1.5 million; services (business/health/tourism) 30%; government 18%; trade 17%; construction 15%; manufacturing 9%; retail 9%; other 2%

Major industries: Aerospace, bio-tech, electronics, manufacturing, oceanography, shipbuilding, software, telecommunications, tourism

Did You Know?

• A recent study ranked San Diego as one of the least segregated cities in the nation.

• Scientist Kurt Benirschke coined the phrase "extinct is forever" when doing work with endangered species at the San Diego Zoo.

• After the New York Yacht Club lost the America's Cup for the first time in 132 years in 1983, it was the San Diego Yacht Club, representing the U.S., that won it back from Australia in 1987 and successfully defended it in 1988 and 1992.

- San Diego gained 215,000 legal and illegal immigrants in the 1990s, increasing its foreign-born population to more than 600,000.

- Greater San Diego is about the same size as the state of Connecticut.

- San Diego skateboarder Danny Way holds the world record for the highest air on a skateboard. On April 17, 2002, he performed a "method air" off the top of a ramp and reached 18.25 feet before coming down, safely.

- A recent U.S. report estimated that more than 20 million gallons of untreated sewage was being discharged near Tijuana and carried by currents onto U.S. beaches, many in San Diego.

- Among the things kept at the San Diego Supercomputer Center at UCSD is the largest single repository of protein structure data on earth and one of the world's top 20 supercomputers, capable of doing more than 1.7 trillion calculations per second.

- One of La Jolla's most famous residents was Theodor Seuss Geisel, better known as Dr. Seuss. The author once said that his greatest work was the Lion Wading Pool that he donated to the San Diego Wild Animal Park in 1973.

PARADISE FOUND

SUNSHINE YEAR-ROUND, miles of white-sand beaches, laid-back friendliness, history and Hispanic culture, and family-oriented outdoor entertainment at SeaWorld and the world-famous San Diego Zoo are enough to draw 14 million visitors annually to "America's finest city." But there's more than meets the eye here. If you look beyond the obvious, you'll discover why many longtime vacationers eventually become residents, and why residents have a hard time ever moving.

San Diego, occupying the southwest corner of California, boasts an almost perfect year-round climate. Most days are sunny, averaging 70°F and humidity is low. The cool coastal climate is ideal for the area's most colorful industry—flower growing. Summer temperatures frequently reach 100°F inland, particularly at the Wild Animal Park near Escondido; even so, nights are cool enough to make it a good idea to have a sweater or jacket handy.

San Diego is a big city, where locals take pride in its small-town feel. With more than 1 million people living within the city limits, San Diego is second only to Los Angeles in population among California cities and ranks as the seventh-largest municipality in the United States. It also covers a lot of territory, roughly 400 square mi of land and sea.

Central San Diego is delightfully urban and accessible. You can walk the entire downtown area—explore the exciting and trendy Gaslamp Quarter, stop and shop at whimsical Horton Plaza, dine Italian, hear a rock band, attend a play, take a sunset harbor stroll, picnic in the park, or visit a historic building. Downtown you can catch the trolley or take the bus to the Balboa Park museums and the zoo, Old Town historic sites, Mission Bay marine park, Qualcomm Stadium, diverse urban neighborhoods, and Tijuana.

To the north and south of the city are 70 mi of beaches. Hiking and camping territory lie inland, where a succession of long, low, chaparral-covered mesas are punctuated with deep-cut canyons that step up to savannalike hills, separating the verdant coast from the arid Anza-Borrego Desert. Unusually clear skies make the inland countryside ideal for stargazing.

You'll find reminders of San Diego's Spanish and Mexican heritage throughout the region—in architecture and place-names, in distinctive Mexican cuisine, and in a handful of historic buildings in Old Town. The San Diego area, the birthplace of California, was claimed for Spain by Juan Rodríguez Cabrillo in 1542. The first European community, Mission Alta California, was established here in 1769, when a small group of settlers and soldiers set up camp on what is now called Presidio Hill. Franciscan Father Junípero Serra, leader of the settlers, celebrated the first Mass here in July of that year, establishing the Mission San Diego de Alcalá, the first of the 21 missions built by Spanish friars in California. San Diego, along with the rest of California, ultimately came under Mexican rule before entering the United States as the 31st state in 1850.

In 1867 developer Alonzo Horton, who called the town's bay-front "the prettiest place for a city I ever saw," began building a hotel, a plaza, and prefab homes on 960 downtown acres. The city's fate was sealed in 1908 when the U.S. Navy's battleship fleet sailed into San Diego Bay. The military continues to contribute to the local economy, operating many bases and installations throughout the county; San Diego is home to the largest military complex in the world.

San Diego has taken an orderly approach to inevitable development with the adoption of a general plan to run through the year 2020. More than 50 projects are under way or on the drawing board for downtown. The most recent opening is a new ballpark for the Padres.

Links between the south-of-the-border communities of Tijuana and Ensenada continue to strengthen. More than 50 million people cross the border at San Ysidro annually, indicative of the two-nation nature of San Diego. In recent years Tijuana has grown into one of the biggest, most exciting cities in Mexico. You'll discover a sophisticated, pulsating city marked with excellent restaurants, trendy bars and dis-cos, chic boutiques, discount malls, sports-betting parlors, broad boulevards congested with traffic, and new high-rise hotels.

Without question, San Diego is one of the warmest and most appealing destinations in the United States. As you explore, you'll make your own discoveries that will lead you to agree with most locals that this corner of California is just this side of paradise.

— Bobbi Zane

BOOKS & MOVIES

Books

There's no better way to establish the mood for your visit to Old Town San Diego than by reading Helen Hunt Jackson's 19th-century romantic novel, *Ramona*, a best-seller for more than 50 years and still readily available. The Casa de Estudillo in Old Town has been known for many years as Ramona's Marriage Place because of its close resemblance to the house described in the novel. Richard Henry Dana Jr.'s *Two Years Before the Mast* (1869), based on the author's experiences as a merchant sailor, provides a masculine perspective on early San Diego history.

Other novels with a San Diego setting include Raymond Chandler's mystery about the waterfront, *Playback*; Wade Miller's mystery, *On Easy Street*; Eric Higgs's gothic thriller, *A Happy Man*; Tom Wolfe's satire of the La Jolla surfing scene, *The Pump House Gang*; and David Zielinski's modern-day story, *A Genuine Monster*.

Movies

Filmmakers have taken advantage of San Diego's diverse and amiable climate since the dawn of cinema. Westerns, comedy-westerns, and tales of the sea were early staples: *Cupid in Chaps, The Sagebrush Phrenologist* (how's that for a title?), the 1914 version of *The Virginian,* and Lon Chaney's *Tell It to the Marines* were among the silent films shot in the area. Unlike many films in which San Diego itself doesn't figure into the plot, the screen version of Helen Hunt Jackson's novel *Ramona* (1936), starring Loretta Young as the title character, incorporated historical settings (or replicas).

Easy-to-capture outdoor locales have lured many productions south from Hollywood through the years, including the following military-oriented talkies, all or part of which were shot in San Diego: James Cagney's *Here Comes the Navy* (1934); Errol Flynn's *Dive Bomber* (1941); John Wayne's *The Sands of Iwo Jima* (1949); Ronald Reagan's *Hellcats of the Navy* (1957, costarring Nancy Davis, the future first lady); Rock Hudson's *Ice Station Zebra* (1968); Tom Cruise's *Top Gun* (1986); Sean Connery's *Hunt for Red October* (1990); Charlie Sheen's *Navy Seals* (1990); and Danny Glover's *Flight of the Intruder.*

In a lighter military vein, the famous talking mule hit the high seas in *Francis in the Navy* (1955), in which a very young Clint Eastwood has a bit part. The Tom Hanks–Darryl Hannah hit *Splash* (1984), *Spaceballs* (1987), *My Blue Heaven* (1990), *Hot Shots* (1991), *Wayne's World 2* (1993), and Ellen DeGeneres's *Mr. Wrong* (1996) are other comedies with scenes filmed here. The city has a cameo role in the minihit *Flirting with Disaster* (1996), and one of the best comedies ever made, director Billy Wilder's *Some Like It Hot* (1959)—starring Marilyn Monroe, Jack Lemmon, and Tony Curtis—takes place at the famous Hotel Del Coronado (standing in as a Miami resort).

Other movies including San Diego as either a co-star or surrogate for fictional locales include *Jurassic Park: The Lost World* (1997); *Pearl Harbor* (2001); *Traffic* (2000); *The Scorpion King* (2002); *The Antwone Fisher Story* (2002); *Bruce Almighty* (2003); and *Anchorman* (2004).

The amusingly low-budget *Attack of the Killer Tomatoes* (1980) makes good use of local scenery—and the infamous San Diego Chicken. The producers must have liked what they found in town as they returned for three sequels: *Return of the Killer Tomatoes* (1988), *Killer Tomatoes Strike Back* (1990), and—proving just how versatile the region is as a film location–*Killer Tomatoes Go to France* (1991).

Television producers zip south for series and made-for-TV movies all the time. The alteration of San Diego's skyline in the 1980s was partially documented on the hit show *Simon & Simon*. Other productions that have filmed here include *Silk Stalkings, Baywatch, High Tide, Renegade,* and *Nip/Tuck*.

INDEX

NOTES

NOTES

NOTES

NOTES

NOTES

NOTES

NOTES

NOTES

NOTES